Constructivism: The New Paradigm

From Theory to Practice

J.K. Mohapatra
M. Mahapatra
B.K. Parida

ATLANTIC

PUBLISHERS & DISTRIBUTORS (P) LTD

Published by

ATLANTIC

PUBLISHERS & DISTRIBUTORS (P) LTD

7/22, Ansari Road, Darya Ganj, New Delhi-110002
Phones : +91-11-40775252, 23273880, 23275880, 23280451
Fax: +91-11-23285873
Web: www.atlanticbooks.com
E-mail: orders@atlanticbooks.com

Branch Office
5, Nallathambi Street, Wallajah Road, Chennai-600002
Phones : +91-44-64611085, 32413319
E-mail: chennai@atlanticbooks.com

Printed in India at Nice Printing Press, A-33/3A, Site-IV, Industrial Area, Sahibabad, Ghaziabad, U.P.

The book is dedicated to those noble souls
who became teachers,
not out of compulsion or convenience,
but out of choice,
conviction and commitment

Preface

Constructivism, according to Matthew Daniel Eddy, is a theory of knowledge that argues that knowledge and meaning are generated by people from an interaction between their experiences and their ideas. It has influenced a number of disciplines, including psychology, sociology, education, and the history of science. Various approaches in pedagogy derive from constructivist theory. They are generally suggestive of the fact that learning is accomplished best using a hands-on approach. Learners do not learn well by being told what will happen in a particular situation but by experimentation in which they make their own inferences, discoveries and conclusions.

The book explains what is the need for constructivism and answers various questions relating to the justification, and logicity of epistemological evolution of constructivism. It delves into various pathways in constructivism, and how they help in acquiring knowledge in different domains. Conceptual change as the basic process of constructivism, and concept map and constructivism have been described in exclusive chapters. A learner-centered input-output model, and some important teaching models along with their respective frameworks, have been explained with examples. A teacher is a guide, facilitator, innovator, negotiator, catalyst, experimenter, and researcher—all rolled into one. These roles of the teacher have been discussed, providing do's and don'ts for the teacher, including those in ALCON's framework.

With changing time there has been a paradigm shift in the comprehension about the nature and process of human learning. This shift has been engineered through a natural process of cognitive evolution, a necessity to meet the challenges of new and demanding experimental evidences, and a desire to optimize the degree and quality of meaningful learning by the learner. As a result, the shift has slowly but conclusively moved from behaviourism to cognitivism and now to constructivism (Cooper, 1993). This shift and how it has impacted teacher education has been discussed in a separate chapter.

Over the years, constructivist thinking has permeated many diverse fields like art, history, communication, ethnology, industrial management, law, and linguistics, among others. Constructivism has also enjoyed considerable success in science and mathematics education. It has been instrumental in generating a large amount of research-based empirical data which has led to a greater understanding of the characteristic of the learners, the process of learning, and the general problems of teaching-learning. This has been taken up in the last chapter.

The book is an outcome of our 25 years of research on Piaget, Pupils' Alternative Conceptions, Concept Map Technique, Constructivism and Constructivist-informed Teaching Models. That is why a fair amount of examples appear in the entire book. Tables and figures have been given at appropriate places to support the text. Each chapter has references of the sources used to develop the matter.

We have made a sincere effort to avoid jugglery of words to improve the readability of the text. However, we admit that for the discerning reader, the treatment, presentation, structure, composition, and language of different chapters may appear to be different, which is but natural as three authors have written the book. In this context one may not lose sight of the fact that being the dedicated researchers in constructivism, we mutually agreed that in the context of the chapters assigned, each will have the freedom to choose the details of presentation, because such a freedom is a prerequisite in dealing with constructivism.

We hope that the book will be well received by teacher-educators, teachers, curriculum framers, textbook authors, and students in particular, and educationists in general. It will also prove beneficial for researchers in the field.

J.K. Mohapatra
M. Mahapatra
B.K. Parida

Acknowledgements

I take this opportunity to express my deep sense of gratitude to Prof. J.D. Novak, Cornell University, Cornell, for his keen interest and constructive comments on the concept map technique proposed by us. My co-authors and I are grateful to him for his note of appreciation about the model of the four-dimensional hypothetical space, PACT, proposed by us.

I am thankful to Prof. G.L. Claxton, King's College, London, for an in-depth informal discussion about pupils' alternative conceptions, their background and structures, in 1985, when I visited King's College as a British Council Fellow. I express my thanks to Prof. M. Monk, who initiated me into the area of Pupils' Alternative Conceptions.

I also record my gratitude to Prof. L.C. McDermott, University of Washington, Seattle, for her keen interest in my work on 'force' and 'motion', and for regularly sending me the reprints of her latest papers in this area. I will be failing in my duty if I do not acknowledge my thanks to late Prof. R. Driver and her active research group at Leeds University, Leeds, for the fruitful discussion I had with the group.

My special thanks are due to Prof. J.K. Gilbert, the University of Reading, Reading, for his academic patience to go through many of my papers and for recommending them for publication in the *International Journal of Science Education*.

I am also indebted to Prof. H. Pfundt and Prof. R. Duit, University of Kiel, Kiel for sending me regularly their updated "Bibliography of Students' Alternative Frameworks and Science

Education" which has been a great source of reference for keeping track of various research studies in the area and quoting from the data contained in their bibliography for necessary background and justification, in some chapters of this book.

Thanks are due to Prof. Mohit M. Mohanty for many meaningful discussions and for providing background materials while writing the book.

My co-authors and I owe special thanks to the science education group of Regional Institute of Education, Bhubaneswar for a number of fruitful interactions. Special thanks are also due to the students and teachers who gleefully cooperated with us when various tests were administered on them.

J.K. Mohapatra

Contents

1 Why Constructivism

1.1 Introduction

In the last decade and a half, whenever in the framework of constructivism, we have conducted orientation programmes (as a matter of fact we have been conducting 20+ such programmes per year) for teachers of all categories, primary, secondary, and higher secondary, they very often raise a common question:

- Sir, we have been teaching our subjects for the last 20 years, our students have been performing very well in the examinations, hence we are happy, our authorities are satisfied and parents are happy. So why should we change our teaching technique? For that matter why constructivism?

When we further coax them a little and request them to ask any other queries (because helping learners to ask questions is one of the main components of constructivist informed teaching), which they may have, they ask:

- Do we have to learn about constructivism, because that is the new fashion?, or
- Do we, of necessity, must learn about constructivism?

These three questions clarify quite a few issues.

(a) The first question depicts the mindset of the ultimate clientele group.

(b) It raises a major question, which justifies the title of the first chapter of this book, as the book boasts to take the reader from theory to practice.

(c) It also shows by default that because of their academic isolation, they suffer from cognitive myopia.

(d) It also confirms that for them whatever is relevant for examination, is relevant for education. This is their personal construct, built out of societal expectations.

(e) The 2nd and 3rd questions indicate the teachers' resistance to learn anything new. They have conveniently forgotten that a teacher is first a learner, then a teacher and for a teacher, continuous

- Learning is imperative, and
- Learning is not optional.

In passing we note that even teacher educators ask the 2nd and 3rd questions whenever they attended constructivist informed orientation programmes.

It is hoped that by the end of this chapter all the questions will have negotiated, acceptable answers and the justification, necessity as well as logicity of the epistemological evolution of constructivism will be more transparent.

The growth of epistemology and pedagogy, in general, and science education, in particular, in the second half of the 20th century has been so rapid that even the fastest runners are unable to remain static unless their efforts are an integral part of a larger group at work, so varied that efforts by an individual to develop some amount of expertise in any particular branch demands an equally good knowledge of other branches, so integrated that specifying anchoring concepts in any domain in isolation from others, sometimes even diverging concept domains, has become more and more difficult, so phenomenal that its impact is now felt at all levels of the society through the daily use of various kinds of terminologies and IT appliances of such dimensions of sophistication as were unheard of in hundred years, prior to that.

In such a framework education has evolved within the philosophy of 'freedom of necessity', a necessity which is defined by the demands of the changes in and needs of the society and a freedom for the individual with a right to choose. As a result of this the focus of education has changed, its domain of operation has been expanded beyond the walls of the classroom, its structures have been restructured to meet the ever evolving situations, its form has been redefined, its operational modalities have been modified beyond recognition, and assessment procedures have undergone a metamorphosis.

We divide this second half of the 20th century into three periods. In section 1.2 we discuss pre-1960 scenario, section 1.3 contains post-1960 – pre-1980 scenario and post-1980 scenario is presented in section 1.4. Section 1.5 gives our concluding remarks.

1.2 Pre-1960 Scenario

In this period the teaching-learning process (TLP) is verily described as the Transmissionist or Teacher-centered approach.

This approach broadly comes under the erklaren tradition in which explanation and hence instruction (not teaching) is the goal. It is realist in outlook, showing allegiance to an empiricist-inductivist view of knowledge, with a firm belief in the value of a reductionist approach to phenomena, the use of replicable experimental methods in search for casual mechanisms. Gaining knowledge from this framework has been described as diligent gathering of facts and then the drawing out of generalities, called, 'concepts'. The empiricist observes, collects, analyses, classifies and infers. He goes out into the world and collects his data or facts systematically, he puts them together, analyses them and then he draws out relations between them, called, concepts, principles and laws.

The long and massive influence of this Baconian empiricist—inductivism on the philosophy and growth of knowledge, in general, and science, in particular, is well recorded (Quinton, 1980). Chalmers (1978) synthesizes this philosophy into three basic features:

- Within realism, the world exists in an absolute sense such that absolutely true discoveries of ontological realities could be made by suitably trained observers.
- 'Singular statements' (a particular occurrence or state of affairs at a particular place and at a particular time) can be produced by faithfully recording observations made with an unprejudiced mind and using unimpaired sense organs along with dependable, reliable instruments.

- 'Universal statements' (which refer to all events of a particular kind at all places and at all times), or concepts, as we would now call them, can be obtained by inductive generalization from a suitably large number of diverse singular statements.

The spirit and content of the above assertions are contained in the following famous statement.

> The Great Book of the universe lies forever before our eyes but which we cannot read since we have not learnt the script in which it is written.
>
> —Galileo

Galileo's metaphor of the 'Great Book' encapsules the positivist aspect of nature and knowledge, in general and science, in particular, in the erklaren tradition. From this perspective science is portrayed as a pursuit leading to the revelation of the ultimate truths which have an absolute existence, and knowledge is regarded as an understanding of the fruits of these discoveries which confirm to the agreed-upon standards of a community of scholars.

One of the basic core assumptions of empiricism is that (Harris, 1982) there are two types of knowledge, non-theoretical and theoretical. For the empiricist it is the non-theoretical knowledge that makes up the building blocks for his construction, while the theoretical knowledge acts as both mortar and blue print.

The non-theoretical knowledge is simply "given". It is "out there" simply to be discovered, observed and known. Finally comprehension has to come through inductive generalizations. This basic tenet of empiricism, despite its long history and manifold acceptance, is badly conceived (Harris, 1982).

Similarly, practitioners and advocates of inductivism argue that its merit lies in its ability to arrive at generalizations from a number of particular instances. The inherent flaw in this is that it neither proves those generalizations to be true nor establishes high probability levels of their being true. Thus a central problem concerning inductively derived conclusions is that they are not simply logically valid, nor are they empirically binding.

By 1960, discerning researchers were becoming more and more concerned about these limitations and lacunae about this empiricist-inductivist's method of gathering knowledge.

Questions were being asked. But there were no satisfying answers.

On the other hand while the empiricist-inductivist view of knowledge was having its hay day, in the decade following the 1920's, psychology was dominated by behaviourism. Passivity of mind was emphasized, with the environment providing an '**input**' which is directly transmitted to, and accumulated by, the organism. The resulting behaviour was called as the '**output**'. This **input-output** (stimulus-response) model aimed to produce a blue print of human behaviour by conducting experiments on lower organisms in the belief that conclusions, arrived at, could be transferred to describe the behaviour of higher organisms, like the human beings, which were seen as differing only in complexity.

Behavioural psychology, as the name suggest, is a study of the change in manifest behaviour. So it was no surprise that in its framework learning was perceived as a process of changing or conditioning observable behaviour as a result of selective reinforcement of an individual's response to stimuli that occur in the environment. In this context one particular reminder is the Pavlov's dog experiment, where the dog will rush for its food as soon as the bell is rung. Here the mind of the pupil is seen as an empty vessel to be filled with facts (i.e. concepts, representation, laws, objective reality), and facts and more facts so that the world comes to be perceived and interpreted by the pupil in the perspective of the absolute truths.

Following seventeenth century philosopher John Locke, behaviourist sometimes interpret the above process of passive learning by the pupils by stating that pupils come to school as "tabula rasa" (i.e. blank slates) to be written upon by teachers (Wenning, 2008).

Thus the salient feature of behaviouristic epistemology is that pupils endeavor to accumulate knowledge (i.e. absolute truths) about the natural world and teachers transmit the same in a classroom for the benefit of the pupils. Hence, this epistemology centers on a transmissionist approach which is largely passive, teacher-directed and controlled.

Therefore, the nomenclature for the teaching-learning process during this period is "transmissionist" or "teacher-centered" approach.

The confluence of empiricist-inductivist view and behaviouristic view on TLP occurred because for both—

- The world of knowledge consists of irrefutable objective facts and world of truths, called ontological realities.
- This knowledge is like a commodity which can be transported and transmitted by the teacher using communication (both verbal and non-verbal) as the conveyance.
- Learning, as an accumulation of isolated facts, takes place in a rigid, hierarchical progression. (Udavari-Solner and Thousand, 1995)
- Rigidity of their principles is non-negotiable.

Some people call this the objectivist epistemology (Jonassen, 1991). He states,

> Objectivist believes in the existence of reliable knowledge about the world. As learners, the goal is to gain this knowledge; as educators, to transmit it.... Learners are told about the world and are expected to replicate its content and structure in their thinking.

These discussions show that the transmissionist approach or the teacher-centered approach which was in practice till 1960 was enmeshed in two sets of salient principles. They are the following:

Basic Principles

- Concepts, principles and laws have an absolute, objective, singular existence in a state of isolation which is unaffected by the environment, including individuals (the teachers, the learners). (Principle of absolute truths and ontological reality.)
- Concepts to be learned by a child of a particular class have been enshrined in the curriculum by the considered

views and recommendations of experts (Principles of primacy of curriculum).

- The textbooks elaborate on and describe these concepts with examples, non examples and activities.
- The teacher's job is to transmit these static and unchallengeable concepts in a classroom situation. (Transmissionist Principle)
- The child, viewed as a passive learner, shall have to only receive, what is transmitted. (Principle of passivity of learning.)
- The degree of learning by the child is measured by assessing his/her change in behaviour through reading more of the world and/or adding more to his/her bag of truths and/or facts about the world, as well as by his/her ability to regurgitate (as and when asked for) the accepted explanation and methodology expostulated by the teacher. (Murphy, 1997)

Thus the pupil as an entity had a passive existence imprisoned within the walls of objective knowledge. The above set of basic principles along with the crucial inputs is presented diagrammatically in Fig. 1.1.

Operational Principles

- The teacher knows everything and the pupils do not know anything (Reflection of the Principle of "tabula rasa").
- The teacher lectures and the pupils listen.
- The teacher demonstrates and the pupils observe.
- The teacher asks questions and the pupils answer them.
- The teacher enforces his/her authority and the pupils obey it.
- The teacher can punish (sometimes for the wrong reasons) by imposing his/her authority of knowledge and the pupils are to tolerate the punishment as meek lambs.
- The teacher acts and the pupils are to show as if they are also taking part in the acting.

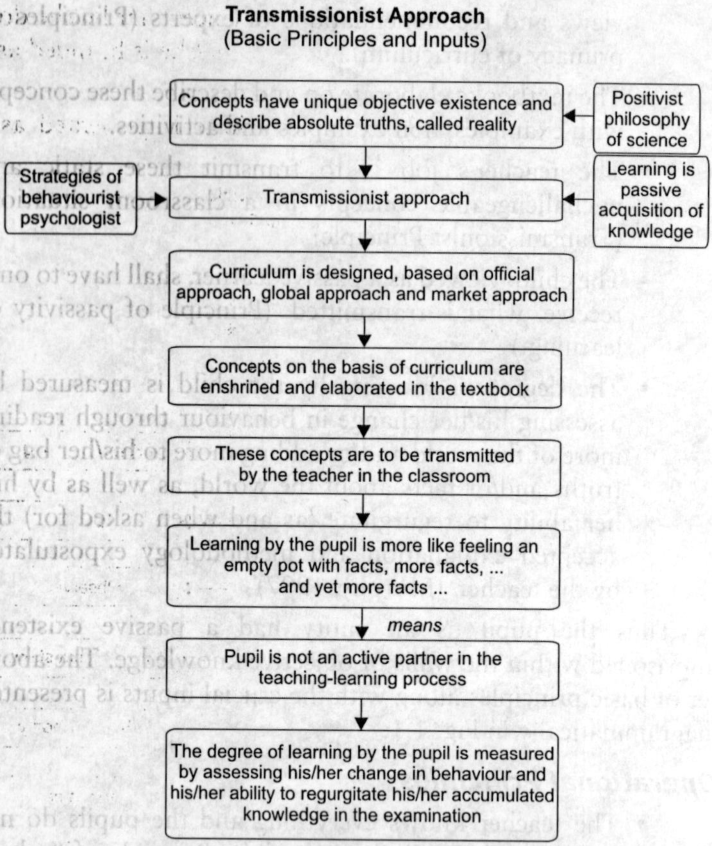

Fig. 1.1

Within the framework of such sets of principles:

- Nowhere any concern is shown for the poor pupil.
- Because of the above, a state of alienation is induced in the mind of the pupil.
- As a result, the pupil sits in the class but does not belong to the class.

This teaching-learning situation was academically unhealthy and cognitively repulsive. It was, as if, the teacher brings an apple and orders the pupil to eat it. The pupil has to eat it even if he/she does not like apples. If he/she eats the apple with even a semblance of smile on his/her lips, as if he/she is enjoying it, he/she is called a good student. If he/she voices that he/she does not like an apple and also does not eat it, he/she is branded as a bad student.

The above set of operational principles is presented as a concept map in Fig. 1.2.

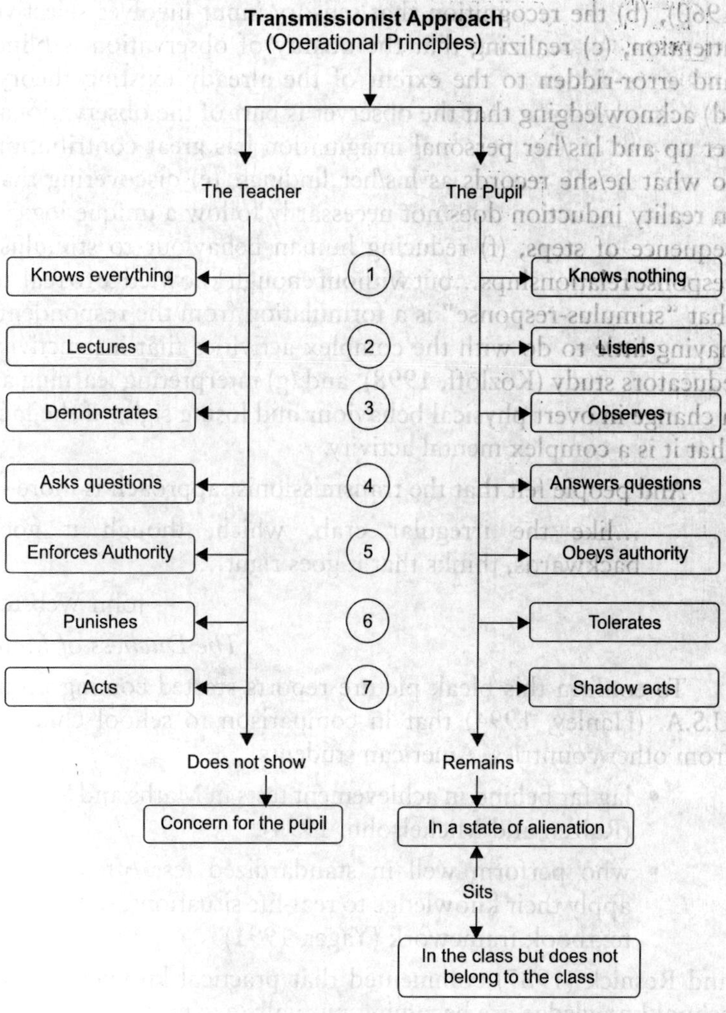

Fig. 1.2

By 1950, the experts got disillusioned with the transmissionist approach. Behaviourism coupled with Empiricist-inductivism and its corollary, the transmissionist approach to science teaching got weakened by the late 1940's although it had a temporary strengthening through the emergence of logical positivism. This weakening was caused by (a) new body of experimental data which was embarrassing to its underlying tenets (Berlyne, 1960), (b) the recognition that sensory input involves selective attention, (c) realizing that the quality of observation is blind and error-ridden to the extent of the already existing theory, (d) acknowledging that the observer is part of the observational set up and his/her personal imagination has great contribution to what he/she records as his/her findings, (e) discovering that in reality induction does not necessarily follow a unique logical sequence of steps, (f) reducing human behaviour to stimulus-response relationships...but without enough knowledge to realize that "stimulus-response" is a formulation from the respondent, having little to do with the complex activities that instructivist educators study (Kozloff, 1998), and (g) interpreting learning as a change in overt physical behaviour and losing sight of the fact that it is a complex mental activity.

And people felt that the transmissionist approach is more—

> ...like the irregular crab, which, though it goes backwards, thinks that it goes right....
>
> —John Webster
>
> *The Duchess of Malfi*

To confirm this bleak picture reports started coming up in U.S.A. (Hanley, 1994) that in comparison to school children from other countries, American students,

- lag far behind in achievement tests in Maths and Science (Raizen and Michelsohn, 1994),
- who perform well in standardized test often fail to apply their knowledge to real-life situations, outside the textbook framework (Yager, 1991)

and Resnick (1987) commented that practical knowledge and school knowledge are becoming mutually exclusive.

Hence, by mid 1950s empiricist-inductivist view of knowledge and behavioural psychology based epistemology was fast approaching towards its logical and natural extinction, as they have miserably failed in the struggle for existence under cognitive evolution.

The last nail on their coffin was put in 1957.

1.3 Post-1960 – Pre-1980 Scenario

In 1957 Russia sent the Sputnik-I into space. This was the wakeup call for the Western World. They realized that science education in their countries is lagging behind that in Russia. As a result, they, perforce, had to abandon empiricist-inductivist view and epistemology based on behaviourism.

Thus transmissionist/teacher-centered approach lost its charm and was put down on the way side.

Educationists of the Western World, in general, and U.S.A., in particular, searched for alternative approaches in epistemology and pedagogy. They discovered the Cognitive Psychologists whose studies and conclusions were in stark contrast with those of the behaviourist psychologists. For them the child, i.e. the learner, instead of the teacher, was the focus of their study and conclusions. Their argument was it is not important, who teaches; it is important, who learns. Three of the leaders of this cognitive psychology movement were Piaget, Bruner and Ausubel.

To understand the emergence of Constructivism, a brief review of their related works is in order for completeness.

1.3.1 Piaget

In epistemology Piaget occupies the same prime position as Darwin in the domain of Biological Evolution. Only those portions of his work which were relevant during 1960s in the search for alternative approaches will be briefly reviewed here. For a more comprehensive study of all the dimensions of his works one may refer to Modgil and Modgil (1982).

Piaget made a quantum jump when through diligent studies and careful observations he revealed that concepts

- are not just cognitive entities having specific connotations,
- but have hierarchical logical structures and can be arranged in a higher and higher cognitive demand scale.

For a detailed review of these cognitive demands of concepts one may refer to Adey (1979), Shayer and Adey (1981), Mahapatra (1994) and Mohapatra and Mahapatra (1999).

The obvious next logical step was to study and analyse the ability of the child's mind to handle and internalize the logical structures of the concepts. Thus his epistemology is both a theory of knowledge and a theory of cognition. In this context, his work on genetic epistemology can be broadly classified into two domains.

- Stage Dependent Theory
- Stage Independent Theory.

Stage Dependent Theory

Under this, Piaget's approach and investigation of the problem fall under three main areas (Gruber and Voneche, 1977).

- He emphasized the importance of activity in the growth of intelligence.
- He proposed that certain underlying pervasive logico-mathematical structures can be found repeatedly in these diverse activities.
- He explored in depth the growth of the child's thinking in relation to certain universals in the contents of human experience.

Piaget and Inhelder investigated the behaviours exhibited by children in different task situations and formulated an explanation in a framework of some logical structures. As an obvious outcome of these intensive and extensive studies, Piaget and Inhelder were able to identify four definable developmental stages of a child which are differentiated from one another by distinct, discernable logical structures.

The main characteristics of the stage theory are (Inhelder, 1956; Inhelder and Piaget, 1958; Piaget, 1960, 1972; Flavel, 1963, 1972; Piaget and Inhelder, 1969; Elkind and Flavel, 1969; Inhelder, Sinclair, 1971; Dasen, 1972):

- "Each stage is characterized by an overall structure in terms of which the main behavioural patterns are determined". (Piaget and Inhelder, 1969: 153)
- The order of appearance of each stage is invariant. However, the chronological age during which children can be expected to develop behaviour, representative of a particular stage is not fixed. The concept of fixed sequence or order of the stages is called "ordinality". Piaget's proposed stages are ordinal stages. A "Bright" child may go through the stages rapidly and a "Dull" child may progress more slowly, some never reaching the last stage (Wadsworth, 1989), but the sequence is strictly maintained.
- Each stage incorporates the successes of the previous stage.
- Each stage may be seen as a preparation for the following stage, while the achievement of a new stage is seen as the reaching of a state of equilibrium.

Thus each stage contains an initial period of preparation and a final period of achievement and sandwiched between these two will be many sub-stages of micro cognitive developments. Commenting on the sub-stages Inhelder (1956) writes:

> I am always struck by the fact that among developing children the dispersion within a stage is relatively small compared with the wide differences between behaviour at one stage and another.

Piaget's comment (1960) on the same issue is the following, "As soon as we try to pin these intermediary stages down, we enter a sort of a cloud-dust (Sic) of sub-intermediaries because of their instability."

However, the above views do not mean that Piaget believed in sudden jumps in thinking style as the child proceeds from one stage to the next. In fact he advocates that the transition is always a smooth one because it is a continuous evolutionary process.

The broad four stages are:

STAGE – 0, Sensori-motor (Pre-verbal) stage ... 0-2 years

STAGE – 1, Pre-operational stage ... 2-7 years
STAGE – 2, Concrete operational stage ... 7-11 years
STAGE – 3, Formal operational stage ... 11 or 12 – 14 (or) 15 years.

The chronological age of the child shown against each stage is simply a statistical indication of the age limits where the particular stage may manifest, but the age boundaries of the various stages are not rigid. However, what is rigidity true is that each child passes through the stages in exactly the same sequence, i.e. a child cannot develop say, formal operation abilities just after the pre-operational stage without going through the stage of concrete operation. The main characteristics defining each stage are the following.

The most striking feature of the sensory-motor stage is the absence of language and mental representations. During this stage the practical knowledge which constitutes (Piaget, 1964) the substructure of later representational knowledge is developed. To begin with, the child's world remains a world of "Here and Now".

Gradually, the child then evolves into his pre-operational stage. He develops some ability to mentally co-relate objects on the basis of some of their characteristics. For example—all men are "Daddy" and all women are "Mummy". In other words, he develops the ability to deal with single classes, but he cannot reason about subclasses nested within larger classes. His thinking at this stage is mostly controlled by his perception which led Piaget to formalize his scheme of correspondence and constituent function (Piaget, 1977, 1978).

The concrete operational stage may also be thought of as a process of reordering and recombination and is richer than the previous stage (Piaget, 1974). Although the actual presence of objects is no intrinsic condition (Sinclair, 1971) for this stage, the mechanism of "reflexive abstraction" associated with this stage still features mainly the physical and mental "manipulations" of concrete objects.

In the final stage the thinking of the child is no more restricted to the concrete or the potentially real. The child can now reason on hypothesis, construct operations at propositional logic, and attain new structures, which are on the one hand combinatorial and on the other hand more complicated group structures. In short, the formal operations associated with this stage are the hypothetico-deductive ones. Further the operations in this combinatorial stage are non-local in the sense that they are mobile (Piaget, 1964).

This brief discussion on Piaget's model about the hierarchically sequenced logical structure of concept with consequent specific cognitive demands and review of Piaget's stage dependent theory was critically essential, because

- for the design of the new curriculum and textbooks during the period post-1960 – pre-1980, they provided the bench mark for easy reference, and
- they helped in the design of tools to ascertain any match/mismatch between (Mohapatra & Mahapatra, 1998; Mahapatra & Mohapatra, 2006).
  (a) the cognitive demands of concepts included in the curriculum and textbooks for any standard, and
  (b) the developmental stage in which the students of that standard are likely to be.

Such a match/mismatch data is functionally needed before a curriculum is designed or a textbook is drafted.

We note in passing that Piaget's and his 'Geneavian School of psychologists' above discussed works are based primarily on the philosophy of "Structuralism". Structuralists are different from others by their conviction (Gardner, 1973; Tomlinson-Keasey, 1982) that there is a pattern or organization underlying mental functioning, by their belief that this structure can be discovered through orderly analysis, and by their notion that structures have a generality and coherence that extend beyond a specific instance. However, Piaget is a little more than a structuralist in the sense that he not only recognized the necessary and intrinsic sequence of the structures but explained them by invoking an innate programme (Inhelder, 1976). It is because of this that he is often referred to as a "constructivist" (O'Loughlin, 1992), which we discuss in Chapter 2.

For completeness we record that although during 1960s and 1970s Piaget's genetic epistemology was the most influential work in the context of Cognitive Psychology, design of curriculum and drafting of textbook, some authors did point out certain flaws in Piaget's model of developmental stage. The flaws are:

- The model has the problem of horizontal and vertical decalages (Lovell and Ogilvie, 1960; Uzgiris, 1964; Smedshund, 1961).
- There is heterogeneity of behaviours and characteristics of a given stage (Beilin, 1971; Brown and Desfortes, 1977; Schwebel, 1975).
- There is the problem of 'Precocity' (Gelman and Tucker, 1995).
- Each stage consists of a structure d'ensemble (Novak, 1978; Cornell, 1978; Odom, 1978; Ennis, 1978).

In view of the above it is interesting to note that the idea of stages of cognitive development has been under almost continuous attack for 50 years, without showing any sign of being prepared to lie down or die.

Stage Independent Theory

In the stage independent theory Piaget visualized that the intellectual development of concepts in the mind of a child goes through four cognitive processes. They are:

- Schema
- Assimilation
- Accommodation
- Equilibration

We call this stage independent theory, because these four processes, which are the active agents to generate learning, are not specific to any stage.

(a) Schema: Schemata (plural of schema) are intellectual structures, those organize events as they are perceived by the organism, and classified into groups according to common characteristics. They are repeatable psychological events in the sense that a child will repeatedly classify a particular event in a manner which is consistent in his/her mental structure. As for example, if a child consistently classifies cows as dogs, then it will be safe to infer that in his/her personal constructs consisting of such schemata as "Four Legs", "Bigger than Cats", "Friendly", "Wet Nose" (Wadsworth, 1989) he/she is unable to differentiate between a cow and a dog.

Schemata are the child's tool bag of actions and responses to make things happen. At birth, schemata are mostly reflexive and rudimentary in nature, such as grabbing and mouthing objects. As the child grows, schemata become more differentiated, less sensory, and more numerous. The network they form becomes increasingly more and more complex. These schemata, which do not have any physical counterpart, are not observable entities, are inferred to exist, and are hypothetical structures of cognitive development, those do change with years. The adult's schemata are different from those of the child, but are derived from the sensory-motor schemata of the child. The processes responsible for this change and attainment of new structures are assimilation, accommodation and equilibration.

(b) **Assimilation:** Assimilation is the cognitive process by which the child integrates new experiences of the outside world into the existing schemata, without changing their structures, but potentially at the cost of "squeezing" the external perception to fit the existing schemata. Assimilation is a continuous process which goes on all the time. Assimilation theoretically does not result in a change in schemata. But through this processes the child tries to perceive new things in the framework of the existing structures or he/she may see old things in a new way.

(c) **Accommodation:** This is the process which is responsible for generating changes in the schemata. When a child encounters a new event he/she tries to assimilate it into existing schemata. Four possibilities are there. The new event may

- exactly fit into the existing schemata, or,
- fit after minor alternation or restructuring of the existing schemata, or,
- need the extension of the cognitive domain by adding new structures into the existing ones, i.e. by potentially generating new scheme, or,
- be in total dissonance with the schemata of the child and he/she may reject it totally.

All the above four activities are part of the process of accommodation leading to a change of the schemata. Accommodation thus accounts for a qualitative development of the form and structure of the schemata in contrast with assimilation, which accounts for the quantitative development of schemata (Wadsworth, 1989).

(d) **Equilibration:** The processes of assimilation and accommodation are necessary for cognitive growth and development. They remain active in tandem, flip-flopping between them in the process of progressive growth of schemata. Equilibration is a steady state of balance reached through assimilation and accommodation. It allows external experience to be incorporated into internal structures. When such integration is not possible, dis-equilibration occurs, leading to "Cognitive Conflict" and providing motivation for the child to seek equilibration through further assimilation and/or accommodation. This involves self-reflection and auto-regulation.

Over and above this theoretical presentation of the key four processes of Piaget's stage independent theory, a common, real life example is in order so as to go from theory to practice for the benefit of the teacher.

Example

The real life situation is like the following:

The child daily goes to her school from her house by walking. There is a post office near the house. The Post Office is connected to the house by a road. On the other hand, the school is connected to the house and to the Post Office by different roads. This situation is depicted in Fig. 1.3.

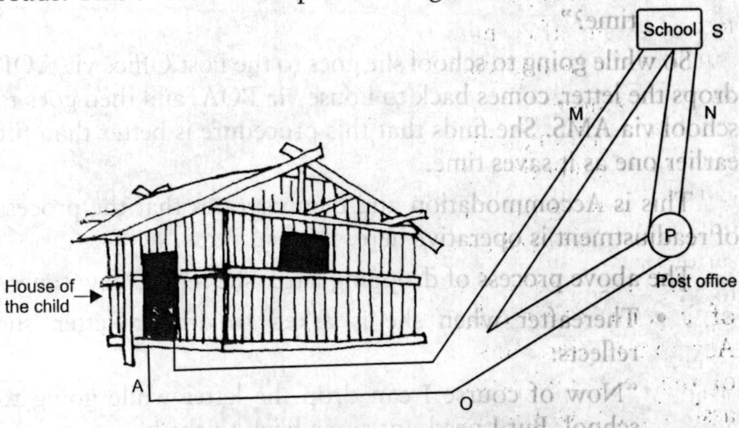

Fig. 1.3

- The Schemata in the mind of the child are that:
  - there is a road AMS, connecting her house and her school,
  - there is a separate road SNP, connecting her school to the Post Office, and
  - there is another road AOP, connecting her house to the Post Office.

Father of the child hands over a letter to her and asks her to drop the letter in the Post Office while coming back from the school.

- The child goes to school via AMS. When the school closes she takes the path SNP, goes to Post Office and drops the letter in the post-box. There after she goes back to school by the road PNS and then comes to her house via SMA.

Thereafter for the next few times whenever her father asks her to drop a letter in the Post Office she repeats the process, stated above. This is Assimilation.

- But after few times when she is asked to drop a letter she starts thinking:

"I can drop the letter in the Post Office while I am going to school instead of while I am coming back from school. Will it make any difference? Will this save time?"

So while going to school she goes to the Post Office via AOP, drops the letter, comes back to house via POA, and then goes to school via AMS. She finds that this procedure is better than the earlier one as it saves time.

This is Accommodation and demonstrates that the process of readjustment is operative here.

The above process of dropping letter she repeats few times.

- Thereafter when she is asked to drop a letter, she reflects:

  "Now of course I can drop the letter while going to school. But I need not come back to the house again. I can go to school straight from the Post Office via PNS."

  She does that and finds that the procedure is still better. She also discovers that she can drop the letter while coming back from school by taking the path SNP and then reach the house via POA and that this procedure is identical to the procedure of taking the path AOP and then PNS.

  She has reached a state of Equilibration by using the processes of reflection, assessment, readjustment and self-regulation.

The discussion on the above four processes was needed as at a later stage (particularly in Chapter 2) one can see that the genetic roots of Constructivism are present in them. Thus it is justified to call Piaget a constructivist.

1.3.2 Bruner

Bruner (1978) on the other hand tried to find out the characteristics of a concept. He concluded that a concept must have five elements, i.e. a name, examples (positive and negative); attributes (essential and non-essential) attribute values and a rule defining the specific essential attributes of a concept. In some cases, the attributes may have a range of values within which the attributes are acceptable. Noising or distractive attributes are non-essential ones which make it difficult to find the common essential features of the concept.

Bruner et al. (1977) further differentiated between concept formation and concept attainment. Bruner and his associates viewed the environment to be a complexity consisting of innumerable objects, events and phenomena. To cope with the environment, we are engaged in the process of categorizing which means that we render discriminately different things equivalent, responding to them in terms of class membership rather than their uniqueness. In other words, we invent categories and form concepts. Categorizing helps reduce complexity of the environment because we do not have to respond to each stimulus as if it were entirely different and had its own label or to learn it at each encounter. Hence, categorizing is the basic thinking process. All categorizing activity involves identifying and placing events into classes on the basis of certain cues and ignoring others (Joyce and Well, 1980). According to Bruner, categorizing activity has two components; the act of concept formation and the act of concept attainment. The former is the first step towards the later. Concept formation is the act by which new categories are formed; it is an act of invention. But in concept attainment the concept is already formed.

In concept attainment teaching, a teacher needs an array of examples that are alike in some ways and different in others. As the learner encounters the examples, he/she is required to find out whether the instance exemplifies the concept or not. At each encounter with an example, the learner formulates hypothesis about the concept, and simultaneously he/she gets information about the characteristics and attribute values of the concept. In the process of treating each example against the frame of reference of the concept, the learner is constantly applying the various 'elements' of the concept in practice. Thus, the learner is engaged in correctly distinguishing examples from non examples before he/she verbalizes the concept. The strategies people use to attain concepts are basically of two kinds—selection and reception. The reception model of concept attainment is considered an ideal strategy—one that minimizes strain and maximizes performances. It is more direct in teaching students the elements of a concept.

It may be noted that Concept Formation (CF) and Concept Attainment (CA) are distinctly different from each other in their objectives in the sense that CF's objective ends mostly with categorization, whereas CA's objective starts mostly after categorization. Hence, the mental activity, thinking process, reflection and analysis associated with CF and CA are not same. So the function of each for a child needs different teaching strategy.

1.3.3 Ausubel

Ausubel's (1963, 1968) Advance Organizer's model, which aims at meaningful verbal learning by the learner, starts with the premise that each academic discipline has a structure of concepts and these are organized hierarchically. The mind is an information processing system. Like the disciplines, the mind has a hierarchically organized set of ideas that provides anchors for information and ideas that serve as a storehouse for them. New ideas can be usually learnt and retained only to the extent that they can be related to already available concept or proposition that provides ideational anchors.

As per Ausubel, Advance Organizers is the basic process for strengthening cognitive structures and enhancing retention of new information. Its primary objective is to provide the scaffolding for explaining, integrating and interrelating the concept to be learnt with the concepts already learnt by the child. In it is also inbuilt the ability to help the child to differentiate between the concept to be learnt and the concepts already learnt. As a corollary if the new concept is strongly in dissonance with the concepts already learnt by the child so that he/she is not able to locate or generate any ideational linkage then the child may reject the new concept (In our model the 'Conceptual Rejection' as an output, is discussed in Chapter 5, may be compared with this view of Ausubel).

Advance organizers are of two types: (a) expository and (b) comparative. Expository organizers are specially useful for they supply cognitive girders when the child is exposed to unfamiliar material or situation. It also provides a general model of class relationships as a general subsume for a new class, subclasses and species. On the other hand, comparative organizers handle mostly with familiar materials. They provide a fusion/integration of old concepts with the new concept when it has some similarity with the old ones. But it does not treat the old and new concept as one and the same. It also has the ability for differentiation between the two.

Unlike Bruner who stresses on the need for the learners to discover knowledge directly in a final form, Ausubel terms his approach to learning as Reception Learning or Meaningful Verbal Learning. He emphasizes that Reception Learning is important, because, the understanding that the learner acquires, both in and out of school, are presented, rather than discovered. Further, even if knowledge is acquired by using discovery approaches, it has to be followed by internalization through Reception Learning.

Perhaps the word 'Meaningful' in the present context needs a little elaboration at this point, because this word is very frequently used under constructivism. For the comprehension of "meaningful learning" Ausubel sets forth three cardinal characteristics. They are:

- The "meaningfulness" of a material presented depends on the learner and the material and neither on the presenter, nor on the method of presentation.

  (This is a very strong statement and by a single stroke renders the teacher-centered approach redundant and meaningless.)
- A strong connection between the new concepts to be learnt with the already existing cognitive structures of the learner determines the degree and quality of meaningful learning.

  (This is again a very strong statement and will delineate the role of learner's alternative conception for meaningful learning, which will be discussed in Chapter 7.)

- Meaningful learning puts emphasis on the readiness of the learner to comprehend, relate and reconcile what he/she knows with what he/she is going to learn, rather than to memorize verbatim the later.

  (This eliminates the basic philosophy of Transmissionist Approach.)

The discerning reader may look into the studies by Ausubel (1960), Ausubel and Fitzgerald (1962), Ausubel et al. (1968) for details about meaningful learning.

Ausubel advocated that Reception Learning takes place through two processes, viz. Progressive Differentiation and Integrative Reconciliation. Under the former, the more general and inclusive ideas of a discipline are presented first. Gradually, step by step, the concepts are differentiated in terms of 'details' and 'specificity'. Thus, as learning proceeds an individual organizes the contents of a particular discipline in a hierarchy, in which the more inclusive concepts occupy a position at the apex of the structure and subsume progressively less inclusive and more highly differentiated, sub-concepts. The rationale given is that new ideas and information can be efficiently learnt and retained only to the extent that more inclusive and appropriately relevant concepts are already available in the cognitive structure to serve a subsuming role, or to furnish ideational anchorage. For instance, molecular arrangement and molecular motion are inclusive or subsuming concepts. A structure of knowledge on states of matter can be cognized by learners if the subsuming concepts are presented at the outset. Now, information regarding kinetic theory, evaporation's, condensation, change of state, etc. can be efficiently and meaningfully learnt once the inclusive concepts are internalized. Such subsuming concepts may be found in every discipline of study. Once the inclusive concepts are presented and organized within a learner, new ideas are taken in and relationships are explored between ideas, to point out the similarities and differences and reconcile inconsistencies. As a result of this mental exercise new learning takes place. This is called integrative reconciliation. In meaningful learning, potentially meaningful material enters the cognitive field and interacts with, and is appropriately subsumed, indexed in a relevant and more inclusive system. Therefore, existing cognitive structure in the mind of the learner is a major factor affecting meaningful learning and retention.

We note in passing that the seminal ingredients of the Concept Map technique (Novak, 1990; Matthews et al., 1984; Mohapatra and Parida, 1995), which is a powerful one in a constructivist informed TLP and which will be discussed in Chapter 4, are present in the process of progressive differentiation.

1.3.4 Chinese Dictum

At around the sametime when the entire western world was intensely engrossed in studying, analyzing and distilling out essential ingredients from the works of cognitive psychologists for use in (i) designing science curriculum, (ii) drafting science textbooks, and (iii) formulating innovative teaching techniques, they also discovered a Chinese dictum which states:

- I read I forget,
- I see I remember, and
- I do I understand.

The last of the above three principles propounded the role of activities by the child for promotion of comprehension.

1.3.5 Child-centered/Activity Based Approach

Piaget's works, which focus on

- hierarchically arranged logical structures of concepts,
- cognitive developmental mental levels of the child,
- role and importance of the match and mismatch between the cognitive demand of a concept, cognitive developmental level of the child, and
- assimilation, accommodation and equilibration as the three basic processes used by the child to learn a concept,

and Bruner's works, which emphasize

- the five characteristics of each concept, and
- concept attainment which is more desirable than concept formation,

and Ausubel's works, which advocate

- the advance organizer model,
- the promotion of meaningful verbal learning, and
- the process of progressive differentiation and integrative reconciliation,

culminated in the child-centered approach and the Chinese dictum induced the Activity-based approach. Finally, the teacher-centered approach went into oblivion and the child occupied the center-stage in the TLP.

We classify the child-centered approach into two types (Mohapatra, 1994).

- Child-centered by the child (CCBC),
- Child-centered for the child (CCFC).

1.3.5a CCBC

In 1967 massive curriculum reform processes were underway. In particular the first wave of the Nuffield science projects were published in England and Wales and the *Physical Science Study Committee* (PSSC) and the *Biological Science Study Committee* (BSSC) books got published in U.S.A. These books caught the interests of many countries in the world. The slogan behind this movement was *'I do I understand'*. In these exciting new courses,

- The existing pupils activities were redesigned to ensure greater participation 'by' the pupils,
- New and innovative pupils' activities were added to the already existing ones so that pupils may have the opportunity to learn science 'by' investigating science without being told the answers in advance, and
- More emphasis was laid on exploration 'by' the pupils than on mundane instruction only.

Greater teacher-pupil interaction was promoted through redrafting of textbooks. Doing 'by' the pupils and not hearing lectures was stressed. Teacher became a co-partner in the activities performed 'by' the pupils with the help of suggestive but not prescriptive guidelines. Pupils were seen spending major portion of their time pushing trolleys up run ways, gathering cutting and sticking tangling metres of ticker tape, marbles were rattled around in trays simulating solids, liquids and gases, batteries and bulbs were clicked in and out of specially designed circuit boards.

We call this CCBC because the entire gamut was geared to promote greater active participation "BY" the pupils.

The above referred textbooks had another novelty associated with them. Each carried with it another set books called Teacher's Guide/Handbook. These books were meant to

- make the teacher aware of his/her new role,
- provide more content and pedagogical inputs for the teacher for his/her enrichment of knowledge,
- suggest the teachers to design innovative activities, and
- suggest better assessment procedure to make the evaluation of pupil's meaningful learning more reliable.

1.3.5b CCFC

During the operationalisation of the Nuffield, PSSC and BSSC type projects, researchers started asking very loaded questions like curriculum for 'what' and for 'whom'. People started searching answers to salient question—Did the concern 'for the child' as an evolving organism decides the form, focus, structure and content of the curriculum? Here, of course one must keep track of three types of curricula (Mohapatra and Mahapatra, 1996):

- The 'Official Curriculum' which is a policy document of the National Government or State Government or institutions like National Council of Educational Research and Training, New Delhi, and which delineates the broad objectives as seen by the Government or Institutions.
- The 'Operational Curriculum', is the curriculum along with the accompanying textbook which is designed and/or approved by various educational Boards and Universities and which is expected to be transacted in the classroom situation. Primarily 5 different approaches

(Eraut, 1990) go into the designing of the 'Operational Curriculum'.

- The 'Functional Curriculum', is what the child finally learns as indicated by the formal assessment systems.

To bridge the gap between the 'Functional Curriculum' and the 'Operational Curriculum' and because of the concerns 'for' the readiness of the child, efforts were made to design curriculum with, say, minimum mismatch between the cognitive demands of the concepts and the cognitive developmental level (a la Piaget) of the pupils, and salient inputs from the works of Bruner and Ausubel.

We call this CCFC because in this approach the concern is 'FOR' the child.

1.3.6 Impact

After all these efforts, educational administrators, curriculum framers, textbook writers, researchers, teachers and parents expected a quantum jump in the meaningful learning of science by the pupils.

By 1975, impact studies were undertaken.

Soon evidences from those studies showed that in the framework of pupils' conceptualization of science concepts, the dictum 'I do I understand', in reality, got transformed to 'I do and I am even more confused' (Driver, 1983). Research workers concluded that for the children to develop an understanding of the concepts and principles of science, more is required than simply providing practical experiences and innovative activities. This is also voiced by Chisman (1992) when he wrote that although Nuffield type approaches made science more interesting, the focus was still on the science content and not on the needs of and the intrinsic parameters associated with the pupils.

Similarly, by the late 1970's research studies indicated that textbooks and pedagogy based on cognitive approaches (i.e. on the basis of the findings of Piaget, Bruner and Ausubel) contribute marginally to the degree and quality of meaningful learning by the pupils.

A 20-year experiment, with lots of promise, at least on paper, had proved to be unsuccessful. The western world was in a fix, because they were back at square one.

The essence of this child-centered approach/activity-based approach, which theoreticians sometimes refer to as Cognitive-approach, along with the consequences are shown diagrammatically in Fig. 1.4.

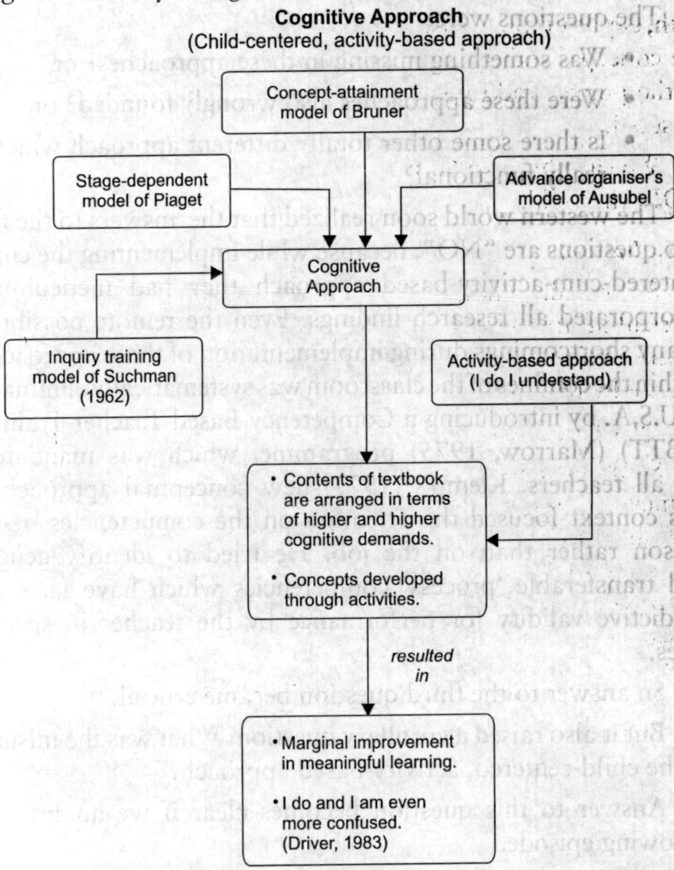

Fig. 1.4

1.4 Post-1980 Scenario

The results of the impact studies look to be logically inconsistent. Because, the only two human inputs inside the classroom, where the TLP is in operation, are the teacher and the child (pupil/learner). The failure of the Teacher-centered approach was natural because the approach, in the framework of TLP, was, of course, wrongly founded. But the child-centered approach, the activity-based approach..., why should they fail to produce the desired results? There were several questions which needed answers.

The questions were:

- Was something missing in these approaches? or,
- Were these approaches also wrongly founded? or,
- Is there some other totally different approach which is really functional?

The western world soon realized that the answers to the first two questions are "NO", because while implementing the child-centered-cum-activity-based approach they had meticulously incorporated all research findings. Even the remote possibility of any shortcomings during implementation of these approaches within the confines of the classroom was systematically eliminated in U.S.A. by introducing a Competency-Based-Teacher-Training (CBTT) (Marrow, 1975) programme, which was mandatory for all teachers. Klemp's (1977) new conceptual approach in this context focused the attention on the competencies of the person rather than on the job. He tried to identify generic and transferable 'process' competencies which have face and predictive validity for performance by the teacher in specific roles.

So answer to the third question became crucial.

But it also raised a corollary question: What was the mistake in the child-centered, activity-based approach?

Answer to this question becomes clear if we analyse the following episode.

Episode

One Mr. Roberts was a very popular figure in his community, because by profession he was a teacher in the school of the community. He had a dog, Daniel, of the golden glade variety, which was disciplined and faithful. Once a news went round in the community that Roberts has taught his dog, how to whistle. So every resident of the community became proud of Roberts for this rare achievement.

One day, while Mr. John was taking his morning walk, he met Roberts. John was very curious to hear the whistling of Daniel, the dog. So he said, "Roberts, I heard that you have taught Daniel, how to whistle."

Roberts smiled and said, "Yes, Yes, I have taught him how to whistle."

John said, "Then, let us hears how he whistles."

Roberts replied, "I taught him how to whistle, but he did not learn."

Here in lies the reason of the failure of the child-centered approach as well as the suggestion for what should be the approach.

In the episode, Roberts, being a good teacher, was sincere, committed in his efforts to teach Daniel, how to whistle. He might have even taken the help of electronic musical instruments to repeat the production of whistling sound. And, Daniel, the student, was faithful, obedient and disciplined. But, the end result is Daniel did not learn how to whistle. This is so because Roberts' focus was on his effort and on the disciplined behaviour of Daniel. But, Roberts did not, at first, tried to learn, how a dog learns.

The same mistake was committed in the Teacher-centered approach (where the focus was on the teacher, his/her techniques, his attitude, knowledge base, competencies, etc.), in the child-centered approach (where the focus was on the child, his/her mental developmental level, involvement, active participation, activity performing ability and interest, etc.) and nobody emphasized to know how does a child learn. Since TLP is an output oriented activity it is essential and imperative that one should search to find an answer to the question,

How does the child learn a concept?

So around 1980 search was on to find out an answer to this all-important, specific question. It is then that educational researcher came across a potentially loaded statement of Ausubel (1968). He states,

> If you ask me to identify the single most important factor that determines the degree and quality of learning, I will say ascertain what the child knows and teach him accordingly.

This statement has two important, complementary parts.

- Ascertain what the child knows.
- Teach him accordingly. (It means teaching of the child should depend wholly on what the child knows.) This will be taken up in Chapter 6.

The first part is likely to provide greater insight into the cognitive domain of the child and hence will possibly help in the formulation of a new and functional epistemology. On the other hand, the second part will generate crucial bench marks for a novel and pragmatic pedagogy.

Perhaps the first serious research study on "What the child knows?" was done by Late Prof. R. Driver. It completely shattered the perception-based conclusions that "The child learns and hence knows whatever is taught in the classroom" (here classroom is used in a very broad sense). There followed a spate of research studies about what the child knows, i.e. child's concepts about concepts.

1.4.1 Child's Concept About Concepts

We will make a brief and relevant review of this area of research. The research efforts were focused on mainly three broad areas.

A. Obviously the major efforts (for a comprehensive list Pfundt and Duit, 1994 may be seen) were directed to diagnose, collect, collate, classify and map these children's concepts in various concept domains. For diagnosis, old techniques were refined and new techniques were developed. Some of the techniques were,

- asking questions,
- encouraging pupils to ask questions,
- engaging pupils in activities,

- generating situations for reflection and voicing opinion,
- brain storming sessions,
- generating cognitive conflict and disequilibrium,
- presenting bridging analogies, and metaphors,
- organising group discussion,
- providing interactive computer programmes,
- presenting multiple situations for visualizing a concept,
- providing open-ended questions with no fixed response, and
- creating conceptual dilemma.

B. Search for a nomenclature: The total emphasis on the study of pupils' concept about concepts in science resulted in a proliferation of terms that describe these concepts which were mostly at variance with the connotation of formal concepts in science. These terminologies emerged from two approaches, namely,

- a negative approach based on empiricist philosophy,
- a positive approach based on the new constructivist philosophy.

Negative Approach

In this approach pupils' conceptions of natural phenomena are viewed as inferior to the formal or experts' view. This view, being embedded in empiricism (Abimbola, 1988), has a long history. Though not in the present context, as early as 1940, Matteson and Kambly (1940) called the pupils' conceptions as "erroneous concepts". Terms like: "misconceptions" (Ralya and Ralya, 1940; Doran, 1972; Novick and Menis, 1976; Goldsmith, 1978; Brumby, 1979, 1984; Champagne et al., 1979, Nussbaum, 1979; Helm, 1980; and Fisher, 1986), "misunderstandings" (Brumby, 1979), "erroneous ideas" (Champagne et al., 1979), and "mistakes" (Gowin, 1983) were used. The most commonly used term is "misconceptions", perhaps because it is possible to clearly delineate (Markle and Tiemann, 1970) many of these concepts as "insects" or "elements" in terms of "critical attributes" that define them. They are viewed as "misconceptions" to the extent that they very often treat a non-example as an example. However, we argue that in that sense is not the Lamarckian theory a misconception? But in the hierarchy of the theories of evolution, instead of being termed as a "mis theory", it is still regarded as a theory, because in a Lakatosian spirit we not only appreciate the limitations of the framework in which it was proposed but also believe in the philosophy that even a wrong theory also does contribute to the growth of science. Therefore, we reject such a nomenclature, i.e. 'misconception', because

- a negative viewpoint about what the pupil conceives is built into it, and
- as a result it is likely to create an unfriendly, non-conducive, alienated psychological classroom climate, where pupils are to learn what we expect him/her to learn.

Positive Approach

In the positive approach pupils' prior conceptions are viewed (West, 1982) as an interpretative framework on which to anchor the new learning. Saltiel and Malgrange (1980) and Saltiel and Viennot (1985) use the term "Spontaneous reasoning" to describe pupils' conceptions. But, it may be noted that the "reasonings" used by pupils are not "spontaneous" or "on the spot" or "on the spur of the moment". They are usually based on very sound reasoning and logic in their framework enmeshed in their ideas. The process behind the reasoning they adopt has direct similarity to that of a scientist (Driver, 1983). As for example a group of pupils responded that 'fire is a living thing' and when asked as to why they think it to be so they replied, "Fire can create fire, fire can move from one place to another place, fire respires oxygen, fire needs food (dry leaves, twigs, etc.) for survival, fire responds to stimulus, because if you strike fire, flashes come out." Obviously the reasoning is very sound in the conceptual background of the pupil and is definitely not "spontaneous". So we reject the term "spontaneous reasoning".

On the other hand, in the context of the nomenclatures, "mini-theories" by Claxton (1983, 1985), "alternative theories" by Hanson (1984), "naive or intuitive theories" by Mc Closkey (1983), and "Common sense theories" by Hills (1989), not only do the objectives, used in conjunction with the word 'theory', differ among researchers but so does the meaning and use of the word 'theory' itself (Rankin, 1995).

Mc Closkey (1983) views theories of students as being naive in the sense of being incorrect or primitive when compared to scientific theories. Di Sessa (1988), in contrast, believes that: "...intuitive physics is nothing much like a theory in the way one uses that word to describe theories in the history of science or professional practice." Also McClelland (1984) asserts that: "To suppose that children are scientists of a sort when they think about such phenomena seems to me to misconstrue totally the meaning and purpose of science." Hills (1989) believes that an interpretation of the word 'theory' as it is used in formal science is unwarranted, because one need not adopt the canons upon which scientific theories are based in using the word 'theory' to describe students' understanding of natural phenomena.

We argue that any of these terms containing the word 'theory' may not be considered as a viable nomenclature because most of these informal, untutored ideas of the pupils are not necessarily substantiable by experiments and have obviously poor predictive qualities in terms of what really happens, except perhaps in the local-specific, macro-world of pupil's layman experiences. Hence, if due consideration is given to the purpose for which these informal ideas serve in the everyday affairs of the students then these common sense conceptions/ideas can be best viewed as neither being naive or primitive but rather alternative to the scientific conceptions (Rankin, 1995).

It is from such considerations that Driver and Easley (1978) proposed the term "Alternative frameworks". From the definition of 'framework' 'as given in *Webster's New Collegiate Dictionary* and the *Advanced Learner's Dictionary of Current English* it should be clear (Abimbola, 1988) that "Alternative frameworks" are just the undergirders that anchor the ideas. Ideas are not the same thing as their framework, although ideas reflect their framework and vice versa. We agree with Abimbola (1988) that—"framework refers more to the organization of ideas rather than the ideas themselves. 'Frameworks' then are not what are revealed to us in research about students' existing conceptions; they are what we infer from what the students tell us during interviews or while using any other assessment techniques. We need to note, too, that our inferences are fallible."

Osborne and Gilbert (1980) and Hewson (1981) proposed the term "Alternative conceptions" and are in line with Engel and Driver's (1985) suggestion of "Alternative ideas". The term "Alternative Conceptions" is more inclusive than "Alternative frameworks". If some conceptions are held by the students strongly and persistently then it is better to call them conceptions with the prefixed adjective 'Alternative' to be contrasted with "Scientific conceptions". We prefer the term "Alternative Conceptions" (which is now mostly accepted) because, it,

- tends to treat the informal ideas of the pupils on the same footing as the formal concepts in science so that psychological resistance from the pupils to receive and consider formal concept will possibly be less intense as compared to the situation where the term 'misconception' is used,
- has the scope to give equal weightage to the various ideas that each group of pupils may have about the same natural phenomena so that no pupil will feel neglected or alienated in the framework of his/her conceptions, and
- has the latitude to also include the so-called "misconceptions" until they are actually rejected by the pupils themselves through activities, discussion, debate and other experiences.

We will be very often referring "Alternative Conceptions", as "ALCONs" in an abbreviated form.

C. Pupils' ALCONs in most cases, were so unexpected and so much at variance with the accepted meanings of those concepts that it was imperative to know how could such ALCONs be formed in the cognitive domain of the pupils.

We will keep the discussion on this query to the last part of this chapter, because therein lies the answer to the question: How does a child learn a concept?

However, at this point, it is but natural to present few indicative and illustrative exemplars of pupils' ALCONs, from various research studies.

1.4.1a Exemplar 1

One of the earliest studies investigated pupils' ALCONs about the concepts "Living", "Animal" and "Plant". That was so, because a pupil is exposed to this classification of 'objects' into 'living', 'non-living' and 'living' into 'animals', 'plants' very early, i.e. in standard III and IV. Bell (1981), Bell & Barker (1982) observed that 78 per cent of 11-year-olds of New Zealand categories 'spider' as not an animal. Even 35 per cent of Primary teacher trainees responded the same. This was obviously a surprising revelation (Villabi and Lucas, 1991). It was difficult for the researchers to believe this result. Since they used the interview-about-instances approach, they naturally wanted to find out the reasons for such a discrepant response. The result of the intensive interview showed, that—the reason for categorizing something as an animal, or, not was based on such considerations, by the pupils, as

- the number of legs (animals are expected to have four legs),
- size (animals are big),
- habitat (animals are found only in land),
- coating (animals have fur), and
- noise production (animals make a noise).

Since neither any science textbook, nor any classroom teaching by a teacher ever state the above criteria for identification of 'animals', then the obvious question, that was asked, was—

> How could such criteria, defining cognitive images about the concept 'animal' be formed in the minds of the pupils?

Mohapatra (1994) also investigated pupils' ALCONs about the concepts 'animal', 'living', and 'plant'. Since these concepts are taught in classes III and IV, the subjects for his study were 222 pupils of class VI(P1), and 216 pupils of class VII(P2), because, it was expected that by that time fairly stable states of conceptualization of these concepts must have been ingrained in the minds of the pupils and these will be reflected in their responses. As regards taking pupils of two classes as subjects it was thought that this variation may indicate any desirable modification that may have been effected in pupils' mental structures about these concepts, over the school years.

The Tool consisted of three types of questions for each of the concepts, 'animal', 'plant' and 'living'. The first type contained a list of objects from which the pupils are to pick, say 'animals'. The second type contained questions with Yes/No type responses and the pupils were asked to justify their answers. The third type asked them to write five names of animals. Finally, there was clinical interview of few subjects.

The results of this study are given in Table 1.1, Table 1.2 and Table 1.3.

Table 1.1: Per cent of subjects responding to specific names as example of 'animal'

Sl. No.	Specific names of animals	Subjects	
		P1	*P2*
1.	Examples of big animals, like cow, dog, elephant, etc.	97.7	98.5
2.	Examples of small animals, like ant, mosquito, fly, etc.	0.0	5.6
3.	Examples of birds, like crow, eagle, parrot, etc.	1.2	1.6
4.	Examples of reptiles, like snake, lizard, etc.	0.7	1.0
5.	Examples of human beings, like, father, mother, friend, etc.	0.0	0.0

Table 1.2: Per cent of subjects responding to specific names as examples of 'plant'

Sl. No.	Specific names of plants	Subjects	
		P1	*P2*
1.	Examples of big plants like mango tree, banyan tree, etc.	95.8	98.6
2.	Examples of small plants like rose plant, paddy plant, tomato plant, etc.	1.3	3.5
3.	Examples of very small plants, like grass, moss, etc.	1.1	3.4
4.	Examples of creepers like, money plant, pumpkin plant, etc.	0.8	1.7

Table 1.3: Per cent of subjects who gave specific names as examples of 'living' being

Sl. No.	Specific names of living beings	Subjects	
		P1	*P2*
1.	Animals (including man)	45.2	48.2
2.	Plants	50.3	51.3
3.	Non-living objects	4.5	0.5

Table 1.4 is special because it gives per cent of subjects who categorized certain very specific non-living objects as living beings. The responses were special because the explanations they gave for their answer were special and they highlight the objective of this chapter.

Table 1.4: Per cent of subjects who categorized very specific inanimate objects as 'living' being

Sl. No.	Very Specific objects	Subjects	
		P1	*P2*
1.	Fire	7.7	6.2
2.	Cloud	11.5	10.4
3.	Robot	15.6	13.7
4.	Motor Car	7.2	6.3

From the above four tables the visible pupils' ALCONs are:

- human beings are not animals (very strong ALCON),
- even birds, reptiles are not animals,
- ant, mosquito, etc. are not animals,
- creepers are not plants,
- grass and moss are not plants,
- even rose plant, paddy plants are not plants,
- fire is a living being,
- cloud is a living being,
- robot is a living being, and
- motor car is a living being.

The obvious question is,

> How could such ALCONs (which definitely are neither part of the textbook nor part of the classroom teaching) be formed in the minds of the pupils?

The answer to which will gradually emerge in this chapter.

The purpose of presenting the results of Mohapatra (1994) is to arrive at three important conclusions:

C1: Although Mohapatra's studies were undertaken 13 years after Bell and Barker's studies, the pupils ALCONs, those were diagnosed, were identical. This indicates a strong resilience of these ALCONs, against change of time and situation.

C2: The form, structure and characteristics of these two independent studies are mostly identical although in one case the subjects were from New Zealand and the other case they were from Odisha, India. Thus this shows that these ALCONs are culture, geographical boundary and classroom teaching practices independent. Spoken differently, these ALCONs have a strain of 'universality' in them. This raises a question; do they depend on the mental developmental level of the pupil within the framework of Piaget's stage dependent theory? Answer to such queries can be seen in Chapter 5.

C3: The similarity between the ALCONs of the subjects P1 and P2 indicates that these ALCONs resist modification or erasement, with advancing school years.

At this point three sample clinical interviews, one for each of the three concepts is in order to have a peep into the operational cognitive structures of the pupils.

Clinical Interview-I (Concept 'Animal')

Interviewer	:	Is 'house-fly' an animal?
Pupil	:	No, Sir. (Very convinced tone)
Interviewer	:	Why?
Pupil	:	It is not like...say...a dog.*
Interviewer	:	Anything else....
Pupil	:	(Feels encouraged).... It does not have fourlegs.*

Thus for the pupil the critical attributes (*asterisked ones) to identify an animal are—

- animals are big in size, and
- animals should have four legs (here 'four' is the essential attribute value, as per Bruner).

Coupled with these if one combines the findings of from the interview of other pupils, two more critical attributes of the concept 'animal' emerge. They are—

- animals must have a tail, and
- animals have a wet nose.

The question is…"Where from the pupils collected these as the critical attributes of the concept 'animal'?"

The answer to this question was glaring at the researcher and the answer is—

> The pupil has himself/herself constructed the knowledge that these are the critical attributes to identify an animal.

Once we accept this answer many things fall into place and many puzzles about ALCONs get solved and one arrives at the conclusion—

> Knowledge is constructed by the pupil.

and the corollary is—

> Knowledge cannot be instructed.

Other conclusions also follow. They are:

1: Pupil's ALCON is real and valid for him/her.

Because by using his/her ALCONs he/she comprehends and organises his/her experimental world. Each pupil has his/her own connotation for a concept, like, 'Animal'. Once this is accepted as a fact, then from the pupil's (i.e. learner's) point of view.

2: Concepts lose their absolute, objective, singular existence.

This is the principle of relativism. Searle (1995) argued that as humans, we create (read, 'construct') systems of representation. Any one or more of these systems of representation can viably (read, not truly) represent the same reality. Searle names it

'Conceptual relativity'. Mohapatra (1994) calls it 'connotative relativity'. Matthews (1992) terms it 'relavist epistemology'.

We note in passing that the spirit of the Sapir-Whorf hypothesis (Sapir, 1956; Whorf, 1956) in its 'weaker form' is somewhat similar to this principle.

Thus:

Relativism licenses multiplicity of truths, representations and realities in the cognitive world of the pupils.

An analysis of the connotative relativity, manifesting as concepts expressing a single concept yields a matrix of four states (Pavlik, Schweers and Popejoy, 1982).

$$\begin{pmatrix} C_c \\ C_f \\ F_c \\ F_f \end{pmatrix} = \begin{pmatrix} \text{Concrete concept shaped within concrete language.} \\ \text{Concrete concept shaped within formal language.} \\ \text{Formal concept shaped within concrete language.} \\ \text{Formal concept shaped within formal language.} \end{pmatrix}$$

While teaching the seemingly simple term 'animal', the teacher is in the state of F_f whereas the child is in the state of C_c, and likes to continue to be there as it does not in any way conflict with his/her 'world of science' and 'world of experience'.

These, above conclusions lead to two questions:

Q. 1. How could the pupil construct such an unexpected concept about the concept 'animal'?

An answer to this question needed intensive clinical interview which have been conducted. And the result is the following. The pupil for the first time encounters the concept 'animal' as 'domestic animal'. In every home animals like horse, cow or dog, etc. are called "domestic animals". Whereas pet birds, like, parrot or peacock are never called as 'domestic animals'. Thus the pupil associates with the concept 'animal' the attributes, large in size, having four legs, a tail and wet nose. These constructs are then his/her **personal** ALCON, which is not influenced by the textbook or formal teaching in the class. However, he/she does remember the formal teaching in the class.

He/she does remember the formal concept for regurgitation in the examination.

Similarly, no textbook gives 'human being' as example of 'animal'. Further at the entrance of most hospitals and malls it is written that 'Animals are not allowed inside'. These experiences are functionally utilized by pupils to construct the concept that human beings are not animals.

In this connection an interesting research report is worth mentioning here. Bell and Freyberg (1985) in their case studies of New Zealand pupils' ALCONs about the concept 'animal' observed that some pupils have ticked human beings as 'animals'. Under normal circumstances a researcher would have been happy by receiving this correct response. But since their objective was to diagnose pupils' ALCONs, they engaged these specific pupils in a group discussion-cum-clinical-interview. The result was totally unexpected.

Transcript of the discussion with one of the pupils is given below.

Teacher : Is a person an animal?
Class : No! (Chorus)
Jane : Yes, it is!
Class : No, it's not!
Jane : Yes, it is. We are all animals.
Teacher : Why do you say that Jane?
Jane : Well, we are all Kiwis, aren't we?

(It may be noted that New Zealanders are sometimes known as Kiwis, after a flightless bird, unique to that country.)

This is a case of 'wrong reason-correct answer'. But, the answer also shows an ALCON, which is a manifestation of 'connotative relativity'.

Q. 2. Is this 'connotative relativity' specific to the concept 'animal'?

The answer is definitely 'No' and as proof, two more samples of clinical interview are presented below (Mohapatra, 1994).

Clinical Interview-II (Concept 'Plant')

Interviewer	:	You have given a cross mark in the box against 'moss'. What actually you mean?
Pupil	:	Sir, I mean—'moss' is not a plant.
Interviewer	:	But why? There has to be some reason.
Pupil	:	(Thinks a little) Yes... Sir, you... see..., 'moss' is not like a mango tree.*
Interviewer	:	So
Pupil	:	It is so small..., it does not have branches... And...*
Interviewer	:	And...
Pupil	:	And it does not have a stout stem.*

The asterisked statements definitely show ALCONs, because in the pupil's cognitive structures a 'plant' must

- be large in size, like a mango tree,
- must have a stout stem, and
- must have branches.

Clinical Interview-III (Concept 'Living')

(Group of pupils who ticked 'fire' as a living thing)

Interviewer	:	So you feel that 'fire' is a 'living thing'.
The group of Pupils	:	(In chorus) Yes, Sir.
Interviewer	:	Why?
		(Pupils raised their hands to give replies. Interviewer points his finger at one of the pupil.)
Pupil 1	:	Sir, fire can move from one place to another place.*
Interviewer	:	Why do you say so?

Pupil 1	:	Sir, I have seen.
Interviewer	:	Where have you seen?
Pupil 1	:	I have seen it in my village. Once fire started in one house soon it moved to other houses and they caught fire.**
Interviewer	:	(Points at another pupil.)
Pupil 2	:	Sir, I agree with her. (Points at Pupil 1.)
Interviewer	:	Any other reason?
Pupil 3	:	(Stands up) Sir, fire can create fire.* (Looks happily at his classmates)
Interviewer	:	Have you seen what you said?
Pupil 3	:	Yes, Sir. By using a burning match stick we light the gas stove.*
Interviewer	:	(Feels astonished at this statement and depth of observation) Anything else.
Pupil 4	:	Yes, Sir. We need oxygen. Fire needs oxygen.*
Interviewer	:	But...
Pupil 5	:	(Stands up) Sir, if we stop inhaling oxygen we will die. Without oxygen fire will also die.**
Pupils of the group	:	Yes, Sir.... Yes, Sir....

The single asterisked statements are definite indications of ALCONs, because in pupils' cognitive structures, 'motion' and 'spreads', 'create' and 'procreate', 'respiration' and 'needs' are three pairs of synonymous words/concepts.

The double asterisked statements not only show the depth of observation by the pupils but also indicate their scientist-like reason-based thought process, as proposed by Driver (1983).

1.4.1b Exemplar 2

Happs (1982, 1984) reported views (read structures) held by 11-17-year-old pupils about 'rock'. Of course to an earth-scientist, 'rock' is a material which consists of minerals. This is also mentioned in the textbook and taught by the teachers. But when pupils were interviewed, they expressed very different views. Their classification criteria for 'rock' were,

- weight (i.e. heaviness),
- colour
- size, and
- jaggedness.

For example, a fist-sized sample of dull looking, jagged, grey wake was readily described as 'rock' by 80 per cent of the interviewees, but only 28 per cent acknowledge a small rounded piece of pumice stone as 'rock'. To many pupils pumice was 'too light to be a rock'.

Taking cue from this study Mohapatra (1994) investigated pupils' ALCONs about the concept 'Heavy'. The subjects were 45 students of Class VIII. Mohapatra presented before the class two transparent plastic bags, one containing potato and the other containing brinjal. He also carried with him a digital weighing machine. He asked the students to find out the weight of each of the bags. The students vied with each other to do the task with alacrity and observed that the weight of each bag was 1 kg.

Then Mohapatra asked, "Which of the two bags is heavier?"

In the constructivist mental framework of the class teacher and Mohapatra, the question was very simple and all the students were expected to give the correct answer.

But more than 30 per cent of the pupils replied that the bag containing potato is the heavier one. When they were asked, "What is the reason for your answer?" they replied, "Potato is so hard and brinjal is so soft. So the bag containing potato is heavier."

This was a totally unexpected discovery of pupils' ALCON about the concept 'Heavy', and obviously this ALCON was self-constructed by the pupils.

1.4.1c *Exemplar 3*

This exemplar again consists of a simple situation. The pupils of standard III were shown a glass, full to the brim with water. They were also shown a brass ball and were asked, "what will happen, if the brass ball is dropped into the water?"

There were four types of answers. The pupils were then divided into four groups as per their responses and each group was engaged with discussion. The results were the following.

Group 1:

We : You have answered that there will not be any change in the glass of water.

Pupils : (In a single voice) Yes, Sir.

We : Why do you say so?

Pupil 1 : I have seen this.

We : (being surprised) Where have you seen?

Pupil 1 : Sir, I have seen my mother putting a spoonful of sugar in a cup of tea, and nothing happens. Sugar is solid, brass is also solid.

Group 2:

(Answer of this group was the same as that of group 1. But the reason, they advanced, was different. Incidentally, this group had only 2 pupils.)

We : You have replied that there will be no change in the glass of water if the brass ball is dropped into it.

Pupil 1 : Yes, Sir.

We : Why do you say so?

Pupil 1 : Sir, I have seen this.

We : Where have you seen?

Pupil 1	:	Sir, I belong to Paradip, the port. I have seen huge ships of steel coming there. But there is never any change in the level of seawater. (Then he smiles as he feels that he has given a satisfactory reason.)

Group 3:

We	:	You have replied that the level of water will go down in the glass, if the ball is dropped into it.
Pupils	:	Yes, Sir.
We	:	Why do you say so?
Pupil 1	:	Sir, when I sit on a couch, the couch get squeezed, because I am heavy.
We	:	So...!!
Pupil 1	:	Since brass is heavy, if it is dropped into the glass of water, water will get squeezed.

Group 4:

We	:	You have replied that, if the ball is dropped into the glass, some amount of water will flow out. (In fact we were happy that there was a group who gave the correct answer.)
Pupils	:	Yes, Sir.
We	:	Why do you say so?
Pupil 1	:	Sir, I have seen this happening.
We	:	(Surprised) Where have you seen this activity?
Pupil 1	:	Sir, when my mother puts me in the bath tub, water flows out.

It may be noted that in all the four cases the replies, i.e. constructed knowledge, were based on the personal ALCONs of the pupils and were not based on any formal knowledge, instructed in the class.

In this connection Donaldson (1978) writes,

> "When a child interprets what we say to him, his interpretation is influenced by at least three things—
>
> - his knowledge of the language,
> - his assessment of what we intend (as indicated by our non-linguist behaviour), and
> - the manner in which he would represent the physical situation to himself if we were not there at all."

The last factor is somewhat reflected in the reasons, advanced by each group, to justify their replies. The key words in the last factor are, 'represent the physical situation to himself', which indicates continuous self-construction.

To highlight the indisputable fact that the child constructs his/her knowledge we will present only two more exemplars.

1.4.1d Exemplar 4

The subjects were pupils of standard II. The madam teacher had taught the pupils the subtraction of two digit numbers, involving borrowing, like, subtraction of 19 from 36. Madam had used for her TLP the standard techniques of—

- lecturing,
- asking question,
- suggesting answers, if necessary, and
- appreciating correct answer given by any pupil.

The pupils had done their class work and homework correctly. In the traditional sense the lesson was a successful one.

Before madam had moved over to the next lesson, we entered the scene. We thought that since subtraction by borrowing is cognitively a conceptual process its learning needs different types of comprehension, internalization, reflection and application. So we wanted to investigate what are the personal constructs, i.e. ALCONs, of the pupils with regards to the concept 'borrowing'.

We asked the madam, "You developed and taught the lesson well by using the useful conventional technique of asking questions. Did the pupils ask any question?"

(In this section we have stated that 'encouraging the pupils to ask question is one of the techniques to diagnose pupils ALCONs, because sometimes the type of question one asks gives a better picture of one's cognitive structures than the answer one gives to questions.)

Madam replied, "Sir, they are small kids. What question they can ask?"

(That small kids are incapable of asking questions is an ALCON of the madam.)

We said, "Still...."

Madam said, "No Sir, they did not ask any question."

We said, "With your permission, should we encourage them to ask question?"

Madam shyly told, "Sir, all of you are my teachers. You don't have to seek my permission."

Then we coaxed the small cute kids to ask questions, if any, about the use of this borrowing technique being used for subtraction. The pupils were visibly afraid to ask questions to us, because they perhaps were thinking, "How can we ask question to Sirs, who are teachers of our madam."

Ultimately after lots of coaxing, cajoling and presenting toffees as gift and with promise from the class teacher that she will not get angry, a small, cute, sweet girl stood up. She was almost on the verge of crying because of the fear that later she will probably be severely reprimanded by the madam. Her name was Madhu. Finally she spoke up with an unsteady voice.

Madhu: Madam has taught us 'borrowing' is a bad habit. Sir, you can check my notes. But madam is borrowing now...!! How...??

(In standard II, a single madam teaches all the subjects. In the EVS class madam has taught: "Borrowing is a bad habit." She has also asked the pupils to take it down in their notebooks. That concept has been ingrained in the epitaxy of cognitive structure of the pupils. Hence, it has formed an ALCON. So in a different context when "Borrowing" word is used she cannot accept the new connotation and she is in a severe cognitive conflict.

(This could not have been diagnosed without persuading her to ask question.)

Once Madhu stood up and asked her question, others gradually mustered courage to speak. Sanat spoke out.

Sanat: Sir, Do the family members of madam not give her enough money so that she has to borrow in the class?

(Here the knowledge construction of Sanat is totally different from that of Madhu. For Sanat 'borrowing' is used only in the context of borrowing money. May be his family is going through a financial crisis and they are frequently discussing to borrow money to climb over the crisis. Sanat is applying his ALCON about, 'borrowing' in the context of subtraction. This is highly peculiar, but this is the reality.)

It is clear that such a concept about the concept 'borrow' was Sanat's own construction which has led him to ask this serious societal question.

The case with Raghav, who stood up next, was different. He did not ask any question. But he was enmeshed in a cognitive problem and he needed our help to solve it.

We: Yes, Raghav, you want to speak something.

Raghav: Sir, I have understood this subtraction by borrowing. But, I am unable understand this borrowing method.

We: (We were surprised by his statement) You understand 'borrowing', but you don't understand the method…!!

Raghav: Yes, Sir.

We: What do you exactly mean by that?

Raghav: Sir, if I have 6 rupees with me and I borrow one rupee, then it becomes only 7 rupees.

But in this subtraction there was the digit '6', madam borrowed '1' and it became '16' instead of becoming '7' only. I am unable to understand this method. If I know the method, I can apply the same when I borrow money from my father.

(Here the conceptual problem of Raghav is different from those of Madhu and Sanat. He desires to transport the borrowing of digits with their place value, to borrowing of money in the home context. Regarding the two processes to be similar is an ALCON which is constructed by Raghav himself.)

The cases discussed under Exemplar 3 and Exemplar 4 exemplifies the representation of a physical situation using one's own constructed ALCON. These cases again highlight knowledge construction by pupils.

1.4.1e Exemplar 5

This exemplar's speciality was that in this case:

- the child was only 4 years old,
- she had already constructed an ALCON, purely on her own effort, and
- she was trying to explain her experiential world by applying her ALCON in a way which she thinks, is correct and viable.

It was a chilly Sunday morning in London. Mohapatra and his friend Sunit, who had gone to London as British Council Fellow, went to meet one of their Indian friends, who was by then obtained the citizenship of England. On reaching Vikram's house they pressed the calling bell, even though the outer door was half open. As is commonly seen, on hearing the sound of the bell, a small cute girl came running to the door, with smiles on her face.

But very soon Mohapatra saw that total astonishment has covered her face and she was looking at Sunit with eyes wide open and mouth gaping. Mohapatra was surprised by seeing such unexpected reaction from the child and looked at Sunit.

After remaining in that dazed position for few seconds, she rushed inside. Thereafter Vikram came, they sat in the drawing room. Soon the child came, sat with Vikram and again started looking at Sunit in a dazed manner.

Then she said, “Papa, papa, uncle has a telephone in his mouth.”

This statement was a shock for Mohapatra and he again looked at Sunit’s mouth. What he observed there, generated a comprehension in Mohapatra, which was beyond imagination.

Soon the girl said in her sweet voice, expressing deep concern, “Papa, papa, the telephone has caught fire.”

The cause of the girl’s such an unexpected reaction was the following. Sunit was smoking a pipe (Fig. 1.5). Now in the girl’s cognitive domain:

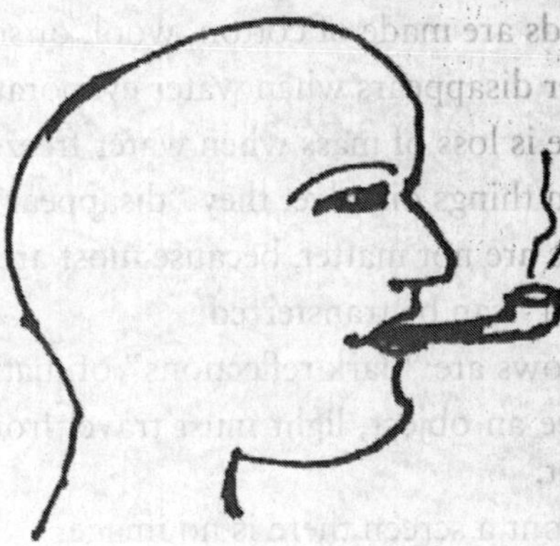

Fig. 1.5

- She had a mental image and constructs for a telephone, on the basis of shape and colour.
- For her the pipe resembled a telephone and for her, half of the telephone was inside Sunit’s mouth. She cannot believe a fact (at least in the domain of reality of the child) that a man can do such a thing.
- And seeing the smoke coming out from the pipe (for her from the telephone) she expresses her concern.

Finally,

- Our mental constructs of reality (i.e. telephone) are different from her mental constructs of reality.
- This exemplifies multiplicity of reality and representations. This is manifested relativism.

For a classified list of pupil's ALCONs one may refer to Phillips (1991), Hapkiewicz (1992, 1999). However, we give below a short-list of few interesting ALCONs, constructed by pupils.

An interesting list of ALCONs

1. Earth is larger than sun.
2. Gravity cannot exist without air.
3. Rain comes from holes in clouds.
4. Clouds are made of cotton, wool, or smoke.
5. Water disappears when water evaporates.
6. There is loss of mass when water freezes.
7. When things dissolve, they "disappear".
8. Gases are not matter, because most are invisible.
9. "Cold" can be transferred.
10. Shadows are "dark reflections" of matter.
11. To see an object, light must travel from the eye to the object.
12. Without a screen there is no image.
13. Red light travels faster than violet light.
14. When light passes through a prison, colours are added to the light.
15. When light passes through a filter, colour is added to the light.
16. The tip of a shadow always moves along an east-west line.
17. Moon and sun are about the same size. Stars are smaller than sun or moon.
18. Air and oxygen are the same gas.
19. Particles of solids have no motion.

20. Things "use up" energy.
21. An object at rest has no energy.
22. The terms "energy" and "force" are inter-changeable.
23. If energy is conserved why are we running out of it?
24. The distance travelled by a body is equal to its displacement.
25. If an object has a speed of zero, it has no acceleration.
26. If a body is at "rest", no force is acting on it.
27. Only animate objects can exert force.
28. When dropped in vacuum, objects fall with constant speed.
29. Constant motion requires a constant force.
30. Mass and volume are same.
31. An object's volume is greater in water than in air.
32. Electricity is produced in the wall socket.
33. All the electrons that make up an electric current are initially contained in the battery or generator.
34. Wire is hollow like water hose and electrons move inside the hollow space.
35. If one cuts down a plane mirror to half its size then image of only half of an object will be seen inside it.
36. Laws of reflection are valid only in the case of reflection from a plane mirror.
37. All metals are attracted by a magnet.
38. Heat is a substance.
39. The temperature of a substance depends on its size.
40. Pressure and force are synonymous.
41. Moving fluids contain higher pressure.
42. Objects sink in water, because they are "heavier" than water.
43. Rainwater is neutral in PH.
44. Plants, fungi, eggs and seeds are non-living.
45. Man produces his own food, like cereals and vegetables.
46. Plants feed by absorbing food through their roots.

47. Sunlight is food. It contains vitamin D.
48. Plants produce oxygen for our benefit.
49. The pupil of the eye is a black spot on the surface of the eye.
50. The size of an image depends on the size (diameter) of the lens used to form the image.
51. Electrons change into light when a lamp is turned on.
52. Rivers start from the ocean and fall on the hills.
53. Sound can travel in vacuum.
54. If you stand erect and your stretched left hand points towards east, then your head points towards north.

1.5 Conclusion

The discussions in the section 1.4 and the four exemplars involving 7 concepts as well as the list of illustrative 54 ALCONs indicate conclusively that:

- No child enters a class devoid of concept. [The principle of tabula rasa (blank slate) is completely shattered by this.]
- Concepts (read knowledge) cannot be instructed.
- Knowledge is actively constructed by the child. (Piaget's stage independent theory, where he advocates that acquisition of knowledge by the child goes through the processes of assimilation, accommodation and equilibration, and the model of Schema in fact reflects the above finding.)
- Child's ALCONs control the degree and quality of knowledge construction and hence the degree and quality of meaningful learning.

From these conclusions the following principles logically follow:

- **Principle of knowledge construction:** Knowledge is actively constructed through an autogenic process by the cognizing subject, and not passively received.
- **Principle of viability:** Viability decides the knowledge construction rather than validity and truth.

- **Principle of relativism:** In the child's framework, concepts, truths, reality and representations have a plurality ascribed to them, instead of an uniqueness. (von Glasersfeld, 2006)
- **Principle of character:** The character of cognition is functional and adaptive. (This follows from the 2nd principle)
- **Principle of purpose:** The purpose of cognition is to serve the child in comprehending and organising his/her experiential world.
- **Principle of invention:** Concepts are invented by the child rather than discovered.

[This is true even for scientists. In fact this principle is accepted by those who take a critical realist position and also by those who are on the idealist side of ontology. Strike (1987) argues that this principle is accepted by almost all who come from both traditional and constructivist perspectives (Ernest, 1993).]

The four important conclusions and the six basic principles stated above, are the cardinal characteristics of what is known now as 'CONSTRUCTIVISM'. Thus the emergence of 'Constructivism' as the most promising new paradigm of the theory of knowledge and the theory of learning was a natural outcome of cognitive evolution through the processes of struggle for existence, survival of the fittest and natural selection. This process of cognitive mutation became a reality because of the contributions from various educational thinkers and philosophers.

For the completeness of this chapter we mention below some of the key ideas and contributions from educational thinkers and philosophers for the growth of constructivism.

Vico:

- "God knows the world, because He created it, human beings can know only what they themselves have made."

  (Latin: verum ipsum factum)
- Whatever a man thinks and knows can therefore never represent an ontological reality.

(Latin: Deus naturae artifex, homo artificiorum deus)

[von Glasersfeld (1984) calls Vico "the first true constructivist", and thus traces the intellectual genealogy of constructivism.]

Kant:

- "Logical analysis of actions and objects lead to the growth of knowledge and the view that one's individual experiences generate new knowledge."

  [quoted from Brooks and Brooks (1993)]
- "Our understanding of the external world has its foundations not merely in experience, but in both experience and *a priori* knowledge."

  (Note: *a priori* knowledge is nothing but ALCONs.)
- "Our cognition begins with experience", but experience is a composite of both matter and form, with 'matter' being "what we receive from impressions" and the 'form' being "what our cognitive power supplies from itself".
- His 'categories' are predecessors of what are now called 'constructs' and 'schema'.

Dewey:

- Human mind is a meaning making organ, relentlessly driven to make sense of its world. (Dewey, 1933)

  (This provides the background for constructivism and active learning.)
- Development of knowledge is an adaptive human response to environing conditions, aimed at an active restructuring of those conditions.

  (Reflection of the principle of character, stated above, can be seen in this view.)

- Knowledge is a perception of those connections of an object which determine its applicability in a given situation. Our beliefs are only hypothesis, theories, suggestions, and guesses and are to be entertained tentatively and to be utilized as indications of experiments to be tried. (Dewey, 1916)

  (The above stated principle of purpose can be seen here. In the second part of this view, roots of constructivism are present.)

Vaihinger:
- The primary purpose of mind and mental process is not to portray or mirror reality, but to serve individuals in their navigation through life circumstances.

  (This resonates with the principles of purpose, stated above.)

Hayek:
- "Much that we believe to know about the external world, is, in fact, knowledge about ourselves. (Hayek, 1952)

  (This basically leads to the principle of relativism.)

Kelly:
- People organize their experiences by developing bipolar dimensions of meaning, or personal constructs (Kelly, 1970, 1991a, 1991b).

  People continually test their personal constructs by tracking how well they predict real life events and by modifying them as and when they are judged deficient.

  (These two for the first time use the phrase 'personal construct' and state that autogenic cognitive construction is a continuous active process.)

Ausubel:
- If you ask me to identify the single most important factor that controls the

degree and quality of learning, I will say, "Ascertain what the child knows and teach him accordingly." (Ausubel, 1968)

Piaget:

- Stage independent theory which advocates that a child learns through the processes of assimilation, accommodation and equilibration (Piaget, 1972).

  (The back and forth activity between assimilation and accommodation is sometimes referred as a "dynamic dance" of reflection, adaptation, change and growth. Piaget refers this as "constructivism".)
- Model of Schemata. (This envisages reframing of existing schemata (conceptual models) of the external world to fit new experiences. Thus schemata are always in a state of flux.) (The above two dimensions of Piaget's theory represent the principle of knowledge construction.)
- Intelligence organizes the world by organizing itself.

Lakatos:

- Presented a revolutionary 'activist' view of knowledge (Lakatos, 1970).
- It is we who create our 'prisons' (read cognitive structures) and we can also critically demolish them (i.e. to construct new structures).

  (Constructivism is embedded in these two loaded pronouncements.)

Kuhn:

- Knowledge acquisition is achieved by conceptual change, effected through continuous and discontinuous pathways (Kuhn, 1970).
- Replaced the 'realist' philosophy by the 'relativist' one.

(Kuhn introduced the model of 'conceptual change' which explains the mechanism of knowledge construction. His second view introduced the principle of relativism.)

Popper:
- Theory of falsification, which states that Science progresses (read knowledge growth) through the process of falsification (Popper, 1959).

  (This advocates that cognitive structures of knowledge are proved to be deficient by using the principle of falsification and are replaced by new structures, which are more encompassing and more inclusive.)

Vygotsky:
- Language is not only a vehicle for communication and meaning making, but also is a tool for constructing mental images and cognitive structures (Vygotsky, 1962). A word is microcosm of human consciousness.

  (This emphasizes the importance of language in shaping cognitive structures.)
- During the course of knowledge development everything occurs twice. Once for social interaction and communication. Then the knowledge gets internalized and individualized, resulting in "inner speech" (Vygotsky, 1978). (The above two theories form the basis of social constructivism.)
- With a little prop from the teacher a child can enter into his/her zone of proximal development (ZPD) and start constructing concept in his/her now potentially active zone.

Bruner:
- The constructivism tenet—reality is constructed by the individual.

- The perspectival tenet—the meaning of a concept is dependent on the context of the child. The context is also related to the domain of the content.
- The constraints tenet—meaning making is constrained by the framework developed by the culture as well as by the evolution of the child in that culture.
- There are three information processing systems, namely, the enactive representation, the iconic representation, and the symbolic representation and what he calls "integration" is the building of higher order ensembles of the three (Bruner, 1990).
- "Knowing is a process, not a product" (Bruner, 1966). "Thinking about thinking" has to be a principal ingredient of any empowering practice of education (Bruner, 1996).
- Learning and thinking are always situated in a cultural setting and always dependent upon the utilization of cultural resources.
- Knowledge, after all, is justified belief.

  (Justification is in the framework of the learner and leads to the principle of relativism and principle of viability).

von Glasersfeld:

- Knowledge cannot be instructed. It is actively constructed through an autogenic process by the cognising subject, the learner.
- The character of cognition is functional and adaptive. Adaptation does not mean adequation to an external world of things existing in themselves, but rather improving the organism's equilibrium, i.e. its fit, relative to experienced constraints.

- The purpose of cognition is to serve the learner in comprehending and organising his/her experiential world and not to discover an objective ontological reality.
- Concepts, representations, truths and reality are subjective and hence have a relativistic existence in the learner's cognitive domain.

  (This follows as a corollary from the first principle, above.)
- The emphasis is on the viability of human perception and knowledge and not on its validity.
- Absolute meaning of words is unattainable.

  von Glasersfeld (1995) is the proponent of radical constructivism. For a review one may see Staver (1998).

Maturana:

- Organisms are, by definition, self-creating and self-sustaining systems. This is the concept of autopoiesis (Maturana, 1988).
- Living systems are cognitively closed. When living systems think they are mapping an external world, they are actually experiencing and processing their own structurally determined responses.
- A closed system never comes into direct contact with reality. What is "outside" never gets "inside".

  (The above strong views brand Maturana as even more radical constructivist than others.)

Gergen:

- The term "Constructionism" is preferred to the term "Constructivism", because Social Constructionists are of the opinion that constructivism is too "interiorized", thereby condemning the individual to self-imprisonment in his/her own subjective experiences (Gergen, 1995).

- Reality is socially negotiated.
- Each individual has multiple, "multiphrenic" selves, which are socially constituted within the boundaries of culture, context and language (Gergen, 1991; Raskin, 2002).
- Persons use words and symbols not just descriptively, but persuasively to accomplish goals in a society.
- Human identity (language, knowledge, etc.) is fluid and constituted within the parameters set forward by social surroundings (Gergen, 1991, 1994).
- Individuals have constructed identities those are negotiated within cultural contexts.

Due to the emergence of constructivism the post-1980 Scenario is justifiably called the age of the "Constructivist Approach", or Learning-Centered Approach, a compact picture of which is presented in Fig. 1.6, with some succinct features.

We are conscious that the picture is neither comprehensive or inclusive of all possible strains. Its importance is its brevity for researchers and classroom practitioners.

As an outcome of the above discussions we conclude this chapter by stating three notable features of constructivism.

First

Because of the latitude for the interpretation of the core ideas of constructivism, views of quite different thinkers and researchers from diverse disciplines, like Psychology, Philosophy, Epistemology, Pedagogy, Science, Mathematics, Technology, Sociology, Linguistics, etc. got integrated in the evolution of constructivism. In other words constructivist views served as a rallying point for many, as is indicated in Fig. 1.6. That is why

Matthews (1993) uses the metaphor of constructivism being a mansion with many rooms (discussions on which will be taken up in Chapter 2).

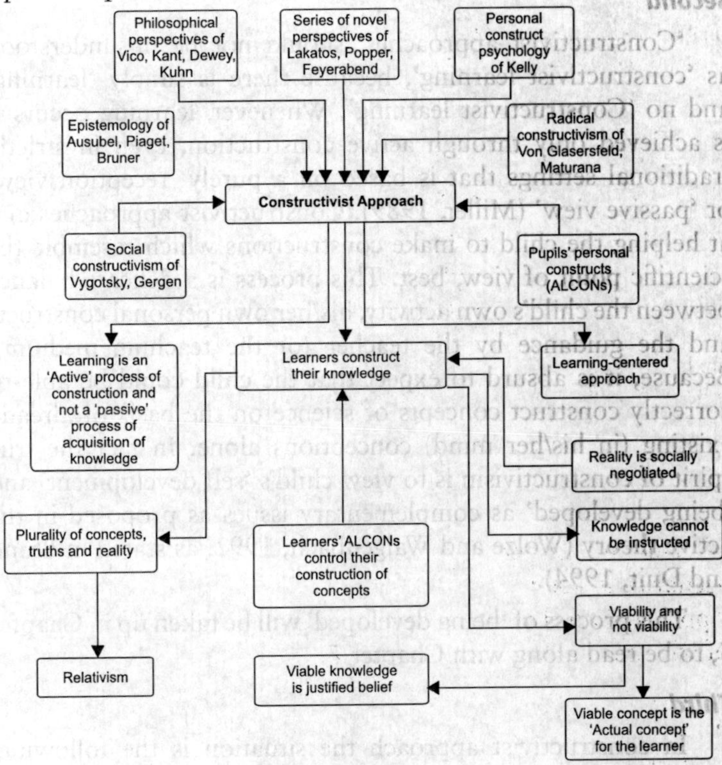

Fig. 1.6

This openness has with it, its associated pitfalls in the sense that non-constructivist sometimes enter this mansion slyly because there seems to be a desire among the researchers to be a member of the fashionable constructivist party in order to be taken seriously and in order to be part of mainstream research. As a result the constructivists form a very heterogeneous group with (a) researchers who are already constructivists before they know (the 'Real' ones), (b) researchers who claim to be constructivists, but in fact are not or at least in superficial way (the 'Fake' ones), and (c) researchers who share major ideas with those in the constructivist party but do not want to be called constructivist because they have some reservations about and objections to constructivism (the 'Moderate Conservatives').

Second

'Constructivist approaches' should not be misunderstood as 'constructivist learning', because there is simply 'learning' and no 'Constructivist learning'. Whenever, learning occurs it is achieved only through active construction, even in strictly traditional settings that is based on a purely 'reception view' or 'passive view' (Miller, 1989). Constructivist approaches aim at helping the child to make constructions which resemble the scientific point of view, best. This process is a delicate balance between the child's own activity, his/her own personal constructs and the guidance by the teacher (or the teaching medium). Because, it is absurd to expect that the child could be able to correctly construct concepts of science on the basis of already existing (in his/her mind) conceptions alone. In fact the true spirit of constructivism is to view child's 'self development' and 'being developed' as complementary issues as proposed in the active theory (Wolze and Walgenbach, 1992; as stated in Pfund and Duit, 1994).

This process of 'being developed' will be taken up in Chapter 5, to be read along with Chapter 7.

Third

In constructivist approach the situation is the following, the child with his/her personal constructs enters the learning set-up, the classroom, he/she is exposed in a guided way to the concepts to be learnt, active construction involving reflection/modification/erasement/rejection/absorption starts, and finally those constructions "Survive" that prove to be successful in dealing with the world around the construction. It is interesting to note that the above steps have a direct resemblance with the three basic principles of Darwin's theory of Evolution, namely, the Law of Natural Selection (here, by the Child of the concept), the Law of Struggle for Existence (here, between the personal constructs and the concepts during the period of construction) and the Law of Survival of the Fittest (here the final concept internalized by the child on reaching the state of equilibration).

The nitty-gritty of this construction of knowledge by the child are discussed in Chapters 3 and 5.

References

Abimbola, I.O. (1988). The problem of terminology in the study of student's conceptions in science. *Science Education*, Vol. 72(2): 175-84.

Adey, P. (1979). *Science curriculum and cognitive development in the Caribbean.* Ph.D. thesis, University of London, London.

Ausubel, D.P. (1960). The use of Advance Organisers in the learning and retention of meaningful verbal material. *Journal of Educational Psychology*, Vol. 51, pp. 267-72.

—— (1963). *The psychology of meaningful verbal learning.* New York: Grun and Stratlon.

—— (1968). *Educational Psychology: A Cognitive View.* New York: Holt, Rinehart and Winston.

Ausubel, D.P., and Fitzgerald, D. (1962). Organiser, general background and Antecedent learning variables in Sequential verbal learning. *Journal of Educational Psychology*, Vol. 53, pp. 243-49.

Ausubel, D.P., Stager, M., and Gaite, A.J.H. (1968). Retroactive facilitation of meaningful verbal learning. *Journal of Educational Psychology*, Vol. 59, pp. 250-55.

Belin, H. (1971). Developmental stages and developmental process. In D.R. Green, M.P. Ford, and G.B. Falmer (Eds.), *Measurement and Piaget.* New York: McGraw-Hill.

Bell, B. (1981). When is an animal not an animal? *Journal of Biological Education*, Vol. 15(3): 213-18.

Bell, B., and Barker, M. (1982). Towards a scientific concept of "Animal". *Journal of Biological Education*, Vol. 16(3): 197-200.

Bell, B., and Freyberg, P. (1985). Language in Science classroom. In R. Osborne and P. Freyberg (Eds.). *Learning in Science: The implications of children's science.* London: Heinemann.

Berlyne, D.E. (1960). *Conflict, arousal and curiosity.* New York: McGraw-Hill.

Brooks, J., and Brooks, M. (1993). *The Case for a Constructivist Classroom.* Alexandria, VA: ASCD.

Brown, G., and Desforges, C. (1977). Piagetian psychology and education. *British Journal of Educational Psychology*, Vol. 47, pp. 7-17.

Brumby, M.N. (1979). Problems in learning the concept of natural selection. *Journal of Biological Education*, Vol. 13(2): 119-22.

—— (1984). Misconceptions about the concept of natural selection, held by medical biology students. *Science Education*, Vol. 68(4): 493-503.

Bruner, J. (1966). *Towards a Theory of Instruction.* Cambridge, MA: Harvard University Press.

—— (1978). *The Process of Education*. Cambridge: Harvard University Press.

—— (1990). *Acts of Meaning*. Cambridge, MA: Harvard University Press.

—— (1996). *The Culture of Education*. Cambridge, MA: Harvard University Press.

Bruner, J., Goodnow, J.J., and Austin, G.A. (1977). *A study of thinking*. New York: Jon Wiley.

Chalmers, A.F. (1978). *What is this thing called Science?*. Milton Keynes: Open University.

Champagne, A.B., Klopfer, L.E., & Anderson, J.H. (1979). *Factors influencing the learning of classical mechanics*. Pittsburgh: University of Pittsburgh Learning Research and Development Centre, #1979/23.

Chisman, D. (1992). Changes in Science and mathematics education since 1966. *Science Educational News Letter*, No. 100, January 1992, British Council.

Claxton, G. (1983). *School Science: Falling on stony ground or choked by thorns?* Mimeograph. Centre for Science and Mathematics Education, Chelsea College, University of London.

—— (1985). Teaching and acquiring scientific knowledge. In T. Keen and M. Pope. (Eds.), *Kelly in Classroom: Practical Applications of Personal Construct Psychology.*

Cornell, E.H. (1978). Learning to find things: A reinterpretation of object permanence studies. In L.S. Siegel and C.J. Brainerd (Eds.), *Alternatives to Piaget: Critical Essays on the theory*. New York: Academic Press.

Dasen, P. (1977). *Piagetian Psychology: Cross cultural contribution*. New York: Gardner Press.

Di Sessa, A. (1988). Knowledge in pieces. In G. Forman and P. Pufall (Eds.), *Constructivism in the Computer age*. Hillsdale, NJ: Lawrence Erlbaum.

Donaldson, M. (1978). *Children's Minds*. Fontana/Collins.

Doran, R.L. (1972). Misconceptions of selected science concepts held by elementary school students. *Journal of Research in Science Teaching*, Vol. 9(2): 127-37.

Driver, R. (1983). *The Pupil as scientist?* Milton Keynes: The Open University Press.

—— (1989). Student's conception and the learning of science. *International Journal of Science Education*, Vol. 11(5): 481-90.

Driver, R., and Easley, J. (1978). Pupils and paradigms. A review of literature related to concept development in adolescent science students. *Studies in Science Education*, Vol. 5, pp. 61-84.

Elkind, D., and Flavell, J.H. (1969). *Studies in cognitive development*. New York: Oxford University Press.

Engel, C.E., and Driver, R. (1985). What do children understand about pressure in fluids? *Research in Science and Technology Education*, Vol. 3(2): 133-34.

Ennis, R.H. (1978). Conceptualization of children's logical competence: Piaget's propositional logic and an alternative proposal. In L.S. Siegel and C.J. Brainerd (Eds.), *Alternatives to Piaget: Critical Essays on the Theory*. New York: Academic Press.

Ernest, P. (1993). Constructivism, the psychology of learning and the nature of mathematics: Some critical issues. *Science Education*, Vol. 2, pp. 87-93.

Fisher, K.M. (1985). A misconception in Biology: Aminoacids and translations. *Journal of Research in Science Teaching*, Vol. 22, pp. 53-62.

Flavell, J.H. (1963). *The Developmental Psychology of Jean Piaget*. New York: D. Van Nostrand Company.

—— (1972). An analysis of cognitive developmental sequences. *Genetic Psychology Monographs*. Vol. 86, pp. 279-350.

Gardner, H. (1973). *The quest for mind: Piaget, Levi-strauss, and the structuralist movement*. New York: Knof.

Gelman, R., and Tucker, M.F. (1975). Further investigation of the young child's conception of number. *Journal of Child Development*, Vol. 46, pp. 167-75.

Gergen, K.J. (1991). *The saturated self: Dilemmas of identity in contemporary life*. New York: Basic Books.

—— (1994). *Realities and Relationships*. Cambridge, MA: Harvard University Press.

—— (1995). Social construction and the education process. In L.P. Steffe & J. Gale (Eds.), *Constructivism in Education*. Hillsdale, NJ: Lawrence Erlbaum.

Goldsmith, R.H. (1978). Changes in the importance of certain popular science misconceptions. *School Science and Mathematics*, Vol. 73(1): 31-36.

Gowin, D.B. (1983). Misconceptions, metaphors and conceptual change: Once more with feeling. In H. Helm and J.D. Novak (Eds.), *Proceedings of the International Seminar, Misconceptions in Science and Mathematics*. Ithacca, NY: Department of Education, Cornell University.

Gruber, H.E., and Voneche, J.J. (1977). *The Essential Piaget*. New York: Basic Books.

Hanley, S. (1994). http://www.towson.edu/csmc/mctp/Essays/Constructivism.txt

Hanson, K. (1984). Alternative theories in classroom. In C. Anderson (Ed.), *Observing Science Classrooms: Observing Science Perspectives from Research and Practice*. Columbus, OH: Association for the Education of Teachers in Science.

Hapkiewicz, A. (1992). Finding a List of Science Misconceptions. *MSTA Newsletter*, Vol. 38, pp. 11-14.

—— (1999). http://www.msta-mich.org

Harris, K. (1982). *Education and Knowledge*. London: Routledge & Kegan Paul.

Hayek, F.A. (1952). *The Sensory Order*. Chicago: University of Chicago Press.

Helm, H. (1980). Misconceptions in physics amongst South African students. *Physics Education*, Vol. 15, pp. 92-105.

Hewson, P.W. (1981). A conceptual change approach to learning science. *European Journal of Science Education*, Vol. 3(4): 383-96.

Hills, G. (1989). Students' untutored beliefs about natural phenomena: Primitive Science or common sense? *Science Education*, Vol. 73, pp. 155-86.

Inhelder, B. (1956). *Discussion on child development*. Volume I. In Tanner and B. Inhelder (Eds.). Tavistock Publication.

—— (1976). *Forward in Piagetian Research: Complication and Commentary*. Vol. I. (Eds.) S. Modgil and C. Modgil. UK: NEFR Publishing Company.

Inhelder, B., and Piaget, J. (1958). *The Growth of Logical Thinking*. London: Routledge Kegan Paul.

Jonassen, D. (1991). Evaluating constructivist learning. *Educational Technology*, Vol. 34(4): 34-37.

Joyce, B., and Weil, M. (1980). *Models of Teaching*. Englewood Cliffs. NJ: Prentice-Hall International Inc.

Kelly, G.A. (1970). A brief introduction to personal construct psychology. In D. Bannister (Ed.), *Perspectives in Personal Construct Psychology*. San Diego: Academic Press.

—— (1991a). *The psychology of personal constructs: Vol. 1, A Theory of Personality*. London: Routledge.

—— (1991b). *The psychology of personal constructs: Vol. 2, Clinical diagnosis and psychotherapy*. London: Routledge.

Klemp, G.O. (1977). *Three factors of success in the field of work: Implications for curriculum in higher education*. Boston, Massachusetts: McBer & Co.

Kozloff, M.A. (1998). http://people.unew.edu/kozloffm/ContraConstructivism.html.

Kuhn, T. (1970). *The structure of scientific revolution*. Chicago: Chicago University Press.

Lakatos, L. (1970). Falsification and the methodology of Scientific research programmes. In L. Lakatos and A. Musgrave (Eds.), *Criticism and Growth of Knowledge*. Cambridge: Cambridge University Press.

Lovell, K., and Ogilvie, E. (1960). A study of conservation of weight in the junior school child. *British Journal of Educational Psychology*, Vol. 30, pp. 109-18.

Mahapatra, M. (1994). *Piagetian Stages of the Pupils of Secondary Schools of Orissa and the Cognitive Demands of the Physics Curriculum of C.B.S.E. – A match/mismatch analysis*. Unpublished Ph.D. thesis, Utkal University, Orissa, India.

Mahapatra, M., and Mohapatra, J.K. (2006). Towards a science of curriculum design, Part-I. *Indian Educational Review*, Vol. 42(2): 3-25.

Markle, S.M., and Tiemann, P.W. (1970). 'Behavioural' analysis of 'Cognitive' content. *Educational Technology*, Vol. 10, pp. 41-45.

Marrow, G.G. (1975). The politics of competence: A review of competency-based-teacher-education, *Basic Skill Programmes on Teaching*. Washington, D.C.: National Institute of Education.

Matteson, H.D., and Kambly, P.E. (1940). Knowledge of science possessed by pupils entering seventh grade. *School Science and Mathematics*, Vol. 40, pp. 244-47.

Matthews, M. (1993). Constructivism and science education: Some epistemological problems. *Journal of Science Education and Technology* 2, Vol. 1, pp. 359-69.

Maturana, H.R. (1988). Reality: The search for objectivity or the quest for a compelling argument. *The Irish Journal of Psychology*, Vol. 9, pp. 25-82.

McClelland, J. (1984). Alternative frameworks: Interpretation of evidence. *European Journal of Science Education*, Vol. 6, pp. 1-6.

Mc Closkey, M. (1983). Naïve theories of motion. In D. Genter and A.L. Stevans (Eds.), *Mental Models*. Hillsdale, NJ: Lawrence Erlbaum.

Milter, R. (1989). Constructive criticisms. *International Journal of Science Education*, Vol. 11, pp. 587-96.

Mohapatra, J.K., and Mahapatra, M. (1998). Are the Science Reasoning Tasks good discriminators of the Piagetian Stages?—A study under Indian conditions. *Indian Educational Review*, Vol. 33(1): 40-51.

—— (1999). *New Dimension of Science Curriculum*. New Delhi: Commonwealth Publishers.

Murphy, E. (1997). http://www.cdli.ca/-elmurphy/emurphy/cle2b.html

Novak, J.D. (1978). An alternative to Piagetian Psychology for science and maths. Education. *Science Education,* Vol. 5, pp. 1-30.

Novick, S., and Menis, J. (1976). A study of students' perception of the mole concept. *Journal of Chemical Education*, Vol. 53(11): 720-22.

Nussbaum, J. (1979). Children's conceptions of the earth as a cosmic body. *Science Education*, Vol. 63(1): 83-93.

Odom, R.D. (1978). A perpetual salient account of decalage relations and developmental change. In L.S. Siegel and C.J. Brainerd (Eds.), *Alternatives to Piaget: Critical Essays on the Theory*. New York: Academic Press.

O'Loughlin, M. (1992). Rethinking Science Education: Beyond Piagetian constructivism, towards a socio-cultural model of teaching and learning. *Journal of Research in Science Teaching*, Vol. 29(8): 791-820.

Osborne, R., and Gilbert, J.K. (1980). A technique for exploring students' views of the world. *Physics Education*, Vol. 6, pp. 376-79.

Pavlik, R.A., Schweers, R.R. Jr., and Popejoy, W.D. (1992). A proposal for bonding language and concept development. In R.W. Bybee and R.B. Sund (Eds.), *Piaget for Educators*. London: Charles E. Merrill Publishing Company.

Pfundt, H., and Duit, R. (1994). *Student's Alternative Frameworks and Science Education.* Kiel: Institute fiir die PadagogiK der Naturwissenchaften an der Universitat Kiel (IPN).

Phillips, W.C. (1991). Earth Science Misconceptions. *Science Teacher*, Feb. '91, pp. 21-23.

Piaget, J. (1960). *Discussions on child development.* Volume 8. In Tanner and B. Inhelder (Eds.). Tavistock Publication.

—— (1964). Cognitive development in children: Piaget, Part-1, Development and learning. *Journal of Research in Science Teaching*, Vol. 2, pp. 176-86.

—— (1972). *The Principles of Genetic Epistemology.* London: Routledge Kegan Paul. (Trans.) by Wolfe Mays.

—— (1977). *The development of thought: Equilibrium of Cognitive Structures.* New York: Viking Penguin.

—— (1978). *Correspondence and Transformation: Impact of Piaget's Theory.* (Ed.) F.B. Murray.

—— (1974). *Adaptation Vitale at psychologiedel intelligence: Selection organique at Phenocopic.* Paris: Hermann.

Piaget, J., and Inhelder, B. (1969). *The Psychology of the Child.* London: Routledge Kegan Paul.

Popper, K. (1959). *The logic of scientific discovery.* London: Hutchinson & Co.

Quinton, A. (1980). *Francis Bacon.* London: Oxford University Press.

Raizen, S.A., and Michelsohn, A.M. (1994). *The Future of Science in Elementary Schools.* San Fransisco: Jossey-Bass.

Ralya, L.L., and Ralya, L.L. (1940). Some significant concepts and beliefs in astronomy and geology of entering freshman and the relation of these to general scholastic aptitude. *School Science and Mathematics*, Vol. 40, pp. 727-34.

Rankin, G. (1995). A challenge to the theory view of students' understanding of natural phenomena. *Science Education*, Vol. 79(6): 693-700.

Raskin, J.D. (2002). Constructivism in psychology, Personal construct psychology, Radical constructivism, Social constructivism. *American Communication Journal*, Vol. 5(3): 1-17.

Resnick, L.B. (1987). Learning in school and out. *Educational Researcher.* Vol. 16, pp. 13-20.

Saltiel, E., and Malgrange, J.L. (1980). 'Spontaneous' ways of reasoning in elementary kinematics. *European Journal of Physics*, Vol. 1, pp. 73-80.

Saltiel, E., and Viennot, L. (1985). What do we learn from similarities between historical ideas and the spontaneous reasoning of students? In P.L. Lijnse. (Ed.), *The many faces of teaching and learning mechanics.* Conference of Physics Education. Utrecht: GIREP/SVO/UNESCO.

Schwebel, M. (1975). Formal operations in first year college students. *Journal of Psychology*, Vol. 91, pp. 133-41.

Shayer, M., and Adey, P. (1982). *Towards a Science of Science Teaching.* London: Hienemann.

Sinclair, H. (1971). Piaget's theory of development: The main stages. In L. Steffe and S. Taback (Eds.), *Piagetian Cognitive Development Research and Mathematical Education.* Washington, D.C.: National Council of Teachers of Mathematics.

Smedslund, J. (1961). Conservation of substance and weight-II. *Scandinavian Journal of Psychology*, Vol. 2(2): 71-84.

Staver, J.R. (1998). Constructivism: Sound theory for explicating the practice of science and science teaching. *Journal of Research in Science Teaching*, Vol. 35(5): 501-20.

Strike, K.A. (1987). Towards a coherent constructivism. In J.D. Novak (Ed.), Proceedings of the *Second International Seminar on Misconceptions and Educational Strategies in Science and Mathematics*, Vol. 1, Ithaca, NY: Cornell University.

Suchman, R. (1962). *The elementary school training programme on Scientific Inquiry*, Report to the US office of Education, Project Title VII, Project 216. Urbana: University of Illinois.

Tomilinson-Keasey, C. (1982). Structures, functions and stages: a trio of unresolved issues in formal operations. In S. Modgil and C. Modgil (Eds.), *Jean Piaget: Consensus & Controversy.* New York: Rinehard and Winston.

Udavari-Solner, A., and Thousand, J.S. (1995). Promising practices that foster inclusive education. In R.A. Villa & J.S. Thousand (Eds.), *Creating Inclusive Schools.* Alexandria, VA: Association for Supervision and Curriculum Development.

Uzgiris, I.C. (1964). Situational generality of conservation. *Child Development*, Vol. 35, pp. 831-41.

Viennot, L. (1985). Analysing students' reasoning in science: A pragmatic view of theoretical problems. *European Journal of Science Education*, Vol. 7, pp. 151-62.

Villalbi, R.M., and Lucas, A.M. (1991). When is an animal not an animal? When it speaks English! *Journal of Biological Education*, Vol. 25(3): 184-86.

von Glasersfeld, E. (1984). An introduction to Radical Constructivism. In P. Watzlawick (Ed.), *The Invented Reality.* London: W.W. Norton and Co.

—— (1995). *Radical Constructivism: A way of knowing and learning.* Washington, DC: Falmer Press.

—— (2006). http://srri.nsm.umass.edu/vonGlasersfeld/ online Papers/html/geneva/

Vygotsky, L.S. (1962). *Thought and Language.* Cambridge, MA: MIT Press.

—— (1978). *Mind in Society*, Cambridge, MA: Harvard University Press.

Wadsworth, B.J. (1989). *Piaget's theory of cognitive and affective development*. 4th Ed. New York: Longman Inc.

Wenning, C.J. (2009). Dealing more effectively with alternative conceptions in science. *Journal of Physics Teacher Education*. Online, Vol. 5(1): 11-19.

West, L. (1982). The researchers and their work. In C. Sutton and L. West (Eds.), *Investigating Children's Existing Ideas*. The report and analysis of a research seminar held in April, 1982, at the University of Leicester, U.K.

Wolze, W., and Walgenback, W. (1992). Naturwissenshaftliche Bildung als systembildung. In P. Hau Bler (Ed.), *Physikunterricht and Menschenbildung*. Kiel, Germany: IPN at the University of Kiel.

Yager, R. (1991). The constructivist learning model, towards real reform in science education. *The Science Teacher*, Vol. 58(6): 52-57.

2 Pathways in Constructivism

2.1 Introduction

In the previous chapter it was logically shown how and why constructivism gradually emerged as a necessary paradigm to seek reliable answers to the question—"How does a learner learn?" The basic philosophy, principles and operational frameworks of constructivism are drastically different from those of behaviourism. Constructivism has offered itself as a more viable and reliable approach to knowledge acquisition in many different domains. However, unlike behaviourism, constructivism appears in a large variety of forms (Good et al., 1993; Phillips, 1995; Geelan, 1997), some more prominent than the others. Ernest (1995) goes on to say that there are as many varieties of constructivism as there are researchers. Riegler (2003) finds constructivism a 'veritable jungle'. Matthews (m.matthews@ unsw.edu.au) observes, "Thus constructivism is clearly a 'Broad Church' doctrine, and this presents problems for its appraisal. These 'identity problems' are exacerbated when some educational constructivists simply identify constructivism with non-behaviourist learning theory."

The different types of constructivism, however, have overlapping characteristics because of which they cannot be put in watertight compartments. Some of the different varieties of constructivism are elaborately discussed in the literature because of their realistic appeal and broad range of applicability, whereas some others are only briefly mentioned. Let us call the former varieties as *major pathways in constructivism* and the latter as *minor pathways in constructivism*. In this chapter we shall first take a look at the origin and connotation of the term 'constructivism'. We shall then discuss in some detail the various major pathways, which enjoy large following and wide deliberations. In addition, we shall prepare a list of the minor pathways cited in the literature and highlight the main features of some of them depending on their accessibility. The minor varieties have their own subtleties which need to be recognized for a fuller appreciation of constructivism.

2.2 Origin of the Term 'Constructivism'

In order to appreciate the broad perspective enjoyed by constructivism we begin with the origin of the term 'constructivism'. The term appears to be Russian in origin [*konstruktivizm*].

According to *The Oxford Dictionary of Difficult Words* (2002: 95):

"Constructivism is a style or movement in art in which assorted mechanical objects are combined into abstract mobile structural forms. The movement originated in Russia in the 1920s and has influenced many aspects of modern architecture and design."

The Chambers Dictionary (1995: 366) defines constructivism as

"A non-representational style of art, especially sculpture and architecture, using man-made industrial materials and processes such as twisting and welding" and also as "non-realistic style in stage sets, using steps, platforms, etc. (also 'constructionism')".

The New Encyclopaedia Britannica (1985) elaborates:

"**Constructivism,** Russian artistic and architectural movement that was first influenced by Cubism and Futurism and is generally considered to have been initiated in 1913 with the 'painting reliefs'—abstract geometric constructions—of Vladimir Tatlin. Antoine Pevsner and Naum Gabo joined Tatlin and his followers in Moscow, and upon publication of their jointly written *Realist Manifesto* in 1920—they became the spokesmen of the movement. It is from the manifest that the name

Constructivism was derived; one of the directives was 'to construct' art. Because of their admiration for machines and technology, Functionalism, and modern industrial materials such as plastic, steel, and glass, they were also called artist-engineers."

Thus the term 'constructivism' seems to have originated in the field of art and architecture. However, over the years, it has exerted a lot of influence in the various fields of knowledge and learning, though, across the fields, the basic connotation of the term remains—"to construct".

Historically, the tenets of constructivism, as used in the field of knowledge, is said to have emerged as early as the sixteenth century in the writings of Giambattista Vico or Giovanni Battista Vigo (1668-1744), an Italian philosopher. His proposition of 1710, *verum esse ipsum factum* ("true itself is fact" or "the true itself is made") is taken as an early instance of constructivist epistemology. The proposition states that truth is verified through creation or invention and not through observation as taught by Descartes. It is also translated as, "The human mind can know only what the human mind has made" (von Glasersfeld, 1995: 21). von Glasersfeld (1995) observes, "The treatise from which this statement is taken, is the first constructivist manifesto." von Glasersfeld (2000) also quotes Giambattista Vico thus: "God knows the world, because He created it, human beings can know only what they themselves have made." Vico further states, "*Deus naturae artifex, homo arti-ficiorum dues*", which simply means—Whatever a man thinks and knows can therefore never represent an ontological reality (Jha, 2009). According to Vico, it is impossible to compare our image of reality with a reality outside. This is because in order to check whether our representation is a 'true' picture of reality we should have to have independent access not only to our representation but also to that 'outside reality' before we get to know it. And because the only way in which we are supposed to get at reality is precisely the way we would like to check and verify, there is no possible escape from the dilemma (von Glasersfeld, 1987).

According to Noddings (1990) constructivism also emerged from the work of Ulric Neisser (act psychology), and Noam

Chomsky (innate linguistic structures of mind). Neisser (born 1928) is an American psychologist who is credited with the modern growth of cognitive psychology. Chomsky (born 1928) is an American linguist, philosopher and cognitive scientist. He is recognized as the father of modern linguistics and a very influential person in the academic and scientific community.

2.3 Major Pathways in Constructivism

In constructivism three major traditions have been identified. These are: (i) philosophical constructivism, (ii) sociological constructivism, and (iii) educational constructivism. The latter two have further sub-classification as we shall see below.

2.3.1 Philosophical Constructivism

Philosophical constructivism probably originated in the ancient Greek philosophy. Socrates (469-399 BC) used the technique of 'dialogue' in which he asked directed questions leading his pupils to realize for themselves the weakness in their thinking. The Socratic dialogue has been recognized as an important tool in constructivism. It is used to assess students' knowledge and plan new learning experiences. More recent origins of constructivism may be seen in George Berkeley's (1685-1753) philosophy of science, the philosophy of Immanuel Kant (1724-1804), Thomas Kuhn's (1922-96) *Structure of Scientific Revolutions* (1962), Richard Rorty's (1931-2007) *Philosophy and the Mirror of Nature* (1979), Dewey's insight about human knowledge and knowing, and Derrida's philosophy of deconstruction.

Berkeley was a well-known Irish philosopher on human knowledge, who opposed *materialism* and defended *idealism* announcing that there are no mind-independent things: *esse est percipi* (to be is to be perceived). This subjective idealist said, "...all those bodies which compose the mighty frame of the world, have not any subsistence without a mind..." (Sampson, 1908: 181).

Kant, regarded as one of the most influential thinkers of modern Europe, was a German philosopher who theorized that objective experience is actively constituted or constructed by the functioning of the human mind. He stated (Kant, 1787 and its translation by Werner S. Pulhan, 1996) the following in very clear terms:

- Human reason can grasp only what she herself has produced according to her own design.
- Logical analysis of action and objects lead to the growth of knowledge and one's individual experiences generate new knowledge (Brooks and Brooks, 1993).
- It is beyond doubt that all our knowledge begins with experience.
- Our understanding (*read* knowledge) of the external world has its foundations not merely in experience, but in experience and a priori knowledge (*read* alternative conceptions which control the degree and quality of knowledge construction).

The intellectual giant, John Dewey is normally viewed as an unorthodox realist with respect to debates about human knowledge and knowing. Some even view Dewey as an early exemplar of 'social constructivism'. He recognized the importance of the subjective experience of individuals in so far as acquisition of knowledge is concerned. Some of the relevant views of Dewey are the following:

- Human mind is a meaning making organ, relentlessly driven to make sense of its world. (This is similar to the present notion of constructivism and active learning.)
- Knowledge and ideas (*read* concepts) come only from a situation where the learner has to draw them out of experience that has meaning and importance (*read* serve and organize the learner's experiential world) to her.
- Classroom could be the place where the learner could move about, form groups, plan and execute activities, in short, learns for herself under the direction and guidance of the teacher.
- Learning is active. It involves reaching out of the mind. It involves organic assimilation starting from within. It

is the learner and the subject matter which determine both quality and quantity of learning.

- The teacher is not in the school to impose certain ideas (*read* concepts) or to form certain habits in the learner (Dewey, 1916).

Jacques Derrida is rarely referred to under constructivism because he was the proponent of the philosophy of deconstruction. But we would like to refer him in passing because of our perception that like every learning involves some amount of 'unlearning', every mental construction also involves some amount of 'deconstruction'. Derrida fastens on to the element of 'subjectivity' which he sees to be still at work (Norris, 1986) once the transcendental reduction has been carried through. He regarded that certain phenomena of consciousness belong more to individual psychology than to any universal structure (*read* ontological reality). This indicates that (in the framework of constructivism) for the learner, her universe consists of structures constructed by her consciousness. Derrida further advocates (Derrida, 1982) that the mind whose operations are experienced and analyzed is a form of conscious self-surveillance critically trained upon its own logical workings and thus redeemed from errors and uncertainties of common mental experience.

The philosophical view of constructivism revolves around the concept of *materialism* vs. *idealism*. Materialist philosophers regard *matter as primary* and *consciousness as secondary* and as a derivative of matter. According to them the *world is knowable*. Idealist philosophers, on the other hand, believe that *consciousness is primary*; it existed prior to matter and brought matter into being. There are two kinds of idealists: (i) *subjective idealists*, who argue that the world is "created" by the consciousness of the individual—the subject, and (ii) *objective idealists*, who insist that the world is "created" by some kind of an *objective consciousness* (*super individual*). Idealists are divided on the matter of *knowability of the world*. Some of them, called *agnostics*, declare that the world is unknowable. Other idealists believe that the world is knowable, but man cognises his own thoughts and emotions (subjective idealists), or a mystic idea, a universal spirit (objective idealists), and not the objective world, nature (Afanasyev, 1980).

Thus, according to the philosophical view of constructivism, our beliefs and perceptions of the world are actively constructed (not discovered) by us on the basis of our experiences and active processes of developing knowledge rather than through a passive reception of sense data. This basic principle of philosophical constructivism in fact governs all other kinds of constructivism.

2.3.2 Sociological Constructivism

Experts in the history of science, philosophy of science, sociology, anthropology and computer science often indulge in the debate concerning the role of social factors in scientific advancement relative to rational, empirical and other scientific factors. This has led to the notion of *sociological constructivism.* According to sociological constructivism the progress of science and technology and the generation of the public body of knowledge are due to changing social conditions and interests. It is guided by theories of Sociology of Scientific Knowledge (SSK) (e.g. Bloor, 1976; Collins, 1985; Woolgar, 1988). SSK, primarily associated with the sociology of science, concerns with social influence on science. It argues that all knowledge is constructed and interpreted socially in the frame of science and technology studies. Though the physical world is not socially constructed, our knowledge of the physical world is socially constructed in the sense that interpretation of the sensations coming through our sense organs is socially constructed by people interacting with each other. The changes in theories and philosophical commitments of science are not directly linked to the explanatory power of cognitive content and rational reasoning. The sociologists treat the individual mind as a 'black box' whose inputs are sociological concerns and outputs are in the form of statements of belief (*read* knowledge) which may be true or false.

Three varieties of sociological constructivism have resulted from different schools of thought (Boudourides, 1998): *strong* form, *mild* form, and *actor-network theory*. Though Boudourides uses the term 'social constructivism' in place of 'sociological constructivism' owing to the traditional practice, we shall use the term 'sociological constructivism' in our discussion. Differences between these two terms will become clear when we consider social constructivism in the next subsection.

The strong form of sociological constructivism originates from the theory of Social Construction of Technology (SCOT) (Bijker et at., 1987; Collins, 1985; Woolgar, 1988; Grint and Woolgar, 1997). It says that technological change is a genuine social process; is governed by social practices; is stabilized through the processes of interpretation, negotiation and closure in which different social actors take part.

The mild variety of sociological constructivism is associated with the notion of Social Shaping of Technology (SSOT) (e.g. MacKenzie and Wajcman, 1985; MacKenzie, 1991). In this approach, besides social factors, weightage is given to non-social factors like the inherent properties and effects of technology in the shaping of technology. It contends that these properties and effects are due to social or political biases embodied by the technology in a particular social context.

The third variety follows the principles of the Actor-Network Theory (ANT) (e.g. Callon, 1986; Latour, 1987). It argues that the development and stabilization of scientific and technological matters arise from "the construction of heterogeneous networks, which are concrete alignments between human actors, natural phenomena, and social or technical aspects. In the processes of stabilization of technology, all actors (or 'actants') in the network, either human/natural or social/technical, are analyzed through the same impartial prism and the same terms and methods are symmetrically applied to different entities. However, special preference is given to the explanatory role of social elements, such as social groups and interpretation processes" (Boudourides, 1998).

2.3.3 Educational Constructivism

Educational constructivism is concerned with knowledge construction in teaching-learning situations including classrooms. It is also known as *psychological constructivism* (Phillips, 1995) and has two categories: (a) *personal constructivism*, and

(b) *social constructivism*, depending upon whether an individual or a group is involved in the process of construction. Personal constructivism in turn is supposed to have two versions: a *mild* or *trivial* version (*cognitive constructivism*) due to Piaget, Bruner, and Ausubel, and *radical constructivism* due to von Glasersfeld. Social constructivism is ascribed to Vygotsky.

Personal Constructivism

Cognitive Constructivism

The most influential thinker and realist in the development of constructivist ideas was Jean Piaget (1896-1980). Piaget was a structuralist. Hence he was a constructivist because every construction assumes the existence of structures, which are being or to be constructed, be it the physical world of a building or the cognitive world of concepts and knowledge. He identified structures in three different planes (Piaget, 1970, 1972, 1977):

Plane I : Piaget was able to classify concepts into a spectrum of sequentially higher and higher logical structures and thus having distinguishable cognitive demands (Shayer and Adey, 1981).

Plane II : Piaget advocated that the cognizing subject builds knowledge by a process of active interaction with the environment and this process has three structures: *assimilation*, *accommodation*, and *equilibration*. In assimilation the learner arranges experiences within her current structures of understanding. She views the world through the eyes of her personal constructs in an effort to organize and preserve her personal world of schema and meanings. As she confronts new information and experiences, she modifies changes and adjusts her existing mental structures to accommodate the new experiences and create new mental images/structures. This progression of knowledge construction occurs because of the reciprocal roles of assimilation and accommodation, finally leading to a state of equilibration. As in biological adaptation where the species goes through changes within the principle of *survival of the fittest*, the above three processes taken in totality can be viewed as cognitive adaptation by the learner to accept, understand and organize her experiential world. Thus, in Piagetian theory, as in constructivism, there is no objective ontological reality. In this framework, conceptual structures, which we consider to be 'knowledge', are the products of active knowers who shape their thinking to fit the constraints of their experience.

Plane III : Piaget also identified four sequential stages (structures) in the mental development of a child. They are (i) *the sensorimotor stage* (0-2 years), (ii) *the preoperational* or *symbolic stage* (2-7 years), (iii) *the stage of concrete operations* (7-12 years), and (iv) *the stage of formal operations* (adolescence and adulthood). Each stage is discernible by the child's ability to handle, organize and internalize specific logical structures *vis-à-vis* concepts. Further, these stages do not vary in their sequence and no stage can be skipped. However, some research studies show that a child can be programmed to go through cognitive acceleration (Adey, 1988).

Thus Piaget provided strategic insight into the three crucial components of constructivism namely,

- the cognitive ability of the cognizing subject,
- the processes involved in actual construction of knowledge, and
- the cognitive demands of concepts.

After Piaget, Jerome Seymour Bruner was one of the most prominent cognitive psychologists who influenced the theory of constructivism. While Piaget provided a gradation of the concepts as per their logical cognitive demands, Bruner went a step further and presented a structure of the concepts themselves. He stated that every concept has a *name*, an *example*, a *non-example* (non-examples are essential as they can help distinguish between concepts), *attributes*, *attribute values*, and *rule governing the attributes* (Bruner, 1990).

Bruner is very clear (Bruner, 1996) when he says that the reality that we impute to the world we inhabit is a constructed one. In other words, reality is constructed, not discovered. In this framework each step of the growth of science is basically construction of a better mental model to represent the reality but is not the reality. This is in fact the truth and the basis for the often repeated statement that 'Science is tentative'.

In this connection Piaget (1970: 57-58) says, "What remains is construction as such, and one sees no ground why it should be unreasonable to think it is ultimate nature of reality to be in continual construction instead of consisting of an accumulation of ready-made structures".

According to Bruner, learning is an active social process in which the learner 'constructs' new ideas or concepts based on her current or past knowledge. The learner chooses and permutes the knowledge, constructs hypotheses, makes decisions, and while performing these she relies on her cognitive structuring skill. Her cognitive structures help her to grasp the meaning of and organize her experiences, and enable her to go beyond the given information. That is why, Bruner (1996) emphasizes that 'Thinking about thinking' has to be the principal ingredient of any empowering practice of education.

In *The Course of Cognitive Growth* Bruner identifies three human information processing systems, i.e. *enactive representation*, *iconic representation*, and *symbolic representation*. What he calls *integration* is the building of higher order units, chunks or ensembles by using the above three. Since these constructed representations are obviously subjective, they open up the possibility of pluralistic connotations of concepts which is an important corollary of constructivism.

Bruner proposes nine tenets of education, which are as follows:

(a) *The perspectival tenet*: Meaning is related to the frame of reference, stance, perspective of the interpreter and its context within some content.

(b) *The constraints tenet*: Forms of meaning making are constrained by the evolution of the species and the symbolic processing system developed by a culture.

(c) *The constructivism tenet*: Reality is constructed by the individual.

(d) *The interactional tenet*: Human exchange occurs only in an interacting sub-community (humans have an astonishingly well-developed talent for intersubjectivity).

(e) *The externalization tenet*: Human activities result in oeuvres (works, external products) which are developed through interaction in sub-communities (he suggests class ethnographies here).

(f) *The instrumentalism tenet*: Education is an instrumental factor in later life within a culture; ergo, "the chief subject matter of school, viewed culturally, is the school itself".

(g) *The institutional tenet*: In the developed world, schooling is an institution with all the powers and constraints of such institutions of culture and government.

(h) *The tenet of identity and self-esteem*: Humans universally perceive the self and recognize the selfness of others with two key properties of agency and evaluation.

(i) *The narrative tenet*: The mode of thinking and feeling that helps children (indeed, people generally) create a version of the world in which, psychologically, they can envisage a place for themselves—a personal world.

It may be seen that the tenets (a), (b), and (c) above reflect the principles of constructivism.

Ausubel (1968) has made a very crucial statement about 'learning' by a child. He states,

> If you ask me to identify the single most important factor that determines the degree and quality of learning I will say, 'Ascertain what the child knows and teach him accordingly.'

This statement has two parts, (i) 'Ascertain what the child knows', and (ii) 'Teach him accordingly'. As discussed in Chapter 1, field studies in the first area provided crucial evidences which led to the formulation of constructivism, during the 1980s and 1990s.

Radical Constructivism

Ernst von Glasersfeld (1983, 1984, 1987a, 1987b, 1989, 1990a, 1990b, 1993, 1995, 1999, 2000) is justifiably regarded as the leading proponent of *radical constructivism*. It is 'radical' because (von Glasersfeld, 1987) it rejects the traditional *philosophical materialism/realism* according to which

- An absolute reality (ontological reality) exists, which is a world 'out there'. It exists irrespective of whether we know or experience about it or not.
- The purpose of acquisition of knowledge is to understand and possibly build a model which represents that ontological reality.

From the point of view of *realism*, every concept has a unique, objective existence because it describes a unique, objective absolute reality. Once we accept this viewpoint, a corollary (which the behaviourist profusely used because they assumed it to be true and valid) follows that a concept (a la knowledge) can be transferred from one person (teacher) to another (learner) by using suitable methods of communication.

However, on the basis of thousands of field study-based evidences about learner's *alternative conceptions*, Glasersfeld advocated the following:

- The sole purpose of knowledge acquisition by a child is to comprehend and organize her experiential world. Thus it has no need-based correspondence with the existence/non-existence of any ontological reality.
- The process involved in acquiring knowledge is a process of cognitive adaptation within the framework

of the theory of evolution. As in the case of natural evolution a living system changes, modifies itself within the principle of 'survival of the fittest', so also a child changes, modifies, deconstructs, reconstructs her mental structures so as to adapt to her cognitive world.

- Glasersfeld opines that the child's efforts are geared to arrive at a viable construct. He creates a theory of knowledge evolution by stating that the character of cognition is functional and adaptive.
- Knowledge is the result of an individual subject's constructive activity, and not a commodity that somehow resides outside the knower and can be conveyed as a distilled entity by diligent perception or linguistic communication. Knowledge is not a transferable commodity and communication is not a conveyance (Glasersfeld, 1987b, 1990a).

Some very crucial conclusions may be derived from the above observations of Glasersfeld:

- Knowledge cannot be instructed. It is constructed by the cognizing subject.
- The traditional view of the existence of an experiencer-independent ontological reality, called the 'truth', does not have any importance for the construction of knowledge. Thus, from this perspective, constructivism may be regarded as a 'theory of knowing' rather than a 'theory of knowledge'.
- In the learners' frameworks every concept has now a pluralistic connotation and not a unique, objective connotation. This is because the mental structure associated with a concept by an individual learner is true and valid for her in so far as her experiential world is concerned, and this structure may vary from learner to learner. Thus the meaning of every concept becomes learner-relative.
- Language is then a continuous ongoing process of interpretation, reinterpretation, leading to cognitive adaptation. von Glasersfeld (http://www.mcgill.ca/

douglas/fdg/kjf/17-TAGLA.htm) says, "To find a fit simply means not to notice any discrepancies." This is drastically different from matching something with something else (reality), because there is no way to validate a 'correct match'. There is a lot of similarity between Glasersfeld's statement as above and Derrida's parallel comments.

According to von Glasersfeld, 'knowledge' does not represent the world at all—it comprises action schemes, concepts, and thoughts, and it distinguishes the ones which are considered advantageous from those that are not; in other words, it pertains to the ways and means the cognizing subject has conceptually evolved in order to fit into the world as she experiences it.

Further, in this connection, the following statements of von Glasersfeld are worth contemplating:

> The word 'knowledge' refers to a commodity that is radically different from the objective representation of an observer-independent world which the mainstream of the Western philosophical tradition has been looking for. Instead, 'knowledge' refers to conceptual structures that epistemic agents, given the range of present experience within their tradition of thought and language, consider *viable*. (von Glasersfeld, 1989: 124)

> Our knowledge is useful, relevant, viable, or however we want to call the positive end of the scale of evaluation, if it stands up to experience and enables us to make predictions and to bring about or avoid, as the case may be, certain phenomena (i.e. appearances, events, experiences).... Logically, that gives us no clue as to how the 'objective' world might be; it merely means that we know one viable way to a goal that we have chosen under specific circumstances in our experiential world. It tells us nothing...about how many other ways there might be. (von Glasersfeld, 1987a: 199)

von Glasersfeld also justifies the name *radical constructivism* in the following lines:

> Radical constructivism, thus, is *radical* because it breaks with convention and develops a theory of knowledge in which knowledge does not reflect an 'objective' ontological reality, but exclusively an ordering and organization of a world constituted by our experience. The radical constructivist has relinquished 'metaphysical realism' once and for all. (von Glasersfeld, 1987a: 199)

Matthews calls the ideas of von Glasersfeld as the *von Glasersfeld's principle*, or *von Glasersfeld's philosophy* (VGP) (m.matthews@unsw.edu.au.). He makes the following list of epistemological and ontological theses therein:

(1) Knowledge is not about an observer-independent world.

(2) Knowledge does not represent such a world; correspondence theories of knowledge are mistaken.

(3) Knowledge is created by individuals in a historical and cultural context.

(4) Knowledge refers to individual experience rather than to the world.

(5) Knowledge is constituted by individual conceptual structures.

(6) Conceptual structures constitute knowledge when individuals regard them as viable in relationship to their experience; constructivism is a form of pragmatism.

(7) There is no preferred epistemic conceptual structure; constructivism is a relativist doctrine.

(8) Knowledge is the appropriate ordering of an experiential reality.

(9) There is no rationally accessible, extra-experiential reality.

VGP appears to have influenced a number of researchers such as G. Wheatley (Wheatley, 1991: 10), and S. Fleury (Fleury, 1998: 157-58). Some of the elements of VGP may also be seen in an earlier work of R. Driver (Driver and Oldham, 1986: 109). On the other hand, VGP is criticised to have major problems of the following types: its empiricist conception of knowledge, its confusion of real and theoretical objects of science, its individualism, its account of concept acquisition, its inherent philosophy of solipsism, and its idealism. See for instance the work of W. Suchting (Suchting, 1992: 247).

Social Constructivism

Lev Semyonovich Vygotsky (1896-1934), a leading Russian developmental psychologist, is the propounder of social constructivism. In it he brings to focus the role of the society in the process of knowledge acquisition by a learner. According to him *collaboration* is the key in knowledge construction. His theories about language, thought, and their mediation by society (Bruffee, 1983) have significant impact on modern constructivism. Previously, learning was considered to be an almost individual enterprise following the behaviourist and Piagetian principles. Vygotsky's theories have forced educationists to recognize the role of the society in learning. Vygotsky's main ideas can be found in the posthumously published works, *Thought and Language* (1986) and *Mind in Society* (1978).

Vygotsky delineated the proactive role of language and society *vis-à-vis* indigenous culture for the cognitive development of the child. He visualized the child not as a physically isolated and intellectually segregated individual but as a prosensitive individual who is being constantly exposed to social interaction and social context, right from her birth onwards. He states (Vygotsky, 1978), "Every function in the child's cultural development appears twice: first, on the social level, and later, on the individual level; first between people (interpsychological) and then inside the child (intrapsychological). This applies equally to

- voluntary attention,
- logical memory, and
- formation (*read* construction) of concepts.

All the higher functions originate as actual relationships between individuals."

In Vygotsky's theoretical system of social constructivism, every individual member always brings to the group a personal contribution (*read* personal construct) at their own levels, and, between individuals, their unique contributions interchange, interact and auto-modify, as a result of which the collective construction forever becomes larger than the total number of separate individual constructions (Liu and Matthews, 2005).

Vygotsky made experimental study of a child's reasoning when she worked independently and when she worked with an adult. The difference between the two scenarios led him to introduce the notion of the '*Zone of Proximal Development*' (ZPD) (Vygotsky, 1978) which is defined as the intellectual potential, a child acquires when assisted by a knowledgeable adult or a more advanced peer. Assistance is provided through *cues* and *scaffolding* (sometimes called the 'other regulations') which eventually leads to the child's intellectual growth and 'self-regulation'. ZPD is to be distinguished from the actual domain of development of the child and can be a true measure of the child's achievement. It also means, a learning environment should comprise interactive communication besides the child and learning material. Interactive communication needs to involve guided interaction that should enable the child to reflect critically on her conceptions and go for necessary changes.

From his experiments involving children in the activity of grouping-sorting objects, Vygotsky discovered that children pass through *four stages of conceptual development*: (1) the *syncretic grouping* stage, in which the child groups things seemingly at random, (2) the *complex formation* stage, in which the child makes recognizable collections of groups of objects, (3) the *pseudo-concept formation* stage, in which the child chooses the right attributes but cannot explain the choice as the concept has actually been learnt by rote and not yet by an abstraction of any general rule, and (4) the *abstract concept formation* stage, in which the child forms abstract concepts like adults by focusing on at least one attribute accurately and being able to explain the type of the chosen grouping by naming the attribute. Though these stages appear to be similar to those of Piaget there are important differences between them. Vygotsky concludes that (i) no rigid maturational progress exists through these stages, (ii) role of tutor is important in the development of these stages, and (iii) verbal labels are easily acquired independently of the formation of the corresponding true concepts.

Concerning the stages of cognitive development, Vygotsky believes that learning precedes development, whereas Piaget believes it is just the opposite. Vygotsky contends that the child's mind is inherently social in nature and her speech moves from communicative social (interpersonal) to inner egocentric (intrapersonal). Piaget, on the other hand, argues that the speech of the child is egocentric to begin with, which goes away with maturity, getting transformed into social speech. Since the development of thought follows that of speech, Vygotsky claims that thought develops from society to the individual and not the other way.

Vygotsky argues that all higher mental functions are social in origin and are embedded in the sociocultural fabric. These higher mental functions are primarily interpsychological (two or more persons) in nature, originating between and among individuals. Then an individual's mental processes convert them to an intrapsychological (individual) form for the individual. Thus, learning may be viewed as developing first in group settings before becoming individual (Wertsch, 1979).

Vygotsky's image as a linguistic constructivist stems from his following important and loaded statements (Vygotsky, 1986):

- Word without a meaning (not necessarily the correct meaning) is not a word.
- Word must be a part of inner speech and language.
- There is an explicit and profound connection between oral language and development of mental images and constructs. [Perhaps an example is in order. In some parts of western Orissa (now Odisha), India, the term 'cottage cheese' (*chhena*) conveys the meaning and mental image of 'cow dung'. That shows the strong influence of language and its social context on mental constructs of the child.]
- Thought is not merely expressed in words; it comes into existence through them (because thought corresponds to mental constructs).

- A word devoid of thought (i.e. mental constructs) is a dead thing, and a thought unembodied in words remains a shadow.
- During development when a child learns a language, the first utterances have a communicational purpose, but once internalised they become 'inner speech' (that reflects internally constructed cognitive structures).

Social constructivism views individual knowledge and social knowledge to be one and the same. It suggests that construction of knowledge is facilitated by the vast cultural repertoire of artefacts, ideas, assumptions, concepts and practices which an individual inherits or born into. Thus, learning is a form of cultural apprenticeship. It may also be perceived as a process of enculturation in which "the learner of a culture learns from her tutors" and that "novices are introduced to a community of knowledge through discourse in the context of relevant task" (Driver et al., 1994). Gergen (1985, 1995) argues that knowledge is created and legitimized by means of social interchange in its many forms. In this context, Gergen (1995) sets forth four essential points (Staver, 1998). First, social interdependence is the conduit through which we attain meaning in language. Second, within language, its meaning is dependent on the context of the social interdependence. Third, the function served by language is primarily communal and it is paramount in continuing relationships among individuals in communities. Fourth, similar to the purpose of cognition in von Glasersfeld's radical constructivism, the purpose of language is not to reflect the external world in an ontological manner. Thus social constructivism sees knowledge as primarily fashioned and made by human discourse (Osborne, 1996).

Kim (2001) notes that social constructivism is based on specific assumptions about reality, knowledge, and learning.

Reality : Social constructivists believe that reality is constructed through human activity. Members of a society together invent the properties of the world (Kukia, 2000). For the social constructivist, reality cannot be discovered: it does not exist prior to social invention.

Knowledge : To social constructivists, knowledge is a human product and is socially and culturally constructed (Prawat and Folden, 1994; Gredler, 1997; Ernest, 1999). Individuals create meaning through their interactions with each other and with the environment they live in.

Learning : Social constructivists view learning as a social process. It does not take place only within an individual, nor is it a passive development of behaviours that are shaped by external forces (McMohan, 1997). Meaningful learning occurs when individuals are engaged in social activities.

It is interesting to note that some authors like to call 'sociological constructivism' by the name 'social constructivism', which may lead to confusion with social constructivism as propounded by Vygotsky (e.g. Boudourides, 1998) (See our observations in the subsection pertaining to sociological constructivism above). In this connection we would like to point out that though basic processes such as collaboration/cooperation, interaction and exchange of ideas/perceptions between individuals are common to both types of constructivism, differences between them are tangible. Sociological constructivism is concerned with public bodies of knowledge, like science and technology, and how they are negotiated and governed by the changing social conditions and interests. Social constructivism, on the other hand, is concerned with an individual's learning and how it is influenced by other members of the society. Accordingly, the scope, parameters and details of dynamics involved are not the same in these two forms of constructivism.

The different categories of major pathways in constructivism, as discussed above, are depicted in Fig. 2.1.

To conclude the present section, in our discussions so far we have given some details of the well-known varieties of constructivism namely philosophical constructivism, sociological constructivism, cognitive constructivism, radical constructivism, and social constructivism. A summary of the basic features of same is presented in Table 2.1 which gives a compact comparative view of the major pathways in constructivism.

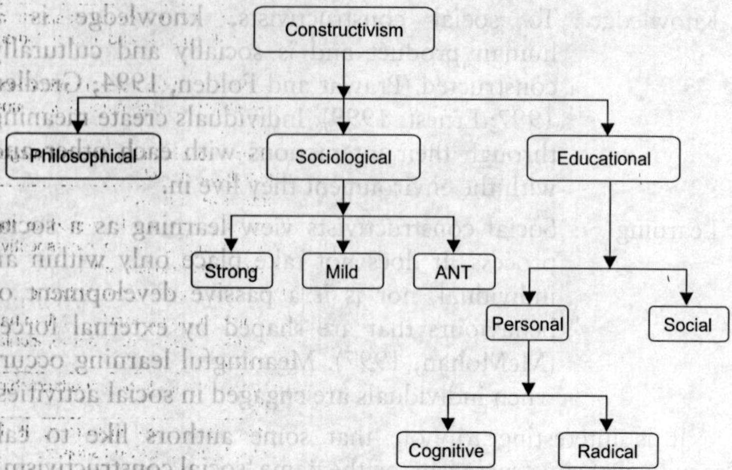

Fig. 2.1

Table 2.1

Major pathways in constructivism	Leading proponents	Basic features
Philosophical constructivism	Vico	The human mind can know what the human mind has made.
	Kant	Human reason can grasp only what she herself has produced according to her own design.
	Dewey	Human mind is a meaning making organ, relentlessly driven to make sense of the world.
	Derrida	Certain phenomena of consciousness belong more to individual psychology than to any universal structures.
Sociological constructivism	Bloor	All knowledge is constructed and interpreted socially in the frame of science and technology studies.
	Collins, Bijker et al., Woolgar	Technological change is a genuine social change. (Social Construction of Technology, SCOT)
	Makenzie and Wajeman	Besides social factors, non-social factors in a particular social context also influence construction of technological knowledge. (Social Shaping of Technology, SSOT)
	Callon, Latour	Development and stabilization of scientific and technological matters arise from the construction of heterogeneous networks. (Actor-Network Theory, ANT)

Contd...

<table>
<tr><td rowspan="7">Educational constructivism</td><td rowspan="4">Personal</td><td rowspan="3">Cognitive</td><td>Piaget</td><td>• Classification of concepts into a spectrum of sequentially higher and higher logical structures.
• Knowledge is built through the processes of assimilation, accommodation, and equilibration.
• Child goes through four sequential stages of mental development.</td></tr>
<tr><td>Bruner</td><td>• Concepts have structures.
• Meaning of a concept is related to the frame of reference, stance, and perspective of the interpreter (a la learner).
• Reality is constructed by the individual.
• Human information processing system has three representations, i.e. enactive, iconic, and symbolic.</td></tr>
<tr><td>Ausubel</td><td>Ascertain what the child knows and teach him accordingly.</td></tr>
<tr><td>Radical</td><td>Glasersfeld</td><td>• Knowledge cannot be instructed. It is constructed by the cognizing subject.
• The purpose of knowledge acquisition by a child is to comprehend and organize her experiential world.
• The process involved in acquiring knowledge is a process of cognitive adaptation.
• Knowledge is not a transferable commodity and communication not a conveyance.</td></tr>
<tr><td rowspan="3" colspan="2">Social</td><td>Vygotsky</td><td>• Collaboration is the key to knowledge construction.
• Learning is a form of cultural apprenticeship.
• Every function in the child's cultural development appears twice: first, on the social level, and later, on the individual level.
• A word devoid of thought (i.e. mental constructs) is a dead thing, and a thought unembodied in words remains a shadow.
• Word without a meaning (not necessarily the correct meaning) is not a word.</td></tr>
<tr><td>Driver</td><td>Knowledge is created and legitimized by means of social interchange in its many forms.</td></tr>
<tr><td>Gergen</td><td>• Social interdependence is the conduit through which we attain meaning.
• Within language, its meaning is dependent on social context.
• The function served by language is primarily communal.
• The purpose of language is not to reflect the external world in an ontological manner.</td></tr>
</table>

If one analyzes the above skeletal table depicting the essence of the major pathways in constructivism one can perceive four seminal undercurrents connecting them. They are:

- Knowledge is constructed by the cognizing subject. The teacher/the society/the indigenous culture are only facilitating/defining agents.
- The purpose of acquisition of knowledge is to comprehend and organize one's experiential world and thus to live an error-free, acceptable life in a community.
- Knowledge acquisition takes place through a process of cognitive adaptation.
- Language (not necessarily spoken or written) and learner's alternative conceptions are girders on which the learner constructs her own cognitive structures.

2.4 Minor Pathways in Constructivism

The different varieties of constructivism discussed above are the main types of constructivism or major pathways in constructivism. Besides them there are many other types of constructivism cited in the literature as well. Though they have their own significance, they appear to be of limited scope, and hence not widely followed or discussed in the literature. We therefore consider them as 'minor pathways' in constructivism as compared to the well-known varieties. Given below is a list of 25 of the minor varieties in alphabetical order. The list, however, may not be exhaustive.

(i) Communal constructivism
(ii) Computational constructivism
(iii) Constructionism
(iv) Contextual constructivism
(v) Critical constructivism
(vi) Cultural constructivism
(vii) Cybernetic constructivism
(viii) Dialectical constructivism
(ix) Didactic constructivism
(x) Empirical constructivism
(xi) Human constructivism
(xii) Information-processing constructivism

(xiii) Mathematical constructivism
(xiv) Methodological constructivism
(xv) Moderate constructivism
(xvi) Physical constructivism
(xvii) Pragmatic constructivism
(xviii) Psychiatric/Therapeutic constructivism
(xix) Rational constructivism
(xx) Realist constructivism
(xxi) Sociocultural constructivism
(xxii) Socio-historical constructivism
(xxiii) Sociotransformative constructivism
(xxiv) Trivial constructivism
(xxv) Weak constructivism

A perusal of literature suggests that some of the above forms of constructivism are not readily accessible. In view of this we now briefly introduce 19 of the above list of 25 forms of constructivism.

Communal Constructivism

B. Holmes and others (Holmes et al., 2001) introduced the term communal constructivism in 2001, in view of the increasing influence of Information and Communication Technology (ICT) and networked learning on construction and sharing of knowledge. In this model, apart from developing their own knowledge base, students and teachers create knowledge for the benefit of other students. All the students and teachers involved may be thought of as members of a kind of community who help one another in the generation and sharing of knowledge making use of ICT. Communal constructivism thus suggests a way of converting the principles of social constructivism into practice in teaching-learning situations. In the words of Holmes et al. (2001), "What we argue for is a communal constructivism where students and teachers are not simply engaged in developing their own information but actively involved in creating knowledge that will benefit other students. In this model students will not simply pass through a course like water through a sieve but instead leave their own imprint in the development of the course, their school or university, and ideally the discipline."

Computational Constructivism

Computational constructivism is structured on the neural basis of cognitive development. Its proponents are Quartz, and Sejnowski (1997) and Westermann (2000). It addresses questions like, "How do minds emerge from developing brains?" It suggests that the representational features of concepts are built from the dynamic interactions between neural growth mechanisms and environmentally derived neural activities. A both theoretical and applicative picture of the operations of the brain can be obtained from 'How the mind works' by Pinker (1998).

Constructionism

As a variant of constructivism, constructionism (Papert, 1991, 1993) emphasizes that in order to learn about abstract concepts it is necessary for a learner to create and experiment with 'artifacts'. A link between this view and that of the original Russian connotation of constructivism may be seen. Today constructionism may be facilitated by computers in which virtual artifacts may be created and experimented upon. Constructionism implies that besides being an active constructor of knowledge, a learner needs to go for particular constructions of the subject that are external and shared, thereby bringing understanding and experience together.

Contextual Constructivism

An individual constructs her knowledge upon a foundation or in a context. Contextual constructivism recognizes the significance of context in learning. Contextual constructivism is about understanding the fundamental beliefs which both students and teachers bring to the classroom, and how these beliefs are supported by culture. According to Cobern (1993) contextual constructivism is nothing but the impact of culture on the teaching and learning of science. In such a picture contextual constructivism may be regarded as a subset of social constructivism. In contextual constructivism the student, the content, and the context are intimately connected. The student builds an understanding of content in context and the context mediates student understanding of content. Context shapes student learning and is in turn shaped by both content and the student.

Critical Constructivism

The roots of critical constructivism (Kincheloe, 1993, 2005, 2008) are said to lie in a series of articles which appeared in the journal *Critical Inquiry* (1991). It argues that besides 'truth' and 'reality', other research tools like 'evidence', 'document', 'experience', 'fact', 'proof', etc. are also important in a social and ideological construction, and these are also subject to criticism. It applies to many disciplines including natural science such as physics and biology, statistics, history, law, etc. According to Kincheloe (1993): "Critical constructivism concerns the attempt to move beyond the formal style of thinking which emerges from empiricism and rationalism, a form of cognition that solves problems framed by the dominant paradigm, the conventional way of seeing."

Watts and Jofili (1998) raise an interesting debate on 'constructivist teaching' claiming that the term is an oxymoron as it combines two contradictory actions: 'construction' and 'instruction' (teaching). They argue that "…constructivist teaching itself should be superseded in favour of 'critical constructivism', an approach which undertakes a broader critique of the relationships between teacher and taught, between learner and subject matter, and between schooling and society". According to them, "To be critical constructivists, teachers must possess critical awareness: an understanding of themselves, their perspectives, their approaches to the construction of knowledge, and ways in which their own consciousness has been shaped by society (and schools)." They further observe that "Inside a critical constructivist classroom, learners reflect on the lives they lead, ask questions to discover meanings and values. Their learning experiences now include a self-reflective dimension around themes from daily life. …This aims to push them into becoming active participants in shaping the economic, social and cultural environment in which they live. These learners also become actively and critically involved in controlling their own learning, and teachers need to work towards the 'liberation' of learners, instead of their 'domestication'." The authors produce empirical evidence of teachers moving from constructivism towards critical constructivism in classroom transactions through in-service professional development course and action research.

In short, according to critical constructivism the learner is expected to question the answers, the evidences, and the so-called facts.

Cultural Constructivism

According to cultural constructivism, knowledge and reality, as perceived by a community of people, are dependent upon its culture, which may also dictate the methodology and approach. To give an example, for scientific studies, Western cultures use *objects* whereas Native American culture uses *events*. Superstitions and blind beliefs are also peculiar to cultures. Under cultural constructivism knowledge construction is perceived as a process of *enculturation*. Cultural constructivism appears to be a subset of the broader social constructivism.

Cybernetic Constructivism

Cybernetics is the study of self-organizing systems. Cybernetic constructivism owes its origin to cybernetic developments in biology, neurophysiology, and cognition, in particular, cybernetics of self-organization or second order—mode 2—cybernetics (von Foerster, 1984). It is based on the concept of *autopoiesis* (self-formation) originally developed to study cell biology. Autopoietic systems are self-contained and self-referential units. Besides biology the concept has been applied to physical, cognitive and psychic systems (Mingers, 1995) and social, communication, and legal systems (Luhmann, 1989, 1990, 1995).

Cybernetic constructivism supports the basic notion of philosophical constructivism as a self-referential process of maintaining identity. Autopoiesis is said to manifest its constructivist character at the level of 'closure' of the nervous system in the sense that action and cognition depend on each other and not on any outside system. von Foerster (1984) has argued that this happens when human brain interprets signals received from different sensory organs. Thus living beings are autopoietic systems. Accordingly Maturana and Varela (1980) have claimed that cognitive apparatus is an organizationally closed system. Riegler (2003) terms this biological constructivism. In this connection von Glasersfeld claims that "Contemporary neurophysiological models may be compatible with a constructivist theory of knowing but can in no way be integrated with the notion of transduction of 'information' from the environment that any realist epistemology demands" (von Glasersfeld, 1989).

Dialectical Constructivism

Dialectical constructivism is concerned with the interaction between a learner and her environment. It recognizes that traditional views of cognition are not sufficient and both psychological and sociological factors are important for learning. The blending of psychology and sociology helps one to understand how individuals orient and learn from their surrounding and, further, how these interactive influences shape their mental processes. Dialectical constructivism is also called blended constructivism as it brings out the importance of the blending of psychology and sociology in the context of learning. It is linked to the joint efforts of psychologists and sociologists to understand learning from the perspective of 'contextualism' (Brunning, Schraw, and Ronning, 1999).

Didactic Constructivism

Didactic constructivism is linked to the problem of operationalizing radical constructivism in teaching (Brink, 1991). Here the term 'didactic' has the connotation 'to realize'. The verb 'to realize' in turn has two components: 'to construct', and 'to confront'. In this process the learner constructs a conceptual representation and then confronts it with the ideas of the others. It enables one to discover mistakes which could not be perceived earlier. Similarity between this and the Socrates' 'dialogue' discussed earlier in the context of philosophical constructivism may be seen.

Human Constructivism

Human constructivism (Sharma, 2006), due to J.D. Novak (Novak, 1993), basically proposes that the process of meaningful learning, as understood through assimilation theory, is fundamental to both the psychological process of cognitive development of individuals and the epistemological process of new knowledge construction. It avers that learning and research are nothing but meaning making mechanisms. A researcher as well as a new learner constructs meaning out of a new experience by connecting it to their existing knowledge framework. This means that a scientist and a learner use the same cognitive processes in the construction of new knowledge. The consequent conceptual change may occur in small incremental steps resulting in a 'weak' form of knowledge reconstruction or in a rapid and abrupt manner resulting in a 'strong' form of knowledge reconstruction. This is valid for both a scientist and a learner. According to human constructivism, knowledge is an idiosyncratic, dynamic construction of human beings and in identical situations two human beings may construct two different meanings. This brings out the 'human' aspect of a scientist's work, which is often ignored in teaching-learning situations.

Information-processing Constructivism

According to information-processing constructivism (McInerney and McInerney, 2002) ability of an individual in information processing is crucial in the process of learning. It suggests that a learner has an independent capacity to self-actualize, i.e. the learner can actively organize his/her own learning experiences with clear ideas of means and ends.

Mathematical Constructivism

Mathematical constructivism (Riegler, 2003) is a reaction to Platonism in mathematics. Its proponents, such as L.E.J. Brouwer, Arend Heyting, and Jean Paul van Bendegem claim that mathematical objects exist only if they can be constructed by a method. For this reason they oppose, for example, the notion of infinity.

Physical Constructivism

There exists a 'physical' approach to cognition (Riegler, 2003). The proponent and physicist O. Diettrich (2001) argues that the perceived patterns and regularities are just invariants of inborn cognitive (sensory) operators. Different sets of cognitive operators generate different cognitive phenotypes. Laws of nature are, therefore, human specific. According to the physicist G. Grossing (2001) the perceived non-classical structure of space and time in relativistic cases are human-specific artefacts based on neurophysiological processes.

Pragmatic Constructivism

According to Rieber (1993), pragmatists are those teachers and researchers who have developed a broad and general constructivist perspective through their disposition, reading and professional development programmes, but have a narrower view of the same in classrooms.

Psychiatric/Therapeutic Constructivism

This constructivism is used as a family therapy to solve interpersonal problems (Watzlawick et al., 1974). It aims at disrupting the pattern of symptomatic interpretation of a habitual situation by 'reframing' the situation. The procedure is to "place a conceptual and/or emotional setting or viewpoint in another frame which fits the 'facts' of the same concrete situation equally well or even better and thereby change its entire meaning". This way the patients are enabled to find alternative constructions of their worldview. This in fact amounts to an extension of the operational domain of cognition of a learner.

Socio-historical Constructivism

This form of constructivism basically suggests that humans are social beings, situated within the culture and history of a society, which shape their thinking process. The importance of this approach is the consideration of history as an agent for knowledge construction.

Sociotransformative Constructivism

The sociotransformative constructivism (Rodriguez, 1998) was conceived to help teachers in making their science and mathematics classes more gender-inclusive, socially relevant, and student-centerd. It attempts to unite social constructivism as a theory of learning and multiculturalism as a theory of social justice.

Trivial Constructivism

This advocates the thesis that all knowledge is human construction (von Glasersfeld, 1993). It, however, has 'discovery of ontology' as its purpose (Osborne, 1996). It also means that the worldviews, which are differently constructed, gradually converge towards a knowledge system that represents the world objectively.

Weak Constructivism

Paul Ernest (1995) describes weak constructivism as one in which individuals construct their own knowledge (a local notion), while accepting the existence of objective knowledge (a global notion).

In Table 2.2 we give a summary of the basic features of the different minor pathways in constructivism discussed above.

2.5 Conclusion

In this chapter we have taken a tour of the fascinating landscape of constructivism. Beginning with a glimpse into the meaning and origin of the term 'constructivism' we came across a large variety of constructivism. Of them five major varieties of constructivism namely philosophical constructivism, sociological constructivism, cognitive constructivism, radical constructivism, and social constructivism are generally widely discussed and disseminated in the literature. Besides discussing them in some detail in this chapter under the heading of 'major pathways in constructivism' we have tried to highlight some of the less prominent varieties of constructivism whose significance can be judged on their merit. We have named them 'minor pathways in constructivism'. It must be pointed out that these varieties

Table 2.2

Minor pathways in constructivism	Basic features
Communal constructivism	Students and teachers as a community; Members help one another in knowledge acquisition; Each member creates knowledge for self and others; Use of ICT and networked learning
Computational constructivism	Cognitive development of learner; Neural dimension of cognition
Constructionism	Knowledge construction facilitated by construction of and experimentation with artifacts
Contextual constructivism	Significance of context in learning; Impact of culture on learning
Critical constructivism	Construction has a critical dimension; Construction has a self-reflective dimension
Cultural constructivism	Knowledge and reality depend upon culture; Knowledge construction is a process of enculturation
Cybernetic constructivism	Concept of autopoiesis; Cognitive apparatus is an organizationally closed system
Dialectical constructivism	Interaction between learner and environment; Blending of psychological and sociological factors for learning; Contextualism
Didactic constructivism	Operationalizing radical constructivism in teaching; Construction and confrontation; Discovering mistakes
Human constructivism	Knowledge as idiosyncratic and dynamic human construction; Learning and research use similar meaning making mechanisms; Weak and strong forms of knowledge reconstruction
Information-processing constructivism	Information-processing; Self-actualization
Mathematical constructivism	Mathematical objects exist if they can be constructed by a method
Physical constructivism	Inborn cognitive operators; Cognitive phenotypes; Neuro-physiological processes
Pragmatic constructivism	Broad constructivist perspective gained through reading, disposition and professional development but narrower view of constructivism in classrooms
Psychiatric/Therapeutic constructivism	Solving interpersonal problems; Reframing a habitual situation; Alternative worldviews
Socio-historical constructivism	Humans as social beings situated within culture and history; Thinking process shaped by culture and history
Sociotransformative constructivism	Uniting social constructivism as a theory of learning and multiculturalism as a theory of social justice
Trivial constructivism	Knowledge is human construction; Discovery of ontology
Weak constructivism	Own knowledge as local notion; Objective knowledge as global notion

are not less important; rather they attempt to bring to the fore some subtle but significant issues in constructivism. They are only limited in their domains of operation. They appear to be less global and more local in their scope. Some of them may be directly traced to the major varieties whereas some others appear to have an independent stance. They appear less widely in the literature. This is one reason why we have given here a brief account of only 19 of the list of 25 forms of constructivism we came across in the literature. However, it may not be far from truth if we conclude that these minor varieties constitute some 'fine structures' of the major varieties of constructivism. Whereas the main principles of the major varieties have already found their way into teaching learning models developed for classroom transactions (see Chapter 5 of the present book for some of these models) the minor varieties perhaps are yet to make their presence felt. In view of their individual significance it is important to recognize their existence and use them to further enrich teaching learning situations, in respective contexts.

References

Adey, P. (1988). Cognitive acceleration: Reviews of Prospects. *International Journal of Science Education*, 10(2): 121-34.

Afanasyev, V.G. (1980). *Marxist Philosophy* (Moscow: Progress Publishers).

Ausubel, D.P. (1968). *Educational Psychology: A Cognitive View* (New York: Holt, Rinehart, and Winston).

Bijker, W., Pinch, T. and Hughes, T. (Eds.) (1987). *The Social Construction of Technological Systems: New Directions in the Sociology and History of Technology* (Cambridge, MA: MIT Press).

Bloor, D. (1976). *Knowledge and Social Imagery* (London: Routledge and Kegan Paul).

Boudourides, M.A. (1998). *Constructivism and education: a shopper's guide.* Paper contributed to the International Conference on the Teaching of Mathematics, Samos, Greece, July 3-6, 1998. http://www.duth.gr/~mboudour/

Brink, J. van den (1991). Didactic constructivism. In E. von Glasersfeld (Ed.), *Radical Constructivism in Mathematics Education* (Kluwer Dordrecht), 195-227.

Brooks, J. and Brooks, M. (1993). *In search of understanding: The case for constructivist classroom* (Alexandria, VA: Association for Supervision and Curriculum Development).

Bruffee, K.A. (1983). Writing and Reading as Collaborative or Social Acts: The Argument from Kuhn to Vygotsky. In N. Hays et al. (Eds.), *The Writer's Mind: Writing as a Mode of Thinking* (Urbana: NCTE).

Brunner, J. (1990). *Acts of Meaning* (Cambridge, MA: Harvard University Press).

—— (1996). *The Culture of Education* (Cambridge, MA: Harvard University Press).

Brunning, R.H., Schraw, G.J., and Ronning, R.R. (1999). *Cognitive Psychology and Instruction* (Upper Saddle River, NJ: Merrill), 218.

Callon, M. (1986). The Sociology of an Actor Network." In Callon, M., Law, J. and Rip, A. (Eds.), *Mapping the Dynamics of Science and Technology* (London: Macmillan).

Cobern, W. (1993). Contextual constructivism: the impact of culture on learning and teaching of science. In K. Tobin (Ed.), *The Practice of Constructivism in Science Education* (Hillsdale, NJ: Lawrence-Erlbaum), 51-69.

Collins, H.M. (1985). *Changing Order: Replication and Induction in Scientific Practice*. London: Sage. Ernest, P. (1995), The one and the many. In L. Steffe and J. Gale (Eds.), *Constructivism in Education* (459-86) (New Jersey: Lawrence Erlbaum Associates, Inc).

Derrida, J. (1982). *Margins of Philosophy* (trans. Alan Bass) (Chicago, Illinois: Chicago University Press).

Dewey, J. (1916). *Democracy and Education: An Introduction to the Philosophy of Education* (Columbia: Macmillan Company).

Diettrich, O. (2001). A Physical Approach to the Construction of Cognition and to Cognitive Evolution. *Foundation of Science*, 6(4): 273-341.

Driver, R., and Oldham, V. (1986). A Constructivist Approach to Curriculum Development in Science. *Studies in Science Education*, 13: 105-22.

Driver, R., Asoko, H., Leach, J., Mortimer, E., and Scott, P. (1994). Constructing Scientific Knowledge in the Classroom. *Educational Researcher*, 23: 5-12.

Ernest, P. (1995). The One and the Many. In L. Steffe & J. Gale (Eds.). *Constructivism in Education* (459-86) (New Jersey: Lawrence Erlbaum Associates, Inc).

—— (1999). Social Constructivism as a Philosophy of Mathematics: Radical Constructivism Rehabilitated? Available on internet.

Fleury, S.C. (1998). Social Studies, Trivial Constructivism, and the Politics of Social Knowledge. In M. Larochelle, N. Bednarz & J. Garrision (Eds.). *Constructivism and Education* (Cambridge University Press), 156-72.

Gergen, K.J. (1985). The social constructionist movement in modern psychology. *American Psychologist*, 40: 266-75.

—— (1995). Social construction and the educational process. In L.P. Steffe and J. Gale. (Eds.). *Constructivism in Education* (pp. 17-19) (Hillsdale, N. J.: Erlbaum).

Geelan, D.R. (1997). Epistemological Anarchy and the Many Forms of Constructivism, *Science & Education*, 6(1-2): 15-28.

Good, R., Wandersee, J., and St. Julien, J. (1993). Cautionary Notes on the Appeal of the New "Ism" (Constructivism) in Science Education. In K. Tobin (Ed.) *Constructivism in Science and Mathematics Education* (AAAS, Washington DC), 71-90.

Gredler, M.E. (1997). *Learning and Instruction: Theory into Practice* (3rd Ed.). (Upper Saddle River, NJ: Prentice Hall).

Grint, K., and Woolgar, S. (1997). *The Machine at Work: Technology, Work and Organization* (Cambridge, UK: Polity Press).

Grössing, G. (2001). Comparing the Long-Term Evolution of "Cognitive Invariances" in Physics with a Dynamics in States of Consciousness. *Foundation of Science* 6(4): 255-72.

Holmes, B., Tangney, B., FitzGibbon, A., Savage, T., and Meehan, S. (2001). *Communal constructivism: Students constructing learning for as well as with others.* Proceedings of SITE 2001, Florida.

Jha, A.K. (2009). *Constructivist Epistemology and Pedagogy* (New Delhi: Atlantic Publishers and Distributors (P) Ltd.).

Kant, I. and Pulhan, Werner S. (tr.). (1996) [1781, 1787]. *Critique of Pure Reason* (Indianapolis: Hackett Publishing Company).

Kim, B. (2001). Social Constructivism. In M. Orey (Ed.). *Emerging Perspectives on Learning, Teaching, and Technology.* Available on website http// www.coe.uga.edn/epltt/social constructivism.htm.

Kincheloe, J.L. (1993). *Towards a Critical Politics of Teacher Thinking. Mapping the Postmodern* (London: Bergin & Garvey).

—— (2005). *Critical Constructivism Primer* (NY: Peter Lang).

—— (2008). *Knowledge and Critical Pedagogy* (Dordrecht, The Netherlands: Springer).

Kukia, A. (2000). *Social Constructivism and the Philosophy of Science* (New York: Routledge).

Latour, B. (1987). *Science in Action* (Cambridge, MA: Harvard University Press).

Liu, C.H. and Matthews, R. (2005). Vygotsky's philosophy: Constructivism and its criticisms examined. *International Educational Journal*, 6(3): 386-99.

Luhmann, N. (1989). *Ecological Communication* (Cambridge, UK: Polity Press).

—— (1990). *Essays in Self-Reference* (New York: Columbia University Press).

—— (1995). *Social Systems* (Stanford: Stanford University Press).

MacKenzie, D. (1991). *Inventing Accuracy: A Historical Sociology of Missile Guidance* (Cambridge, MA: MIT Press).

MacKenzie, D. and Wajcman, J. (Eds.) (1985). *The Social Shaping of Technology* (Milton Keynes: Open University Press).

Matthews, M.R. *Constructivism in Science and Mathematics Education.* m.matthews@unsw.edu.au.

Maturana, H. and Varlea, F. (1980). *Autopoiesis and Cognition: The Realization of the Living. Boston Studies in the Philosophy of Sciences.* Vol. 42 (Boston, Dordrecht: D. Reidel).

McInerney and McInerney (2002). *Educational Psychology* (Australia: Pearson Custom Publishing).

McMohan, M. (1997). Social constructivism and its worldwide web: a paradigm for learning. Paper presented at the ASCILITE Conference, Perth, Australia.

Mingers, J. (1995). *Self-Producing Systems: Implications and Applications of Autopoiesis* (New York: Plenum).

Noddings, N. (1990). Constructivism in mathematics education. In R. Davis, C. Maher, & N. Noddings (Eds.), *Constructivist views on the teaching and learning of mathematics* (7-18) (Reston, Va: National Council of Teachers of Mathematics).

Norris, C. (1986). *Deconstruction: Theory and Practice* (Methuen and Co. Ltd.).

Novak, J.D. 1993. Human constructivism: A unification of psychological and epistemological phenomena in meaning making. *International Journal of Constructivist Psychology*, 6(2): 167-93.

Osborne, J.F. (1996). Beyond constructivism. *Science Education*, 80, 53-82.

Papert, S.A. (1991). Situating Constructionism. In I. Harel & S. Papert (eds.), *Constructionism* (1-12) (Norwood, NJ: Ablex).

Papert, S. (1993). *The Children's Machine: Rethinking School in the Age of the Computer* (New York: Basic Books).

Phillips, D.C. (1995). The Good, the Bad and the Ugly: The Many Faces of Constructivism. *Educational Researcher*, 24(7): 5-12.

Piaget, J. (1970). *The Science of Education and the Psychology of the Child* (NY: Grossman).

—— (1972). *To Understand is to Invent*. (NY: The Viking Press Inc.).

—— (1977). *The Development of Thought: Equilibration of Cognitive Structures* (NY: The Viking Press Inc.).

Pinker, S. (1998). *How the mind works* (London: Penguin Books).

Prawat, R.S., and Folden, R.E. (1994). Philosophical perspectives on constructivist views of learning. *Educational Psychologists*, 29(1): 37-48.

Quartz, S. and Sejnowski, T.J. (1997). The neural basis of cognitive development: A constructivist manifesto. *Behavioural and Brain Sciences*, 20(4): 537-96.

Rieber, L.P. (1993). A pragmatic view of instructional technology. In K. Tobin (Ed.), *The Practice of Constructivism in Science Education* (Hove: Lawrence Erlbaum).

Riegler, A. (2003). The Key to Radical Constructivism. http://www.univie.ac.at/constructivism/key.html

Rodriguez, A.J. (1998). Strategies for counter resistance: Toward sociotransformative constructivism and learning to teach science for diversity and for understanding. *Journal of Research in Science Teaching*, 36(6): 589-622.

Sampson, G. (Ed.) (1908). *The Works of George Berkeley.* Vol. I. London.

Sharma, S. (2006). Constructivism. In S. Sharma, *Constructivist Approaches to Teaching and Learning: Handbook for Teachers of Secondary Stage*, 4-5 (New Delhi: NCERT).

Shayer, M. and Adey, P. (1981). *Towards a Science of Science Teaching*. (London: Heinemann Educational Books).

Staver, J.R. (1998). Constructivism: Sound theory for explicating the practice of science and science teaching. *Journal of Research in Science Teaching*, 35(5): 501-20.

Suchting, W.A. (1992). Constructivism Deconstructed. *Science & Education*, 1(3): 223-54.

The Chambers Dictionary (1995) (New Delhi: Allied Chambers (India) Limited).

The New Encyclopaedia Britannica (1985) Volume 3. Micropaedia: 576.

The Oxford Dictionary of Difficult Words (2002) (New York: Oxford University Press).

von Foerster, H. (1984). *Observing Systems* (Salinas: Intersystems Publications).

von Glasersfeld, E. (1983). Learning as a constructive activity. In J. C. Bergeron and N. Herscovics (Eds.), *Proceedings of the Fifth Annual Meeting of the North American Chapter of the International Group for the Psychology of Mathematics Education* (41-69) (Montreal: University of Montreal).

—— (1984). An introduction to radical constructivism. In P. Watzlawick, *The Invented Reality* (17-40) (New York: W.W. Norton & Company).

—— (1987a). *Construction of Knowledge* (Intersystems Publications, Salinas CA).

—— (1987b). Learning as a constructive activity. In C. Janvier (Ed.), *Problems of Representation in the Teaching and Learning of Mathematics* (Hillsdale, NJ: Lawrence Erlbaum).

—— (1989). Cognition, Construction of Knowledge and Teaching. *Synthese*, 80(1): 121-40.

—— (1990a). An exposition of constructivism: Why some like it radical. In R.B. Davis, C.A. Maher and N. Noddings (Eds.), *Constructivist Views on the Teaching and Learning of Mathematics* (19-29) (Reston, VA: NCTM).

—— (1990b). Environment and Education. In L.P. Steffe & T. Wood (Eds.), *Transforming Children's Mathematics Education: International Perspectives* (200-15) (Hillsdale, NJ: Lawrence Erlbaum).

—— (1993). Questions and answers about radical constructivism. In K. Tobin (Ed.), *The Practice of Constructivism in Science Education* (23-38) (Washington, DC: AAAS Press).

—— (1995). *A Way of Knowing and Learning* (The Falmer Press, London).

—— (1999). How do we mean? A constructivist sketch of semantics. *Cybernetics and Human Knowing*, 6(1): 9-16.

—— (2000). *Radical Constructivism and Teaching*. http://srri.nsm. umass.edu/ vonGlasersfeld/onlinePapers/html/geneva/

Vygotsky, L. (1978). *Mind in Society* (Cambridge, MA: Harvard University Press).

—— (1986). *Thought and Language*. (Transl. and Ed.) A. Kozulin (Cambridge, MA: The MIT Press). (Originally published in Russian in 1934.)

Watts, M. and Jofili, Z. (1998). Towards critical constructivist teaching. *International Journal of Science Education*, 20(2): 173-85.

Watzlawick, P., Weakland, J., and Fisch, R. (1974). *Change: Principle of Problem Formation and Problem Resolution* (New York: W.W. Norton).

Wertsch, J.V. (1979). From social interaction to higher psychological processes. *Human Development*, 22: 1-22.

Westermann, G. (2000). *Constructivist Neural Network Models of Cognitive Development*, Ph.D. thesis at the University of Edinburgh.

Wheatley, G.H. (1991). Constructivist Perspectivists on Science and Mathematics Learning. *Science Education*, 75(1): 9-22.

Woolgar, S. (1988). *Science: The Very Idea* (London: Routledge).

3 Conceptual Change: The Basic Process of Constructivism

3.1 Introduction

The child interacts with the environment, peer group and family members and acquires considerable knowledge and ideas about the natural and technological world before his/her formal education. That is why one of the tenets of constructivism is that 'No child enters a class devoid of concepts'. Most of these ALCONs differ from the accepted scientific views. ALCONs may be formed in any field of knowledge/concept/idea. These ALCONs are intuitive and found to be extremely resistant to change. For example—Sun rises in the east—the child observes it every day morning and taken it to be granted that—sun is moving from east to west, however scientifically it is wrong. The truth is earth is moving and sun is static/fixed. The Earth is revolving around the Sun. This is a good example of alternative conception. It is difficult to make the child understand this simple scientific concept. Even after many years of formal education many adults possess such alternative conception. In this situation the intuitive conception is replaced or modified by the scientific concept. Effective learning suggests that learning involves changing a person's conception rather than simply adding new knowledge to what already exist. ALCONs resist to change as these concepts are correct in learner's domain because of their viability. Acquisition of the scientifically approved concept requires conceptual change (Vosniadou and Skopeliti, 2005) which helps in construction of knowledge.

Over the last forty years an active research in the area of children's conceptual understanding in science has been undertaken. This research includes detailed information about children's conceptions at various ages in different scientific domains (Carry, 1985; West et al., 1985). Basically this research programme deals with children's existing conception about natural phenomena. Here learning is visualized in terms of conceptual development or change rather than piecemeal addition of new knowledge to the existing one, which is the basis of knowledge construction i.e. constructivism.

Based on two main observations of cognitive psychology about learning namely,

(a) Learning is a purposeful, intentional, autogenic (Glasersfeld, 1992) sequence of construction of cognitive structures, and
(b) Learning is pervasively influenced by the ALCONs of the pupils.

Posner et al. (1982) and Hewson (1981, 1982) developed the conceptual change model of learning. In this model child is visualized as an inquiring knower (De Vries and Kohlberg, 1987). Whenever the child encounters a new concept, event or instance, an interpretative and/or integrative interaction of it with his/her own existing conceptions immediately starts. The outcome, resulting in a conceptual change which depends on the form and structure of existing ALCONs and of the interaction.

3.2 Pathways for Conceptual Change

There are different pathways for conceptual change from the ALCONs towards the correct conceptions. Fig. 3.1 presents an attempt to categorise these pathways.

As depicted in Fig. 3.1 conceptual change can take place due to teaching task undertaken in the classroom by the teacher or it can be longitudinal conceptual change which occurs due to progress in age. When the students go to higher and higher classes or progress in age their schema gets refined and conceptual change occur. Teaching task based conceptual changes are intentional conceptual changes. Again both types of conceptual change can occur due to knowledge acquisition through conceptual change underlying the differentiation between continuous and discontinuous pathways, namely a gradual process of growth and a quantized discrete process, characterized by stages of growing expertise. Alluding to the distinction by Kuhn (1970) they may be also termed as "Evolutionary" (West, 1982) or "Revolutionary" (Nussbaum, 1989). The level to which conceptual change occurs determines whether it is a part of an evolutionary process or a revolution (Thagard, 1992). In evolutionary pattern of conceptual change the student maintains substantial elements of the old conception while gradually incorporating individual elements from the new one. Conceptual change is not seen as a sudden shift from one theory to another, but a continuous process which is controlled by the different kinds of constrains, and particularly those that belong to the framework theory (Vosniadou, 1994a). Evolutionary conceptual changes are weaker conceptual change.

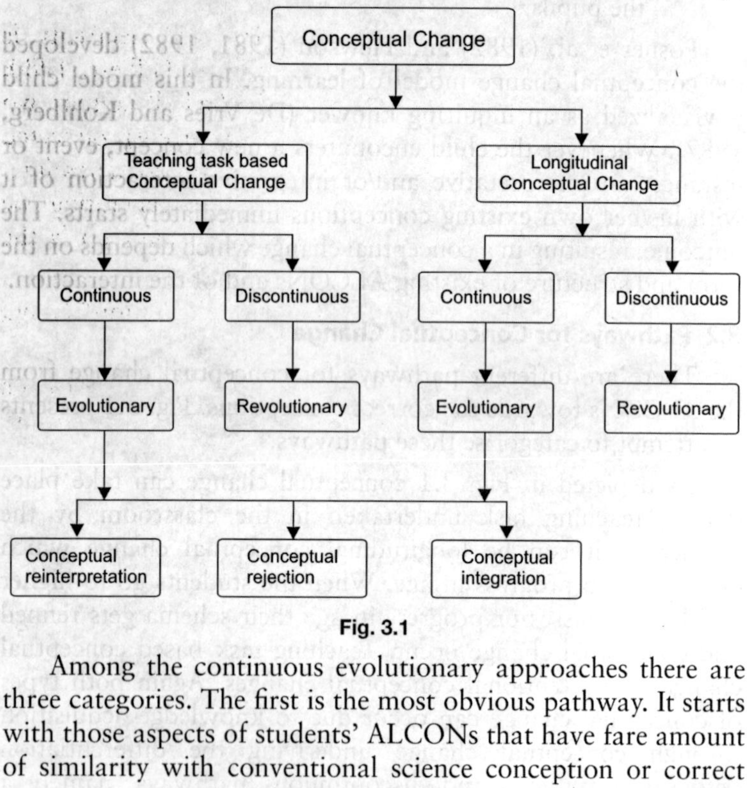

Fig. 3.1

Among the continuous evolutionary approaches there are three categories. The first is the most obvious pathway. It starts with those aspects of students' ALCONs that have fare amount of similarity with conventional science conception or correct conception. Brown and Clement's (1989) strategy of "bridging analogies" is such an approach that tries to generate a continuous pathway. A few examples in this framework is in order.

(a) The modification of pupils' ALCONs that only four-legged large land animals are animals (Bell, 1981; Bell and Barker, 1982; Mohapatra and Das, 1996) to include mosquito, snail and ant as animals is a sign of extension in both meaning and richness of the concept "animal" in the personal schema of pupils.

(b) Pupils' gradual learning that bodies at rest do have forces acting on them to be contrasted with the concept that bodies at rest do not have any forces acting on them (Mohapatra and Bhattacharya, 1989) is a process of evolutionary change towards the meaningful learning of the 'concept of rest'.

(c) A well-known pupil ALCON in basic electricity is that current is used up (Osborne and Gilbert, 1980; Osborne, 1981; Osborne, 1983) in the bulb so that two ammeters (instrument for measuring current) connected on each side of the bulb will show different reading. The reinterpretation process results in generating the modified comprehension that what is used up is the energy not the current.

These are examples of "Conceptual reinterpretation" (Jung, 1986) under the evolutionary conceptual change.

If the new concept does not convey any meaning to the learner, he/she will reject it without trying to modify the concept. Even this conceptual rejection is an evolutionary change in the same sense as the state of rest is a state of motion with zero velocity.

If the new concept convey any meaning (may not be the correct one) then the learner may modify the structure of the existing ALCONs and try to accommodate the new conception. This is what we call conceptual integration (Hewson, 1981; Posner et al., 1982).

Conceptual integration and conceptual reinterpretation which are "Evolutionary" changes make the pupils ALCONs richer in structures, more precise in their usable meanings and more specific in their domain of operation.

On the other hand if the assimilation of the new concepts/ experiences require large scale change of accommodation (Posner et al. 1982) resulting in a deep restructuring of knowledge then one may call that as 'Revolutionary Change' (West, 1982). Modification of the ALCON that heat is a fluid, so as to accept the scientific connotation that heat is a form of energy is a revolutionary conceptual change. Similarly pupils' ALCON is that matter and energy are different entities. But when they learn that matter and energy are inter-convertible, it demands revolutionary change. Thus conceptual change is both an evolutionary learning process and a revolutionary paradigm change.

In an input-output framework the final states of conceptual change will be delineated in Chapter 5.

3.3 Is Conceptual Change Global or Domain Specific?

Learning in a particular content area is always domain specific (Seiler, 1973). Hennessy (1993) supported this insight by showing that the knowledge achieved is quite substantially linked with the situation in which it was developed. Conceptual changes in science are always domain specific. It is different for different science concept in different domains like optics, thermodynamics, genetics. Thus the kind of changes necessary is different for different domains and even sub-domains.

Conceptual change is not specific to science and can be used in business, industry and fields of education, i.e. in every domain of knowledge acquisition. Thus, conceptual change is related to all field of knowledge. The advancement in science and technology has initiated change in restructuring industries and companies. Hospitals are now as "medical centres" and treated as profit making industries. The 'patients' are now named as "Clients". The concept of bank transaction has changed to ATM and computerized operation. From time to time companies change their models of operation and employees are trained to re-conceptualize their roles and responsibilities and modify their way of operation. Banks now even name their new customer linked schemes as 'products'. Though conceptual change is domain specific but for construction of knowledge conceptual change is a necessity in all fields of knowledge.

3.4 Theoretical Origins of Conceptual Change

Researchers in 1980s saw the growth of studies investigating the development of students' pre-instructional conceptions towards the intended science concepts in conceptual change approaches, which placed conceptual change as embedded in various theoretical frames with epistemological, ontological and affective orientations (Duit and Treagust, 2003).

One of the most prominent conceptual theory which is based on Kuhn's notion of paradigm shift and Piaget's notion of accommodation was proposed by Posner et al. (1982). They proposed—if a learner's current conception is functional and if the learner can solve problems within the existing schema, then the learner does not feel a need to change the current conception. Even when the current concept does not successfully solve some problems, the learner may make only moderate changes to his/her conceptions. This is called "conceptual capture" (Hewson, 1981) or "weak restructuring" (Carey, 1985). For conceptual change to occur the learner must be dissatisfied with an initial conception in order to self-modify/erase it and accept a scientific conception. This is called "conceptual exchange" (Hewson, 1981) or "radical restructuring" (Carey, 1985). The approach presented by Posner et al. (1982), called classical approach, emphasizes and assumes logical and rational thinking (only cognitive domain). However, it ignores the affective (e.g. motivation, values, interest) and social component of learning. This theory is criticized by many because it is based on learner's cognition only and not learner as a whole. It does not consider the teacher and other students, school environment, society as factors which influence the learning process of a learner.

Strike et al. (1992) recognized these deficiencies in their original conceptual change theory and revised it by including the influence of affective and social factors in their original model. In the revised theory: (1) A learner's conceptual ecology was made larger than what was suggested by the original theory to include motives and goals not related to the epistemological factors suggested by the history and philosophy of science, (2) Current conceptions are themselves part of the learner's conceptual ecology and ALCONs are generated which lead them to their preconceptions. (3) Conceptions can exist in different modes of representation and articulateness.

According to (Hewson et al., 1998), conceptual change is influenced by social factors and is achieved through cognitive apprenticeship. These views on learning perceive discussion among students and instructor as a means of promoting conceptual change. For conceptual change, the factors to be taken into account (Duit, 1999) are:

- Cognitive factors
- Affective factors
- Social factors
- Contextual factors.

Thus in recent years researchers have raised issues of motivational, affective and contextual factors to achieve conceptual change (Gregoire, 2003; Murphy, 2007). Jonassen argues that conceptual change is more than a realignment or restructuring of ideas but rather, it results from interactions of mind with other minds in the world (Lee and Jonassen, 2012). These interactions are crucial for viable and meaningful (at least in the framework of the learner) construction of knowledge and contribute primarily to the principles of constructivism. With the exponential growth in online communication such as face book and twitter, learner's ideas and conceptions are constantly exposed to the challenges posed by friends and community members.

The different views and perspectives on conceptual change are as follows:

- An epistemological perspective of conceptual change.
- An ontological perspective of conceptual change.
- An affective perspective of conceptual change.
- An intentional perspective of conceptual change.

- Multidimensional perspective of conceptual change.
- Framework theory view of conceptual change.
- Mental model theory of conceptual change.
- Domain specific restructuring view of conceptual change.
- Knowledge-in-pieces view of conceptual change.
- Knowledge as theory perspective and knowledge as element perspective view of conceptual change.

3.4.1 An Epistemological Perspective of Conceptual Change

Posner et al. (1982) introduced the classical conceptual change approach in which teacher design teaching strategy after knowing the students' ALCONs. The teaching strategy consists of ideas that do not fit students' existing conceptions and leads to dissatisfaction. It is followed by introducing a new framework based as formal science, which explain the anomaly. However, after instruction students' conceptual progress towards understanding the concept and the principle is still limited (Duit and Treagust, 1998). The best that can be achieved is a peripheral conceptual change (Chinn and Brewer, 1993). Initial idea of the learner merge with parts of the new idea (given by the teacher) to form a hybrid concept (Jung, 1993) or synthetic model (Vosniadou and Brewer, 1992). Student's dissatisfaction with a prior conception was believed to initiate dramatic or revolutionary conceptual change. The researchers have measured student's conceptual change from an epistemological position using the terms Conceptual Status and Epistemological Profiles.

3.4.2 An Ontological Perspective of Conceptual Change

In this perspective, conceptual change is viewed as ontology, namely, how students view the nature of the conception and seeks to examine the ways that students consider scientific conceptions in terms of their personal perception of reality. Thus ontological perspective refers to students' personal view on nature, or reality. Chinn and Brewer (1993) described ontological beliefs as being about "the fundamental categories and properties of the world". Carey (1985) argued that "some of the child's concepts are incommensurable with the adults" and needs strong knowledge restructuring during childhood. This sort of conceptual change is called radical restructuring by Vosniadou (1994). In terms of framework theory radical restructuring can be explained as revision to central "framework theories" which involve both ontological and epistemological changes. Strongest ontological changes are referred to as 'tree switching' (Thagard, 1992) and 'tree swapping' (Chi, et al., 1994). Examples of ontological conceptual changes are a conception of heat from a flowing fluid to kinetic energy in transit and a conception of a gene from an inherited object to a biochemical process. The ontological shift view of conceptual change (Chi, 2005) emphasizes that many pre-concepts are incorrectly assigned to the broad ontological category. Conceptual change in this view involves constructing the new ontological category and reasoning the concept to the correct category. For example: A child categorizes Whale as 'fish' but when the child grows and comes to know what is a mammal, the child recategorizes it and an ontological shift is said to have taken place in the mind of the child.

According to Chi the conceptual change process is hard because either,

- the student assigns the concept to a different (wrong) ontological category, or
- the student lacks an appropriate category to which the concept could be assigned.

If student become aware of their ontological commitments, they can then become aware of how the scientific theory does not fit with their existing knowledge structure. In this situation students assign the concept into a correct category by revising their ontological commitments, categories and presuppositions.

3.4.3 An Affective Perspective of Conceptual Change (Student)

Affective dimensions like students' interest, motivation, emotion and intention play a key role in supporting conceptual change. However, these aspects have not been addressed in classical conceptual change approach. Research studies reveal that students' self-efficacy and control beliefs, the classroom social context, and the individual's goals, intentions, purposes, expectations and needs are as important as cognitive strategies in concept learning. Pintrich et al. (1993) review of social and motivational literature highlights the importance of interest, personal and situational beliefs to students' engagement in learning activities. The teachers who ignore students' social and affective aspects may limit students' conceptual change. Zembylas (2005) argued that both cognitive and emotional aspects equally influence conceptual change.

3.4.4 An Intentional Perspective of Conceptual Change

Conceptual change is individual specific as learner has to construct his/her knowledge. This view considers that learners need to be active and to have the intention to learn. Learner should play an active intentional role in the process of knowledge restructuring (Sinatra and Pintrich, 2003). In this situation conceptual change depends not only on cognitive factors such as recognition of conflict, but also on meta-cognitive, motivational and affective process that can be brought under the learner's conscious control and may determine the form and structure of change. Intentional perspective of conceptual change is analogous to that of mindfulness (Salomon and Globerson, 1987), a "construct which reflects a voluntary state of mind and connects among motivation, cognition and learning".

3.4.5 Framework Theory Approach

The framework theory (Vosniadou et al. 2008) view of conceptual change suggests that when new ideas are encountered, basic ontological commitments influence how new ideas are assimilated. Successful conceptual change in this view requires strategic changes in the interfering ontological commitments.

The framework theory perspective is consistent with Chi's (1992) argument that conceptual change requires an ontological shift. Researchers of these perspectives suggest that radical changes like these do not take place suddenly. These changes are gradual and time-consuming process because the students have to revise and restructure their ALCONs. Vosniadou and Ioannides (1998) suggested that along with ontological change the students should be guided through instruction to internalize the concept.

The framework theory approach is based on cognitive development research and attempts to provide a broad theoretical basis for understanding the process of conceptual change. According to this approach concepts are embedded in domain specific 'framework theories' which represent different explanatory frameworks from currently accepted science and mathematics (Carey, 1991). These framework theories are constructed by the children when they interpret their everyday experiences in the context of lay culture. Framework theories are domain specific.

3.4.6 Mental Model Theory

Conceptual change process can be visualized in terms of changing mental models (Ioannides and Vosniadou, 2002; Vosniadou and Brewer, 1992). According to Vosniadou and Brewer (1992) elementary school students construct earth models in disc or rectangular flat shape basing on their every day experience. This model of earth is called "Initial model" which is not influenced by any instruction. After instruction knowing earth is spherical the student construct "synthetic model". The students in their synthetic model visualize earth as hollow sphere, hemisphere, flattened sphere, etc. Synthetic model is scientifically incorrect but it is an indication that students begin to synthesize the scientific theory by restructuring their initial model or framework theories. This synthetic model gets restructured and helps the student to learn the actual concept.

3.4.7 Domain Specific Restructuring

Carry (1991) put forth her "domain specific restructuring" by challenging Piaget and "Global restructuring" leading to conceptual change process. According to Carry, children restructure their own theory/naïve theory structures by increasing their knowledge in a specific domain. As children are exposed to new experiences instructions they gradually replace their theory like conceptual structures with scientifically correct conceptual structures. Restructuring of concepts results from social interactions, increased knowledge in a specific domain and variety of dis-equilibrating influences, partially influenced by development of logical structure of the child.

3.4.8 Knowledge-in-Pieces

The "knowledge-in-pieces" di Sessa (1988) views both pre-concept (naïve) and scientific conceptual understanding as grounded in multiple small knowledge resources that can be considered "sub-conceptual". Since both naïve and scientific conceptions are grounded in the same broad pool of sub-conceptual resources, conceptual change can be visualized as the re-organization of these resources. In this view, prior knowledge is not so coherent or stable and knowledge is conceived as consisting of many fine grained bits of knowledge. This is the same as knowledge-as-element perspective and the P-prime.

3.4.9 Multidimensional Perspectives of Conceptual Change

The multidimensional perspectives of conceptual change consider epistemological, ontological and affective domains in order to address the complexity of teaching and learning process (Duit, 1998). Venville and Treagust (1998) utilized four different perspective of conceptual change namely Posner et al. (1982) conceptual change model, Vosniadou's (1994a) framework theory and mental model, Chi et al. (1994) ontological categories and Pintrich et al. (1993) motivation perspective to teach genetics in secondary school using analogies.

3.4.10 Knowledge as Theory Perspectives and Knowledge as Element Perspectives View of Conceptual Change

Researchers in conceptual change have made significant progress on two prominent theoretical perspectives regarding knowledge structure (Ozdemir et al., 2007) and they are characterized under two broad categories:

(1) Knowledge as theory perspectives

(2) Knowledge as element perspectives

Knowledge-as-theory perspectives examines learner's knowledge as a coherent unified framework of theory like character (Carey, 1999; Chi, 2005; Ioannides and Vosniadou, 2002; Wellman and Gelman, 1992) whereas in knowledge-as-element perspectives student knowledge is considered as an ecology of quasi-independent elements (Clark, 2006; di Sessa et al., 2004; Linn et al., 2004).

3.4.10a Knowledge-as-Theory Perspectives

Knowledge as theory perspective is based on Piaget's concepts of assimilation and accommodation, Kuhn's concept of normal science, scientific revolution and paradigms shift (Kuhn, 1970), radical restructuring (Carey, 1985), conceptual exchange (Hewson, 1981) conceptual capture (Hewson, 1981) or Weak restructuring (Carey, 1985), higher level ontological shift (Chi, 1992), Framework theories and mental models (Vosniadou, 1994a, b).

One of the proponents of knowledge-as-theory advocates that change between concepts can be achieved through three processes (Carey, 1991).

- Replacement,
- Differentiation, and
- Coalescence.

Replacement: One concept displaces another concept where the two concepts are fundamentally different.

Differentiation: In this process the initial concept splits into two or more new concepts. For example plants differentiated into herbs, shrubs and creepers.

Coalescence: It is opposite process of differentiation. Coalescence involves two or more original concepts coalescing into a single concept.

Knowledge-as-theory perspectives suggest revolutionary (Nussbaum, 1989) process of conceptual change where one theory is replaced by another theory like understanding.

3.4.10b Knowledge-as-Element Perspective

The proponents of this theoretical perspective basically belong to science education community. di Sessa (1993) proposed that the knowledge structures of novices consist primarily of unstructured collections of many simple elements called P-primes (short for Phenomenological Primitives). P-primes are developed through a sense-of-mechanism that reflects our interaction with the physical world. The learner merely assumes that "something happens because that is the way they are". These presuppositions influence learners reasoning when they interpret the world (Ueno, 1993). P-primes do not have the status of a theory because they are not produced or activated under highly organized system like framework theories proposed by knowledge-as-perspective theory. This P-prime concept was supported by Southerland et al. (2001) and Clark (2006). According to knowledge-as-element perspective conceptual change is a piecemeal process. This perspective hypothesizes that naïve knowledge structures consist of multiple conceptual elements. Novices spontaneously connect and activate these knowledge pieces according to the relevance of the situation. Conceptual change process begins with quasi-independent small knowledge elements that get connected to create more complex conceptual structures by adding new knowledge elements, recognizing connections and/or modifying existing simple knowledge elements through an evolutionary (West, 1982) process. Evolutionary process is the most obvious pathways. It starts with the aspects of students' pre-instructional conceptions that are mainly in accord with science conceptions or correct conceptions.

3.5 Conditions of Conceptual Change

Construction of new conception is possible only on the basis of already existing conceptions (Duit, 1999). Two major components which influence conceptual change are:

- Conditions that need to be satisfied for a person to experience conceptual changes.
- Person's conceptual ecology that provides the context in which conceptual change occurs.

Here we discuss only the conditions which should be satisfied for conceptual change to occur. For successful conceptual change the following four cognitive conditions should be satisfied during learning process (Posner et al., 1982). Three major conditions of conceptual change are:

- Intelligible
- Plausible
- Fruitful

The fourth condition refers to the extent to which the learner is dissatisfied with a conception. The other important component is the conceptual ecology, through which a conception is depicted as occupying a "niche" among such cognitive factors as the other knowledge, analogies and metaphors, past experience, and epistemological commitments of a learner.

(i) **Intelligibility:** The new conception should convey meaning (not necessarily the correct meaning) to the learner. Posner et al. (1982) argued that for learner to accommodate a new conception he/she must find it intelligible. Without intelligibility a conception has no status (Hewson and Thornley, 1989) for the learner. Schollum and Osborne (1985) call this the criteria of relevance. This relevance they specify by stating that the new concept should be related to learner's personal experience outside classroom. Learners must find a new conception intelligible before they can begin to consider its plausibility or fruitfulness and thus accommodate it into their cognitive structures (Hewson, 1981). Strike and Posner (1985) explicated the meaning of intelligibility and the other conditions for conceptual change by relating them to the components of conceptual ecology. The essence of the idea of intelligibility lies in the manner in which a conception is represented mentally and in classroom discourse by learners and to learners (Thornley, 1990). Conception can be made potentially intelligible, through symbolic definitions, images, analogies or any of several other modes of expression. The essence of the intelligibility of an idea is seen to lie in the learners' ability to represent the idea using several modes of representations. For example let us take the concept of 'electric current'. One can represent current (Thornley et al., 1996).

- as a linguistic definition such as "rate of transfer of electric charge" or symbolically $i=\frac{dq}{dt}$.
- in terms of a critical attribute such as that it involves the flow of matter as well as energy.

- as an example such as "something" or "stuff" that flows in a vacuum cleaner's power cord.
- as an analogy for example to the flow of water in a pipe.

Thus the learner can represent ideas by linguistic expressions, criterial attributes, examples, images, analogies or metaphors, other modes of representation like auditory, olfactory, etc.

(a) **Linguistic expressions:** Linguistic representations have their value in their memorizability not meant for a test but for the way in which they can be used as a later check on an act of classification, or a plan for some action. It includes labels, definitions or formulas, expressed in natural, formal or symbolic language.

(b) **Critical attributes:** Critical attributes often overlap with "Linguistic Expressions". Definitions often incorporate statements of critical attributes. Critical attributes are useful when two potentially confusable conceptions are to be discriminated. Critical attribute is important in discriminatory between similar conceptions.

(c) **Images:** Critical attributes are often best represented as images. For example, showing leaf shapes while teaching about types of leaves (or) showing a picture of tetrahedral bond configuration facilitates understanding of molecular geometry.

(d) **Action as representation:** If the concept is intelligible one can transform it to action for explaining it to others. For examples 'pushing' gesture when describing forces.

(e) **Exemplars:** Exemplars play a special role in representation. If a concept is intelligible to a teacher he/she can find appropriate exemplar to represent the concept. In Shulman's (1986) framework, prototypes are one type of case knowledge which together with propositional and strategic knowledge, constitute pedagogical content knowledge (PCK). As Shulman notes, "...[Prototype] exemplify, illustrate and bring alive the theoretical propositions that are potentially the most powerful tools teacher can have".

Representations of Intelligibility

Intelligibility is nothing but the representation that learners and teachers do, and that is where the various modes of representation come explicitly into play. If the concept is intelligible to the learner or the teacher he/she will be able to find a way of representing the conception. The individual must be able to grasp how experience can be structured by a new conception sufficiently to explore the possibilities inherent in it (Strike and Posner, 1985). One can represent a intelligible concept's wing criterial attributes if he/she will be able to represent or communicate it to another person. Exemplars for representations of intelligibility are—I can understand it, I can talk to other people about it, I can carry on a conversation about it. One of the examples in the literature is "the moon is made of green cheese". It is a proposition that everyone would find the concept to be intelligible but not plausible and thus distinguish between the concepts of intelligibility and plausibility. Analogies and metaphors can be useful for illustrating intelligibility.

An Intelligible Conception of Refraction

Hewson and Hennessey (1992) explained that for a concept to be intelligible students must know what the concept means and should be able to describe it in their own words. The concept of refraction is intelligible for the learner which is evident from the following interview of a Class X student after facilitating an activity to explain refraction, allowing a beam of light passing through a glass slab. The teacher explained that the bending occurs because light slows down when it enters the glass slab and speeds up when leaves the glass slab.

Interviewer : Can you tell me what happens here to make the light beam bend?

Student : Because it is passing through materials of different densities...making the light bend.

Interviewer : How does the density affect the beam to make it bend?

Student : Do not know, what happens inside the slab.

Interviewer : Do you have any idea what happens here to make it bend?

Student : The light slows down when it enters the slab.

Interviewer : Are you very sure about the light speed being different in different medium?

Student : I am not very sure. It may or may not be due to different densities.

Here the student demonstrated that the concept of refraction is related to light changing speed in media with different densities was intelligible to the student.

(ii) **Plausibility**: For a concept to be plausible the concept must first be intelligible and students must believe that this is how the world actually is and that it must fit in with other ideas or concepts that students know about or believe. Plausibility means the learner can justify his/her ideas and explanation. The concept is plausible if the learner can persuade others that his/her ideas are true or reasonable. Different modes by which one can say that the concept is plausible to him/her are as follows:

(a) Consistency with other accepted ideas. For example, one conception can be deduced from another accepted idea.

(b) Consistency with beliefs about causes and effects. For example, understanding causes and effects in a causal mechanism.

(c) Consistency with past experiences. Past experiences, which are true, helps the learner to realize the plausibility of the concept.

(d) Consistency with laboratory experiences: The concept is plausible if it is consistent with the result of the laboratory experiences. For example, the time period of a simple pendulum depends on the length of the pendulum, this concept is plausible if it is concluded from the result of the pendulum experiment.

(e) Consistent with analogous situation. For example, one can give an analogous situation like, an atom is like the solar system.

(f) Consistent with beliefs about the basic nature of the world or universe. For example, when you throw a ball, it falls down or comes back to you.

(g) Concepts fit with the beliefs about the way the world is or must be. The learner is able to fit his/her ideas to a "ontological" categories.

Representation of Plausibility

Plausibility can be represented by linguistic expressions, criterial attributes, exemplars, analogies and metaphors.

Using linguistic expression one can say that the conception is potentially true and is consistent with the learner's worldview (Hewson and Hewson, 1984) so that the concept is plausible. In contrast the characterization as "anticipated degree of fit... into an existing conceptual ecology" (Posner et al., 1982) reflects a "psychologists" perspective of representing plausibility of a concept. For representing using criterial attributes one must relate to the possibility of a conception being true of the world actually being or working in that way.

Plausibility can be represented by exemplars. For example "Physicists prior to the 20th century were reluctant to accept what geologists were claiming about the age of the world since they had no theory that would allow the sun to provide energy for that period of time" (Posner et al., 1982). Analogies and metaphors are useful tools for representing plausibility of any concept.

Plausible Conception of Refraction

For a concept to be plausible, the concept must first be intelligible. The teacher taught the concept refraction using analogy. The analogy used is called wheel analogy. The teacher analogically compared the ray of light to a pair of wheels as they rolled obliquely from a hard to a softer surface.

In the following interview the plausibility of the concept is evident.

Interviewer : How the pair of wheels (Toy car) helped you to understand bending of light idea?

Student : Yes, I think it helped.

Interviewer : Why do you think that it helped?

Student : I can just imagine that I have seen it in the class (when the teacher demonstrated) that the toy can changes its direction of motion when it goes from a hard to a smooth surface.

Here the concept of refraction is plausible because it fitted with the idea of a toy car as to what actually happens and how the world actually is and it fitted his/her picture of the world.

Thus the new conception not only intelligible but also seem to be true and valid to the learner. The learners should be able to decide on their own about how a new concept fits into their ways of thinking.

(iii) **Fruitfulness:** For a concept to be fruitful, it must first be intelligible and plausible and should be seen as something useful to solve problems or be a better way of explaining things. Fruitfulness controls the motivation for learners to either cling to old ideas, or be prepared to struggle to understand new ones. Even just mental satisfaction could be a strong indicator of a concept being fruitful. Fruitfulness is multidimensional like plausibility.

Degree of fruitfulness of a concept motivates the learner to either understand it by sticking with the concept an idea or give it up for a new one. The concept should have power to explain a lot or it should work in a lot of different situations. The concept should be is better than the available alternatives. The concept is fruitful for the learner if it helps in getting a good grade or helps the learner to impress the teacher. A fruitful concept is associated with a highly respected figure, e.g. if Sir Isaac Newton believed it, it is obviously worth trying to understand.

Representation of Fruitfulness

A new conception will appear fruitful if it not only resolves its predecessor's anomalies but also leads to new insights and discoveries (Posner et al., 1982). Mode of representations by using criterial attribute of a fruitful concept must show some advantage for the learner in seeing things in a particular way.

A concept is fruitful if it can be represented using exemplar e.g. heat is a result of the kinetic energy of particles and is not a fluid (White and Gunsione, 1989).

A Fruitful Conception of Refraction

A fruitful conception means it is also intelligible and plausible. The following interview depicts that how a fruitful conception of refraction is represented. The Interviewer put a pen partly immersed inside the water contained in a glass and asked the following questions:

Interviewer : Can you explain your friend why the pencil appears to be bent?

Student : No, I cannot because I myself do not know.

Interviewer : I have used one analogy when I taught you refraction.

Student : Yes, I remember. You used a toy car and explained when it moved from carpet to paper how it bent its path.

Interviewer : Can you tell what happened when the wheels went from carpet to paper?

Student : It bent because one wheel got on to the paper first.

Interviewer : So what happened to the wheel which got on to the paper first?

Student : It went faster so it turned away instead of going straight.

Interviewer : So the wheels changed direction because it changed the speed in different medium.

Student : Oh! yes.

Interviewer : Can you compare it with light?

Student : Yes, light speed is different in water and air.

Interviewer : See your activity and tell what happens when the beam of light hits the surface between water and air?

Student : It may bend like the toy car.

Thus without wheel/toy car analogy the student was not interested in the phenomena of the partly immersed pen appearing bent. But when the analogy was recalled by the teacher/interviewer the student became enthusiastic leading to conceptual change. Using analogy and metaphors conceptual change can be initiated.

(iv) **Dissatisfaction:** The concept could be a source of dissatisfaction to the learner. This state will arise if (a) the learner finds that the new conception leads to conclusions which are in conflict with the existing ALCONs. Or, (b) the new conception does not seem to be plausible or fruitful to the learner.

In addition to these conditions one can add another condition, "openness". The learner himself should show his/her willingness to listen and evaluate new ideas and methods, his/her willingness to discard old beliefs so as to undergo conceptual change. Several additional conditions are necessary for effective conceptual change. First there must be dissatisfaction with the pre-existing conception. Learner will never try to change the existing concept until he/she finds them inadequate. Second new concept must be intelligible and plausible. Learners must be able to make sense of new concept which he/she can use for resolving inconsistencies in their belief systems. Third the new concept should be fruitful in the sense that it can be used to solve different problems, i.e. the new concept must also suggest ways to "approach the world" and "open new avenues". After the above conditions are satisfied learning takes place within the learner's "conceptual ecology". A conceptual ecology is the conceptual context by which concepts are "understood and appraised" in the context of the learner's prior knowledge.

3.6 Conceptual Change Teaching Strategies

Suitable teaching strategies facilitate conceptual change within the learner. Westbrrok and Rogers (1992) stated that the process of using "strategies to bring children's thinking into line with that of scientists...has become known as conceptual change". Thus, teaching strategies are key to conceptual change. Teaching strategies for conceptual change can mainly be grouped into two categories (Scott and Driver, 1991).

(i) Teaching strategies based upon cognitive conflict and its resolution.

(ii) Teaching strategies based upon the development of ideas consistent with the science point of view.

(i) Teaching strategies based upon cognitive conflict and its resolution: Several studies concluded that cognitive conflict has an positive effect on conceptual change (Lee et al., 2003).

Cognitive conflict: The origin of the concept of conflict can be traced into the stage independent Piagetian model where Piaget conceived that cognitive conflict is one of the primary catalytic input to initiate the process of equilibrium. This framework recognizes the importance of the dissonance between what the child really thinks to exist and what really does exist. This dissonance leading to cognitive conflict can be due to one of the following reasons:

(a) Encounter with discrepant events.

(b) Encounter with mutually conflicting ALCONs.

(c) Occurrence of identical confrontation between pupils.

(a) **Encounter with discrepant events:** (Discrepant events are very powerful ways to stimulate interest, motivate students to challenge their ALCONs and promote higher order thinking skills.) In the framework of the ALCONs a fact/event/instance/concept is "physical"/"logical" for the child to the extent that it has a real "mental" existence in the mind of the "incipient scientist", the child. On encountering a new event/concept the child tries to explain it using his/her—

- ALCONs and may arrive at a solution which is different from what actually happens. Such an event is called a "discrepant event" (Nussbaum and Novick, 1982a; 1982b). An Example: on being taught that the strength of current is the rate of flow of charge the child incorrectly generalizes that when one makes a switch 'on', charges flow from the switch to the bulb and then only bulb glows. And since there is very little time gap between the 'switching on' and the 'glowing of the bulb', the child concludes that the velocity of charges through the wire is very very high and is equal to the speed of light.

Now if the pupils are presented with the experiment which demonstrates the movement of permanganate ions on soaked blotting paper when the two ends of the blotting paper are connected to a battery, they can observe that the movement of the ions is very very slow. Thus a cognitive conflict is generated between their ALCONs and what really happens. This activity with implications and conclusions is discussed in detail in Chapter 7 while presenting the role of a teacher as a 'motivator'.

(b) **Encounter with mutually conflicting ALCONs:** This arises when child faces a situation where he/she can explain the same event by two different cognitive structures which are at conflict with each other. In this context the investigations of (Stavy et al., 1980) focus on conflict between pupil's "qualitative-intuitive description" and "quantitative-numerical description" of temperature. An example: on being questioned—are there any force acting on a body at rest (like a book on the table), the pupils have two ALCONs to fall back upon; (i) they have the ALCON arising out of an induced incorrect generalization from the Newton's laws of motion that no force acts on a body at rest, (ii) they also have the concept that all bodies on the earth are acted upon by the force of gravity. These two conclusions give rise to a conflict.

(c) **Occurrence of identical confrontation between pupils:** Different pupil may have different ALCON involving the same concept. When all these ALCONs are explicitly brought out and each pupil is encouraged to present his/her analysis of the same phenomenon using his/her ALCON, there is high probability that a stage of conflict between pupil's ideas will be generated. Example: Class fifth students have different ALCONs about solar eclipse as follows: solar eclipse occurs because (i) thick clouds cover the sun, (ii) sun changes its shape, (iii) demons eat the sun for some time. In the class if the teacher allows them to discuss, cognitive conflict will be generated and the teacher may act as facilitator to bring conceptual change and give them the correct scientific concept.

When a child interacts with the environment, peer group, society, family members and elders he/she constructs many inappropriate generalizations (for example—Sun is moving from east to west every day) which become very strong in the mind of the learner and difficult to change as it is true in his/her framework. Such conceptions very often give rise to ALCONs and cognitive conflict.

Cognitive conflict approaches involve promoting situations where the student's existing ideas about some concept are made explicit and are directly challenged in order to create a state of cognitive conflict. Attempt to resolve cognitive conflict leads to subsequent learning. Cognitive conflict is a personal event that may not be experienced by all learners in the same way. Thus, the effect of cognitive conflict on learner's conceptual change is directly related to learner's ability to experience the conflict presented to him/her.

There are different pedagogical strategies for promoting and resolving cognitive conflict.

(1) One of the strategies suggested by Nussbaum and Novick (1982a, b) consists of a teaching sequence which was based upon the Piagetian notion of accommodation and includes four steps:
   - Initial exposure of students' preconception through their responses to an exposing event. This is the exposition phase.
   - Sharpening student awareness of their own and other students' frameworks. This is the awareness phase.
   - Creating conceptual conflict by attempting to explain a discrepant event. This is the conflict phase.
   - Encouraging and guiding cognitive accommodation and the invention of a new conceptual model

consistent with the accepted science view. This is the resolution phase.

(2) Casgrove and Osborne (1985) proposed a teaching strategy entitled "Generative Learning Model of Teaching" which was organized into four phases.

- **Preliminary Phase:** Teacher explores learner's view.
- **Focus Phase:** Learners are given opportunity to explore the context of the concept, preferably within a 'real' everyday situation. Learners to engage in clarification of own views.
- **Challenge Phase:** Learners debate their views with each other and the teacher. Teacher may introduce the correct concept wherever necessary.
- **Application Phase:** Opportunities for application of new ideas across a range of contexts, is presented.

(3) Rowell and Dawson (1985) proposed a strategy in which first the new concept is introduced and then the resolution between students' prior knowledge and new conception occurs. Their strategy is based on history and philosophy of science and Piaget's equilibration theory.

(4) Teaching strategies based upon the development of ideas consistent with the science point of view. In these strategies student builds knowledge on his/her existing ideas.

The teaching model proposed by Clement et al. (1987) belongs to this category. This teaching strategy aims to "increase the range of application of the useful intuitions and decrease the range of application of the detrimental intuitions". The strategy assumes that conceptual change can be encouraged by providing opportunities for students to build up qualitative intuitive understanding of phenomenon before mastering quantitative principles. Such understandings are developed by forming ontology relations between target concept and an anchoring example. The bridging strategy is used to develop the above relationship. The bridging strategy as given by Brown and Clement (1989) consists of four steps:

- The students' misconceptions relating to the topic under consideration are made explicit using a target question.
- The teacher suggests a case (anchoring example) consistent with the students' intuitions.
- The teacher asks the students to make an explicit comparison between the anchor and target cases in an attempt to establish the analogy relation. This is the step where cognitive conflict is likely to become transparent.
- If the student does not accept the analogy, the instructor then attempts to find a 'bridging analogy'. The bridging analogy is intermediate between target and anchor. In this step the conflict gets resolved.

Thus, Clement's basic strategy is to use analogy to generate and resolve conflict, and to develop 'useful' conceptions rather than challenging the misconception.

Problems with the Strategy of Cognitive Conflict

Although the strategy of cognitive conflict is contrived to place the pupil in an intellectually challenging position, the following problems are associated with it (Mohapatra, 1997).

- It is difficult to generate cognitive conflict situation in every context and for each concept. On the other hand if a conflict is designed simply for the sake of creating a conflict, then it may lose its potential with respect to cognitive challenge, motivation for learning and conceptual change.
- The other problem arises out of the import of attitudes by the pupils into classroom. It is observed (Dreyfus et al., 1990) that less able pupils tried to avoid the conflicts to protect their self-image. "They were most characteristically apologetical when confronted with a conflict which, to them, seemed to represent another failure. Also Stavy (1991) expressed a similar opinion when she stated that conflict strategies may cause loss of self-confidence and sometimes even initiate regression.

While the first problem is associated with the innovative and resourceful ability of the teacher, the second one is concerned about the careful handling of the less able/unsuccessful pupils by the teacher.

The following strategies can also be used for conceptual change:

- Conceptual change texts
- Concept cartoons
- Analogy
- Concept mapping—discussed in detail in Chapter 4
- Scaffolding
- Using technology.

Conceptual change texts: In these texts possible misconceptions that the students might have are written down and the inadequacy and mistakes of their misconception are made clear to students. The teacher can also add texts examples that could be useful for the exact and correct comprehension of the subject, if necessary. After convincing the students what they thought to be true was a misconception, the exact correct comprehension of concepts is taught to the students with necessary examples, explanation and proof. Then the students are allowed to study the texts either individually or in groups and compare their previous knowledge on the subject to the information given in the text and think of it. Conceptual change texts are usually given to the students during the presentation of the subject and are asked to analyze the texts either of their own or in groups. After making sure that students complete their reading and analysis of the text, they are expected to start a class discussion on the subject and have an exact and correct comprehension of the concepts.

Concept cartoons: The concept cartoon is one of the useful tools that can be used to point out different viewpoints to students and motivate them to start a discussion about the concept. Concept cartoons were proposed by Brenda Keogh and Stuart Naylor in 1991. The features of a typical concept cartoon (Naylor et al., 2007) are the following:

- Visual representation of scientific ideas
- Minimal text in dialogue form

- Alternative viewpoints on the situation
- Application of scientific ideas in everyday situations
- The rest of the options should also be relevant and include alternative concepts. This is a proposal for science teaching; however, it can be extended to all subjects. It can be used at the beginning or end of a topic or concept example.

Activity: An example of a concept cartoon related to shape of the earth is the following:

Three friends are discussing—

Acquisition: Shape of the Earth.

Who is correct? Mark in one of the following boxes.

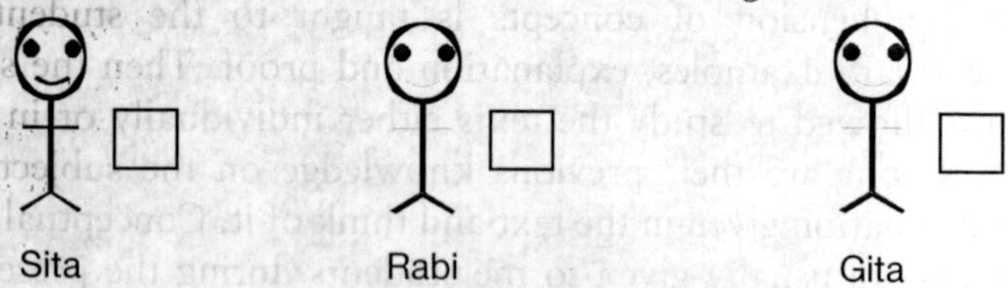

Fig. 3.2

A typical concept cartoon has the following features:

- Text in speech bubbles
- Different viewpoints on the situation
- One being the scientific viewpoint and others are alternative but logical views
- Characters are usually shown from behind to avoid the children basing their decisions on the character rather than on the viewpoint
- Sometimes a blank speech bubble is presented to encourage children to contribute their own ideas

- There is option for group or individual thinking. At the end, question like—what do you think? is asked.

This can be used for a variety of topics other than science, such as

- Literacy promotion in schools
- Teaching English as a second language
- Teaching mathematics

Cartoons when used for the teaching-learning process have some positive effect in the learner. They:

- Engage attention
- Serve as entertainment
- Present information in a non-threatening manner.

Analogy: Analogies have been used as concept building tools for children and adults since the beginning of the recorded history (Harrison et al., 1993). Analogies enhance student learning through a constructivist pathway (Duit, 1991). Teacher use analogies to build conceptual bridges for students between what is familiar (an analog concept) and what is new (a target concept). An analogy is a comparison of the similarities of two concepts. If the analogy and the target share similar features, an analogy can be drawn between them. For example an analogy can be drawn between a camera and the human eye, flow of water and flow of electricity. The teaching with analogies (TWA) model (Glynn, 1995) includes the following six steps:

- Introducing the target concept
- Review the analog concept
- Identify relevant features of the target and analogy
- Map similarities
- Indicate where the analogy breaks down
- Draw conclusions.

Generally TWA method is used for teaching science; however, it can be used for teaching different subject.

Example I:

For teaching Coulomb's Law of electrical force the prescribed six steps could be the following:

1. Introduce the target concept to the learner. Here the teacher introduces Coulomb's law of electrical force to learners.
2. As the students know Newton's law of gravitational force the teacher reminds them about the law.
3. The teacher helps the students to identify relevant features of Newton's law and Coulomb Law. For example in Newton's law of gravitation the force is proportional to the product of masses, whereas in Coulomb's law the electrostatic force is proportional to the product of the charges.
4. The teacher helps the students to connect similar features of the laws.
5. Students draw conclusions about the laws.

The teacher has to tell the limitation of this analogy. The analogy breaks at certain point such as gravitational force is always attractive whereas electrical force can be attractive or repulsive.

Example II:

Why we see the light first then hear the sound during lightening? To explain this to them one has to know the concept of speed. Six steps are:

1. Target concept is light travels faster than sound.
2. The student knows that speed of a car is greater than speed of a cycle.
3. The relevant feature of light and sound are, they have speed.
4. If light speed is analogous to car speed and sound speed is analogous to cycle speed then which will cover a distance of 60 km first. The students will tell that car will reach first as it is having higher speed.

5. The student will conclude that during lightening we see the light first then hear the sound, because speed of light is more than the speed of sound.

Scaffolding: It is a strategy of guiding the learner from what is presently known to that which is to be known. Scaffolding allows students to perform tasks that would normally be slightly beyond their ability without the assistance and guidance of the teacher. Scaffolding is a strategy for construction of knowledge by helping the student to perform just beyond the limits of his/her ability.

Technology for Conceptual Change

In the past to achieve conceptual change cognitive conflict was thought to be sufficient but in recent years researchers have raised issues of motivational, affective and contextual factors to achieve conceptual change (Gregoire, 2003; Murphy, 2007). According to Lee and Jonassen (2012) conceptual change is more than realignment or restructuring of ideas which results from interactions of mind with other minds in the world. With the exponential growth in online communication such as face book, twitter and different search engines like Google, learners' ideas and conceptions are constantly exposed to challenges posed by friends and community members.

Simulations can be used to present exposing or discrepant events in classroom situation. Multimedia Educational Resources for learning and online teaching (MERLOT) (Ref. *http://www.merlot.org*) contains simulations in different subject areas. Teachers may explore new simulations, situations, projects on the internet for effective teaching-learning process.

3.7 Conceptual Change Model (CCM)

Learning driven by ALCONs, suggests that learning may involve changing a person's conceptions in addition to adding new knowledge to the existing one. This view was developed into a model of learning as conceptual change by Posner, Strike, Hewson and Gertzog (1982) and extended by Hewson (1981, 1982). Here, learning is viewed as interaction between new and existing conceptions with the outcome being dependent on the nature of interaction. There are the following two major components on which CCM is based:

- Conditions that need to be met by the new concept in order for a person to experience conceptual change.
- Person's conceptual ecology that provides the context in which the conceptual change occurs. The conceptual ecology consists of many different kinds of knowledge, the most important of which may be epistemological commitment (e.g. generalizability, Hewson & Hewson, 1992), metaphysical beliefs about the world (e.g. the nature of time) and analogies and metaphors which may serve to structure new information.

Learners use their conceptual ecology (i.e. existing knowledge) to determine whether the new conception is intelligible (knowing what it means), plausible (believing it to be true), and fruitful (finding it useful).

Thus, a key principle of conceptual change model is that learners must find a new conception intelligible before they can begin to consider its plausibility or fruitfulness and accommodate into their cognitive structure (Hewson, 1981). The essential idea of intelligibility lies in the manner in which a conception is represented mentally and in classroom discourse, by learners and to learners (Thorley, 1990). There are many CCM consisting of three to six steps. Barnes (1976) and Cosgrove & Osborne proposed four stage teaching sequence CCM.

All the constructivist teaching models are meant to promote conceptual change. Instructional strategy based on CCM helps the students to learn by challenging their preconception. These instructions place the students in an environment that encourages them to challenge their preconceptions and then work towards resolution and conceptual change, thereby acquiring meaningful knowledge.

We present below only two exemplars from CCMs, one each from 6-stage and 4-stage ones.

CCM 1:

A six step CCM suggested by Joseph I. Stepans (1998) is as follows and is depicted in Fig. 3.3.

1. **Commit to an outcome:** The teacher helps the students to become aware of their own thinking by responding to a question or by attempting to solve a problem or challenge. In this stage the teacher uncover the students' preconception about a concept.
2. **Expose beliefs:** The students are allowed to express their individual ideas and beliefs. In a classroom situation the students get chance to hear different views. In this process the students interact with the peer group and try to accept different ideas as being possible alternatives.
3. **Confront beliefs:** Student recognizes the differences between his/her ideas and the ideas of the peer group as they share and discuss their ideas. For confronting their preconception they are exposed to experiments, collection of data, texts, and activities.

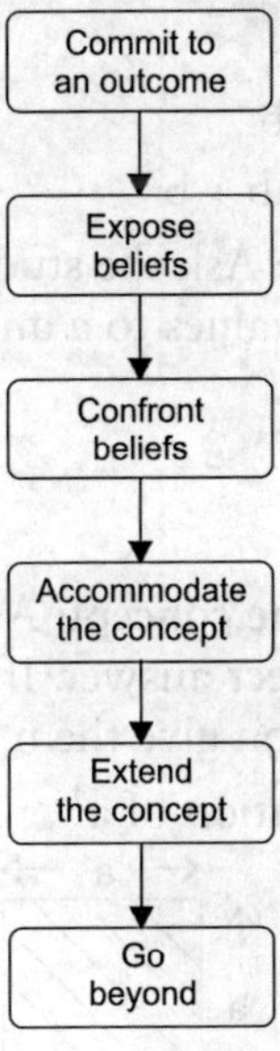

Fig. 3.3: A typical CCM proposed by Joseph I. Stepans.

4. **Accommodate the concept:** The teacher facilitates the students to develop new understanding by resolving conflicts. The students accommodate the new (correct) concept by modifying or replacing their preconception. Thus, students accommodate a new idea (correct concept) or skill by discussing, debating and summarizing.
5. **Extend the concept:** The students will be able to make connections between the concept learned and other situations and areas.
6. **Go beyond:** Students are allowed to pose and pursue new questions, ideas and problems of their own. The teacher in this stage recognizes areas of confusion and tries to resolve it.

Example : $(a + b)^2 = ?$

(i) **Commit to an outcome:** How can we write $(a + b)^2$ without brackets?

(ii) **Expose beliefs:** Tell the students to write down their thoughts on the board. Some possible answers are—

$(a + b)^2 = a^2 + b^2$

$(a + b)^2 = 2a + 2b$

$(a + b)^2 = a^2 + 2ab + b^2$

(iii) **Confront beliefs:** Ask the students to test their ideas by giving different values to a and b.

a = 0, b = 3

a = 2, b = 0

a = 3, b = 5

(iv) **Accommodate the concept:** Ask them how to represent visually the correct answer. If the student cannot come up with suggestion give them one example.

Visual representation of a^2

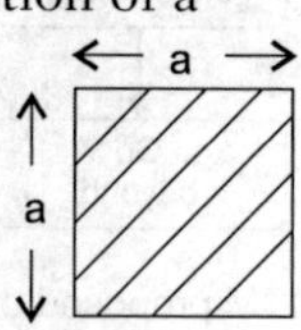

a^2 is the area of a square of side 'a'

Ask again how to represent $(a + b)^2$ visually.

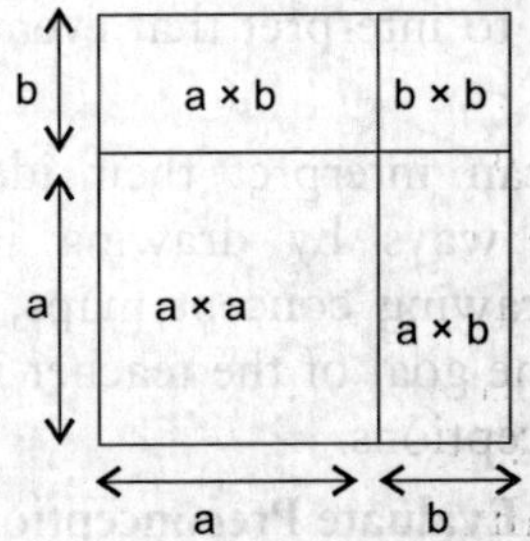

$$\Rightarrow (a + b)^2 = (a \times a) + (a \times b) + (a \times b) + (b \times b)$$
$$= a^2 + 2ab + b^2$$

(v) **Extend the concept:** Ask the students to find out $(a + b)^3$.

(vi) **Go beyond:** How can you express $a^2 - b^2$ with brackets?

The CCM instructional format helps the students to learn by challenging their preconception or existing conceptions.

CCM 2:

Nussbaum and Novick (1982) suggested a conceptual change teaching strategy consisting of four steps as follows:

Step I	:	Reveal student preconceptions
Step II	:	Discuss and evaluate preconception
Step III	:	Create conceptual conflict—with those preconceptions
Step IV	:	Encourage and guide conceptual restructuring.

Step I: Reveal Student Preconceptions

"The key constructivist idea that construction of a new conception (learning) is possible only on the basis of already existing conceptions" (Duit, 1999), this is the basic assumption in teaching for conceptual change. Exploring the preconceptions of a child.

The teacher can reveal student's preconceptions by:

- presenting the exposing event,
- asking students to describe or represent their conceptions.

Exposing event in any situation that requires students to use their preconception to interpret that event (Chinn and Brewer, 1993).

The students can interpret their ideas about the given situation in many ways by drawing illustrations, creating physical models, drawing concept maps, creating simulations in computer, etc. The goal of the teacher is to help the student realize their preconceptions.

Step II: Discuss and Evaluate Preconceptions

In this step opportunity is given to the students to clarify and revise their preconception through peer-interaction and discussion. The teacher acts as a facilitator and receives all explanations and examines whether the arguments/explanations are intelligible, plausible and fruitful in explaining the exposing event and allows the students to discuss each other ideas by forming groups.

Step III: Create Conceptual Conflict

Conceptual conflict begins to build when the learners become dissatisfied with their own conceptions through peer interaction and discussion. The teacher may create a discrepant event. The discrepant event is a phenomenon or situation that may or may not be explained by the student's existing conceptions but can be explained by the revised concept/scientific concept. The teacher may create a discrepant event by presenting anomalous data evidence that contradicts learner's current conceptions (Chinn and Brewer, 1993). If no student has offered the "correct" concept, the teacher may suggest it.

Step IV: Conceptual Restructuring

Conceptual restructuring is nothing but cognitive accommodation. Learner should be given sufficient time to reflect on and reconcile differences between their conceptions and the target theory for fruitful/effective learning. The teacher should facilitate the learning process by incorporating reflective activities to promote cognitive accommodation of the learner's preconception.

For conceptual change learning friendly classroom environment is necessary, where learners are free to discuss and put forth their ideas about a given concept (Bruning, Schraw and Ronning, 1999). The teacher acts as a facilitator of the learning process and the learners are motivated for learning to learn by continuously evaluating and revising their conceptions.

3.8 Conceptual Change; From Theory to Practice

Teaching strategies as mentioned can be incorporated in classroom teaching for achieving meaningful learning. However the teachers usually are not well informed about the recent state of teaching and learning and hold views that are predominantly transmissive (Anderson and Helm, 2001). The quality of science instruction as well as instruction in other domains includes teaching strategies that are oriented toward constructivist conceptual change approaches, i.e. attempts to set constructivism principles of teaching and learning into practice (Beeth, et al., 2003). Research studies on the effectiveness of conceptual change approaches of instructional design show that these approaches are more effective than the traditional or transmissive method of teaching-learning process.

The following factors determine the implementation of conceptual change strategies in the classroom:

- Teacher
- Student
- Classroom environment.

Teacher: Teaching for bringing conceptual change within the learner is a difficult task. The teacher acts as a facilitator in the teaching learning process. The teacher should have the expertise to use different teaching strategies including innovative technologies and teaching aids. Teacher has to consider the learner as active participant not passive listeners. The teacher should set appropriate contexts for classroom activities and interaction. The teacher finds ways of helping students to get dissatisfied with their own ideas. The teacher respects the ideas of the learner and helps the learners to understand other's views. The teacher probe the status of ideas presented by the learner and leads the class to arrive at correct concepts. The major obstacle for achieving conceptual change is identified (Anderson et al., 2001) as—teachers usually are not well informed about the innovative learning process and still follow transmissive and not constructivist approach. Research conducted (Duit et al., 2007) showed that teachers are not well informed about key ideas of conceptual change. Hence, it is essential to encourage teachers to become familiar with the recent state of educational research which will help to develop their views about efficient teaching-learning process (West et al., 2003). Thus successful teaching by bringing conceptual change leading to constructivist way of teaching is perhaps the major challenge for researchers working in the field of conceptual change. In this scenario the conceptual changes of the teacher's beliefs about good and effective teaching-learning are necessary to commence and implement conceptual change views into practice.

Student: The students are motivated to learn by respecting other's idea. The students understand the goal of learning, i.e. to understand the concept being taught. The students trust their own ideas and at the same time have patience to listen, recognize and respect different views. The students share their thinking with others and change when another view is more viable. Thus for constructivist conceptual change the students need to be seen as active, self-responsible, cooperative and self-reflective learners.

Classroom environment: It plays an important role in the learning process. The class has to be without fear. The students are free to ask question and interact. There should be no ridicule for wrong answer. The teacher acts as the manager for generating learning friendly classroom environment (Mahapatra et al., 2008).

3.9 Conclusion

The goal of teaching for conceptual change is to help the students to learn more fruitful conceptions while discarding the ALCONs they bring to the classroom. Teaching for conceptual change is more time consuming than the traditional method of teaching learning. It requires learning friendly classroom environment in which learner feels free and confident to express and discuss his/her ideas. Conceptual change instruction requires well equipped teacher. The teacher should be well versed with the concepts, strategies and technologies for which the teachers need adequate training and orientation.

References

Anderson, R.D. and Helm, J.V. (2001). The ideal of standards and reality of schools: needed research. *Journal of Research in Science Teaching, 38:* 3-16.

Barnes, D. (1976). *From communication to curriculum.* Harmondsworth: Penguin Books.

Beeth, M. et al. (2003). *Quality development projects in science education. Science Education Research in the knowledge based society* (pp. 447-57). Dordrecht. The Netherlands' Kulwer Academic Publishers.

Bell, B. (1981). When is an animal not an animal? *Journal of Biological Education*, Vol. 15, No. 3, pp. 213-18.

Bell, B. and Barker, M. (1982). Towards a scientific concept of "Animal", *Journal of Biological Education*, Vol. 16, No. 3, pp. 197-200.

Brown, D.E. and Clement, J. (1989). Overcoming misconceptions by analogical reasoning: abstract transfer versus explanatory model constructions. *Instructional Science*, Vol. 13, No. 2, pp. 119-22.

Bruning, R., Schraw, G., and Ronning, R. (1999). *Cognitive Psychology and Instruction* (3rd ed.), Upper Saddle River, NJ: Prentice Hall.

Carey, S. (1991). Knowledge acquisition: Enrichment or conceptual change? In S. Carey and R. Gelman (Eds.), *The epigenesist of mind* (pp. 257-91). Hillsdale, NJ: Lawrence Erlbaum Associates.

—— (1999). Sources of conceptual change. In E.K. Scholnick, K. Nelson and P. Miller (Eds.), *Conceptual development: Piaget's legacy*. Mahwah, NJ: Lawrence Erlbaum Associates (pp. 293-326).

Carry, S. (1985). *Conceptual changes in childhood*, Massachusetts, MIT Press.

Casgrove, M. and Osborne, R. (1985). Lesson frameworks for changing children's ideas. In R. Osborne and P. Freyberg (Eds.), *Learning in Science: The Implications of Children's Science*. London: Heinemann.

Chi, M.T.H. (1992). Conceptual change within and across ontological categories: Examples from learning and discovery in science. In R. N. Giere (Ed.), *Cognitive Models of Science* (129-86). University of Minnesota Press, Minneapolis. MI.

—— (2005). Commonsense conceptions of emergent process: why some misconceptions are robust. *The Journal of Learning Sciences*, 14(2): 161-99.

Chi, M.T.H., Slotta, J.D. and de Leeuw, N. (1994). From things to processes: A theory of conceptual change for learning science concepts. *Learning and Instruction*, 4: 27-43.

Chinn, C.A. and Brewer, W.F. (1993). The role of Anomalous data in knowledge acquisition: A theoretical framework and implications for science instruction. *Review of Educational Research*, 63: 1-49.

Clark, D.B. (2006). Longitudinal conceptual change in students' understanding of thermal equilibrium: An examination of the process of conceptual restructuring. *Cognition and Instruction*, 24(4): 467-563.

Clement, J., with the assistance of Brown, D., Camp, C., Kudukey, J., Minstrell, J., Palmer, D., Schultz, K., Shima bukuro, J., Steinberg, M., and Veneman, V. (1987). Overcoming students' misconceptions in physics: the role of anchoring institutions and analogical validity—Novak, J. (Ed.), *Proceedings of 2nd International Seminar on Misconceptions and Educational Strategies in Science and Mathematics*, Cornell University.

De Vries, R. and Kohlberg, L. (1987). *Programs of Early Education: The Constructivist View*, New York: Longman.

di Sessa, A.A., Gillespie, N. and Esterly, J. (2004). Coherence versus fragmentation in the development of the concept of force. *Cognitive Science*, 28: 843-900.

di Sessa, A.A. (1988). Knowledge in pieces, in Forman, G.; Pufall, P., Constructivism in the Computer Age, Hillsdale, NJ: Erlbaum, pp. 49-70.

—— (1993). Towards an epistemology of Physics. *Cognition and Instruction*, 10(2&3): 105-225.

Drayfus, A., Jungwirth, E., and Eliovitch, R. (1990). Applying the 'cognitive conflict' strategy for conceptual change—Some implications, difficulties and problems. *Science Education*, Vol. 75(5): 555-69.

Duit, R. (1998). Towards multi-perspective views of science learning and instruction. Paper presented at the annual meeting of the American Educational Research Association in San Diego.

—— (1991). On the role of analogies and metaphors in learning science. *Science Education*, 30: 1241-57.

—— (1999). Conceptual change approaches in science education. In W. Schnotz, S. Vosniadou, M. Carretero (Eds.), *New Perspectives on conceptual change* (pp. 263-82). Oxford: Pergamon.

Duit, R. and Treagust, D. (1998). Learning in science—from behaviourism towards social constructivism and beyond. In B. Fraser and K. Tobin (Eds.), *International Handbook of Science Education*, Part I (pp. 3-25), Dordrecht, The Netherlands: Kluwer.

—— (2003). Conceptual change: A powerful framework for improving science teaching and learning, *International Journal of Science Education*, 25: 671-88.

Duit, R., Widodo, A. and Wodzinski, C.T. (2007). Conceptual change ideas—Teachers' views and their instructional practice. Reframing the problem of conceptual change in learning and instruction (pp. 197-217). *Advances in learning and instruction series*. Amsterdam—the Netherlands. Elsevier.

Glynn, S.M. (1995). Conceptual bridges: Using analogies to explain scientific concepts. *The Science Teacher*, 62(9): 25-27.

Gregoire, M. (2003). Is it a challenge of a threat? A dual-process model of teachers' cognitions and appraisal processes during conceptual change. *Educational Psychology Review*, 15: 147-79.

Harrison, A.G. and Treagust, D.F. (1993). Teaching with analogies: A case study in grade 10 optics. *Journal of Research in Science Teaching*, 30: 1291-1307.

Hennessy, S. (1993). Situated cognition and cognitive apprenticeship: Implications for classroom learning. *Studies in Science Education*, 22: 1-44.

Hewson, P. and Hennessey, M.G. (1992). Making status explicit: A case study of conceptual change. In R. Duit, F. Goldberg and H. Niedderer (Eds.), *Research in Physics Learning: Theoretical issues and empirical studies* (pp. 176-87). Proceedings of an international workshop. Kiel, Germany: IPN. Institute for Science Education.

Hewson, P.W. (1981). A conceptual change approach to learning science. *European Journal of Science Education*, Vol. 3, No. 4, pp. 383-96.

Hewson, P.W. (1982). A case study of conceptual change in special relativity: The influence of Prior Knowledge in learning. *European Journal of Science Education*, Vol. 4, No. 4, pp. 61-78.

Hewson, P.W. and Hewson, M.G.A.B. (1984). The role of conceptual conflict in conceptual change and the design of instruction. *Instructional Science*, 13(1): 1-13.

—— (1992). The status of students' conceptions. In R. Duit, F. Goldberg and H. Niedderer (Eds.), *Research in Physics Learning: Theoretical issues and empirical studies* (pp. 59-73). Proceedings of an international workshop. Kiel, Germany: IPN— Institute for Science Education.

Hewson, P.W. and Thornley, N.R. (1989). The conditions of conceptual change in the classroom. *International Journal of Science Education*, 11: 541-53.

Hewson, P.W., Beeth, M.E. and Thorley, N.R. (1998). Teaching for conceptual change. In *International Handbook of Science Education*. Tobin, Kenneth George and Fraser, Barry J. (Eds.), pp. 192-218. Dordrecht, Netherlands: Kluwer.

Ioannides, C. and Vosniadou, S. (2002). The changing meaning of force. *Cognitive Science Quarterly*, 2: 5-61.

Jung, W. (1986). Altu gsvor stellungen und das Lernen von Physik and Chemie. *Naturwissenschaften im Unterricht-Physik/chemie*. Vol. 34, No. 13, pp. 2-6.

—— (1993). Hilft die Entwicklungs sychologic dem physikdidaktiker [Does developmental psychology help the physics educator?] In R. Duit and W. Graber (Eds.), *Kognitive Entwicklung and naturwissens chaftlichen*

Unterricht (pp. 86-107). Kiel, Germany: IPN—Institute for Science Education.

Keogh, B. and Naylor. S. (1991). Concept cartoons, teaching and learning in science: an evaluation. *International Journal of Science Education*, 21(4): 431-46.

Kuhn, T. (1970). *The structure of scientific revolution*. Chicago: University of Chicago Press.

Lee, C.B. and Jonassen, D.Lt. (2012). An introduction : technologies for conceptual change. In C.B. Lee and D.H. Jonassen (Eds.), *Fostering conceptual change with technologies*.

Lee, G., et al. (2003). Development of an instrument for measuring cognitive conflict in secondary level science classes. *Journal of Research in Science Teaching*, 640(6): 585-603.

Linn, M.C., Eylon, B. and Davis, E.A. (2004). *The Knowledge Integration Perspective on Learning. Internet environments for science education*. Mahwah, NJ Lawrence Erlbaum Associates.

Mahapatra, J.K. and Mohapatra, M. (2008). Criteria for generating learning friendly classroom environment—Science teacher perception under Indian conditions. *Indian Educational Review*, Vol. 44, No. 2, pp. 17-44.

Mohapatra, J.K. (1997). Taxonomy of Conceptual Change: Review of two anchoring instructional strategies and a functional model for teaching. *Indian Educational Review*, Vol. 32(1): 36-54.

Mohapatra, J.K. and Bhattacharya, S. (1989). Pupils, teachers, induced incorrect generalization and concept of force. *International Journal of Science Education*, Vol. 11, No. 4, pp. 429-36.

Mohapatra, J.K. and Das, S. (1996). Classroom processes leading to connotative relativity—generative cause of primary level pupils' alternative conceptions. *Report of International Seminar on School Effectiveness and Classroom Process at Primary Level*. New Delhi: NCERT.

Murphy, P.K. (2007). The eye of the beholder: The interplay of social and cognitive components in change. *Educational Psychologist*, 42(1): 41-53.

Naylor, S., Keogh, B. and Downing, B. (2007). Argumentation and Primary Science. *Research in Science Education*, 37: 17-39.

Nussbaum, J. (1989). Classroom conceptual change : Philosophical perspectives. *International Journal of Science Education*, Vol. 11: 530-40.

Nussbaum, J. and Novick, S. (1982a). Alternative frameworks, conceptual conflict and accommodation towards a principled teaching strategy. *Instructional Science*, Vol. 11, pp. 183-200.

—— (1982b). A study of conceptual change in the classroom. Paper presented at the *Annual Meeting of the National Association for Research in Science Teaching*. Lake Geneva, Chicago.

Osborne, R. (1981). Children's idea about electric current. *New Zealand Science Teacher*, Vol. 29, pp. 12-19.

—— (1983). Modifying children's idea about electric current. *Research in Science and Technology Education*, Vol. 1, No. 1, pp. 73-82.

Osborne, R. and Gilbert, J.K. (1980). A technique for exploring students' views of the world, *Physics Education*, Vol. 6, pp. 376-79.

Ozdemir, G. and Clark, D.B. (2007). An overview of conceptual change theories, *Eurasia Journal of Mathematics, Science and Technology Education*, 3(4): 351-61.

Pintrich, P.R., Marx, R.W. and Boyle, R.A. (1993). Beyond cold conceptual change: The role of motivational beliefs and classroom contextual factors in the process of conceptual change. *Review of Educational Research*, 6: 167-99.

Posner, G.J., Strike, K.A., Hewson, P.W. and Gerzog, W.A. (1982). Accommodation of a scientific conception : Towards a theory of conceptual change. *Science Education*, Vol. 72, No. 1, pp. 103-13.

Rowell, J.A. and Dawson, C.J. (1985). Equilibrational conflict and instruction: A new class-oriented perspective. *European Journal of Science Education*, 5(2): 203-15.

Salomon, G. and Globerson, T. (1987). Skill may not be enough: the role of mindfulness in learning and transfer. *International Journal of Educational Research*, 11: 623-37.

Schollum, B. and Osborne, R. (1985). Relating the new to the familiar. In R. Osborne and P. Freyberg (Eds.), *Learning in Science: The implications of children's science* (pp. 51-65). Portsmouth, New Hampshire: Heinemann Publishers.

Scott, P., Asoko, H. and Driver, R. (1991). Teaching for conceptual change. A review of strategies, In Duit, R., Goldberg, F., Niedderer, Lt. (Eds.), *Research in Physics Learning: Theoretical issues and empirical studies*. University of Kiel, Germany.

Seiler, T.B. (1973). Die Bereichass pezifizitat formaler Denk strukturen—Konsequenzen fur den peeda gogischen prozess (The domain-specific nature of formal thinking patterns—consequences for pedagogical process). In K. Frey and M. Lang (Eds.), *Kognitions psychologie and natur wissen schaft licher untaricher unterricht* (pp. 249-83). Bern. Switzerland: Huber.

Shulman, L.S. (1986). Those who understand: Knowledge growth in teaching. *Educational Researcher*, 15: 4-14.

Sinatra, G.M. and Pintrich, P.R. (2003). *International conceptual change*, Mahwah, N.J.: Lawrence Erlbaum.

Southerland, S.A., Abrams, E., Cummuns, C.L. and Anzelmo, J. (2001). Understanding students' explanations of biological phenomena: conceptual framework or P-prims. *Science Education*, 85: 311-27.

Stavy, R. (1991). Using analogy to overcome misconceptions about conservation of matter. *Journal of Research in Science Teaching*, Vol. 28(4): 305-13.

Stavy, R. and Berkovitz, B. (1980). Cognitive conflict as a basis for teaching quantitative aspects of the concept and temperature. *Science Education*, 64: 679-92.

Strike, K.A. and Posner, G.J. (1985). A conceptual change view of learning and understanding. In L.H.T. West and A.L. Pines (Eds.), *Cognitive structure and conceptual change* (pp. 211-31), New York: Academic Press.

— (1992). A revisionist theory of conceptual change. In R.A. Duschl and R.J. Hamilton (Eds.), *Philosophy of science, cognitive psychology, and educational theory and practice* (pp. 147-76). New York: State University of New York Press.

Thagard, P. (1992). *Conceptual revolutions*. Princeton, NJ: Princeton University Press.

Thorley, N.R. (1990). *The conceptual model in the interpretation of classroom interactions. Dissertation Abstract International*, 51(09): 3033A. (UNI NO 9100-172)

Thorley, N.R. and Stofflett, R.T. (1996). Representation of the conceptual change model in Science Teacher Education. *Science Education,* 80(3): 317-39.

Ueno, N. (1993). Reconsidering P-Prims theory from the viewpoint of situated cognition. *Cognition and Instruction*, 10 (2 & 3): 239-48.

Venville, G.J. and Treagust, D.F. (1998). Exploring conceptual change in genetics using a multi-dimensional interpretative framework. *Journal of Research in Science Teaching*, 35: 1031-55.

Vosniadou, S. and Brewer, W.F. (1992). Mental models of the earth. A study of conceptual change in childhood. *Cognitive Psychology*, 24: 535-85.

von Glasersfeld, E. (1992). A constructivist's view of learning and teaching. In R. Duit, F. Goldberg and H. Niedderer (Eds.), *Research in Physics Learning: Theoretical Issues and Empirical Studies*. Kiel, Germany: IPN at the University of Kiel.

Vosniadou, S. (1994a). Capturing and modeling the process of conceptual change. *Learning and Instruction*, 4: 54-69.

Vosniadou, S. and Ioannides, C. (1998). From conceptual development to science education: A psychological point of view. *International Journal of Science Education*, 20: 1213-30.

Vosniadou, S. and Skopeliti, I. (2005). Developmental shifts in children's categorization of the earth. In B.G. Bara, L. Barsalou and M. Bucciarelli (Eds.), *Proceedings of the XXVII Annual Conference of the Cognitive Science Society* (pp. 2325-30). Mahwah, NJ: Erlbaum.

Vosniadou, S., Vamvakoussi, X and Skopeliti, I. (2008). The framework theory approach to the problem of conceptual change. In S. Vosniadou (Ed.), *International handbook of research on conceptual change*. New York, JY: Routledge.

Wellman, H.M. and Gelman, S. (1992). Cognitive development. Foundational theories of core domains. *Annual Review of Psychology*, 43: 337-75.

West, J. and Pines, A. (1985). *Cognitive structure and conceptual change*, New York: Academic Press.

West, L. (1982). Investigating children Existing Ideas. In C. Sutton and L. West (Eds.), *The report of seminar* held in April 1982, at the University of Leicester, U.K.

West, L. and Staub, F.C. (2003). *Content focused coaching: Transforming mathematics lessons*. Portsmouth, NH: Heinemann/Pittsburg, PA; University of Pittsburgh.

Westbrrok, S.L. and Rogers, L.N. (1992). Experience is the best teacher. Using the laboratory to promote conceptual change. Paper presented at the *Annual Meeting of National Association for Research in Science Teaching*, Boston, M.A.

White, R.T., and Gunstone, R.F. (1989). Metalearning and conceptual change. *International Journal of Science Education,* II, 577-86.

Zembylas, M. (2005). Three perspectives on linking the cognitive and emotional in science, the cognitive and emotional in science learning; conceptual change, socio-constructivism and poststructuralism, *Studies in Science Education*, 41: 91-116.

4 Concept Map and Constructivism

4.1 Introduction

A *concept map* basically represents the map maker's knowledge organized in some manner and reveals the thought process of the person. Its use is widespread, in almost all walks of life and work. In the field of education, though concept mapping was originally conceived for teaching learning of biology (Novak, 1981a), it is now found useful in all kinds of science education and beyond. It is claimed that concept map is 'the most important meta-cognitive tool in science education today' (Mintzes et al., 1997). The numerous uses of concept mapping include such teaching learning processes as planning, teaching, revision, and assessment (e.g. Edmondson, 2000; Kinchin, 2000). Concept map has been recognized as a powerful tool in the constructivist model of learning, in which students construct their own knowledge from the resources available to them. It helps constructivists to discover and model how students learn (Cliburn, 1990). In fact, concept mapping happens to be a constructivist activity in two essential ways: (i) drawing a concept map elucidating one's knowledge and thought process, and (ii) using a concept map as a tool in the teaching learning process.

A concept map may be considered as similar to a circuit diagram representing the working of an electrical device or the layout plan of a building. Drawing isolated parts of a circuit or a building on a sheet of paper is not enough; different parts need to be properly connected to each other to make a meaningful diagram, which can then be used to construct the actual appliance or the building. As an example, we may cite a 1957

Walt Disney concept map (Disney, 1957) that visually represents the different main parts of Disneyland and their interdependence for smooth functioning of this huge entertainment complex. Coming to education, it is well-known that learning concepts in an isolated manner is not adequate; one needs to understand the interconnections between them (Ausubel, 1968; Ausubel et al., 1978). This is especially true of science. Interrelations between concepts can be beautifully represented through concept maps.

Concept map is now used as a successful tool over a wide variety of disciplines and settings (see e.g. Garcia, 2008) besides being an effective instructional tool as well as a powerful learning strategy in classrooms. The root of concept map lies in the principles of constructivism. In view of its significance *vis-à-vis* constructivism we propose to discuss some important aspects of concept map in this chapter.

4.2 Concept, Map, and Concept Map

The term 'concept' (supposed to have originated from Latin conceptum—"something conceived", dating back to 1554-60) has many connotations (Margolis and Lawrence, 2012) such as 'mental representations', 'abilities', and 'abstract objects'. J.D. Novak, one of the most prominent proponents of concept map, defines (Novak and Canas, 2008) concept "as a perceived regularity in events or objects, or records of events or objects, designated by a label" the label being in the form of word(s) or symbols.

On the other hand, from childhood we are all familiar with the popular meaning of the term 'map', i.e. a geographical map, which gives names and relative locations of different places over a region. From such a map it becomes easy to locate places of interest in direction and distance from a given place. Sometimes roads connecting the different places are also shown in the map by means of lines with the corresponding distances indicated by numerals written beside the lines. In a broader sense a map is a visual representation of a space whose elements may be objects, regions, or themes. A map may be static and two dimensional or interactive and three dimensional. We shall consider a concept map as a two dimensional visual representation of a space whose elements are concepts. A concept map shows the relative positions of the concepts involved and their interrelations. Besides the general observation made above, there appears to be a deeper philosophical and procedural analogy between concept mapping and cartography, the science of map making; in fact, the former may be said to be the 'cartography of cognition' (Wandersee, 1990).

4.3 Concept Mapping: A Brief Historical Account

In the sector of education the technique of concept mapping was introduced by Prof. J.D. Novak and his team of researchers at Cornell University in the 1970s as a representation of learners' knowledge in science (Novak and Gowin, 1984). Some details about the origin of the idea of concept map may be seen in the paper titled "Concept mapping: a useful tool for science education" (Novak, 1990a). Novak's team studied changes in students' understanding of science concepts over a 12-year span of schooling using audio-tutorial (A-T) science lessons. According to Novak, the A-T science programme was based upon Ausubel's (1963, 1968) assimilation theory of cognitive learning, which had the fundamental assumption:

> If I had to reduce all of educational psychology to just one principle, I would say this: The most important single factor influencing learning is what the learner already knows. Ascertain this and teach him accordingly (Ausubel, 1968, Epigraph).

The team developed 60 lessons during the period 1967-1973 out of which 28 were used in the 12-year longitudinal study (Novak, 1990a). They "sought to ascertain what students knew both before and after A-T instruction, and how their knowledge changed in subsequent years". Novak further says, "Given the additional ideas from Ausubel's theory that cognitive structure is organized *hierarchically*, and that most new learning occurs through derivative or correlative *subsumption* of new concept meanings *under* existing concepts/propositional ideas, we developed the idea of hierarchical representation of concepts/ propositional frameworks (Novak, 1977: 88-93), which we later described as "cognitive maps" or "concept maps" (Novak, 1979; 1980; 1981). In our early work, we did not always "label" the lines which linked the concepts to form propositions, but it soon became clear that this was essential to represent concepts/propositional meanings in an explicit hierarchical framework. Thus, the concept map tool evolved over a period of 3-4 years as a way of representing both specific concepts/propositional meanings held by learners before and after instruction, and the changes in cognitive structure which occurred over a period of years."

Novak's team worked with the key hypothesis that, contrary to Piaget's suggestions, children in their late pre-operational and early concrete operational stages of cognitive development could acquire useful levels of understanding of any abstract science concept, with carefully designed instruction. Accordingly, they formulated instructions for six- and seven-year-old (first- and second-grade) children on science concepts including the basic ones such as energy and energy transformations, the particulate nature of matter, and the conservation of matter/energy. The hypothesis stated above thus became the basis of the 12-year longitudinal study and the origin of concept mapping in science education. As a means to assess the cognitive changes in the learners the members of the research team used the interviews with the same student in the second and twelfth grades to draw concept maps. Subsequently, they "found that primary-grade children (Symington and Novak, 1982) are capable of developing very thoughtful concept maps which they can explain intelligently to others". The research team also gradually discovered many other advantages of concept mapping such as helping children "learn how to learn", helping teachers become more effective teachers, etc.

A basic underlying fact in the principle and application of the concept map technique is that every concept has a meaningful and usable existence only in association with other concepts with which it is connected through propositional relationships. A concept has very little effective existence in isolation.

The above brief account indicates the beginning of concept map as a tool in teaching learning situations. The concept mapping introduced by Novak and his research team was qualitative in nature. Subsequently, it has acquired quantitative dimensions as will be discussed later.

4.4 Key Features and Examples of Concept Map

The key features of a concept map are the following (Novak and Canas, 2008):

- *Concepts*, usually enclosed in circles or boxes and arranged in a *hierarchical order* depending on the structure of the knowledge domain and the *context*.
- *Relationships* between concepts indicated by a connecting line linking two concepts.
- A *label* associated with each connecting line, the label being a word(s) or symbol.
- A *focus question* guiding the construction of the concept map.
- *Cross-links* indicating relationships between concepts belonging to different segments of the concept map.
- *Specific examples* clarifying the meaning of concepts.

In the hierarchical arrangement of concepts the *most inclusive concept (most general concept* or *superordinate*) is placed at the top of the map followed by *more specific concepts* (*less general concepts* or *subordinates*) below according to the perceived hierarchical sequence. The context for the concept map is provided by our desire to understand an event or a situation pertaining to the given knowledge domain. Two concepts connected by a link and a label constitute a *proposition* (*semantic unit* or *unit of meaning*), which is a meaningful statement about the perception of the map maker. Cross-links amount to synthesis of the related concepts and may lead to new interpretations. It is to be recognized that in a given knowledge space comprising a given number of concepts there is no single unique concept map. Different persons may construct different concept maps depending upon their understanding and perception. Hence, instead of branding the concept maps as 'correct' or 'incorrect' they need to be interpreted to unearth the underlying thought process. Our ability to create a good concept map and search for and establish new cross-links may improve our creativity.

As an example of concept map we reproduce in Fig. 4.1 one from Novak (1990b), which may be called a 'concept map on concept maps' as it visually illustrates the characteristic features of a concept map in the form of a concept map.

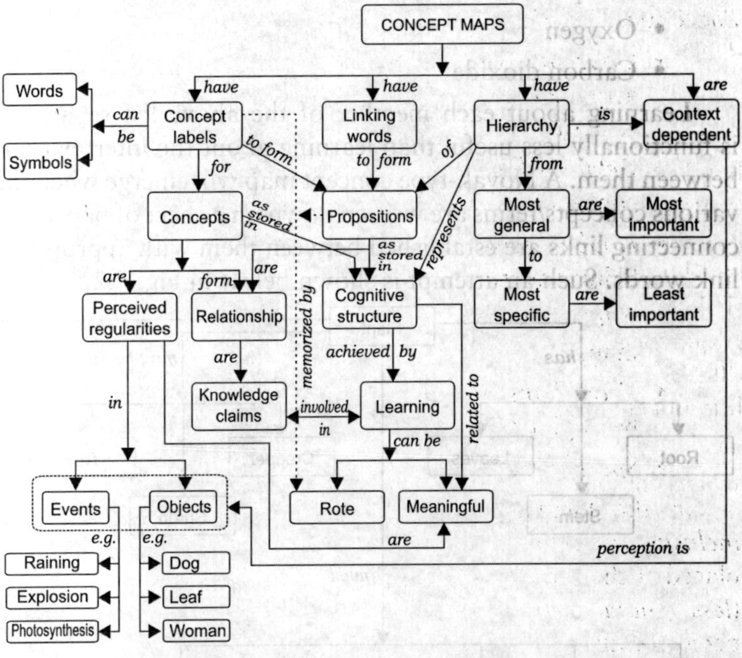

Fig. 4.1

Let us consider another concept map by looking at the following list of concepts and terms related to plant. Note that the words, oxygen and carbon dioxide are not concepts but examples of the concept of gas (e.g. DeCecco and Crawford, 1988).

- Plant
- Root
- Stem
- Leaves
- Flowers
- Fruits
- Shade
- Wood
- Shrub

- Tree
- Creeper
- Oxygen
- Carbon dioxide

Learning about each member of the above list separately is functionally less useful than learning about the interrelations between them. A Novak-type concept map will emerge when the various concepts/terms are written down on a sheet of paper and connecting links are established between them with appropriate link words. Such an attempt is shown below in Fig. 4.2.

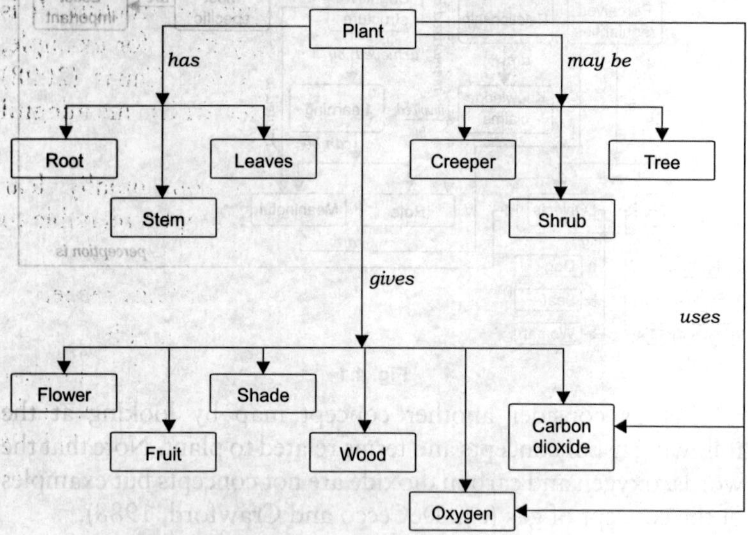

Fig. 4.2

In this concept map all the concepts given in the list above are used. From among the concepts 'Plant' has been chosen as the central (most inclusive) concept to which the other concepts and examples have been connected with link words such as 'has', 'may be', 'gives' and 'uses'. Using such a concept map a lesson on plants can be developed. A learner may use it to write an essay on plant and review her knowledge about plants.

Plenty of examples of concept maps in different domains of knowledge are available in print literature, websites, and you tube, etc. (see e.g. Rao, 2006 for some simple examples). A free concept map software called the IHMC Cmap Tools (Canas et al., 2004; http://cmap.ihmc.us/) is available on the internet, using which one can draw innumerable number of concept maps in any domain of knowledge and share them with others on the net.

4.5 Concept Mapping and Meaningful Learning

There is a deep connection between the process of concept mapping and that of *meaningful (verbal) learning* as enunciated by Ausubel (1963, 1968). Meaningful learning basically refers to a way of learning in which what is being learned is explicitly related with the previous knowledge so that the new knowledge becomes a stable part of the learner's cognitive structure. It is obviously a more effective learning strategy than, for example, *rote learning* which is superficial. Novak and Canas (2008) quote the following three conditions under which meaningful learning can occur.

(i) The material to be learned must be conceptually clear and presented with language and examples relatable to the learner's prior knowledge.

(ii) The learner must possess relevant prior knowledge.

(iii) The learner must choose to learn meaningfully.

The first condition is largely the responsibility of the teacher who needs to have a fair idea of the learner's prior knowledge in the domain under consideration. The teacher uses the principle of *progressive differentiation*, according to which the most general concepts are presented first, followed by the less general ones with a gradual increase in specificity and details. We recognize that concept mapping follows a similar procedure. Concept mapping can also help in discovering learner's prior knowledge.

It is now accepted that a learner does not come to class in an empty mind; she always has some knowledge in her mind related to the topic she is going to learn. This prior knowledge guides the learner's ability to learn. If the prior knowledge base of the learner is not proper and strong it would not be able to anchor the new knowledge, as desired, thereby making learning path of the learner unstable and perhaps wrong. It thus follows that the prior knowledge base of the learner needs to be prepared properly to receive the new knowledge. Concept mapping can help in this as indicated above.

Though condition number three appears to be the sole responsibility of the learner, the teacher can exercise an indirect control on it by motivating the learner to go for meaningful learning instead of the easier but less effective rote learning. The teacher can do this through suitably structured instruction and evaluation in both of which concept mapping can play an effective role. Concept mapping requires the learner to understand the meaning and interrelations between concepts. The learner needs to think in multiple directions involving various levels of abstraction. This fosters deeper level of understanding which in turn helps in clarifying alternative conceptions held by the learner. Concept mapping thus facilitates meaningful learning in which the learner uses the principle of *integrative reconciliation* to anchor the new ideas in the existing knowledge structure.

The significance of meaningful learning may be seen when it is compared with rote learning which requires little or no relevant prior knowledge and the learner makes no conscious effort to connect the new knowledge with the existing knowledge. Clearly, the knowledge gained through rote learning is only temporary and can be easily forgotten unless rehearsed adequately. It also implies that the knowledge base of the learner is not refreshed and her alternative conceptions are not cleared making her stay a poor learner with an uncertain future. In contrast, meaningful learning results in a more permanent, healthy, and strong cognitive structure with a potential future. Creators of new knowledge are considered to have a relatively high level of meaningful learning coupled with a strong urge to search out new meanings (Novak, 1998). Concept mapping can play an effective role in orienting learners toward meaningful learning away from rote learning.

4.6 Concept Mapping Procedure

The following sequential steps are usually recommended for the construction a good concept map (Novak and Canas, 2008):

Step 1 : To begin with, a topic/lesson/text is selected. The map maker ought to be thoroughly familiar with it.

Step 2 : As concept mapping is context specific, a suitable context is identified, if required, with the help of a focus question. Then the portion/domain of the text relevant to the context is identified.

Step 3 : Key concepts (or the terms representing them) are then identified from the selected domain after going through the same. They are listed as they appear in the text.

Step 4 : From the above list of concepts a rank ordered list is generated in which the topmost position is occupied by the most general concept and the bottom-most position by the least general or most specific concept. This list is called a *parking lot* as concepts from it are then moved to their respective positions in the concept map.

Step 5 : A preliminary concept map is then prepared with the help of the parking lot by starting with the most general concept at the top, followed by others in a hierarchical manner. The concepts are enclosed within rectangular boxes or ovals. These structures are called nodes, which are then linked by connecting lines and appropriate propositional link words. In the quantitative type of concept maps the link words are replaced by numerals indicating the link strengths as we shall see later. The lines may be marked with arrows indicating the directionality of the links. Concept maps may be drawn on a sheet of paper, a blackboard/white board, or computer software packages like the IHMC Cmap Tools (Canas et al., 2004; http://cmap.ihmc.us/).

Step 6 : Cross-links are established between different segments of knowledge on the map for fuller appreciation and use of the map.

Step 7 : If required, the preliminary map may be revised any number of times to obtain a final concept map as per the perception of the learner. At the end of the process some concepts may be left behind in the parking lot if the maker cannot find a place for them in the map.

Concept maps may be constructed individually or group-wise in a cooperative mode. In a cooperative learning situation students are instructed to work in small heterogeneous ability groups. Okebukola and Jegede (1988) have found evidence that students engaged in concept mapping tasks cooperatively achieve meaningful learning better than students working alone.

The concept map thus constructed may then be used by the map maker or others for various purposes. As a concept map reflects the knowledge and perception of the map maker the detailed structure of the concept map may vary from person to person. Concept mapping therefore is a good way of discovering alternative conceptions of the persons involved. In a classroom situation the teacher may have to guide the students in the map making process. Of course, the teacher may also prepare her own concept map and use it for planning of teaching learning session and so on.

The Novak-type concept map whose different aspects we have discussed so far is qualitative in nature in the sense that the interrelations between pairs of concepts in the map are described by link words. Besides direct reading of the concept maps, different methods of scoring them have been used from time to time (e.g. Novak and Gowin, 1984; Markham et al., 1994; Liu and Hinchey, 1996; McClure et al., 1999; Nicoll et al., 2001; Kinchin, 2001). According to Kinchin et al. (2000), morphologically concept maps may be classified into three broad categories such as 'spokes', 'chains', and 'nets' with their individual characteristics and interpretations. Borrowed from this paper, examples of these categories of concept maps and their characteristics are reproduced in Fig. 4.3 (a, b, c) and Table 4.1 respectively.

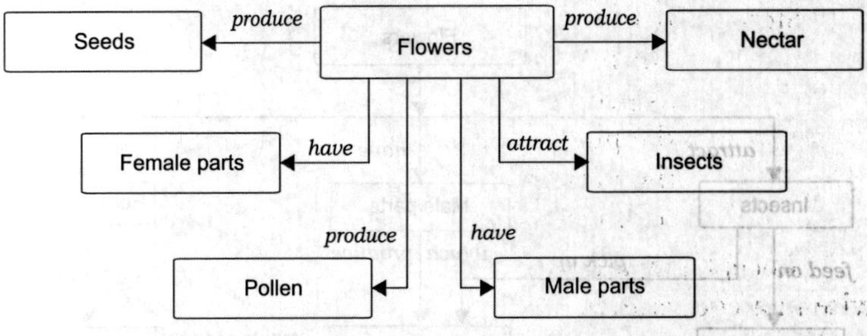

Fig. 4.3a: Spokes

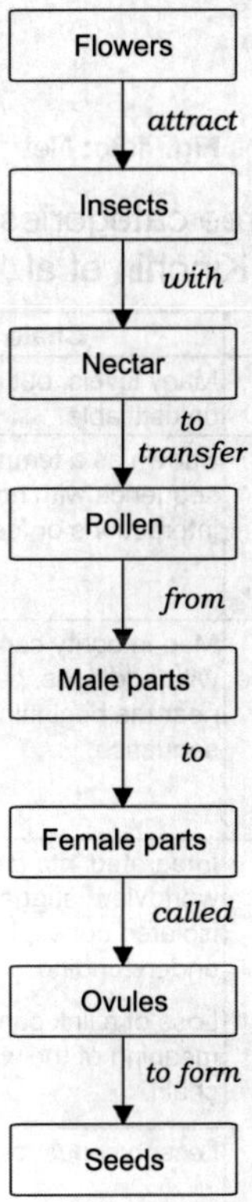

Fig. 4.3b: Chains

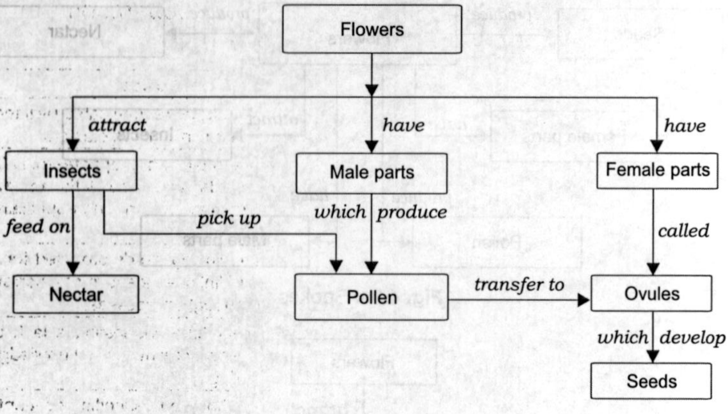

Fig. 4.3c: Net

Table 4.1: The three categories of concept maps (from Kinchin et al., 2000)

	Spoke	Chain	Net
Hierarchy	One level only.	Many levels, but often unjustifiable.	Several justifiable levels.
Processes	Simple association with no understanding of processes or interactions.	Shown as a temporal sequence with no complex interactions or feedback.	Described as complex interactions at different conceptual levels.
Complexity	So little integration that concepts can be added without consequences for 'map integrity'.	Map integrity cannot cope with additions, particularly near the beginning of the sequence.	Map integrity is high. Adding one or more concepts often has minor consequences as 'other routes' are available.
Conceptual development	Shows little or no 'worldview'. Addition or loss of a link has little effect on the overview.	Integrated into a narrow worldview, suggesting an isolated conceptual understanding. Loss of a link can lose meaning of the whole chain.	Can support reorganization to emphasize different components to appreciate a larger world-view or to compensate for a missing link.
Represents	National Curriculum structure.	Lesson sequence.	Meaningful learning.

Kinchin et al. (2000) also identified some 'expertise' indicators which could be used when examining concept maps. This list of indicators is reproduced in Table 4.2.

Table 4.2: Indicators of expertise in concept maps (from Kinchin et al., 2000)

Characteristic	Expert	Novice
Connectedness	Highly integrated structure with numerous cross-links.	Disjointed structure dominated by linear arrangements in isolated clusters.
Link quality	Appropriate linking phrases which add to the meaning of concepts, using the specialist language of the domain.	Links are often inappropriate—usually single words that add little to the meaning and using non-specialist terminology.
Link variety	A diversity of linking phrases illustrating a range of thought processes.	The same linking words are used for a number of links, suggestive of a narrow range of thought processes.
Dynamism	Changes over time, reflecting active interaction with alternative knowledge structures.	Stable over time suggesting a lack of active engagement in knowledge restructuring.
Concepts	Concentration on overarching concepts to create an overview.	Concentration on specific concepts indicating a limited perspective.

We need to point out that several other varieties (Fisher et al., 2000) of knowledge organization tools/qualitative concept mapping technique have been tried out by researchers such as *clinical interview*, *word-association tasks*, *writing or selecting a definition*, *identification of semantic space* (Sutton, 1980), *vee diagrams* (Gowin, 1981), and *concept circle diagrams* (Wandersee, 1987a; 1987b), *SemNet* (Gorodetsky et al., 1994), etc. However, these techniques, with their successes and limitations, are not as widely practised as the Novak-type concept mapping. We shall, therefore, not elaborate on them any further.

4.7 Concept Tree Graph Technique

In 1980s a group of researchers at the University of Oxford came out with a new method of creating concept maps (Matthews et al., 1984a; 1984b; 1985), which may be called a *concept tree graph technique* as the maps look like 'trees' with 'branches'. Though the map making process is similar to that used in the Novak-type concept mapping, here the interrelations between pairs of concepts are indicated by natural numbers instead of link words. The numbers are supposed to describe the 'order' or 'strength' of relationship between the concerned pairs of concepts. The concept mapping thus becomes *quantitative* in nature.

Let us quote the description of the new graph construction method from Matthews et al. (1984a):

In this type of test, pupils are given a list of concept labels. They are then told to choose the two concept labels which they regard as most similar, and link them with a line labelled '1'. Then they may either link another concept label to this pair, or create another separate pair, the only condition being that they form link '2' between the two concept labels which to them are most similar. The pupils then continue the procedure until all the concept labels are linked.

For their study Matthews et al. picked up 10 of the most-used concept labels from the domain of Acids and Bases (Chemistry) and used 250 pupils of the age group 13-15 years chosen from different British schools as subjects. The individual pupil-generated graphs, called *raw tree graphs*, reflect the respective pupils' ability to link the various concept labels. Two representative raw tree graphs shown in Fig. 4.4 are taken from Matthews et al. (1984a).

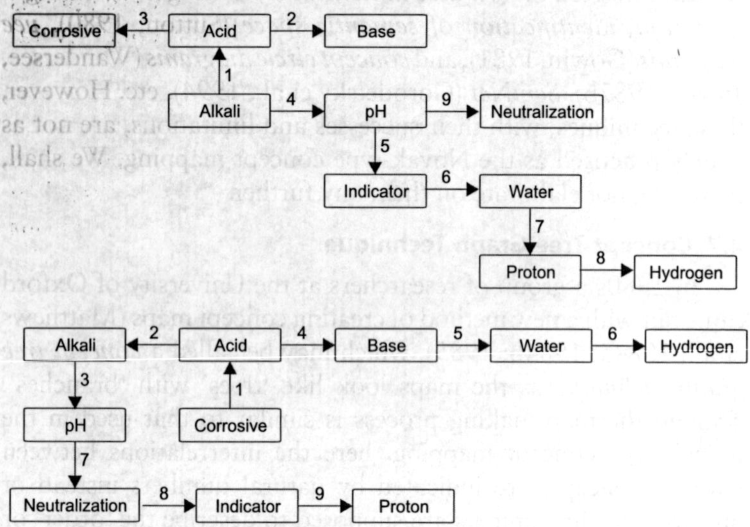

Fig. 4.4

Though individual concept maps are useful for diagnosing the corresponding student's level of cognition they cannot give a direct picture for the entire group of students involved in the map making exercise. For this purpose Matthews et al. (1984a) use the *proximity half-matrix* method by which it is possible to construct an 'average' concept map for the group. They have also used a special algorithm to generate *two-dimensional graphs* from the individual concept maps, which are quite informative. Then in order to measure the cognitive structure of individual students in the domains of (i) acids and bases, and (ii) oxidation and reduction Matthews et al. (1984b) generated *three-dimensional graphs* by adding the Piaget-specific levels as a third dimension to the two-dimensional graphs. The method of Matthews et al., tried on 250 students of age group 13-15 years, in the domain of chemistry, could be applied to a wide range of age and subject area. The results obtained by them were highly informative, interesting and useful, with wide ranging implications for educational administrators, science researchers, teacher-trainers, teachers as well as students (Matthews et al., 1984c).

It may be mentioned that Rapoport (1967) had used a similar method of constructing concept tree graph to study proximity measures among 24 adjectives. In this study there were options for (i) constructing a single tree, and (ii) constructing several sub-trees first and then linking them up.

4.8 Modified Concept Tree Graph Technique

In 1995 Mohapatra and Parida designed and used a modified version of the Matthews type of concept mapping described above in order to investigate pupils' alternative conceptions (ALCONs) about the interrelations between concepts. The ALCONs may be of the following two types:

Type 1 : Pupils may use propositional links (Novak, 1981b, 1984) to connect concepts which are not actually related in a framework of formal science or they may use an incorrect propositional link to connect two related concepts. Novak's (1990b) technique of drawing concept maps has the potential to diagnose (Feldsine, 1983) the conceptions of pupils about the 'integrative reconciliation of meanings' (Novak, 1984).

Type 2 : Pupils may have inappropriate notions about the 'strength of interrelations' between concepts.

This may be illustrated with an example. Formal science says that the law of reflection, i.e. that the angle of incidence is equal to the angle of reflection, is valid for all cases of reflection of light. But pupils feel that it is valid in the case of reflection from a plane mirror and is not/less valid in the case of reflection from a concave or convex mirror (Mohapatra, 1988). In other words, they feel that the concept label 'Plane mirror' is more strongly related than the concept label 'Concave mirror/Convex mirror', to the concept label 'Laws of reflection'.

In order to investigate the second type of ALCONs Mohapatra and Parida (1995) incorporated the following three modifications in the concept tree-graph technique of Matthews et al. (1984a).

(1) *Conceptual modification*: As stated above, in the method of Matthews et al. (1984a) the pupils are given a set of concept labels and are asked to complete a concept tree graph on the basis of 'closest similarity' between the concepts. Thus in the resulting drawing the concept labels are connected by 'similarity links'. However, it can be argued that in science one has 'related concept labels' but not 'similar concept labels'. For instance, terms like 'velocity' and 'speed' are not similar but related concept labels. Consequently, the use of 'similarity' as the criterion to link concept labels was abandoned.

Further, the fact that a set of related concepts has an organized hierarchical structure was noted. In this schema of conceptual hierarchy (Novak, 1990b) the most general, most inclusive concept is placed at the top, with less general concepts and specific examples progressively branching out form it. In view of this, in the modified approach the pupils are asked to identify the most fundamental/basic concept label from the given list, then choose the concept(s) which, in their opinion, is(are) most strongly related to the basic concept, link it(them) to the basic concept with line(s) and label it(them) '1'. They are then asked to continue the process of linking the concepts and designating each subsequent link with a successively higher link number till all the concepts are exhausted.

(2) *Structural modification*: In the method of Matthews et al. (1984a) each link carries a number label which is different from that carried by any other link in the concept tree graph, i.e. no two links will have the same number label. Thus, if there are N concepts, then there will be $(N - 1)$ links, carrying the distinct number labels 1, 2, 3, …., $(N - 1)$.

In the modified technique, the pupils are told that if, at any stage of tree graph construction process they feel that there is more than one concept linked to the preceding concept with equal strength then they should give the same number label to the separate links connecting these concepts to the preceding one. This is justified by the fact that in the growth of scientific concepts, more than one concept may originate simultaneously/ in parallel from a single concept and, thus, may have relations of the same strength with the parent concept. Consequently, there could now be more than one link carrying the same link number in a concept tree graph and, although there will be $(N - 1)$ links corresponding to N concept labels, the sequence of number labels of the links may now terminate at k, where

$$k \leq (N - 1).$$

(3) *Logistic modification*: In the method of Matthews et al. (1984a) one generates a 'similarity matrix' (m) for each tree graph. The elements of each m are then reordered by subtracting each element of m from the largest element, E_{max}, and made more manageable by dividing the elements of the reordered matrix by E_{max}. After these operations the values of the matrix elements, M_{ij} of the new matrix, M, will have values such that

$$0 \leq M_{ij} < 1.$$

In this procedure there is thus always a matrix element of value 'ZERO', meaning that there will always be a pair of concepts having 'zero similarity' or a 'zero significant' link between them. The occurrence of a 'zero' matrix element is justified only when a totally unrelated concept is present in a family of related concepts. The link strength between any two concepts among a family composed entirely of related concepts can, at best, approach this mathematically ideal lower limit of 'zero', but cannot be equal to 'zero'.

In the modified method, this unwanted 'zero' element is eliminated in the reordered matrix by:

(a) forming the sum, *S*, of the largest and the smallest elements of the matrix, *m*;
(b) subtracting each element of the matrix from *S*; and
(c) dividing each element of the reordered matrix by *S*.

This procedure yields a new matrix, *M*, with elements, M_{ij}, such that

$$0 < M_{ij} < 1.$$

The modified concept tree graph technique was used by Mohapatra and Parida (1995) to identify alternative conceptions held by pupils as well as teachers in the domain of 'reflection of light'. 102 pupils of Standard IX (age 15 years), 110 pupils of Standard X (age 16 years), 348 pupils of Standard XII (age 18 years), and 48 practising science teachers of secondary level constituted the population. The following 11 interrelated concept labels, taught in Standard VII, were chosen for the study.

Laws of reflection	Plane mirror
Reduced image	Virtual image
Concave mirror	Shaving mirror
Convex mirror	Magnified image
Real image	Object distance (u) = Image distance (v)
Rear-view mirror	

Typical raw concept tree graphs drawn by pupils of Standard IX, pupils of Standard X, pupils of Standard XII, and teachers are shown in Figs. 4.5(a), (b), (c), and (d) respectively.

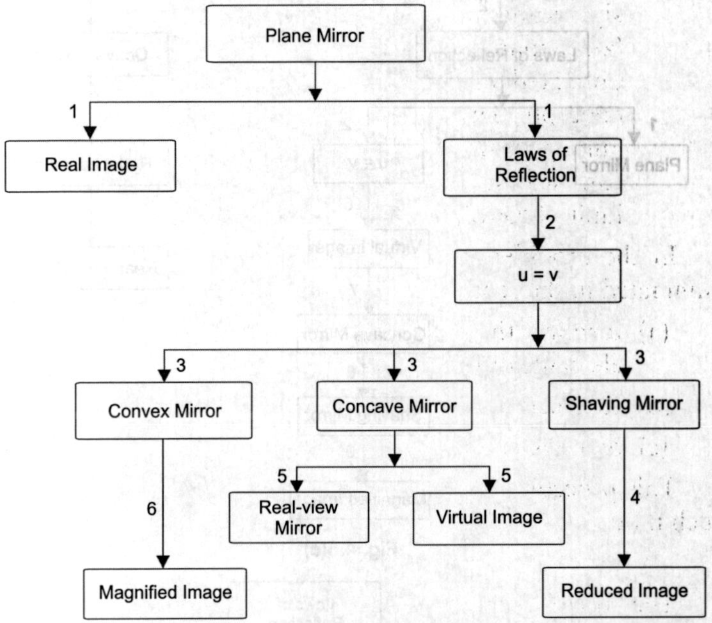

Fig. 4.5(a)

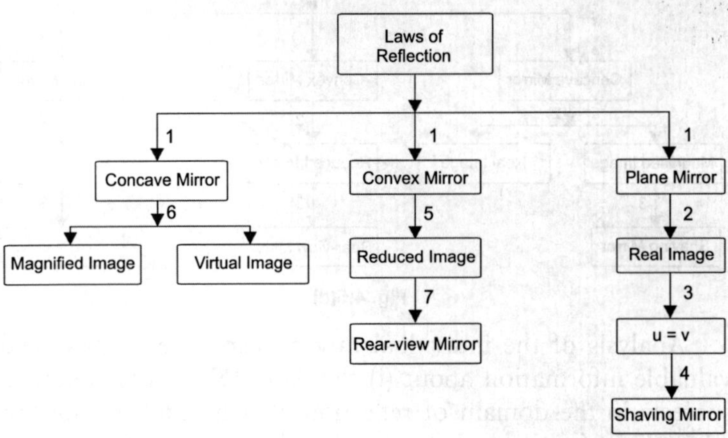

Fig. 4.5(b)

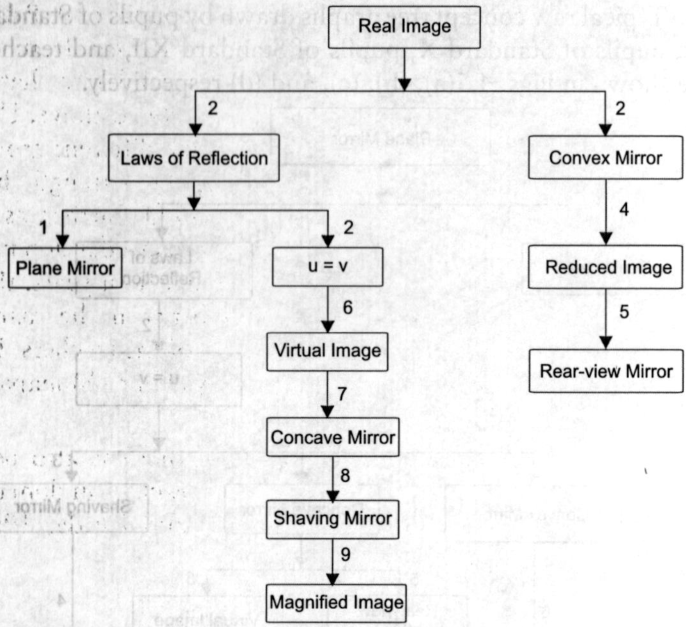

Fig. 4.5(c)

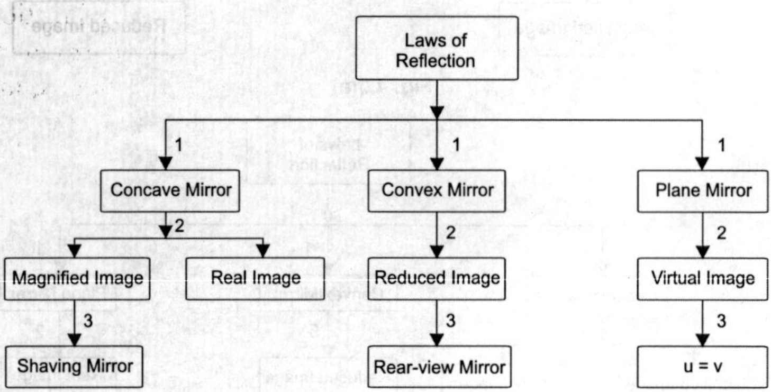

Fig. 4.5(d)

Analysis of the individual raw concept tree graphs yields valuable information about (i) the ALCONs of the concerned subjects in the domain of reflection of light, and (ii) how the ALCONs of pupils change with school years. In order to obtain the relevant information about the thought processes of the different groups of subjects, Mohapatra and Parida (1995) generated group link-strength half matrices from the corresponding raw tree graphs in a manner similar to that of Matthews et al. (1984a) with modifications as stated above. They also drew representative concept maps for the different groups of subjects from the corresponding group link-strength half matrices using arbitrarily chosen lower cut-offs. Further, as an informative way of looking for pupils' progressive development towards meaningful learning with change in school years, they computed the coefficient of correlation between the matrix elements of each group of pupils with those of the teachers. For details of the procedures and results one may refer to Mohapatra and Parida (1995).

The modified concept tree graph technique has also been used to probe ALCONs of pupils as well as teachers in domains other than reflection of light (Mohapatra and Parida, 1993; Mohapatra et al., 1998; Parida et al., 2000).

4.9 Applications of Concept Mapping

Concept mapping has been proved to be a very effective tool for all stakeholders associated with the process of education across disciplines. Pupils, teachers, teacher educators, curriculum framers, and researchers have found concept mapping quite useful for their respective purposes. There is ample research evidence in support of the claim that concept maps are highly reliable knowledge representation tools. Given below is a list of the benefits of concept mapping for different stakeholders.

For Pupils: Concept mapping

- can help in effective note taking.
- helps pupils move towards meaningful learning away from rote learning and retain knowledge in long-term memory for longer durations.
- can help pupils prepare better for examinations through wholesome review/summarization of lessons.
- enables pupils discover their alternative conceptions in a given domain of knowledge and suitably modify

them thereby becoming more effective knowledge constructors.

- encourages them to become autonomous and reflective learners by acquiring the skill of 'learning how to learn' (Novak and Gowin, 1984).
- encourages divergent/creative thinking and discovery of new knowledge/interpretations.
- can enhance language ability.
- can enable pupils improve their social skills, and human values such as respecting others' views, tolerance, negotiation, reaching consensus, etc. when working on concept maps in group situations.
- softwares like Cmap tools facilitate collaborative and distance learning.

Bascones and Novak (1985) found that students using concept maps recorded significantly superior achievement in problem-solving tests in high school physics compared to those not using concept maps. Robertson-Taylor (1985) used concept maps to help college students in introductory biology to acquire a meaningful understanding of biology laboratory work. Feldsine (1987) found that though a majority of his college chemistry students showed initial reluctance to concept mapping, they soon became good makers and users of the technique after realizing how it made difficult concepts become clearer. It has been found that concept mapping is a better learning strategy than other strategies such as *underlining* (Amer, 1994), *note-taking* (Reader and Hammond, 1994), *discussing with co-learners* (Chularut and DeBacker, 2004), and *outlining* (Robinson and Kiewra, 1995). Concept mapping has also been examined as an effective follow-up strategy to learning from texts (Hilbert and Renkl, 2008).

For teachers: Concept mapping

- helps teacher plan and prepare for a lesson.
- can be used to teach curricular subjects as an advance organizer.

- can help improve pupils' problem-solving skills (Pankratius, 1990).
- helps teacher identify learners' prior knowledge and alternative conceptions.
- helps teacher review/summarize a lesson.
- can be fruitfully used in formative as well as summative evaluation.
- can be used in brain-storming sessions.
- can better gauge learners' depth and breadth of knowledge and skill than conventional methods of testing.
- helps teacher link between different lessons.
- enables teacher to discover own alternative conceptions, which helps in becoming a more effective teacher.
- enables teacher to discover and fill the gaps between her own perception and student's perception in a curricular area.
- helps teacher to chart the academic progress of a learner.
- can identify areas to generate cognitive conflict, a major step to knowledge construction.
- can provide pathways for cognitive negotiation, another major step to knowledge construction.
- can make analogy based teaching more effective by making analogy transparent to the learner.
- can help the teacher to identify the zone of overlap between her own cognitive constructs and those of the learner and thereby help her to become a more effective negotiator.

For teacher educators: Concept mapping

- can be used in teacher training/faculty development programmes as an advance organizer tool and also to assess the impact of training.
- has been used to explore preservice teachers' perceptions on effective teaching (Beyerbach and Smith, 1990).

For researchers: Concept mapping

- has been recognized as a valid tool to assess pupils' conceptual changes (e.g. Wallace and Mintzes, 1990; Markham et al., 1994).
- has been used to assess the relationship between conceptual understanding and the use of study strategies by science students (Hegarty-Hazel and Prosser, 1991).
- is widely used for eliciting pupils' knowledge structure in science content (e.g. Kharatmal, 2009).
- is used to discover alternative conceptions existing with pupils and teachers (e.g. Ross and Munby, 1991; Mohapatra and Parida, 1995).
- is used to study the expert-novice differences in knowledge structures (Mintzes, 2007).

For curriculum framers: Concept mapping

- has been recognized as an effective tool for curriculum development, especially for creating interdisciplinary courses and case-based exercises (Edmondson, 1995).

For knowledge archivists: Concept mapping

- has been found to be very useful in capturing and archiving the tacit knowledge of experts, which they often fail to communicate in lectures or books (Coffey et al., 2002).

4.10 Concept Mapping vs. Mind Mapping

The very popular children's story *Peter Pan* (Barrie, 2008) gives the following description of a different kind of map, *the map of a child's mind*:

> I don't know whether you have ever seen a map of a person's mind. Doctors sometimes draw maps of other parts of you, and your own map can become intensely interesting, but catch them trying to draw a map of a child's mind, which is not only confused, but keeps going around all the time. There are zigzag lines on it, just like your temperature on a card, and these are probably roads in the island, for the Neverland is always more or

> less an island, with astonishing splashes of color here and there, and coral reefs and rakish-looking craft in the offing, and savages and lonely lairs, and gnomes who are mostly tailors, and caves through which a river runs, and princes with six elder brothers, and a hut fast going to decay, and one very small old lady with a hooked nose. It would be an easy map if that were all, but there is also first day at school, religion, fathers, the round pond, needlework, murders, hangings, verbs that take the dative, chocolate pudding day, getting into braces, say ninety-nine, three-pence for pulling out your tooth yourself, and so on, and either these are part of the island or they are another map showing through, and it is all rather confusing, especially as nothing will standstill.

This gives a graphic description of how complex a child's mind can be and how difficult it would be to map such a mind in action. Mapping an adult's mind may also yield an interesting scenario, perhaps less complicated than a child's mind.

In literature, mind mapping (Buzan, 1974; Budd, 2004) has been recognized as an effective tool to organize ideas and information, somewhat similar to concept mapping. However, whereas a mind map focuses on a single idea or word (the central governing concept), a concept map connects several ideas or words. A mind map has a radial or tree like structure showing relationships with the central idea, whereas a concept map depicts relationships/links between the concepts.

4.11 Conclusion

In this chapter we have discussed the various aspects of concept mapping, which establish it as a very effective constructivist tool. A large body of research findings exists (e.g. Al-Kunifed and Wandersee, 1990; Garcia, 2008; www.cmappers.net) in support of the utilitarian values of concept mapping. Even a concept map-centered learning environment ('a new model of education') has been suggested (Novak and Canas, 2008). A lot of internet-based support for concept mapping is also available. However, the tool has not yet been integrated into classroom teaching learning process to the extent desired, even in advanced countries like US and UK. Several reasons have been identified (e.g. Kinchin, 2001) for the scenario such as the unwillingness of teachers to learn the technique of concept mapping, lack of time to implement the technique in classroom, pressure for timely completion of curriculum, difficulty in handling large groups of pupils in classroom situations, continued reliance on rote learning to get good grades in examinations, dominance of traditional evaluation strategies, etc. The need of the hour, therefore, is to plan intensive training of teachers to make them comprehend and utilize the huge potential of concept mapping as a tool that enables the pupils to construct concepts in a way they are expected to be constructed.

In India sporadic research studies are conducted on the efficacy of concept mapping. In the sector of school education, serious efforts are being made to improve things in terms of quantity as well as quality under the umbrella of World Bank supported schemes such as Sarva Siksha Abhiyan (SSA) and Rashtriya Madhyamik Siksha Abhiyan (RMSA). Efforts are also on to implement the tenets of constructivism in teaching learning processes along the guidelines of the National Curriculum Framework 2005 (NCERT, 2005). However, no concerted attempt seems to have been made to implement the concept mapping tool in classroom transactions although there are curricular provisions to introduce pre-service as well as in-service teachers to this highly useful technique. Concept mapping as a meaningful learning strategy ought to find its own niche in our teaching learning process.

References

Al-Kunifed, A. and Wandersee, J.H. (1990). One hundred references related to concept mapping. *Journal of Research in Science Teaching*, 27(10): 1069-75.

Amer, A.A. (1994). The effect of knowledge-map and underlining training on the reading comprehension of scientific texts. *English Specific Purposes*, 13: 35-45.

Ausubel, D.P. (1963). *The Psychology of Meaningful Verbal Learning* (New York: Grune and Stratton).

—— (1968). *Educational Psychology: A Cognitive View* (New York: Holt, Rinehart, and Winston).

Ausubel, D.P., Novak, J.D. and Hanesian, H. (1978). *Educational Psychology: A Cognitive View* (second edition) (New York: Holt, Rinehart, and Winston).

Barrie, J.M. (2008). *Peter Pan* (New York: Sterling; www.sterlingpublishing.com/kids).

Bascones, J. and Novak, J.D. (1985). Alternative instructional systems and the development of problem-solving skills in physics. *European Journal of Science Education*, 7(3): 253-61.

Beyerbach, B. and Smith, J. (1990). Using a computerized concept mapping program to assess preservice teachers thinking about effective teaching. *Journal of Research in Science Teaching*, 27: 961-72.

Budd, J.W. (2004). Mind maps as classroom exercises. *The Journal of Economic Education*, 35(1): 35-46.

Buzan, T. (1974). *Use Your Head* (London: BBC Books).

Canas, A.J. et al. (2004). Cmap Tools: A knowledge modelling and sharing environment. In A.J. Canas, J.D. Novak, and F.M. Gonzalez (Eds.), *Concept maps: Theory, methodology, technology. Proceedings of the first international conference on concept mapping* (Vol. I, pp. 125-33) (Pamplona, Spain: Unversidad Publica de Navarra).

Chularut, P. and DeBacker, T.K. (2004). The influence of concept on achievement, self-regulation, and self-efficacy in students of English as a second language. *Contemporary Educational Psychology*, 29: 248-63.

Cliburn, J.W., Jr. (1990). Concept maps to promote meaningful learning. *Journal of College Science Teaching*, 19: 212-17.

Coffey, J.W., Hoffman, R.R., Canas, A.J., and Ford, K.M. (2002). A concept-map based knowledge modelling approach to expert knowledge sharing. In M. Boumedine (Ed.), *Proceedings of IKS 2002—the IASTED international conference on information and knowledge sharing* (pp. 212-17). (Calgary, Canada: Acta Press).

DeCecco, J.P. and Crawford, W.R. (1988). *The Psychology of Learning and Instruction*. (N.J., USA: Prentice-Hall Inc.).

Disney, Walt. (1957). http://www.mind-mapping.org/images/walt-disney-business-map.org

Edmondson, K.M. (1995). Concept mapping for the development of medical curricula. *Journal of Research in Science Teaching*, 32(7): 777-93.

—— (2000). Assessing science understanding through concept maps. In J.J. Mintzes, J.H. Wandersee, and J.D. Novak (Eds.), *Assessing Science Understanding: A Human Constructivist View* (San Diego: Academic Press), 15-40.

Feldsine, J. (1983). Concept mapping: a method for detection of possible student misconception. In H. Helm and J.D. Novak (Eds.), *Proceedings of the International Seminar on Misconceptions in Science and Mathematics*. (Ithaca, NY: Department of Education, Cornell University).

Feldsine, J.E., Jr. (1987). *The Construction of Concept Maps Facilitates the Learning of General College Chemistry: A Case Study.* Unpublished Ph.D. Dissertation. (Ithaca, NY: Department of Education, Cornell University).

Fisher, K., Wandersee, D., and Moody, D. (2000). *Mapping Biology Knowledge* (The Netherlands: Kluwer Academic Publishers).

Garcia, GNA (2008). *An Annotated Bibliography of Concept Mapping* (University of Connecticut).

Gorodetsky, M., Fisher, K.M., and Wyman, B. (1994). Generating connections and learning with SemNet, a tool for constructing knowledge networks. *Journal of Science Education and Technology*, 3(3): 137-44.

Gowin, D.B. (1981). *Educating* (Ithaca, NY: Cornell University Press).

Hegarty-Hazel, E. and Prosser, M. (1991). Relationship between students' conceptual knowledge and study strategies. Part 1: Student learning in physics. *International Journal of Science Education*, 13: 303-12.

Hilbert, T.S. and Renkl, A. (2008). Concept mapping as a follow-up strategy to learning from texts: what characterizes good and poor mappers? *Instructional Science*, 36(1): 53-73.

Kharatmal, M. (2009). Concept mapping for eliciting students' understanding of science. *Indian Educational Review*, 45(2): 31-43.

Kinchin, I.M. (2000). Concept mapping in biology. *Journal of Biology Education*, 34(2): 61-68.

Kinchin, I.M. (2001). If concept mapping is so helpful in learning biology, why aren't we all doing it? *International Journal of Science Education*, 23(12): 1257-69.

Kinchin, I.M., Hay, D.B. and Adams, A. (2000). How a qualitative approach to concept map analysis can be used to aid learning by illustrating patterns of conceptual development. *Educational Research*, 42(1): 43-57.

Liu, X and Hinchey, M. (1996). The internal consistency of a concept mapping scoring scheme and its effect on prediction validity. *International Journal of Science Education*, 18(8): 921-37.

Margolis, E. and Lawrence, S. (2012). *Concepts. Stanford Encyclopedia of Philosophy.* (Metaphysics Research Lab at Stanford University).

Markham, M., Mintzes, J., and Jones, M.G. (1994). The concept map as research and evaluation tool: further evidence of validity. *Journal of Research in Science Teaching*, 31(1): 91-101.

Matthews, G.P., Brook, V.G., and Khan-Gandapur, T.H. (1984a). Cognitive structure determinations as a tool in science teaching. Part 1: A new method of creating concept maps. *European Journal of Science Education*, 6(2): 169-77.

—— (1984b). Cognitive structure determinations as a tool in science teaching. Part 2: The measurement of Piaget-specific levels. *European Journal of Science Education*, 6(3): 289-97.

Matthews, G.P., Brook, V.G., Elliot, G.S., and Khan-Gandapur, T.H. (1985). Cognitive structure determination as a tool in science teaching. Part 3: Results. *European Journal of Science Education*, 7(3): 263-79.

McClure, J.R., Sonak, B., and Suen, H.K. (1999). Concept map assessment of classroom learning: reliability, validity, and logistical practicality. *Journal of Research in Science Teaching*, 36(4): 475-92.

Mintzes, J.J., Wandersee, J.H., and Novak, J.D. (1997). Meaningful learning in science: the human constructivist perspective. In G.D. Phye (Ed.), *Handbook of Academic Learning* (Orlando: Academic Press), 405-47.

Mintzes, J.J. (2007). Knowledge restructuring in biology: testing a punctuated model of conceptual change. *International Journal of Science and Mathematics Education*, 5(2): 181-206.

Mohapatra, J.K. (1988). Induced incorrect generalization leading to misconceptions—an exploratory investigation about laws of reflection of light. *Journal of Research in Science Teaching*, 25(9): 777-84.

Mohapatra, J.K. and Parida, B.K. (1993). Studying pupils' concepts about interrelations between concept labels involving refraction of light: a concept map model. *Indian Educational Review*, XXVIII(1): 27-40.

—— (1995). The location of alternative conceptions by a concept graph technique. *International Journal of Science Education*, 17(5): 663-81.

Mohapatra, J.K. et al. (1998). Location of alternative conceptions in the concept domain of rusting of iron by a concept graph technique, *Indian Educational Review*, XXXII(2): 22-37.

NCERT (2005). *National Curriculum Framework 2005* (New Delhi: National Council of Educational Research and Training).

Nicoll, G., Francisco, J., and Nakhleh, M. (2001). A three-tier system for assessing concept map links: a methodological study. *International Journal of Science Education*, 23(8): 863-75.

Novak, J.D. (1977). *A Theory of Education* (Ithaca, New York: Cornell University Press).

—— (1979). Applying psychology and philosophy to the improvement of laboratory teaching. *The American Biology Teacher*, 41(8): 466-74.

—— (1980). Learning theory applied to the biology classroom. *The American Biology Teacher*, 42(5): 280-85.

—— (1981a). *The use of concept mapping and Gowin's 'V' mapping instructional strategies in junior high school science*. Report of the Cornell University 'Learning How to Learn Project.' (Ithaca, New York).

—— (1981b). Applying learning psychology and philosophy of science to biology teaching. *The American Biology Teacher*, 43(1): 12-20.

—— (1984). Application of advances in learning theory and philosophy of science to the improvement of chemistry teaching. *Journal of Chemistry Education*, 61(7): 607-13.

——— (1990a). Concept mapping: a useful tool for science education. *Journal of Research in Science Teaching*, 27(10): 937-49.

——— (1990b). Concept maps and vee diagrams: two meta-cognitive tools to facilitate meaningful learning. *Instructional Science*, 19: 1-25.

——— (1998). *Learning, creating, and using knowledge: Concept maps as facilitative tools in schools and corporations* (Mahwah, NJ: Lawrence Erlbaum Associates).

Novak, J.D. and Canas, A.J. (2008). The Theory Underlying Concept Maps and How to Construct and Use Them. *http://cmap.ihmc.us/ Publications/ ResearchPapers/TheoryCmaps/TheoryUnderlyingConceptMaps.htm*

Novak, J.D. and Gowin, R. (1984). *Learning How to Learn* (New York: Cambridge University Press).

Okebukola, P.A. and Jegede, O.J. (1988). Cognitive preference and learning mode as determinants of meaningful learning through concept mapping. *Science Education*, 72(4): 489-500.

Pankratius, W.J. (1990). Building an organized knowledge base: concept mapping and achievement in secondary school physics. *Journal of Research in Science Teaching*, 27(4): 315-33.

Parida, B.K., Mahapatra, M., and Goswami, M. (2000). Alternative conceptions of pupils in gravitation. *School Science*, Vol. XXXVIII(1): 67-75.

Reader, W. and Hammond, N. (1994). Computer-based tools to support learning from hypertext: concept mapping tools and beyond. *Computer Education*, 22: 99-106.

Rao, Manjula P. (2006). Concept mapping. In Santosh Sharma (Ed.), *Constructivist Approaches to Teaching and Learning*. (New Delhi: National Council of Educational Research and Training).

Rapoport, A. (1967). A comparison of two tree-construction methods for obtaining proximity measures among words. *Journal of Verbal Learning and Verbal Behavior*, 6: 884-90.

Robertson-Taylor, M. (1985). *Changing the Meaning of Experience: Empowering Learners Through the Use of Concept Maps, Vee Diagrams, and Principle of Education in a Biology Lab Course*. Unpublished Ph.D. Dissertation. (Ithaca, NY: Department of Education, Cornell University).

Robinson, D.H. and Kiewra, K.A. (1995). Visual argument: graphic organizers are superior to outlines in improving learning from text. *Journal of Educational Psychology*, 87: 455-67.

Ross, B. and Munby, H. (1991). Concept mapping and misconceptions: a study of high-school students' understandings of acids and bases. *International Journal of Science Education*, 13(1): 11-23.

Sutton, C.R. (1980). The learner's prior knowledge: a critical review of techniques for probing its organization. *European Journal of Science Education*, 2(2): 107-20.

Symington, D. and Novak, J.D. (1982). Teaching children how to learn. *Educational Magazine*, 39(5): 13-16.

Wallace, J.D. and Mintzes, J.J. (1990). The concept map as a research tool: exploring conceptual change in biology. *Journal of Research in Science Teaching*, 27(10): 1033-52.

Wandersee, J.H. (1987a). Drawing concept circles: a way of revealing what the learner knows. In J.D. Novak (Ed.), *Proceedings of the Second International Seminar on Misconceptions and Educational Strategies in Science and Mathematics* (Ithaca, NY: Cornell University), 1: 506-20.

Wandersee, J.H. (1987b). Drawing concept circles: a way to teach and test students. *Science Activities*, 24(4): 19-20.

Wandersee, J.H. (1990). Concept mapping and the cartography of cognition. *Journal of Research in Science Teaching*, 27(10): 923-36.

www.cmappers.net (Cmappers.Learn).

5 A Learner-Centered Input-Output Model

5.1 Introduction

As discussed in the first chapter, during the second half of the 20th century the teaching-learning process (TLP) as practiced inside the classroom has evolved through three broad paradigms, ensconced within the philosophy of "Freedom of Necessity". The "Necessity" is defined by the demands of—

- Social and cultural changes.
- The explorative investigations, particularly in science, and
- The new evidences about how a learner learns.

On the other hand the individual learner has the "Freedom" to choose the context of learning. As a result of this,

- The focus of TLP has gone through continuous change.
- The domain of TLP operation has expanded beyond the walls of the classroom.
- The structures of TLP have been redesigned to meet the ever evolving situations.
- The form of TLP has been redefined.
- The operational modalities of TLP have been modified beyond recognition.
- Evaluative procedures have been made more functional to meet grassroot realities.

In this process of evolution, the approaches to TLP have changed from the Transmissionist one to the cognitive one, and now to the constructivist one. However, in this process of evolutionary changes (Kuhn, 1970) the two important human inputs, which obviously have remained unchanged, are the teacher and the learner.

The teacher brings with him/her, his/her

- Personality (which could be pleasant, smiling, caring, arrogant, angry, terse, authoritative, etc.)
- Content knowledge (which could be say, in the case of science teachers, textbook science, scientists' science, indigenous science, his/her personal construct-science, etc.)
- Pedagogy knowledge (which could have been acquired through professional training, years of experience, self-developed but operationally effective strategies, orientation programmes, etc.)
- Pedagogical content knowledge (Shulman, 1987) (which might have been developed through his/her innovativeness, socio-cultural context, linguistic expertise, infrastructural facilities available in the school, etc.)
- Creativity (generated and refined over years through self modulated efforts, programmed orientations, etc.)

and perhaps a host of other factors into the classroom. These are inputs by a teacher in a classroom situation. He/she uses them in a way which he/she thinks is effective and expects certain learning outputs in the learner.

Similarly a learner (independent of the teacher), brings with him/her a lot of inputs which he/she then uses in constructing new concepts from events, examples, etc.

Thus an input-output model of learning must then necessarily build upon either a teacher-specific or a learner-specific or perhaps a composite-specific (where perhaps the teacher and the learner can be taken in unison) framework.

However, we are conscious that in this discussion we will not be considering such inputs as textbooks, infrastructure facilities, school specific co-curricular practices, contribution by the society in terms of Village Education Committee and other such organizations, use of electronic media, incentives in the form of scholarships, etc., because they are policy-prescribed inputs over which neither the teacher nor the learner has much of a say.

In 'Reality', the TLP as practised even now in the classroom is mostly a Teacher-centered input-output model (Fig. 5.1). It entails inputs by the teacher. It envisages a prototype output in the learner, confined within the philosophy—'What is relevant for examination is relevant for education'. However, in the context of learning in the constructivist framework, the 'Desirability' of TLP consists of input by the learner leading to output by the learner. One may call this the Lerner-centered input-output model. But, optimization of TLP leading to maximization of meaningful learning cannot afford to consider the teacher and the learner in isolation. Thus in 'Ideality' the composite model for TLP involves inputs by both the teacher and the learner, expecting a planned construction by the learner. This means the 'Reality' should help the 'Desirability' to approach the 'Ideality'.

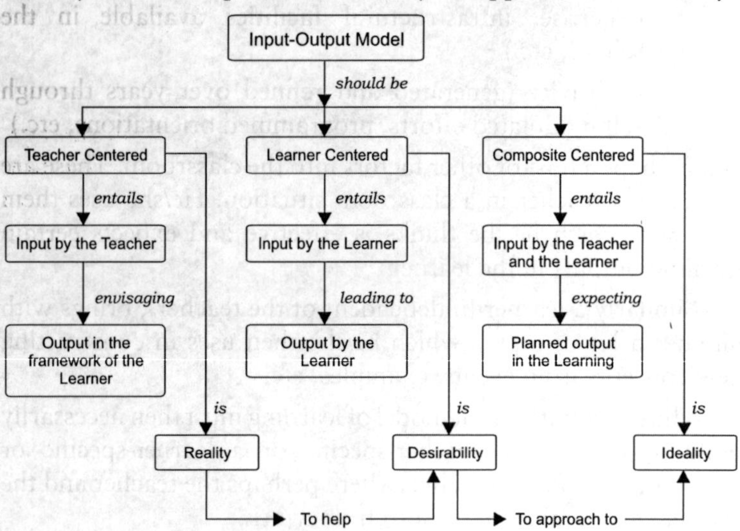

Fig. 5.1

In this chapter we shall confine ourselves to the crucial Learner-centered input-output model. We call this crucial because (as discussed already in earlier chapters) through conclusive field study based evidences constructivism advocates that:

- the learner constructs his/her knowledge,
- no learner enters a class devoid of personal constructs (Alternative conceptions),
- knowledge is constructed through a process of conceptual change (Posner et al., 1982; Hewson and Thornley, 1989).

Thus to maximize meaningful learning in a constructivist framework it is essential to know what are the contributing structures (Inputs) the learner carries with him/her into the classroom and using which he/she is going to construct new structures (Output).

5.2 Inputs

The inputs by the learner have four discernible dimensions, which are,

- Intrinsic inputs
- Constructed input
- Cognitive preference input
- Concept based input.

Dim. 1: Intrinsic inputs: These inputs depend on the age, genetic design, biological growth, as well as socio-cultural background of the learner. These are further classified into two categories, (a) Mental developmental level of the learner and (b) Creativity of the learner.

(a) **Mental developmental level (MDL) of the learner:** When a learner enters a class, obviously his/her mental developmental level or, mental readiness determines the concepts he/she can construct and internalize. If there is a mismatch between the MDL of the learner and the cognitive demand level of the concept, then even the best efforts by a teacher to facilitate the construction by the learner will result in a constructed concept which will be most likely not the desirable one.

Hence, this puts a premium on educational administrators, curriculum framers, textbook authors and classroom teachers to at least ascertain the average

MDL of a group of learners in a particular class before they are exposed to actual learning situations.

Several models are available in the literature to perform this task.

(i) *Piagetian Stage-dependent Model*: In this model it is important to note the following:

- Although the stages form a nominal scale, they can be functionally converted to an ordinal scale for use in a classroom situation.
- In this model the inbuilt lacunae are that the Piagetian clinical interview technique is individualistic in character and is time consuming. These inhibit the technique to be transported, as such, into a classroom situation, involving large number of learners whose MDLs spread over quite a few Piagetian stages.

In spite of this, the Piagetian model is still a fairly reliable reference point and hence there have been large number of efforts to take it into a classroom.

Longeot (1965) was the first to take Piaget into the classroom by overcoming the above limitations of Piaget's method Clinique. His was a test of combinatorial thinking, propositional logic and proportionality. He used scalogram technique to analyze the responses. But he did not give the data on inter-task correlations, or, on the reliability of the task. It was a purely pencil-on-paper test and demanded reading, visual recall and writing abilities. Bruner (1960) had earlier commented that such tests are likely to put the pupils in suspicion. Further the responses in such a test rarely reflect the MDL of the child, measured in terms of the ability to handle specific logical structures.

Raven (1973) developed a test of logical operations. It was again a pencil-on-paper test of classification, seriation, logical multiplication, compensation, proportional thinking, probability and co-relational thinking operations. Thus, although as compared to Longeot's test, Raven broadened the range of logical structures to be tested by a tool; his test suffers from the limitations of a pencil-on-paper test.

Tisher and Dale (1975) went a step forward by introducing an apparatus which should be on view during the administration of their understanding in science test. But the apparatus was never used as an aid to supplement the actual administration of the test. Further it distinguished between only formal and concrete operations, without any finer discrimination.

Rowell and Hoffman (1975) developed a group task to be given in a laboratory with each pupil using an apparatus. The disadvantages are that one needs a spacious laboratory and a large number of apparatus, which in any way does not relate to a realistic classroom situation. Further the responses of any child depended upon how he/she completes the experiment and hence demands on his/her experimental skill which does not necessarily reflect his/her MDL.

To do away with the requirement of a large number of apparatus Issacs (1976) used video-taped presentations. Apart from the fact that this demanded a high level of pictorial perception-to-comprehensional ability, the test also relied heavily on ticked answers, which involved high probability of guessing. Thus the conclusions arrived at from the responses are likely to be quite off the mark.

Shayer and Wharry (1973) developed 7 tasks in which the administrator presented the questions verbally while demonstrating the activities with a simple apparatus. However, they did not provide data on the reliability and validity of the tasks.

The CSMS (Concepts in Secondary Maths and Science) group at Chelsea College, London, in 1974, subjected all the Shayer-Wharry tasks through a thorough psychometric developmental process. The final version of these tasks is called the Science Reasoning Tasks (SRT). These tasks have the following characteristics:

- Their reliabilities are well established.
- Each task requires one very simple equipment for stepwise demonstration of different items.
- They do not impose any constraint on the responses in terms of adequate verbal ability, as they demand short answers from the pupils.

- The provision of short answers also eliminates the uncertain effect of 'guessing' as is common in case of ticked answers.
- The internal consistencies of the tasks as measured (Johnson, 1977) by KR-20 coefficients have values around 0.85.
- The test-retest correlation is also as high as 0.8 (Johnson, 1977).
- Even the task-interview correlations are quite large (Shayer and Adey, 1981) indicating a direct correspondence with Piaget's method Clinique.
- At the end of each demonstration in the context of an item in the task, the pupil is asked,
  - to guess what could happen and
  - to explain what actually happens.

Responses to both these are likely to reflect the mental level of the child.

- Each task is a good discriminator over a range of Piagetian stages.
- They have a cross-cultural validity. In fact, the validity of tasks III and IV, under Indian conditions, have been established by Mohapatra and Mohapatra (1997).

Lawson (1977), without the knowledge of the already developed SRT, designed a set of tasks independently. But they suffered from the defect that the test items were not classified as concrete, or, formal before trial. The stage assigned to each score range was determined by past-hoc inspection of contingency table.

(ii) *Pascual-Leone's M-Power Model*: The proponents of the neo-Piagetian approaches to diagnose and map MDL of pupils advocate that Piaget's theory suffers (Pinard and Laurendeau, 1969) from several drawbacks like horizontal and vertical decalages and low correlation between tasks which are supposed to be passed at about the same age and MDL, such as, conservation, classification and seriation.

Pascual-Leone retained the Piagetian notions of schema, assimilation, differentiation, accommodation and structural invariants, but introduced the concept of M-Power (Pascual-Leone, 1977, 1987). This facilitated the introduction of several hyperfine structures into the stage-dependent model of Piaget. He argued that the instruction does not have to be geared to some general logical structure, but to the specific pre-requisite structures of relevance to the domain in question, together with the M-Power of the learner.

He introduced a new rule for stage transition by stating that the children progress from non-solution to solution of a developmental task when their M-Power increases to the point at which it can activate all the task relevant schematic boosting, namely, schema's own cues, field effects and logical, or, structurally related cues. A reliable and valid tool to measure the M-Power of the child has been developed by Pascual-Leone. Interesting and important case studies involving assessment of M-Power of pupils in a classroom situation can be obtained from Niaz (1988, 1991).

One may use this M-Power framework to assess the MDL of the learner. However, in this formalism, to ascertain the M-demand of any concept, no general taxonomy is available in the literature, as is the case with SRTs (Shayer and Adey, 1981).

(iii) *Processing Space Model*: Case (1985, and references therein) in an information processing framework, propounded that the completion of an item/activity by a learner should not be looked upon in totality, because the process of completion goes through several steps, each demanding a different cognitive ability. Thus the completion of each step should be analysed separately. To operationalise this idea, he advanced the concept of Executive Processing Load

(EPL). EPL is the number of schemes a learner must activate in order to complete one particular step in an executive sequence. The EPL for different steps will be different. He called the maximum instantaneous value of EPL as Maximum Processing Load (MPL). In this model he introduced three variables, Total Processing Space (TPS), Operating Space (OS) and Short Term Storage Space (STSS), which are related by the following equation:

TPS = OS + STSS

Thus a measurement of TPS and OS of the learner will also give an assessment of the learner's effective MDL.

(iv) *Vygotsky's Zone of Proximal Development Model*: Vygotsky's (1962) analysis of the relationship between learning and development is the basis for his concept of the Zone of Proximal Development (ZPD). Vygotsky writes (1978)—"What the children can do with the assistance of others might be in some sense more indicative of their MDL than what they do alone." The abilities which help the child to accomplish this are mature as they must have been internalized by the child for quite some time. These in fact reflect the Actual Developmental Level (ADL). There could be, of course, the abilities which the child cannot exercise at all, even with extensive assistance. These abilities may mature later. But there could be perhaps quite a few abilities which the child can demonstrate with assistance. These abilities could be considered as existing in the process of maturing. They are latent and need little props. These maturing abilities then provide excellent predictive information on how the child will/can perform independently in the near future. Thus assessment of the soon-to-be-mature mental abilities provides a perspective measure of the projected performance ability of the child and reflects the potential developmental level called by Vygotsky, the Zone of Proximal Development (ZPD). Vygotsky asserts that an assessment of ZPD of a child will also indicate the functional mental developmental level. Stated in brief.

$$MDL = ADL + ZPD.$$

In view of the above research findings we recommend the following:

- Taking a broad-based sample of learners one should have a statistically clear picture of the MDL of the pupils in a class before even the curriculum is framed, textbooks are drafted, and the actual classroom teaching takes place, because MDL is the most important intrinsic input by the learner.
- An analysis of the cognitive demands of each concept to be taught in any class be undertaken simultaneously.

(b) **Creativity of the learner:** The learner also brings with him/her his/her creative abilities, which can be measured in terms of the classical model (Torrence, 1965, 1968), involving four parameters, namely, fluency, flexibility, originality, and elaboration. Many culture specific tools (viz. Sudhir and Varpari, 1991) are available in the literature for ready use. One may note that these four parameters are continuous variables and as contrasted to this model, the Oregon University Group, U.S.A. has now proposed the quantum creativity model. One must not lose sight of the fact that creativity also plays a major role for the construction of knowledge by the learner.

Dim. 2: Constructed input: It is now known that the learner constructs knowledge in a continuous autogenic (Glasersfeld, 1992) process. However, as had already been clearly stated by Ausubel (1968), the degree and quality of construction is decided by the Alternative conceptions (ALCONs) of the learner. Since 1980, there have been focused efforts to:

- Diagnose and map learner's ALCONs.
- Refine and innovate new techniques to carry out this diagnosis.

- Study ALCONs' cross-cultural variations, if any.
- Identify genesis of ALCONs, common to a group of learners.
- Study the characteristic of ALCONs.
- Locate implications of ALCONs for TLP.
- Develop and try out teaching models incorporating learner's ALCONs.

Comprehensive reviews and overviews can be obtained from the books by Fensham et al. (1994), Steffe and Gale (1995), Glynn and Duit (1995) and papers by West (1982), Driver and Erickson (1983), Gilbert and Watts (1983), Hashweh (1986) and Mohapatra (1989, 1997). In fact studies on ALCONs were pursued so extensively and intensively that Gilbert and Swift (1985) called these endeavours as 'The Alternative Conception Movement'. To maximize the degree of meaningful construction by the learner it is imperative that the teacher should be equipped with knowledge, techniques, and strategies so as to be able not only to diagnose learner's ALCONs but also to suitably use them through cognitive negotiation in the TLP for an optimal and fruitful output.

Dim. 3: Cognitive preference input: Cognitive preference is a learner's stable mode of perceptual organization of the external environment and the concepts taught to him/her (Tamir, 1985). In fact in the process of learning a concept through construction, cognitive preference of a learner is the self-induced reply to such self-asked question as—'Why shall I learn this concept?' The answer to this question is obviously an input by the learner and becomes the guiding motive force in the process for further learning. Four cognitive preference modes have been identified. They are:

- Recall – It involves acceptance of information for its own sake without consideration of its implications, or, applications. A preference for "Recall" indicates an interest in learning a name, a number, a definition, a formula, an observation, a fact or even a table.

- Principle – A preference for 'Principle' indicates an interest in identifying relationship between variables, or a rule that can be applied to a class of objects, phenomena, or, an interest in explaining a phenomenon leading to a representation of fundamental principles, or, relationships.
- Questioning – A preference for 'Questioning' indicates an interest in critically analyzing and commenting on information for completeness, general validity, or, limitations, or, in generating suggestions and hypotheses for further research.
- Application – A preference for 'Application' indicates an interest in using scientific information to solve problems in commerce, industry, farming, or, in other real life situations.

Cognitive preference ultimately controls the quality of meaningful learning by the learner. Although preference for 'Principle' is perhaps cognitively the best, at the intake point, very few learners have this cognitive preference. However, experimental results show that by suitable intervention techniques (Okebukola and Jedge, 1988) learners originally having preference for 'Recall' can be made to gradually adopt the cognitive preference mode of 'Principle'. But for this the teacher should have a tool (Tamir, 1985) to ascertain the initial cognitive preference of the learners. We note in passing that the mode of cognitive preference adopted by a learner is, many a time, specific to the concept domain and context.

Dim. 4: Concept-based input: Based on the two main observations of constructivism, namely:

- Learning is a purposeful, intentional, autogenic (Glasersfeld, 1992) sequence of construction of cognitive structures by the cognizing subject, and
- Learning is pervasively influenced by ALCONs of the learners.

Posner et al. (1982) and Hewson (1981, 1982) developed the conceptual change model of learning, as discussed in Chapter 3. Activation of the process of conceptual change, when a learner encounters a new concept, requires an assessment of the concept by the learner. This assessment is subjective and purely personal to the learner and hence is a concept-specific input by the learner. Four conditions are associated with this autonomic process of assessment. They are as follows (Hewson and Thornley, 1989; and as discussed in detail in Chapter 3):

C1: The new concept has to be 'Intelligible': In the framework of the existing knowledge of the learner, i.e. the learner's ALCONs in the relevant concept domain, the new concept should convey meaning (not necessarily the correct meaning) to the learner. Without intelligibility a concept has no cognitive status (Hewson and Thornley, 1989) for the learner. Schollum and Osborne (1985) call this the criterion of relevance.

C2: The concept has to be 'Plausible': The new concept should not only be intelligible but also seem to be true and valid to the learner, i.e. it should make sense in the framework of the learner's ALCONs.

C3: The new concept has to be 'Fruitful': The new concept should be such that the learner should find it useful, or, should be convinced that he can achieve something by using it. This achievement could be just logical consistency, leading to mental satisfaction in the learner's framework, or, could seem to have enough potential for fruitful use in future.

C4: The concept could be a source of 'Dissatisfaction' to the learner: This state may arise if (a) the learner finds that the new concept leads to conclusions which are in conflict with the existing ALCONs, or (b) they seem to be valid but are different from those arrived by other pupils using their respective ALCONs, or, (c) the new concept does not seem to be plausible, or, fruitful to the learner, or, (d) the connotation of the concept arrived at by the learner is in conflict with that advanced by the teacher (Dreyfus et al., 1990). Some of these have already been discussed under cognitive conflict but are repeated here to keep intact the framework developed by Posner et al. (1982) and Hewson (1982). The four learner centered inputs are presented in Fig. 5.2.

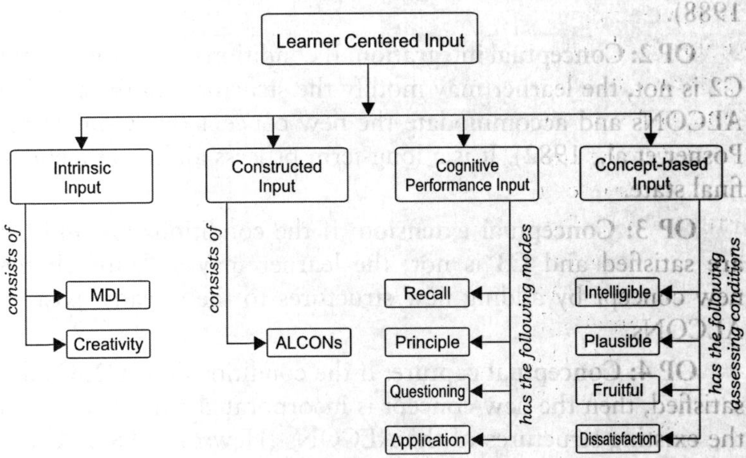

Fig. 5.2

5.3 Output

Out of the four broad inputs by the learner, the intrinsic inputs decide the ability of the learner to assimilate a concept having specific cognitive demand, the constructed inputs decides not only the background but also the mosaic of the new construction, the cognitive preference controls the quality of construction and the concept-bases inputs decide the final states of learning after the construction is complete. When a learner encounters a new concept, he/she makes use of the learner specific four kinds of inputs and is likely to suitably assimilate and accommodate the new concept through needed deconstruction and reconstruction of the epitaxy of his/her cognitive structures, resulting in one of the various possible equilibrated (a la Piaget) states, which we call the output (OP) of learning. They could be one of the following (as discussed in the chapter on conceptual change, Mohapatra, 1997):

OP 1: Conceptual rejection: This will occur if either the new concept does not satisfy the condition C1, or, the MDL of the learner is below the cognitive demand level of the concept. In such a situation the teacher's input (Teacher centered model) has to provide suitable props to ensure that C1 is satisfied, or, that the learner attains some amount of cognitive acceleration (Adey, 1988).

OP 2: Conceptual integration: If condition C1 is satisfied but C2 is not, the learner may modify the structures of the existing ALCONs and accommodate the new concept (Hewson, 1981, Posner et al., 1982). It is a long-term process aiming at a stable final state.

OP 3: Conceptual extension: If the conditions C1 and C2 are satisfied and C3 is not, the learner may still absorb the new concept by adding new structures to the already existing ALCONs.

OP 4: Conceptual capture: If the conditions C1, C2, C3 are satisfied, then the new concept is incorporated straight away in the existing structures of the ALCONs (Hewson, 1981; Posner et al., 1982). There are two possible sub-states under this as listed below:

OP 5: Conceptual dichotomy: If the conditions C1, C2 and C3 are satisfied but the concept is something different from the existing structures and cannot be incorporated into them by trial of various fitments, then the learner faces a problem. On the one hand, the learner is not prepared to abandon the old structures as he/she perhaps does not find anything wrong with them, and on the other hand he/she does not like to reject the new concept, as it satisfies the three basic conditions. In such a case the learner is likely to retain the new concept as a new, independent ALCON, side by side with his/her old ALCONs (Mohapatra, 1989). Villani (1992) also hypothesizes the co-presence of the old and the new knowledge.

OP 6: Conceptual exchange: This will happen when the conditions C1, C2 and C3 are satisfied, and the new concept seems to have better, broader and finer utility value than some of the old ALCONs. Arriving at such a conclusion goes through a process of trial and error, hypothesis formation and testing in so far as organizing his/her experiential world is concerned. In most of such cases a broad scale conceptual change takes place where some of the old ALCONs is/are replaced by the new one.

OP 7: Conceptual indifference: If C4 is strongly satisfied but C1, C2, C3 are also satisfied, the learner may neither accept nor reject the new concept. The learner may prefer, in such a situation, to keep his/her old ALCONs unchanged and remain indifferent to the new concept that is being taught. It may be noted that this is not a case of conceptual rejection.

These outputs are presented in Fig. 5.3. The seven possible outputs, in the event of a learner encountering a new event, instance, or a concept, form taxonomy of outputs (Mohapatra, 1997).

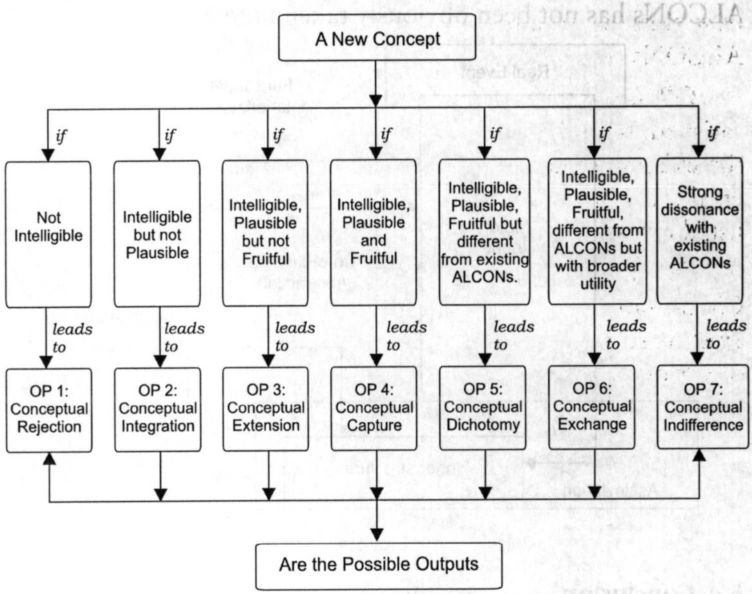

Fig. 5.3

The state of 'conceptual rejection' is also regarded as a constructivist 'output' on two counts: (a) On a dialectical level—rejecting a concept after consideration resulting in 'conceptual rejection' is an 'output' in the same sense as 'rest' is a state of 'uniform motion' with zero velocity, and (b) On a constructivist level—Before rejection the learner must have gone through several attempts of assimilation and accommodation which subsume the autogenic process of construction.

This taxonomy of outputs is more encompassing than other such attempts, like those by Dykstra, Jr. Boyle and Monarch (1992). The three types, 'differentiation', 'class extension' and 'reconceptualization' of conceptual change proposed by them are contained, in spirit and content, in 'conceptual integration', 'conceptual extension' and 'conceptual exchange', respectively, as proposed above.

To appreciate the richness and complexity of the output structures as presented in Fig. 5.3, one may compare it with that of Furth (1969), Fig. 5.4, where explicit account of the ALCONs has not been obviously taken note of.

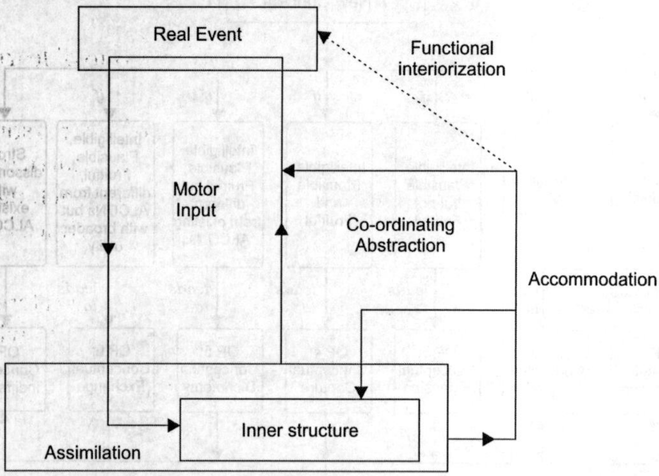

Fig. 5.4

5.4 Conclusion

In a classroom TLP the only two and most crucial human components are the teacher and the learner. The average teacher brings with him/her his/her conformist inputs whereas the learner brings with him/her his/her constructivist inputs. Since the efficacy of a TLP is measured not by the quality of teaching, but by the quality of learning, any input by the teacher will have functional meaning if and only if it works in consonance with the learner's constructivist inputs and endeavours and guides the learner to an output which best approaches the envisaged output of the formal schooling process. In the framework of the above mode, this optimization of learning demands that the following steps be taken:

- A class-wise assessment of the MDL of the learners be undertaken so as to provide crucial statistical picture to the curriculum framers and textbook writers.
- The cognitive demand of concepts, that are to be included in the curriculum for each class, be undertaken to provide informative bench marks to the curriculum framers and textbook writers.
- The learner's ALCONs in each concept domain be diagnosed and mapped to help the teachers to plan teaching strategies.
- If possible genesis of the ALCONs of a group of learners be identified.
- Steps be taken for mass orientation of all personnel involved, right from the planning, to curriculum framing, to textbook writing, to classroom teaching, to evaluation, about the constructivist approach and this learner-centered input-output model.
- Teachers may be apprised of the cognitive preference modes so that they may try to adopt methods which will help the learner to go from the "Recall" mode to the "Principle" mode.
- In all teacher orientation programmes emphasis may be put on the 'Conceptual Change' model and the 7 possible outputs, with the aim in view to impress upon the teachers to use strategies so that the outputs like 'Conceptual Rejection' or, 'Conceptual Indifference' are never manifested.

We have presented here a four dimensional input and made an effort to provide key information for the measurement and/or use of the inputs in a classroom situation. The outputs have been delineated in the conceptual change model of the constructivist approach. It is hoped that this usable model will initiate the much needed step towards a functional and pragmatic composite model.

References

Adey, P. (1988). Cognitive acceleration review and prospects. *International Journal of Science Education*, 10(2): 121-34.

Ausubel, D. (1968). *Educational Psychology: A Cognitive View*. New York: Holt, Rinehart and Winston.

Bruner, J. (1960). *The Process of Education*. Massachusetts: Harward University Press.

Case, R. (1985). *Intellectual Development—Birth to Adulthood*. London: Academic Press.

Dreyfus, A., Jungworth, E. and Eliovitch, R. (1990). Applying the 'Cognitive Conflict' Strategy for conceptual change—some implications, difficulties and problems. *Science Education*, Vol. 74, No. 5, pp. 555-69.

Driver, R., and Erickson, G. (1983). Theories-in-Action: Some theoretical and empirical issues in the study of students' conceptual framework in science. *Studies in Science Education*, Vol. 10, pp. 37-60.

Dykstra, D., Boyle, F.C. and Monarch, I.A. (1992). Studying conceptual change in learning physics. *Science Education*, Vol. 76, No. 6, pp. 615-52.

Fensham, P., Gunstone, R. and White, R. (1994). The Content of Science. *A Constructivist Approach to its Teaching and Learning*. London: Falmer Press.

Furth, H. (1969). *Piaget and Knowledge*. Englewood Cliffs, N.J.: Prentice Hall.

Gilbert, J.K. and Swift, D.J. (1985). Towards a Lakatosian analysis of the Piagetian and Alternative Conceptions research programme. *Science Education*, Vol. 69, pp. 681-96.

Glynn, S. and Duit, R. (Eds.) (1995). *Learning Science in Schools: Research Forming Practice*. Hillsdale, N.J.: Lawrence Erlbaum.

Hashweh, M. (1986). Towards an explanation of conceptual change. *European Journal of Science Education*, Vol. 8, pp. 229-49.

Hewson, P.W. (1981). A conceptual change approach to learning science. *European Journal of Science Education*, Vol. 3, No. 4, pp. 383-96.

—— (1982). A case study of conceptual change in special relativity: The influence of prior knowledge is learning. *European Journal of Science Education*, Vol. 4, No. 4, pp. 61-78.

Hewson, P.W. and Thornley, R. (1989). The condition of conceptual change in the classroom. *International Journal of Science Education*, Vol. 11, No. 5, pp. 541-53.

Isaacs, P.A. (1976). Some conservation concepts in Jamaican grade 6 students. Unpublished M.A. *Thesis, School of Education*, University of West Indies. Mona.

Johnson, D. (1977). *High School Mathematics and Science Concept Profile*, Report written for Saskatchwon Public Board of Education, Saskatchwon, Saskatchwon, Canada.

Kuhn, T. (1970). *The structure of scientific revolution*. Chicago: University of Chicago Press.

Lawson, A.E. (1977). The development and validation of a classroom test of formal reasoning. Paper presented at the *Annual Convention of National Association for Research in Science Teaching*, Cincinati, March 24.

Longeot, F. (1965). *Analyse statistique de trios Genetiques Collectifs*, BINOP 4, Bulletin de L' Institute National D' Etude Du Travail et D' Orientation Professioinalle, pp. 219-37. (Statistical analysis of the Convective genetic tests.)

Mohapatra, J.K. (1989). The fourth dimension of teaching-learning of science: Its characteristics and implications. *Indian Educational Review*, Vol. 24, No. 3, pp. 1-17.

—— (1997). Taxonomy of conceptual change, Review of two anchoring instructional strategies and a functional model of teaching. *Indian Educational Review*, Vol. 32, No. 1, pp. 36-55.

Mohapatra, J.K. and Mahapatra, M. (1997). Usability of Science Reasoning Tasks under Indian conditions: An assessment. *Indian Educational Review*, Vol. 32, No. 3, pp. 124-32.

Niaz, M. (1988) Manipulation of M-demand of Chemistry problems and its effect on student performance: A Neo-Piagetian Study. *Journal of Research in Science Teaching*, Vol. 25, No. 8, pp. 643-57.

—— (1991). Role of epistemic subject on Piaget's genetic Epistemology and its importance for Science Education. *Journal of Research in Science Teaching*, Vol. 28, No. 7, pp. 569-80.

Okebukola, P.A. and Jegede, O.H. (1988). Cognitive Preference and learning mode on determinants of meaningful learning through concept mapping. *Science Education*, Vol. 72, No. 4, pp. 489-500.

Pascual-Leone, J. (1977). A theory of constructive operators: A Neo-Piagetian Model of Conservation and problem of horizontal decalage. Paper presented at the *Annual Meeting of the Canadian Psychological Association*, Montreal.

—— (1987). An organismic process model of Wilkin's field-dependence-independence. In T. Globerson and T. Zelniker, (Eds.) *Cognitive Style and Cognitive Development*, Norwood, New Jersey: Ablex publishing corporation.

Pinard, A. and Laurendeau, M. (1969). Stage in Piaget's cognitive development theory: Exegesis of a concept. In D. Elkind and J.H. Flavell (Eds.), *Studies in Cognitive Development*. London: Oxford University Press.

Posner, G.J., Strike, K.A., Hewson, P.W. and Gerzog, W.A. (1982). Accommodation of a scientific conception: Towards a theory of conceptual change. *Science Education*, Vol. 72, No. 1, pp. 103-13.

Raven, R.J. (1973). The development of a test of Piaget's Logical operations. *Science Education*, Vol. 57, No. 3, pp. 377-85.

Rowell, J.A. and Hoffman, R.J. (1975). Group tests for distinguishing formal from concrete thinkers. *Journal of Research in Science Teaching*, Vol. 12, No. 2, pp. 157-64.

Schollum, B. and Osborne, R. (1985). Relating the new to the familiar. In R. Osborne and P. Freyberg (Eds.), *Learning in Science: The Implications of Children's Science*. London: Heinemann.

Shayer, M. and Adey, P. (1981). *Towards a Science and Science Teaching*. London: Heinemann.

Shayer, M. and Wharry, D. (1973). Piaget in the classroom I: Testing a whole class at the same time. *School Science Review*, Vol. 54, No. 191, pp. 447-57.

Shulman, L.S. (1987). Knowledge and teaching. Foundations of the new reform. *Harvard Educational Review*, 57: 1-22.

Steffe, L.P., and Gale, J. (Eds.) (1995). *Constructivism in Education*. Hillsdale NJ: Lawrence Evebaurn.

Sudhir, M.A., and Varpari, K. (1991). Creativity test in India. *Journal of Creative Behaviour*, 25(1): 27-33.

Tamir, P. (1985). Meta analysis of cognitive preference and learning, *Journal of Research in Science Teaching*, Vol. 22, No. 1, pp. 1-18.

Tisher, R.P. and Dale, L.G. (1975). *Understanding in Science Test*. Victoria: Australian Council of Educational Research.

Torrence, E.P. (1965). *Torrance Test of Creative Thinking: Verbal forms A & B*. Printson, N.J: Personal Press.

—— (1968). Examples and Rationales of Test Tasks for assessing creative abilities. *Journal of Creative Behaviour*, Vol. 2, No. 3, pp. 52-57.

Villani, A. (1992). Conceptual change in science and science education. *Science Education*. Vol. 76, No. 2, pp. 223-37.

von Glasersfeld, E. (1992). A constructivists view of learning and teaching. In R. Duit, F. and Goldbergand, H. Niedderer (Eds.) (1995). *Research in Physics Learning: Theoretical Issues and Empirical Studies*. Kiel, Germany: IPN at the University of Kiel.

Vygotsky, L. (1962). *Thought and Language*. E. Hanfmann and G. Vakar (Eds. and Translators), Cambridge, M.A.: M.I.T. Press.

—— (1978). *Mind in Society: at the development of higher physiological process*. M. Cole, V. John Steiner, S. Scribner and E. Souberman (Eds.). Cambridge, M.A. Harvard University Press.

West, L. (1982). The researchers and their work. In C. Sutton and L. West (Eds.), *Investigating Children's Existing Ideas*, The Report and analysis of a research seminar held in April 1982 at the University of Leicester, U.K.

6 Teaching Models in Constructivist Framework

6.1 Introduction

There is a saying: "The proof of the pudding lies in eating". In the present framework a parallel and more general statement will be: "The quality of a theory, law, model, activity, or technique lies in its applicative and/or predictive efficacy." Thus the quality of the Constructivist Paradigm lies in its applicative efficacy. A conservative list of the major areas where it has to be pervasively applied are,

- Teaching model/methods,
- Learning modes,
- Designing of activities,
- Evaluation techniques,
- Designing of softwares,
- Multimedia approaches,
- ICT,
- Formulation of educational policies,
- Drafting of curriculum,
- Drafting of textbooks, supplementary reading materials,
- Drafting of teachers' manual,
- Refining and redefining of school environment,
- Teacher training protocols.

This chapter deals only with the attempts made in transporting this paradigm into the classroom by designing teaching models. However, to comprehend the viability of these models, one must be very clear about their objectives. Of course in simple words and briefly stated the one point objective of these models, when implemented, is

> To help the learner construct any concept in a way the teacher expects him/her to construct.

But from a macroscopic point of view the broader objectives are four in number:

Objective-1: In constructivism learning is visualized as a purposeful, intentional, ontogenic (Glasersfeld, 1992) sequence of constructions of structures by the cognizing subject. Whenever the learner encounters (not necessarily only inside the classroom) a new concept, event or instance, an interpretative and/or integrative interaction of it with his/her own alternative conceptions immediately starts. This process of conceptual change (Hewson, 1981; Posner et al., 1982) goes on all the time in the cognitive apitaxy of the learner. The learning outcome may or may not conform to the accepted connotation of the concept, event or instance. The teaching model, when implemented, should aim at guiding the learner to adopt the path of correct conceptual change.

Objective-2: Constructivism outlines that the learner's sole purpose in taking a self-designed path of conceptual change so as to learn a concept is (Staver, 1998; von Glasersfeld, 1995) to serve the learner's organization of his/her experiential world. Thus, the learner is simply abandoned (Osborne, 1996) on the ocean of experience condemned to search for knowledge that is 'Viable'. And in future he/she may develop better ideas in the sense that they are 'More Viable'. However, the teaching model should help the learner learn a concept not simply on the basis of 'viability' to organized his/her experiential world, but on the basis of their objective 'Reliability' and 'Validity', which are the key to ensure and acquire scientific knowledge. Thus, the learner should be made conscious of the fact that the touch stone to assess the cognition of any concept by him/her is not 'Viability' but 'Reliability' and 'Validity'.

Objective-3: A learner learns continuously by following a self-designed path of conceptual change and acquires viable knowledge. In other words, the learner in this entire scheme develops and implements his/her own technique to learn how to learn. The teaching model based on constructivism should help the learner to internalize the scientist's technique to learn how to learn. The learner may be encouraged to appreciate the importance of fair testing, the identification and control of variables, the generation of sound hypotheses, the recognition and measurement of sources of error, the criteria by which one theory is distinguished from another, repetition of experimental determination, and the use of averaging. This will ultimately help him/her to distinguish scientific knowledge based on objectivity, reliability and validity from pseudo—scientific knowledge based on viability.

Objective-4: Since the teacher is the basic human input to implement the teaching models, these models should also envisage to bring about essential changes in the teacher through practice and induction. These teaching models should help teacher to transform himself/herself from

- a Director to an equal Actor
- a Dictator to a Negotiator
- a Teacher to a Researcher
- a Transmitter to a Facilitator
- a Mechanical performer to an Innovator
- a Planner for teaching to an Organizer for learning (Vito Perrine, 1991)
- a Rigid guide to a Flexible guide
- a Prescriptor to a Diagnostician
- a conclusion presenter to an Experimenter.

Any teaching model based on constructivism should aim at achieving all or some of the above four objectives. Further, every teaching model should take note of the strongly evidenced fact that the alternative conceptions of the learner pervasively influences (Posner et al., 1982; Hewson, 1981) the degree and quality of learning vindicating Ausubel's (1968) statement,

> If you ask me to identify the single most important factor that determines the degree and quality of learning I will say identify what the child knows and teach him accordingly.

For achieving constructivism the key question is how to change instruction from traditional practices to constructivist way of teaching and what are the teaching path ways. All constructivist teaching models are guided generally by five basic elements (Tolman and Hardy, 1995); activating prior knowledge, acquiring knowledge, understanding knowledge, using knowledge and reflecting on knowledge. The existing constructivist teaching models may be grouped as follows:

1. Earlier models (1980-1990)
2. Later models (1990-2000)
3. Recent models (2000 onwards).

6.2 Earlier Models

(i) **Nussbaum and Novick Model (1982):** This is one of the first constructivist teaching models (Nussbaum and Novick, 1982) for science. According to this model accommodation leads to conceptual change where the central concept is replaced or reorganized. Accommodation will begin when there is dissatisfaction of the learner with an existing conception and it proceeds until and unless the learner considers a new conception to be more intelligible and fruitful. Nussbaum and Novick suggested that accommodation could be facilitated in three steps as follows:

- exposing event
- discrepant event
- elaboration.

"Exposing event" i.e. exposing alternative conceptions, that would require students to state their preconceptions and debate them with each other, creating cognitive conflict which student cannot solve. The student's inability to solve the problem is brought about by presentation of a "discrepant event". A discrepant event is simply an inexplicable condition/statement or situation. The discrepant event creates a state of cognitive dissonance or cognitive disequilibrium. Once the students are in state of disequilibrium they are motivated by curiosity to acquire knowledge, i.e. epistemic curiosity to reduce cognitive dissonance. Traditional teaching methods seldom provide opportunities to encounter cognitive dissonance and motivation for questioning and interactions.

(ii) **Generative Learning Model (1985):** Cosgrove and Osborne (1985) proposed the "Generative Learning Model". Generative learning is the active process of constructing links between new and old knowledge, or a personal understanding how new idea fit into an individual's web of known concept. The essence of this model is that mind or brain is not a passive consumer of information; instead it actively constructs its own interpretations of information and draws inferences from them. Learning takes place when links are generated between the contexts of short-term memory and individual's knowledge base of long-term memory. The above model is organized into four phases:

- **Preliminary phase:** In this phase the teacher ascertains the students' views through surveys or other activities.
- **Focus phase:** The students' attention is focused on a phenomenon and their ideas about that phenomenon. Thus opportunity is given to the students to explore the context of the concept; preferably within daily life or real life situation, i.e. the students clarify their own views.
- **Challenge phase:** In this phase the students present their views to the groups and the teacher presents his/her view (which is correct) and then the views are discussed and compared in order to facilitates accommodation.
- **Application phase:** The students after acquiring the scientific knowledge or the correct concept use the accepted viewpoint to solve a range of problems. Thus the students get opportunities for application of new ideas across a range of contexts.

- Generative model helps teachers to detect zones of proximal development and foster social dynamics that improve cognitive environments for learning.

(iii) **The Ideational Confrontation Model (1985)**: This is a conceptual change instructional model suggested by A.B. Champagne, R.F. Gunstone and L.E. Klopfer in 1985. Like other conceptual change Instructional models (Cosgrove and Osborne, 1985; Chin and Brewer, 1993; Nussbaum and Novick, 1982). This model is also based on:

- Revealing student preconceptions.
- Discussing and evaluating preconceptions.
- Creating conceptual conflict with those preconceptions.
- Encouraging and guiding conceptual restructuring.

This model is especially designed to alter students' concept within a particular domain. It involves the following steps:

- Students make prediction about a common physical situation.
- Each student develops an analysis supporting his/her predictions.
- Students are allowed to discuss, argue his/her viewpoints with the peer group.
- The teacher/facilitator/instructor demonstrate the physical situation and explain the science behind it.
- The teacher allows the students to compare their analyses with the scientific one.

(iv) **Driver and Oldham Model (1986)**: Like the previous models (Nussbaum and Novick, 1982; Cosgrove and Osborne, 1985), this model (Driver and Oldham, 1986) has also two key phases: (i) gathering information about the students' prior knowledge or students' current thinking (elicitation). (ii) Presenting students with some form of stimulus challenging their thinking process. The desired outcome is lead to meaningful, fruitful learning. The constructivist teaching model developed by the children's Learning in Science Project team and given by Driver and Oldham consists of the following five phases:

- **Orientation phase:** The students are given opportunity to develop a sense of purpose and motivation for the topic.
- **Elicitation phase:** The students make their ideas explicit through discussion or writing.
- **Restructuring phase:** Students are exposed to conflicting views of other students or to conflicting situations and the teacher presents the scientific view.
- **Application phase:** The students apply their new conceptions to a variety of situations.
- **Review phase:** students reflect on their change of ideas.

The schematic diagram of the model is depicted in Fig. 6.1

Orientation
↓
Elicitation of ideas
↓
Restructuring of ideas
↓
Clarification and exchange
↓
Explosives to conflict situations
↓
Construction of new ideas
↓
Application of ideas
↓
Review change in ideas

Fig. 6.1: Constructivist teaching model developed by the Children's Learning in Science Project team.

(v) **Niedderer Model (1987):** This model (Niedderer, 1987) aims not to replace students theories (related to real life situation) by scientific theory but to allow them to arrive at a conscious knowledge of both and to learn scientific concepts by learning the differences between every day life thinking and scientific thinking. The model consists of six stages:

- **Preparation:** The teaching process which precedes the intervention and which may contain tools and concepts that may be drawn on.
- **Initiation:** An open ended problem is posed by the teacher.
- **Performance:** This phase includes formulating questions or hypotheses, planning and performing experiments, making observations, theoretical discussions, formulation of findings.
- **Discussion of findings:** The findings of different students are to be discussed in the class.
- **Comparison with science:** Class findings are compared with facts. Differences are stated and possible reasons for those differences are discussed.
- **Reflection:** Students are encouraged to look back on the process of performance and to consider the particular questions or difficulties which have arisen.

The students are given autonomy and opportunity to construct their own knowledge. The author claims that "It seems plausible that their teaching strategy has started for teaching-learning process by letting students come to own results and by comparing those results systematically with the results of scientific research."

(vi) **Needham's Five Phase Constructivist Model** (1987): Teaching-learning process in a constructivist environment should be reflective, collaborative, inquiry-based and evolving. Needham (1987) has introduced five-phase constructivist based learning process. This model requires the students to engage in several phases in order to generate meaningful learning. This model consists of:

- **Orientation:** This phase is intended to gain students' attention and to motivate the students. The teacher needs to present a problem or event with conflicting ideas.

- **Generating ideas:** The students' previous ideas about the concept have to be identified applying techniques like concept mapping or by asking questions.
- **Restructuring ideas:** In this phase the previous ideas need to be expanded or modified through investigation, exploration by allowing the students to do activities (Hands-on and minds-on) that requires science skills, group communication, etc.
- **Applying the ideas:** The ideas are applied to new situations by solving new problems, designing new projects.
- **Reflection:** The students are allowed to reflect on the changes made to the ideas by self-assessment on the change made, or by reflective questioning.

6.3 Later Models

(i) **Neale, Smith and Johnson Model (1990):** This model (Neale, Smith and Johnson Model, 1990) is based on a social constructivist perspective. Six characteristics of conceptual change leading to constructivist teaching practices have been identified as follows:

- Instruction is directed towards contradicting children's mental schemes.
- Links are made to prior lessons and to children's formal experiences.
- Children's conceptions are elicited through predictions and explanations.
- Children test their predication in activities that allow them to discover contradictory evidence and contrasting explanations. Children present their ideas to each other and debate is encouraged.
- The children summarize and contrast alternative views.

This model has been successfully used by the authors in bringing about conceptual change in children.

(ii) **Problem-based Learning Model (1992-95):** Norman and Schmidt (1992) developed three steps for problem-based-learning (PBL) model. In this model the teacher present student with a set of problems then the students are allowed to work in groups to analyse the problem, discuss, research and produce tentative explanation, solution or recommendations. The three steps in the model are:

- acquisition of factual knowledge.
- mastery of general principal or concepts that can be transferred to solve similar problems.
- acquisition of prior examples that can be used in future problem-solving situation of a similar nature.

In this method the students have to conduct research, coordinate with peers and generate unique ideas. This is not a traditional instructional models and may appear risky, scary and uncertain to teacher as well as students, however once adopted this environment is meaningful and rewarding.

PBL helps in engagement in learning due to cognitive dissonance, relevance to real world scenarios, opportunities for critical thinking, meta-cognitive growth, and real-world authenticity that promotes transfer and recall (Frinkle and Trop, 1995). PBL developed by Frinkle and Trop consists of seven specific tacks:

- Determining whether a problem exists.
- Creating an exact statement of the problem.
- Identifying information needed to understand the problem.
- Identifying resources to be used together information.
- Generating possible solutions.
- Analyzing the solutions.
- Presenting the solution, orally or/and in writing.

(iii) **Model Proposed by Yager (1991):** This constructivist teaching model (Yager, 1991) deals with the main issues of conceptual change and conceptual change supporting conditions. Conceptual change can be achieved by following the steps as listed below:

- **Invitation:** Observe surroundings for points of curiosity; ask questions; consider possible responses to questions; note unexpected phenomena identify situations where student perception vary.
- **Exploration:** Engage in focused play; brainstorm possible alternatives; look for information; experiment with materials; design of model; collect and organize data, employ problem-solving strategy select appropriate resources; discuss solutions with others; design and conduct experiments; evaluate choices; engage in debate; identify risks and consequences; define parameters of an investigation, analyse data.
- **Posing explanations and solutions:** Communicate information and ideas; construct and explain a model; construct a new explanation; review and critique solutions; utilize peer evaluation; assemble multiple answers/solutions; determine appropriate closure; integrate a solution with existing knowledge and experiences.
- **Taking action:** Make decisions; apply knowledge and skills; transfer knowledge and skills; share information and ideas; ask new questions; develop products and promote ideas; use models and ideas to elicit discussions and acceptance by others.

(iv) **Model Proposed by Scott (1992):** In this model the students are given many opportunities to make their own experiences and to construct their own meaning of the phenomenon observed. A constructivist scheme of teaching for the particle model of matter has been given by Scott (1992). There are six phases as follows:

- **Orientation and elicitation of pupil ideas:** Pupils are asked to describe and explain some simple phenomena related to properties of matter. In this way their own ideas are made explicit and open for inspection.

- **The nature of scientific theory and theory making:** Pupils are introduced to the nature of scientific theory and theory making through simulations and discussion. This step helps for preparation of the fourth step.
- **A pattern of properties of solids, liquids and gases:** Pupils work to identify and develop a pattern of properties in behaviour of solids, liquids and gases.
- **Pupil theory making:** Pupils develop their own theories as to the nature of solids, liquids and gases. They are encouraged to base their theory making upon the pattern of properties identified in the previous step i.e. step-ii.
- **Review, reflection and movement towards accepted theory:** Pupil theories are compared and evaluated by members of the class. The teacher introduces activities to help pupils towards the accepted scientific view.
- **Application of accepted theory:** Pupils are given opportunity to apply the accepted theory to different situations.

(v) **Glasson and Lalik Model (1993):** This is the language oriented learning cycle model. This model (Glasson and Lalik Model, 1993) consisted of three phases as follows:

- **Exploration:** In which the students experience cognitive disequilibrium through experiences and concrete materials.
- **Clarification:** In this phase the learners construct new knowledge to account for their observations.
- **Elaboration:** In this phase the students are engaged in divergent problem-solving.

(vi) **Model Proposed by Wittrock (1994):** There is raising number of attempts to provide teachers with guidelines how to implement constructivist ideas in planning science instruction. The model worked out by the cognitive psychologist M. Wittrock (Wittrock, 1994) listed the main issues of conceptual change. Conceptual change supporting conditions consisting of five stages are as follows:

(a) **Knowledge, experience and conceptions**
- Learn the students conceptions and beliefs about science, beliefs about their own abilities to learn science, and beliefs about the meaning and usefulness of science in their daily lives.
- Learn the students conceptions of what they must do to learn science.
- Teach the student that learning with understanding is a generative process. It is different from passively reading and remembering information.

(b) **Motivation**
- Teach the students a distinct type of motivation that involves:
  (a) taking responsibility for learning.
  (b) believing that they can and will succeed at understanding science conception and through them gain a deeper understanding of complex everyday experience.
- Design instruction to enable students to experience frequent success at understanding science through using generative learning procedures.

(c) **Attentions**
- Teach students to attend the central problems of constructing meaning for science concepts. Teach them to focus their attention on the problems of generating a structure of information and on the problems of relating science to other subjects and to everyday experience.

(d) **Generation**

- After learning the students models, beliefs and conceptions, teach a scientific model in relation to the students' models. The primary goal is not to "cover the subject matter" or to "present only the scientists' model" or to "show that the students' conceptions are wrong", instead the primary goal is to lead the students to generate a more scientific and more useful model than they now have. The goal may not be attained quickly because it involves student generation of understanding. The generation of meaning requires student effort and thought that go beyond learning from teacher reward or punishment.
- Generate for them, initially at least, examples and applications of the two types of relations that facilitate comprehension: (i) relations among the concepts to be learned, and (ii) relations between these science concepts and student knowledge and experience.
- Lead students to generate these two types of relations as a way to comprehend science.
- Design instruction to involve these two types of relations and to increase student ability to use generative learning strategies that enhance comprehension through relation building.

(e) **Metacognition**

- Teach students to be aware of and to consciously use their thought processes, including learning strategies, comprehension strategies, attention directing strategies, attributions, plans and monitoring strategies to comprehend, transfer, and apply scientific concepts to attain a greater understanding of the world and an enhanced ability to solve everyday problems.

(vii) **ICON Model (1995)**: Robert O. McClintock and John B. Black (1995) of Columbia University Teachers College derived a design model from several computer technology-supported learning environments at the Dalton School in New York. The interpretation construction (ICON) model consists up seven stages:

(a) **Observation**: Students make observations of primary source material embedded in their natural context or simulations thereof.

(b) **Interpretation construction**: Students interpret their observations and explain their reasoning.

(c) **Conceptualization**: Students construct contexts for their explanations.

(d) **Cognitive apprenticeship**: Students serve as apprentices to teachers to master observation, interpretation and conceptualization.

(e) **Collaboration**: Students collaborate in observation, interpretation and conceptualization.

(f) **Multiple interpretations**: Students gain cognitive flexibility by being exposed to multiple interpretations from other students and from expert examples.

(g) **Multiple manifestations**: Students gain transferability by seeing multiple manifestations of the same interpretations.

Using this model exemplar material on the topic motion has been developed as follows:

Exemplar in Science

Grade/Class	:	IX
Text Book	:	Science Text Book (NCERT)
Subject	:	Science
Topic	:	Motion
Concepts	:	Rest and Motion
Duration	:	One and half hour

Learning Objectives

(a) **Process-based:** Students are helped to develop

- Originality
- Open-mindedness

- Reflective thinking
- Flexibility/multiple interpretation
- Concept construction
- Creativity
- Respect for evidence
- Curiosity
- Co-operation
- Intellectual honesty
- The ability to form hypothesis

(b) **Content-based:** Students will be guided to

- Test and refine their own concepts about the concepts, 'Rest' and 'Motion',
- Correlate their reconstructed concepts with various life-centered situation, events, instances,
- Consider and internalize the importance of these concepts in areas other than Kinematics of physics.

The teacher may create the learning situation by asking the students:

Rest

Learning situation: The teacher may create the learning situation by asking the students—Named some bodies at rest,

Students are seen (research findings) to name only those bodies which are present in their immediate surrounding like, chair, table, duster, blackboard, etc.

Note: These replies are not alternative conceptions, but are manifestations of 'Conceptual Situatedness' in their minds, i.e. students have the habit of picking up examples from their immediate vicinity.

To remove this 'situatedness' and infuse 'flexibility' in their thought process ICT can be profitable used.

Observation: While confirming that their answers are correct the teacher may show video clippings/diagrams of

- A mountain

- Their school building
- Big trees in a park/farm/forest
- The village pond
- The road in front of the school.

And ask—

"Are these bodies at rest?"

Possibly there will be three groups of answers:

Group-1 : Students will strongly respond that all the above bodies are rest.

Group-2 : This group will respond that all the above bodies except the trees are at rest, because they have seen that when there is a wind, leaves and branches of the trees shake and move.

Group-3 : This group will respond that all the above bodies except the pond are at rest, because they have seen that when there is wind or if one throws a stone into the pond, waves are created in the water of the pond.

Contextualization: The class can now be divided into three groups along the above lines and a discussion amongst them may be initiated to arrive at a single conclusion. Teacher may channelize the discussion when arguments, advanced by any group, are out of context.

Teacher may help the student to arrive at the conclusions that,

(a) When there is a wind the leaves and branches of a tree do move but the tree as whole does not move from its place (so the trees are at rest and)

(b) When there is a wind or a stone is thrown into the pond, waves, of course, are created on the water surface, but the pond as a whole does not move from its place (so the pond is at rest).

Through this step students will also learn how open-mindedness leads to acceptable and correct understanding which is essential for organizing the experiential world.

Thus now is the time to lead them to a higher level of reflective thinking.

Cognitive apprenticeship: Teacher may ask some leading question—

Q.1: Are you now sure that the above five objects, the video clippings of which you have seen, are at rest?

The students will of course answer in the affirmative. The teacher may then ask,

Q.2: Are you sure? (Students will reply 'YES')

Now state—"So we agree that the 5 bodies are at rest. That is a gentleman's agreement between you and me. Do not go back on your words at a later stage."

This statement will have a dramatic effect on the students, will arouse their curiosity and get them focused in the teaching-learning activity.

Now teacher may show them,

- A working model of the solar system, available in Science Kit box, or
- A simulated video-film of the solar-system, or
- A chart of the solar-system.

Then ask—

"In the solar-system does the earth move round the sun?"

Obviously the unanimous answer from the students will be "Yes".

The teacher may ask, "Are you sure?" so as to dramatize the proceedings.

Some students may laugh on hearing such a redundant question. In any case all will reply, "Yes Sir, we are sure."

Now the teacher may make a statement. "Since the earth is moving constantly, the mountain, the school building, the trees, the pond and the road must also be moving continuously with the earth. Is it not?"

Because of "Inertia of thought" many students will say "Yes, Sir". But others will immediately comprehend the problem.

The teacher may dramatically say, "But a little earlier all of us had a gentlemanly agreement that these bodies are at REST".

On hearing this silence will descend on the entire class. The students will be immersed in a state of 'Cognitive Conflict'. They will ask themselves—what is correct? Are the said bodies at rest or are they moving?

Teacher must realize that generating 'Cognitive Conflict' is one of the most powerful tools for cognitive negotiation.

Collaboration (Group work): The class may be divided into two groups. Group-1: Those who opine that the above objects are at REST. Group-2: Those who opine that the above objects are MOVING.

The groups may be allowed to crystallize their thoughts in 5 minutes and then the leader of each group may present his/her arguments in support of the conclusion of the respective group.

Interpretation construction: Teacher may now again follow the method of cognitive Negotiation and ask the following questions:

Q.1. Those who are of the opinion that these bodies are at the rest, where are they, as observers, located?

Q.2. Those who are of the opinion that these bodies are moving because the earth is moving, where are they, as observers, located?

Q.3. (This question is a corollary to Q. 2) Standing on the earth can you know through meaningful discussion the teacher may help the students to arrive at the following questions.

Q.1. Those who are of the opinion that these bodies are at rest, where are they, as observers, located following conclusions:

(a) The person (say Mary) who opines that the mountains, etc. are at REST is a person who is positioned on the earth.

(b) A person positioned on the earth will not be able to know that the earth is moving. (Teacher many mention in passing that through the use of refined experiment, like the oscillations of the Focult's pendulum, a person positioned on the earth can know that the earth is moving.)

(c) Only by going into outer space in a space shuttle a person (Say Mary) can observe that the earth is moving and so the mountains, etc. are moving.

(d) In (a) and (c) the observer is the same person Mary. But in (a) she is positioned on the earth's surface and in (c) she is positioned in the outer space. So though in both the cases the person is the same, Mary, but as observers she is different.

(e) Thus the state of REST of a body is a conclusion for a specific set of observers. Change the observer and the state of REST of the body will change.

(f) There is nothing called as the state of ABSOLUTE REST of a body.

Motion: Before the discussion of MOTION teacher should ascertain student's concept about MOTION. Because like having a concept that 'REST is 'ABSOLUTE', students do have a concept that 'MOTION' of a body is 'ABSOLUTE'.

Learning situation: Teacher may ask—

"Name some bodies in motion."

Students are seen (researching findings) to name only those moving bodies which are present in their immediate experience, like, car, cycle, train, etc.

This is again a manifestation of 'Conceptual Situatedness.' To remove this 'situated ness' and infuse 'Flexibility' in their thought process ICT can be meaningfully used.

Observation: While confirming that their answers are correct the teacher may show video films (not clippings) or diagrams or pictures of the following:

- Water rushing out from a dam, the sluice gates of which have been opened.

- Launching of a satellite.
- A butterfly flying in a garden.
- Clouds floating in the sky.
- Planets moving round the sun.

On asking: "Whether the above bodies are in motion?" All the students will uniformly reply that the bodies are in motion.

It may be noted that this observation extends their sphere of conceptualization from objects in their immediate surrounding to a much larger domain. This in fact is a manifestation of Vygostky's 'Zone of Proximal Development'.

Contextualization: Now the teacher may show the students a CD film where a car is moving on the road or a train is moving in a natural back drop. The teacher may then make a statement:

> At some time or other each of you must have traveled in car, or in a bus, or, in a train.

The students will nod their heads or say 'YES' in affirmation.

The teacher will again show them the CD film depicting a train moving somewhere and using the technique of 'Thought Experiment' ask—

> Assume that you are sitting inside this moving train. Then as you look out through the open window, then for you, do the trees appear to move or actually move?

All the students will definitely and spontaneously reply—"The trees appear to move."

Cognitive Apprenticeship: Now teacher may ask:

Q.1. Are you sure that the motion of the trees is an appearance? The students will of course answer in the affirmative. Then ask—

Q.2. Are you sure? (Students will answer 'YES'.)

Now state: "So you agree that the motion of the trees is in an appearance. This is a gentleman's agreement between you and me. Do not go back on your words at a later stage."

This statement will have a dramatic effect on the students, will arouse their curiosity and get them focused in the teaching-learning activity.

The strong unanimous reply by the students that the "motion of the trees is an appearance":

- Indicates the 'Conceptual Situatedness' by the students in a new sense. The students have been clearly told that they are sitting inside the moving train, yet at the mental level they are still on the ground with the fixed conception that the trees are always at rest.
- It creates a situation where teacher can be one party and the students, combinedly can be the other party. Thus the teacher ceases to be the 'Director' and becomes an equal 'Actor' in the teaching-learning process. Such a transformation of the teacher's role is an important characteristic of constructivism.
- This also opens up a possibility where the students can argue with the teacher on the academic front and ask questions. This transformation of the role of the students is a positive step to teach them to "learn how to learn", and open up.
- This step will also teach the students the importance of experiments to arrive at dependable conclusions and expose them to the processes of science.

The teacher may make a statement:

"All of you say that sitting in the train when you look outside you see that the trees are moving and that the motion of the trees is an appearance. I do not agree with you. I am of the opinion that sitting in the moving train, for you; the motion of the trees is a reality. So let us proceed scientifically and examine who is correct, I or all of you."

"Do you agree with me?" The reply obviously will be "Yes, Sir."

The teacher may ask "Suppose you are standing at the gate and you observe that a car is moving on the road. How do you know that the car is moving?" Several answers may come:

- Sir, we see that the car is moving.

- Sir, if we measure the distance of the car from us, we will observe that the distance of the car from us is increasing with time, etc.

Teacher may ask: "If we take the photograph of the car in a movie camera or video camera what will we observe?"

The teacher may even show them the video film of a moving car and ask—"By looking at the film how do you know that the car is moving?" and guide them to the conclusion that in the film, from frame to frame the position of the car is changing.

Now the teacher may expose them to a 'Thought Experiment'. It may be noted that 'Thought Experiment' is an important tool for extending the students' domain of active conceptualization.

Teacher may make the following statement-cum-question:

For a moment suppose that you are standing at the gate and a moving car has just crossed you. Further imagine that one end of a roll of twine is tied to the bonnet of the car and the full roll is in your hand. Now if the car is moving and you look at the roll in your hand, what will you observe?

The students will definitely answer: "We will see that the roll of twine will open out."

The teacher may ask: "Do you have any doubt?" The students will answer: "No, Sir."

The teacher will say: "We have reported 4 independent experiments, (a) Your seeing that the car is moving, (b) The distance of the car from you increasing with time, (c) In the movie film position of the car changing from frame to frame, and (d) The roll of twine opening out. All lead to the same conclusion, i.e. the car is moving. So that the car is moving is a reality for you.

This is what Galileo had told ... "if more than one independent experiments give you the same conclusion, then that conclusion is a reality for you."

The teacher will say: "Now for a moment imagines that you are sitting in the train, the roll of twine is in your hand and one end of the twine is tied to a tree. Now if you will look at the roll of twine in your hand what will you observe?"

The students will definitely say, “We will see that the roll of twine will open out.” The teacher will ask, “So what will you conclude?”

It will be observed that there will be two types of responses. Some (few) will say, “The tree is moving.” Others will say, “Sir, really the tree is at rest. The roll in opening out because the train is moving.”

Collaboration (Group Work): The class may be divided into two groups. Group-1: Those who opine that the tree is moving, through the use of logical analogy. Group-2: Those who opine that the motion of the tree is apparent, through the use of conceptual situatedness.

The groups may be allowed to crystallize their thoughts in 5 minutes and then the leader of each group may present his/her arguments in support of the conclusion of the respective group.

Interpretation construction: Teacher may now again follow the method of Cognitive Negotiation and lead the students to conclude:

(a) For a person sitting in the moving train, the motion of the trees is a reality.

(b) For a person on the ground the trees are at rest.

(c) The state of MOTION of a body is a conclusion for a specific set of observers. Change the observer and the state of MOTION of the body will change.

(d) There is nothing called as the state of ABSOLUTE MOTION of body.

Multiple Interpretation

Multiple manifestations: Teacher may now divide the class into 4 groups and ask each group to seek viable answers to the following questions:

Q.1. From your experiences name 2 bodies which are at rest with respect to you but are in motion with respect to some other observer. State the position of the other observer.

Q.2. From your experiences name 2 bodies which are in motion with respect to you but are at rest with respect to some other observer. State the position of the other observer.

Let the groups present their answers, discuss the correctness of them. This will help them to clarify multiple interpretations and multiple manifestations of the concepts 'REST' and 'MOTION'.

Exercises

1. If you are in a bus, for you, your co-passenger is at rest or is he/she in motion?
2. You are sitting in the classroom and when you look outside you saw that a car is passing by your school. For the driver of the car are you at rest or in motion?
3. How can you make the mountain move with respect to you?
4. How can a moving train be at rest with respect to you?
5. If you make a space travel, land on the moon and then look at the earth what will you observe, the moon revolving round the earth of the earth revolving round the moon?
6. Two trains are moving with the same speed, in the same direction, on two parallel railway lines. You are sitting in the last bogie of one of the trains. Is a passenger sitting in the first bogie of the other train at rest or moving with respect to you?
7. You are hiking a cycle. Your friend Ramu crosses you from the opposite direction by hiking another cycle. Then,
   (a) You are at rest with respect to what/whom?
   (b) Ramu is a rest with respect to what/whom?
8. You are sitting in a moving train. A list of objects is given below. Then with resect to you if the object is in motion put M against it and if the object is at rest put R against it.

(a) The door of the engine
(b) Wheels of your boggie
(c) The cigarette puffs coming out from the lisp of your co-passenger
(d) The ward basis of the toilet of your boggie
(e) The driver of your train
(f) The hawker who crosses you
(g) The centre of the wheels of your boggie
(h) The fly flying in your boggie
(i) Your co-passenger who is going to the toilet
(j) Your co-passenger who is standing at the door of your boggie
(k) The mountain which you see through the window
(l) The signal pasts of the station.

(viii) **VOICES Model (1997)**: The acronym "VOICES" has obvious symbolic significance in the sense that in this model voices of all the learners are received, considered, given due weightage, suitable modified/erased/absorbed so that desirable conceptual change is achieved by the pupils themselves. Keeping in view the fact that a conceptual model of learning envisages the learner to surface, articulate, challenge, defined, redefine and reflect on his/her and others constructs (Posner et al., 1982; Hewson, 1985; Driver 1989) and absorbing all good points of the above models, Mohapatra (1997) purposed this model consisting of logically sequenced pragmatic six steps that the teacher may follow in the classroom while teaching a new concept.

Step-1—Voice (V): In the framework of the concept to be taught the teacher has to generate such an atmosphere in the classroom that each learner will voice (v) his/her alternative conception in the specific concept domain.

Step-2—Overlap (O): Once the pupils' alternative conceptions have been diagnosed, the teachers' job will be to locate the zone of overlap (O) between the alternative conceptions and the concept to be taught.

Step-3—Interaction (I): In this step the teaching-learning process will be to generate an atmosphere of interaction (I), in the form of discussions and arguments, between the pupils and between the teacher and the pupils.

Step-4—Choice (C): The teacher has to make choice (C) of the particular strategy (Scott, Asoko and Driver, 1991) to teach the concept in the framework of the short-listed alternative conceptions and teach accordingly.

Step-5—Enunciate (E): The teacher has to enunciate (E) the concept with suitable examples, non-examples, which are likely to be confused as examples and applications. This is the consolidation and reinforcement stage. The pupils need to be given the opportunity to consider the new concept/idea in a range of situations, or across a range of exemplars. This will help the pupils to internalize the new view and realize that it is more reliable than his/her alternative conception.

Step-6—Satisfy (S): The teacher has to, then, by designing and administering a suitable tool satisfy (S) himself/herself that the desirable and envisaged conceptual change of the pupils' alternative conceptions has been achieved. This step is essential not to text how much the pupil know but to evaluate the degrees of efficiency of his/her teaching strategy in the conceptual framework.

By following the above six steps one can teach and achieve meaningful learning in the constructivist framework.

(ix) **5E–Learning Model (1997):** The Biological Science Curriculum Study (BSCS), team along with its principal investigator Roger Bybee developed an instructional model for constructivism, called the "Five Es". This model recommended for science teaching. In this model the process is explained by employing five 'Es'. They are: Engage, Explore, Explain, Elaborate and Evaluate. In this model conceptual change can be achieved by using five district but interconnected phases, as described below:

- **Engage:** In this stage the students first encounter and identify the instructional task. The students make connections between past and present learning experience, lay the organizational ground work for the activities, and head and stimulate their involvement in the anticipation of these activities. The students need to be engaged and focused on the instructional tasks by asking questions, defining a problem, showing a surprising event and acting out a problematic situation. This is the process to motivate the students to create an appropriate situation.
- **Explore:** This stage provide opportunities for students to explore through all senses. The students get directly involved with phenomena and materials and develop experience with the phenomenon. The students are allowed to work together or in teams and build a base of common experience which assists them in the process of sharing and communicating. During exploration the students' inquiry process drives the instruction.
- **Explain:** The teacher interact with students to discover their ideas. In this stage the student begins to put the abstract experience through which he/she has gone into a communicable form. Language provides motivation for sequencing event into logical format. Communication occurs between peers, the facilitation, or within the learner himself/herself. Common language enhances the sharing and communication between facilitator and students. For communication and recorded evidence of learner's development, progress and growth writing, drawing, video or tape recordings may be used.
- **Elaborate:** The students are allowed to expand the concepts they have learned, make connections to other related concepts and apply their understanding to the real life situations. The teacher who acts as the facilitator help the students develop their ideas through additional physical and mental activities.

- **Evaluate:** This the last stage and the fifth 'E'. It is an ongoing diagnostic process that allows the teacher to determine if the student has attained understanding of concept and knowledge. During the instructional process continuous evaluation and assessment may be undertaken by the teacher.

(x) **Model Proposed by Banet and Nunez (1997):** This model is based on posing surprising and attractive activities that would draw the attention of the students and promote cognitive conflict. This teaching sequence consists of the following three phases:

- **Initiation:** This is the initial stage where the students are motivated and their ideas are elicited by exposing them to unusual or thought provoking situations.
- **Restricting of ideas:** Situations provoking cognitive conflict are used which leads to the formation of new knowledge.
- **Application and review:** New ideas are shown to be valid and students are given opportunity to review the change in their original thinking.

(xi) **Model Proposed by Dekkers and Thijs (1998):** This model presents a teaching sequence appropriate for a specific concept in physical science i.e. force. Many students' misconceptions arose from mistaking the meaning attached to scientific terms such as 'Force'. The meaning attached to the term as mistaken by the student is correct in a limited context. By using concept refinement and context expansion the students may move towards a more scientific view. The teaching sequences as outlined in the model are:

- Find a shared meaning of 'force' in limited contexts.
- Refine that partial concept of 'force' and expand these contexts until the meaning is no longer shared.
- Resolve dissonance by comparing and finding shared meanings, based on the already established agreements.

(xii) **Model Proposed by Hewson et al. (1998):** This model is a constructivist teaching model which ensures meaningful learning by bringing in conceptual change. The components are:

- **Ideas:** The ideas of both students and teachers need to be a part of the classroom discourse.
- **Metacognition:** Students are allowed to express their opinions/ideas.
- **Status:** Some ideas become more acceptable to students and other ideas are less acceptable.
- **Justification:** The reasons for ideas and status decisions needs to be justified.

A conducive classroom climate which respect the ideas of others, the teacher as a facilitator of learning, and student willingness to change their views and monitor their learning are some of the factors which supports the execution of the model.

6.4 Recent Models

(i) **Metacognitive Learning Cycle Model** (2000): Blank (2000) proposed a Metacognitive Learning Cycle Model consisting of the following four phases:

- **Concept assessment phase:** In this phase students reflect on their science ideas and the status of those ideas, i.e. whether they are intelligible, plausible and fruitful in consonance with Posner, Strike, Hewson and Gerzog (1982).
- **Concept exploration:** The students explore phenomena related to the concept.
- **Concept introduction phase:** The teacher introduces the main concept in the lesson and the students reflect on any changes in their ideas.
- **Concept application phase:** The students are presented with other examples of the concept and again consider the status of their ideas.

Blank in his field study found that students taught using this approach did not gain a greater content knowledge but there was permanent restructuring of understanding.

(ii) **Constructivist Learning Design Model (2001):** Gagnon and Collay's Constructivist Learning Design (CLD) model (Gagnon and Collay, 2001) aims to present teachers with constructivist perspective on how to arrange classroom events for student learning. CLD is based on the assumptions and processes of constructivist learning theory and offers a different way of thinking about learning and teaching. Learners connect what teachers expect them to learn with their own experience in constructivist approach. CLD consists of a series of learning elements, six in number. Each of these six elements represents an important process in constructivist learning theory in classroom practice. The six basic parts are: situation, groupings, bridge, questions, exhibit, and reflection. In actual classroom teaching these six elements may flow back and forth into one another.

(a) **Situation:** The situation frames the agenda for student engagement by delineating the goals, tasks and forms what Gagnon and Collay call the learning episode. Thus it is the comprehensive overview of the learning episode with a clear statement of your purpose and of the task the teacher expect his/her student to accomplish as they reach the end of the learning episode.

(b) Groupings are the social structures and group interactions that will bring students together in their environment with the tasks and forms of the learning episodes. Groupings of students and material depends in the situation the teacher design and the materials/resources available.

(c) **Bridge:** Bridge refers to the surfacing of students' prior knowledge before introducing them to the new concept. The teacher here choose to determine students' prior knowledge and build a bridge between what the learner already know and what they might learn by accomplishing the task. The task may be in the form of a simple problem, define terms, play a game, construct lists or discuss the topic. The bridge plays an important role in constructivist methodology.

(d) **Questions:** Questions stimulate and synthesize student thinking and communication during a learning episode. The teacher has to ask some guiding questions to introduce the situation, arrange the groupings, set up the bridge, prompt exhibit and encourage reflection. Questions formed by the teacher aim to instigate, inspire and integrate students thinking and sharing of information.

(e) **Exhibit:** The students can present publicly what they learned. The students are allowed to exhibit by making graph, chart, poster, role play, models, visual presentation, audiotape or audiovisual presentations. While doing so the students respond to queries raised by the teacher, by peers, or by visitors.

(f) **Reflections:** Reflections offer students and teachers opportunities to think and speak critically about their personal and collective learning which the students are not going to forget tomorrow. Reflection encourages the learners to crystallize and synthesize their learning, to apply learning artifacts to other part of the curriculum, and to look ahead future learning episodes.

How to use CLD in a Classroom?

Let us take an example: the phases of moon. The teacher is supposed to teach this learning episode to intermediate class i.e. 11th grades.

1. **Situation:** (90 minutes) The purpose of this situation is to provide investigation of a basic science concept where the students are likely to have misconceptions. Students are allowed to work in groups to find out the relationship between the sun, earth, the phases of the moon, connecting it to the properties of light and

formation of shadow. Each group is asked to explain their thinking using diagram.

2. **Grouping:** (5 minutes)
   (a) Students are grouped based on their zodiac sign. Each group with four students.
   (b) Groups work with drawing pictures or use other object to construct models to show the relationship.
3. **Bridge:** (30 minutes) Students are asked to explain why we have seasons. After they present their explanations, they are allowed to watch a film on universe.
4. **Questions:** (20 minutes) The following questions to be asked by the teacher.
   - The groups are asked to draw a diagram showing the relationship between the sun, the earth and phases of moon.
   - What are the phases of the moon?
   - Is the shape of the moon is just the result of the shadow of the earth?
   - Where the moon goes in the day time?
   - Do people on the other side of the earth see the moon in the same phase as we see?
   - Why eclipse does not occur every month?
   - What is an eclipse of the sun?
   - What is the position of the moon in the sky?
   - How big is the moon as compared to the earth?
5. **Exhibit:** (25 minutes) After each group has an opportunity to work out how to represent the relationship between the sun, the earth and the moon, one of the student from each group will present the explanation to the class.
6. **Reflections:** (10 minutes) The teacher will help to summersize the phases and positions of the moon related to the earth and sun. These students describe individually on index cards why people have misconceptions about the phases of the moon.

(iii) **Dual-situated Learning Model (DSLM) (2004):** Hsiao-Ching She, (2004) proposed a Dual-situated Learning Model involving six stages. It was revealed from research study that the model has positive effects in learning of some science concepts such as pressure, osmosis, diffusion, etc. The stages are:

Stage-1: Examining the attributes of the science concept. This stage provides information about which essential mental sets are needed to construct a scientific view of the concepts.

Stage-2: Probing the students' misconceptions of the science concept. This stage requires probing students' beliefs concerning the science concepts.

Stage-3: Analysing which mental sets students lack according to data collected from stage-2. This would reveal which mental sets student lack especially for the construction of a more scientific view of the concepts.

Stage-4: Designing dual-situated learning events. The design of dual-situated learning event is according to stage-3 results, indicating which mental sets student lack. The fourth stage is to design a series of dual-situated learning events.

Stage-5: Instructing with dual situated learning events. This emphasizes giving students an opportunity to make predictions, provide explanations, confront dissonance, and construct a more scientific view of the concepts.

Stage-6: Challenging situated learning events. The last stage is to present the challenging situated learning events, which provides an opportunity for students to apply the mental sets they have acquired to a new situation to ensure that successful conceptual change occurred.

It is reported that this model has a positive effect on students' achievement, especially in reducing misconceptions. Research studies revealed that the concepts of higher hierarchical level would require more dual situated learning events for conceptual change to occur.

(iv) **Motivational Model of Constructivist-informed Teaching (2005):** The motivational model of constructivist-informed teaching was developed by David Palmer (Palmer, 2005). In this model strategy for motivation has been integrated with teaching techniques that can reduce the status of students' misconceptions and increase the status of scientific concepts. This model emphasizes the importance of motivation as a mediator for learning. The three components as suggested by the model are:

- **Selection of concepts that represent appropriate challenge:** In this step the teacher should select concepts that represent achievable challenge considering the conceptual ecologies (including the epistemological and ontological beliefs) of the students in the class. The students get a opportunity to establish the concept in long-term memory. The concepts are so chosen that the students are not allowed to struggle for a long time to achieve accommodation which may lend to optimization of students' motivation.
- **The use of 'dual-purpose' teaching techniques:** Teacher should select teaching techniques that have purpose i.e. development of scientifically acceptable conceptions along with motivation. This may be achieved by class discussion, teacher explanations, appropriate hands-on activities, computer simulations, and application to real-life contexts. The above teaching techniques should not be presented in any particular sequence or series of steps but should be used appropriately for different teaching situation.
- **A classroom climate that encourages positive motivation beliefs:** Along with teaching techniques classroom factors should be given importance to encourage positive motivational beliefs among the students. The teacher should try to create a conducive classroom environment/climate which includes classroom factors like—the teacher should

praise effort and improvement, the teacher should express confidence in students' ability to work at higher level, the teacher should model enthusiasm and how to deal with challenges and the teacher should be supportive, reassuring and attentive as students participate in the learning process. Many such factors may be listed which will help the student to achieve/acquire meaningful learning.

(v) **RIE Model (2008):** A constructivist teaching model has been developed by the faculty members of RIE (Regional Institute of Education, Bhubaneswar) consisting of six steps as follows: Exploration, Analysis, Interaction, Development, Discussion and Evaluation. The format is given below.

FORMAT FOR EXEMPLAR

A Suggested Format for Preparation of Exemplar Material

1. Exemplar No. :
2. Author :
3. Topic :
4. Concepts/Teaching points :
5. Class :
6. Textbook :
7. Processes/Steps :

Processes/Steps

(To be followed in constructivist transaction)

I. **Exploration:** Presentation of evidences / instances / activities / questions / demonstrations / situations / simulations to extract the learner's concepts in the relevant area.

II. **Analysis:** Categorization of learners concepts into useful/non-useful, acceptable/non-acceptable ones.

III. **Interaction:** Presentation of new activities/instances/ problems, etc. to generate group interaction with the aim in view to eliminate non-useful concepts of learners.

IV. **Development:** Development of the concepts to be taught using acceptable concepts of learners and constructivist techniques.

V. **Discussion:** Discussion about new/unfamiliar situations/applications/evidences/instances, etc. leading to extension/consolidation of knowledge through cognitive conflicts, if any, any their solutions.

VI. **Assessment/Evaluation:** To test that the learners have constructed the concepts in a way the teacher expects them to construct. It is a continuous and dynamic process and may involve formative as well as summative evaluation.

Techniques/Strategies

(To be used in the above processes/steps)

- Asking questions
- Helping learners to ask questions
- Demonstration
- Innovative activities
- Discussion about activities/instances
- Generating cognitive conflict
- Using cognitive apprenticeship
- Using analogies
- Use of concept mapping
- Creating brainstorming
- Using interactive software
- Setting problems—conceptual and/or numerical
- Involving learners in collaborative learning situations such as group discussions.

As an exemplar illustrating this model a module has been developed to teach the Class-IV student (NCERT Class-IV textbook on Science) on the topic "Mangoes Round the Year", as follows:

Concepts

- Food gets spoiled with time.

- There is difference between food spoilage and wastage of food.
- Packed food items carry expiry date.
- Food items like bread easily get spoilt due to presence of water/moisture/yeast.
- Some food items can be kept fresh for 1-2 days by simple methods.
- Mango (a seasonal fruit) can be preserved round the year in the form of pickles and Aam papad.

Class : VII
Textbook : NCERT Textbook on Sc.

Processes/Steps

Teacher may carry with him

- A pack of fresh bread.
- A pack of old (say 7 days) bread which is spoilt and on which fungus has been formed.
- Potato curry fresh one and spoilt, sour smelling/tasting potato curry.
- Some packed food items with expiry date printed on it.
- A freshly prepared chappati/roti.
- A stale chappati/roti with mould on it.
- A reading lens.

The item, in pairs, the teacher may keep hidden inside the table drawer.

Exploration: The teacher may ask the students about the items they have brought as Tiffin and write those items on the blackboard under three categories: (a) Cereals (Rice, Roti, etc.), (b) Pulses (Dal, Channa, etc.), and (c) Vegetables (Curry fry, etc.)

Once that is done he may now bring out from the drawer the two types of breads and ask them to examine each one carefully. Then divide the class into four groups and ask each group to write down their observations with regards to colour, smell, details through a lens, about the two breads.

They may now be asked—"Which bread they may eat and which one they should not?"

Thereafter they may be shown the two potato curries as well as the two chappatis/roties. Let them repeat the observation procedure.

Analysis

(a) From the above simple activities the students' conception about spoilage of food can be known.

(b) Some of them may voice that food spoilage and wastage of food are one and the same.

(c) Some of them may opine that if some body has eaten only part of the food served to him/her and leave the rest then leftout food is also spoilt food.

(d) Food items get spoiled with time.

Interaction: Here group discussion may lead the students to understand that:

(a) Spoiled food cannot and should not be eaten. So they are non-edible.

(b) Wastage of food is concerned with food that is edible but is dumped in the dustbin.

(c) Leftover food after somebody has eaten part of it is regarded as non-edible—

  (i) Because the first-person may be carrying some infectious disease, and

  (ii) Due to social customs and taboo.

This step will clarify the concept of spoiled food.

Development: Teacher may distribute slices of fresh bread amongst students formed into groups. Ask them to sprinkle some water on them and leave them on their respective desks. If possible keep them inside a closed box and ask the students to observe the changes in colour, texture, smell, etc. daily. Then each student may prepare an observation table as given in the book and record the findings.

This experiment may take 3-4 days, but it is worth waiting for. In this experiment the reading lens will come handy for observation of details of change in the bread slice.

If bread slice is not available, chappati/roti will also do.

Along with this slice of bread with water sprinkled on it, another slice of bread may also be kept just as such.

This experiment will help them to conclude that presence of water, moisture, hot and humid weather cause the spoiling of food items produce fermentation and accelerate growth of bacteria.

Now the students may be encouraged to classify the seasons into two categories. One—when the food items get spoilt quickly and Two—when the food items do not get spoilt so quickly.

It is time now to ask each group of students to do the following:

- Prepare a list of food items those get spoiled easily.
- Prepare a second list of food items those do not get spoiled easily and stay fresh for pretty long period.

Please note:

(a) These questions/activities do not have any fixed response.

(b) So these questions/activities are open-ended.

Such questions/activities help the students:

- to think
- to recollect events, activities and experiences
- to reflect
- to analyse
- to conclude

and in the process promote the creativity of the students.

Students may not be able to prepare a list of the second group of food items. It is here they need the help of the teacher as the co-participator, facilitator.

Some of the basic food items of the second group are the following:

- Mustard oil (in fact any edible oil)
- Cow's Ghee
- Sugar

- Jaggery
- Haldi
- Cinnamon
- Fenugreek
- Honey

The students may now be asked—

- Name some prepared food items in which the above materials are used to preserve them for longer period.

Note this is again an open-ended activity.

Example: They many come up with answers like oil is used in pickles to preserve them. Even if they have seen they may not have observed—Fried potato (Potato chips) remain fresh much longer than cooked potatoes.

Teacher may now show some packed (empty) spice packet and ask the students to note the expiry date.

6.5 Discussion

Ask the students to discuss with their mothers and report how their mother adopts simple techniques to preserve food items for a day or two.

Example: Fresh milk just left as such gets spoiled within few hours. But milk once boiled for 15-20 minutes and them allowed to cool can remain unspoiled for 1-2 days.

Teacher may mention this is a simple example to Pasteurisation. Then show them a packet of butter and ask them to read, what is written on the packet.

Thereafter teacher may ask the students to discuss with their mother and report

- What are the ingredients used to make mango pickle?
- What is the process to make mango pickle?
- How is Aam pampad prepared?
- What is the process to make Aam pampad?
- What is the food items used in these as preservatives?

This will also highlight the fact that direct sunrays are also an agent to kill bacteria and thus delay spoilage.

Assessment

1. Make a list of food items prepared from milk. Classify them into two categories—(i) those that get spoiled easily, (ii) those that stay fresh for few day. What are the preservatives in the later case?

Discussion

All the above constructivist teaching models are different in several ways however some similarities have been noted as follows:

- Assessment of student's view about a particular concept.
- Students are given opportunity to analyse his/her viewpoint about the particular concept.
- Peer-interaction and student-teacher interaction where teacher acts as a facilitator have been encouraged.
- Sometimes the teacher presents the correct view and facilitates accommodation leading to efficient time management.
- The students after acquiring the correct concept are allowed to apply knowledge across a range of contexts.
- Prescribe inflexible learning pathways.

All researchers agree that the constructivist teaching models are though effective but time consuming than the traditional teaching models. It requires a supportive classroom environment in which students feel confident expressing, exchanging or discussing their ideas. Learning task should not involve high level of difficulty which will take more time to get accommodated and in the process the learner will lose interest and motivation. Hence the concept to be learned should be carefully selected which will be at an achievable level of challenge and students should experience regular feeling of success throughout the learning process (Bandura, 1982).

Though the basic principle of the entire constructivist teaching model is to achieve conceptual change, however there are many differences. To achieve conceptual change different models have prescribed different pathways. It ranges from three to seven steps. In Nussbaum and Novick model (1982) it is only three and Norman and Schmidt (1992) model and ICON model in (1995) there are seven steps. In earlier models (1980-90) a step/phase like restructuring of ideas is common, where the students are exposed to conflicting views of other students or to conflicting situations and the teacher presents the scientific view. The later models (1990-2000) are more elaborate as compared to earlier models. In later models (Dekkers and Thijs, 1998) the use of conflict or confrontation by refining and extending student's existing conception has been minimized. Unlike other models Hewson et al. (1998) avoided the use of step-by-step structure by proposing guidelines for conceptual change.

References

Ausubel, D.P. (1968). *Educational Psychology: A Cognitive View*. New York: Holt, Rinehart and Winston.

Banet, E.O. and Nunez, F. (1997). Teaching and learning about human nutrition: A constructivist approach. *International Journal of Science Education*, 19: 1169-94.

Black, J.B. and McClintock, R.O. (1995). An Interpretation Construction Approach to Constructivist Design. In B. Wilson (Ed.), *Constructivist learning environments*. Englewood Cliffs. N.J.: Educational Technology Publications.

Blank, L.M. (2000). A metacognitive learning cycle: A better warranty for student understanding. *Science Education*, 84: 486-506.

Campagne, A.B., Gunstone, R.F., and Klopfer, I.E. (1985). Effecting changes in cognitive structures among physics students. In L. West and A. Pines (Eds.), *Cognitive structure and conceptual change* (pp. 163-88). Orland, F.L. Academic Press.

Chinn, C.A. and Brewer, W.F. (1993). The role of anomalous data in knowledge acquisition; A theoretical framework and implications for science instruction. *Review of Educational Research*, 63(1): 1-49.

Cosgrove, M. and Osborne, R. (1985). Lesson frameworks for changing children's idea. In R. Osborne and P. Freyberg (Eds.), *Learning in Science: The Implications of Children's Science* (pp. 100-11). Auckland, Newzealand: Heinemann.

Dekkers, P.J.J.M. and Thijs, G.D. (1992). Making productive use of students' initial conceptions in developing the concept of force. *Science Education*, 82: 31-51.

Driver, R. (1989). Students' conception and learning of Science. *International Journal of Science Education*, Vol. II, No. 5, pp. 481-90.

Driver, R. and Oldham, V. (1986). A constructivist approach to curriculum development in science. *Studies in Science Education*, 84: 287-312.

Finkle, S.L. and Torp, L.L. (1995). *Introductory Documents (Available from the center for Problem-based Learning)*. Illinois Math and Science Academy, 1500 West Sullivan Road, Aurora II, 60506-1000.

Gagnon, G.W. and Collay, M. (2001). *Designing for Learning six elements in constructivist classrooms*, Crown Press, INC, California.

Glasson, G.E. and Lalik, R.V. (1993). Reinterpreting the learning cycle from a social constructivist perspective: A qualitative study of teachers' beliefs and practices. *Journal of Research in Science Teaching*, 30: 187-207.

Hewson, P.W. (1981). A conceptual change approach in learning science. *European Journal of Science Education*, 3, 383-96.

—— (1985). Epistemological commitments in the learning of science: Examples from dynamics. *European Journal of Science Education*, Vol. 7, No. 2, pp. 163-72.

Hewson, P.W., and Hewson, M.G.A. (1984). The role of conceptual conflict in conceptual change and the design of science education. *Instructional Sciences*, 13: 1-13.

Hewson, P.W., Beeth, M.E., and Thorley, N.R. (1998). Teaching for conceptual change. In K.G. Tobin and B.J. Fraser (Eds.), International Handbook of Science Education (199-218). Dordrecht, Netherlands: Kluwer Academic Publishers.

Mohapatra, J.K. (1997). Taxonomy of Conceptual change, Review of two anchoring instructional Strategy and a functional model of teaching, *Indian Educational Review*, 32(1): 36-54.

Neale, D.C., Smith, D. and Johnson, V.G. (1990). Implementing conceptual change teaching in primary science. *The Elementary School Journal*, 91: 109-31.

Needham, R. (1987). *Teaching strategies for developing understanding in science*. The University of Leeds Centre for Students in Science and Mathematics Education.

Niedderer, H. (1987). A teaching strategy based on student's alternative frameworks—theoretical conceptions and examples. In Proceedings of the Second *International Seminar—Misconceptions and Educational Strategies in Science and Mathematics*. 2: 360-67, Cornell University.

Norman, G.R. and Schmidt, H.G. (1992). *The Psychological Basis of Problem-based Learning. A Review of the Evidence*, Academic Medicine, 67(9): 557-65.

Novak, J.D., and Gowin, D.B. (1984). *Learning How to Learn*. Cambridge: Cambridge University Press.

Nussbaum, J. and Novick, S. (1982). Alternative frameworks, conceptual conflict and accommodation: Towards a principled teaching strategy. *Instructional Science*, 11: 183-200.

Osborne, J.F. (1996). Beyond Constructivism. *Science Education*, 80(1): 53-82.

Palmer, D. (2005). A motivational view of constructivist-informed Teaching. *International Journal of Science Education*, Vol. 27, 15: 1853-81.

Perrine, V. (1991b). *Designing for Learning, Six elements in constructivist classroom*, George W. Gagnon Jr. & Michelle Collay, Crown Press, INC. California, pp. 13-14.

Posker, G.J., Strike, K.A., Hewson, P.W., and Gertzog, W.A. (1982). Accommodation of a scientific conception: Toward a theory of conceptual change. *Science Education*, 66: 211-27.

Posner, G.J., et al. (1982). Accommodation of a scientific conception: Towards a theory of conceptual change. *Science Education*, Vol. 72, No. 1, pp. 103-13.

Scott, P. (1992). Conceptual pathways in learning science: A case study of the development of one student's idea relating to the structure of matter. In R. Duit, F. Goldberg and H. Niedderer (Eds.), *Research in Physics Learning: Theoretical issues and empirical studies* (pp. 203-24). Kiel, Germany. Institute for Science Education at the University of Kiel.

Scott, P.H., Asoko, H.M. and Driver, R. (1991). Teaching for conceptual change: A review of strategies proceedings of the *Bremen International Workshop on Research in Physics Learning: Theoretical Issues and Empirical Studies*, March, 1991.

She, H.C. (2004). Fostering radical conceptual change through dual-situated learning model. *Journal of Research in Science Teaching*, 41: 142-64.

Staver, J.R. (1998). Constructivism: Sound theory for explicating the practice of science and science teaching. *Journal of Research in Science Teaching*, 35(5): 501-20.

Tolman, M.N. and Hardy, G.R. (1995). *Discovering Elementary Science Method, Content and Problem-solving Activities*. Needham Heights, MA : Allyn & Bacon.

von Glasersfeld, E. (1995). *Radical Constructivism: A way of knowing and Learning*. Washington, D.C.: Falmer Press.

—— (1992). A constructivist view of learning and teaching. In R. Duit, F. Goldberg and H. Niedderer (Eds.), *Research in Physics Learning: Theoretical Issues and Empirical Studies*. Kiel, Germany : IPN at the University of Kiel.

Wittrock, M.C. (1994). Generative Science Teaching. In P.F. Fensham, R.F. Gunstone and R.T. White (Eds.) (1994). *The content of science: A constructivist approach to its teaching and learning*. pp. 29-38. London, U.K.: Falmer Press.

Yager, R.E. (1991). The constructivist learning model. *The science teacher*, 58(6): 52-57.

7 Do's and Don'ts for Teachers in Constructivism

7.1 Introduction

In Chapter 5, the input with which the learner (the Constructor of Knowledge) enters a classroom and the relevance of each input was discussed in detail. Out of all these inputs learner's Alternative Conceptions (ALCONs) happen to be the most crucial input (Ausubel, 1968) in so far as the degree and quality of learning is concerned.

As stated in Chapter 1, it is now known from the conclusive diagnostic studies to identify, analyse and map pupils' ALCONs about natural phenomena that no pupil ever enters the classroom devoid of personal constructs (Kelly, 1955) about any concept, in general and science concepts in particular. These constructs are similar to the formal concepts in science, in the sense that many of them seem to have been internalized through processes not much different (at least in the frame of reference of the learner) from those encountered in the growth of science, construed through experience, experiments, intuitions, trial and error, and logical formulations. But, they are also different from the formal science because most of them usually do not confirm to its format or conclusions. But, their importance from the point of view of the teaching and learning process (TLP) lies not in their similarity or dis-similarity with the formal concepts, but in the effect they are likely to produce on the processes of learning, retention and transfer of knowledge that takes place inside the classroom. Even after three decades of the recognition of the existence and the importance of these ALCONs for TLP, the academic climate about the ALCONs is still in paradigmatic phase in Kuhn's (1970) sense. The observation of Gilbert and

Swift (1985) that "the efforts of individuals have tended to be uncoordinated, terminology has not been agreed upon, a common methodology not shared, ultimate aims not stated, and classroom implications not explored", in detail, is still valid today. In fact Hammer (1996, 2000), Smith et al. (1993-94), Clement et al. (1989) and di Sessa (1988) assert that problems do exist with models of ALCONs and how to deal effectively with them.

Realising the importance of ALCONs, a wide range of pedagogies such as Learning Cycles (Kalplus, 1987), Conceptual Change model of Posner et al. (1982) and Hewson (1981, 1982), Inquiring Knower approach of De Vries and Kohlberg (1987), Microcomputer-based Laboratory Experiences (Thornton, 1987; Thornton and Sokolof, 1990), Disequilibration Techniques (Ministrell, 1989; Dykstra, Boyle and Monarch, 1992), an inquiry approach coupled with Concept Substitution Strategies (Harrison et al., 1999), Bridging Analogies (Clement, 1988, Perschard and Bitbol, 2008), Metaconceptual teaching (Wiser and Amin, 2001), Socratic dialogues with white-boarding (Wenning, 2005; Werning et al., 2006), ECIRR model (Wenning, 2008) have been individually developed to address ALCONs. These umpteen numbers of models do indicate that classroom implications of ALCONs in a constructivist framework are still in a fluid phase of cognitive evolution. In fact, researchers are still constructing their cognitive domain to address this effectively.

To describe the causes for such a situation Hammer (2000) states, "First, (these models) provide no account of productive resources, students have, for advancing in their understanding. Second, descriptions of student difficulties provide no analysis of underlying mechanism, while the perspective of misconceptions cannot explain the contextual sensitivities of student reasoning."

We advocate that the studies in this field continue to be in this phase mostly because, (a) the investigations have been confined to isolated topics instead of a search for a pattern, and (b) the studies have been mostly individualistic even in the framework of the researcher, as is indicated in the Chapter 2. In other words a philosophy of monoism has been pervading this field of research.

In spite of the diverse findings about ALCONs, *vis-à-vis* constructivism, the accurate but still fudgy knowledge base and several laboratory tested models, the ground reality is that the teacher is ultimately responsible to help the learner to construct new concepts, in a way, the teacher expects the learner to construct. For this the teacher has to be knowledgeable enough to appreciate the existence, importance and all pervasive influence of the learner's ALCONs in so far as knowledge construction is concerned. With teacher's very little exposure to research, she has to be provided with discernable patterns and skill-based guidelines to follow in a classroom situation so as to optimize the knowledge construction by the learner.

Keeping this in view we, at a theoretical level, attempt to make a holistic analysis regarding (a) the genesis of ALCONs in section 7.2, (b) the broad characteristics of ALCONs in section 7.3, (c) a hypothetical space in which ALCONs operate in a classroom situation in section 7.4, and at an operation level, discuss the role of the teacher in section 7.5, and enlist the dos and don'ts for teachers in section 7.6. Our concluding remarks are presented in section 7.7.

Such a holistic approach is essential because as a science (construction of concept is a scientific process) it is rooted in the psychological constructs of the learners and as a psychology, it is concerned with the cognitive map of the learner's scientific outlook and skill.

7.2 Genesis

The form, structure and characteristics of learner's ALCONs and their implications for knowledge construction that emerge from the extensive studies are interesting to researchers, informative for curriculum framers, educative for students of education and guiding constraints for pedagogical experts. But, in a framework of **Research for Teaching** and **Teaching for Research** the full potential of these findings in helping the classroom practitioner to improve/modify his/her teaching strategies so that pupils learn better is yet to be realized (Driver, 1989), as evidenced by the proliferation of teaching models in constructivist framework (Chapter 6) which claim apparent to partial success. The advocated usability of the tried strategies in the framework of Research for teaching is hindered by the following limitations:

1. The individualistic character of the ALCONs, i.e. their learner-specific structure, about even any particular concept, has remained the main hurdle that has reduced the applicability of the wealth of knowledge in this area. This observation will be made clear by considering a positive effort in transforming the research results into the classroom situation. Peterson et al. (1986), Haslam and Treagust (1987) and Treagust (1988) designed a two-tier diagnostic test with a structure comparable to the format of the Test of logical thinking of Tobin and Capie (1981). In this two-tiered test, the first part of each item is a multiple choice content area question with two or three choices. The second part of each question contains a set of four possible reasons for each of the answers given to the first part. The structure of the second part is decided by an analysis of clinical interviews conducted earlier and a use of the reported results in relevant literature. Treagust (1988) suggests that administration of such a test and subsequent analysis of the responses are likely to give any teacher a clear idea about learner's ALCONs and hence he can plan functional strategies to transform/erase the ALCONs or to utilize them meaningfully for better construction of knowledge by the learners. However, let us examine the individualism of the ALCONs that will come into play. If in the first step of the test item three choices are given, then once one considers the second step—there will be a total of 12 reasons, four for each choice. There is the likelihood that each of the reasons will be ticked by some learners. Thus, the teacher will have to design strategies to handle all these 12 responses simultaneously. In a classroom situation this task, if not impossible, is very difficult. Thus, the problem is the multiplicity of ALCONs due to their individualism.

2. So far the efforts have been to identify the ALCONs and prescribe teaching strategy, without diagnosing the genesis of the ALCONs. This is like prescribing a medicine for an identified disease without diagnosing its cause. Thus any teaching strategy using the ALCONs as reference point will have limited utility in a classroom situation because a prescription is a prescription to the extent the cause of the process is known.

One of the possible ways to remove these two limitations in a single stroke would be (Mohapatra, 1990) to attempt to locate the genesis (thereby improving the functionality of a prescription) that is likely to produce a common pattern of alternative conceptions in a group of learners (thereby eliminate the problems created by the individualistic character of the ALCONs), so that the research findings can have functionally operational value for classroom teaching.

The nucleus for the search of the occurrence and genesis of a common ALCON exhibited by a group of pupils in a classroom situation was formed out of the following incident. Pupils aged 7 to 8 years, reading in Standard-II of the primary section of the D.M. School, Bhubaneswar, India, were being taught by the mathematics teacher to write in words and in figures all the numbers from 50 to 100. When the teacher reached the number 100 the following conversation ensued between her and one of the pupils, named Pooja.

Pooja	:	Madam! 'Hundred' should be written in red. (It was obviously difficult on the part of the teacher to comprehend this remark.)
Teacher	:	Aa! What did you say?
Pooja	:	Hundred should be written in red.
Teacher	:	(Thinks for a while and says) Yes, yes, I know. Because hundred is an important number, it should be written in red. (*)
Pooja	:	(Laughs at the teacher as if she is a fool and says) No, Madam! That is not the reason.

Teacher : (Looks at her and says) Then....

Pooja : Don't you see; hundred is hund and red.

Teacher : (Laughs at Pooja as if she is a fool).

Instead of trying to analyse in a realistic way as to who is actually the fool, let us try to see why Pooja has this concept, which in our frame of formal thought appears as misconception.

An inspection of the books prescribed for the lower primary classes showed that pupils are taught about the seven colours in either kindergarten or Standard-I. In these books, in the section dealing with colours, there is usually a picture of say, a red flower and by its side the word **red** is written in red colour. This process is repeated for all the rest of the six colours. By watching classroom teaching, it was observed that the pupils are shown, say: a red flower or a green leaf and after asking the pupils questions about the colour of these objects, the teacher writes down their colours on the black board with crayons the colour of which match the colour of the objects. This method of teaching about colours is quite popular among teachers and seems to be effective because pupils learn about the various colours quickly and correctly.

But this juxtaposition of a **red** flower with the word **red** written in red colour or a **green** leaf with the word **green** in green colour has led Pooja to incorrectly generalize an implicit association not only between the word red and the colour of a red object but also between the word **red** and the colour of ink in which it is written. The latter part of the above generalization has

- been induced in her by the repeated unintentional reinforcement in the classroom about the colour red and the word RED, and
- led her to conclude that the word **red**, wherever it appears, should be written in red colour.

We call this generative causation of an ALCON **Induced Incorrect Generalization** or IIG. In this particular case of writing the number 100 in words, Pooja spots the word *red* and voices her conclusion.

Even the asterisk marked statement of the teacher, above reflects such an IIG, i.e. all the words those seem to be important in the mental frame of the reader or the observer should be written in red colour. This is again an evidence of construction of concepts by teachers. The concept of pupils about the concept 'Animal', as discussed in Chapter 1 is again an ALCON generated by IIG.

We thus hypothesize that if this phenomena of IIG affects a group simultaneously it will lead to a group ALCON. The most probable place where such an induction may occur is the classroom itself. So, we focused our attention on the classroom teaching of science.

7.2.1 IIG and Generative Processes

As an exemplar to investigate the existence of IIG as a pervasive genesis we focused (Mohapatra and Bhattacharya, 1989) our attention on the concept of 'Force', because with the statement of Newton's first law of motion, the teacher initiates the pupil into the world of formal concepts in Physics. It is because of this that Newton's laws of motion and the associated concepts of inertia, force, displacement, velocity and acceleration form a cornerstone of the formal concepts of Physics.

The earlier diagnostic studies of Driver (1973), Trowbridge and McDermott (1980, 1981), Gunstone and White (1981), Champagne et al. (1980), Mc Closky et al. (1981), Viennot (1979), Chement (1982), Minstrell (1982), McDermott (1984), Osborne and Freyberg (1985), helped us to keep our tool simple, unambiguous, comprehensible and based on the experiential world of the pupils but was sharp enough to diagnose the existence of IIG.

The tool consisted of six questions. Each question was accompanied by a diagram depicting an event commonly experienced by each pupil. Based on the responses open-ended group discussions were arranged. It was observed (Mohapatra, 1988) that 3 definite generative processes were at work for creating IIG in pupils and teachers. They are presented below. The random sample of subjects for this study was classified into 4 groups. They are 180 pupils of Class IX of local language

(Odia) medium school (P1), 69 pupils of Class IX of English medium schools (P2), 246 students of second year of the +2 programme (P3) and 39 trained graduate science teachers (T1).

7.2.1a Process of Conceptual Reversibility

The first three questions presented 3 common examples of bodies at rest, namely, a body at rest on a table, a body hanging from a rigid support and a see-saw in a balanced position.

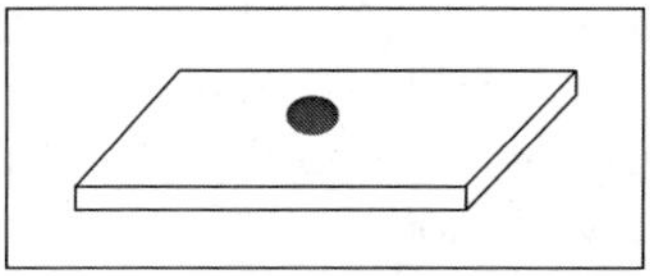

Fig. 7.1

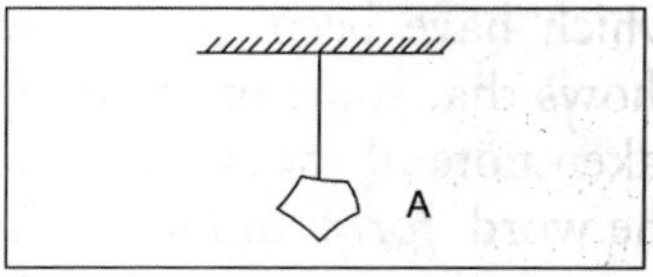

Fig. 7.2

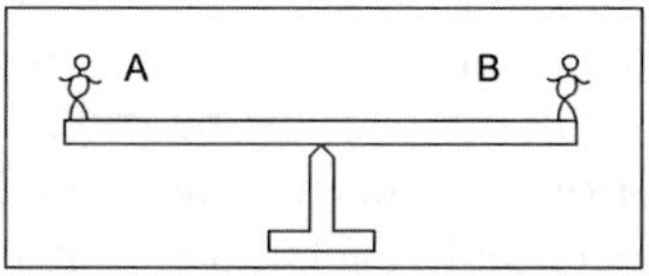

Fig. 7.3

Each diagram carried a question which described the diagram and then asked.... Is there, any force acting on the body? If your answer is 'YES', name the force/s. In all the three cases responses of all the groups (including teachers) showed similar IIG as about 20 per cent of each group responded that NO force is acting on the bodies in all the three cases. Then selected persons from each group were engaged in group discussions to identify the process behind the specific IIG.

We give below part of a conversation with one of the pupils that ensued in the group discussion. This was arranged to discover the genesis of this alternative conception.

Interviewer : You think that there is no force acting on this body at rest on the table?

Pupil : Yes, Sir.

Interviewer : Why do you think so?

Pupil : From Newton's first law of motion one can conclude this.

Interviewer	:	How?
Pupil	:	The law states that only if a force acts on a body at rest, it will change its state. (*)
Interviewer	:	So....
Pupil	:	Since the body continues to be at rest, so no force is acting on it. (*)

There were two definite indicators in two of these replies, which have been marked with an asterisk (*). The first one shows that some of the pupils and teachers have somehow not taken note of the words '*unbalanced*' or '*resultant*' prefixed to the word '*force*' in Newton's first law of motion. This confirms our premise. The second asterisked response shows that students assume that since 'only application of a force can change the state of rest', then the reverse (i.e. 'a body which continues to be at rest has no force acting on it') must be true. Thus the particular alternative conception has been generated by superimposing this process of conceptual reversibility onto the IIG that 'one needs a force to change the state of rest of a body'. Finally, even an appreciable percentage of practicing teachers demonstrated to have the same ALCONs generated through the process of conceptual reversibility.

Question 5 was meant to peep into pupils' concept about the concept 'Force' in the framework of inertia of motion. It was observed that, as above, in these instances also the process of conceptual reversibility was operative.

7.2.1b Process of Conceptual Continuity

One of the concepts that teachers teach and pupils learn in Newton's second law of motion is that the greater the force acting on the same mass, the greater is the acceleration produced by the force. We hypothesize that they are then likely to juxtapose this with the equation of motion, $v = u + at$, and conclude that a greater acceleration means a greater velocity. They start with force, go to acceleration, and proceed further to the concept of velocity. Then they conclude that application of a greater force will produce a greater velocity (Champagne et al., 1980). This we call the process of conceptual continuity. If one superimposes on this the process of conceptual reversibility, one concludes that 'a greater velocity means the application of a greater force'. To test this we posed question 6.

Question 6 presents a situation where two bodies A and B, of equal mass are moving on a frictionless table. A is moving with uniform velocity 2V and B is moving with uniform velocity V, Fig. 7.4. Then the question asks... (a) Is there any force acting on A and B in the horizontal direction? (b) If your answer is 'YES', then is the horizontal force on A more than that on B?

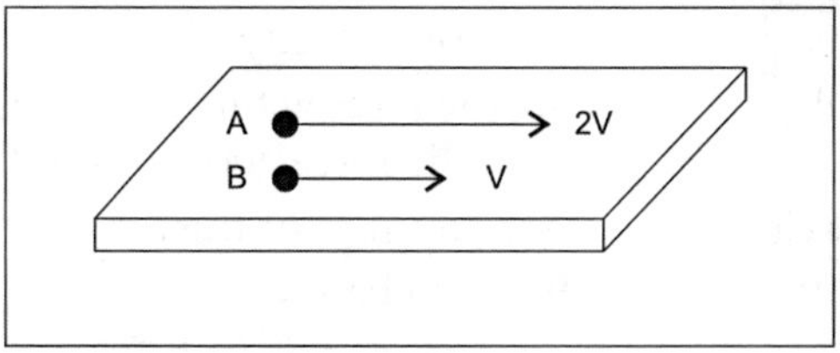

Fig. 7.4

In question 6(a), we categorically ask about forces in the horizontal direction. Table 7.1 shows that a high percentage of pupils and teachers responded that horizontal forces are acting on A and B. In group discussions they very strongly argued that 'there has to be horizontal forces; otherwise, how can the velocity of A be more than that of B?'. As an obvious corollary to this, quite a high percentage of the subjects responded to question 6(b) by saying that the forces on A is more than that on B. Table 7.1 gives the per cent of each group of subjects preferring the indicated response for the questions 6(a) and 6(b).

Table 7.1: Per cent of subjects preferring a particular response to specific questions

Question No.	Particular Response	Subjects			
		P1	P2	P3	T1
6(a)	'Yes'	78.8	81.1	68.2	64.1
6(b)	'Yes'	82.2	76.8	75.2	66.6

At this point presentation of a representative discussion with the pupils is in order.

Interviewer	:	Why do you think that there is a force acting both on A and B.
Pupil	:	It has to be.
Interviewer	:	Why?
Pupil	:	Because they are moving. (*)
Interviewer	:	So....
Pupil	:	If no force will act on them why should they move? (*)
Interviewer	:	But A and B are moving with different uniform velocity.
Pupil	:	So, the force acting on A must be greater than the force acting on B. (*)
Interviewer	:	Are you sure of this?
Pupil	:	It has to be so.

Other pupils and teachers advanced similar arguments for their considered response. It is worthwhile to consider the asterisked answers. They indicate that the subjects feel that velocity is associated with force and greater the velocity greater is the force acting on the body. This confirms our hypothesis that process of conceptual continuity coupled with the process of conceptual reversibility can generate an IIG.

We conclude this sub-section by stating that

- Process of conceptual continuity is a very strong generative cause of IIG, leading to ALCONs in the internalization of at least these specific concepts of 'velocity' and 'force'.
- This generative cause has affected also the teachers.
- ALCONs generated out of this process is very persistent and almost do not get modified with years as can be seen by comparing the per cent of pupils of Class-IX (P1, P2) and those of +2 stage (P3) opting for the ALCON-exhibiting response against questions 6(a) and 6(b) (Table 7.1).
- In the framework under consideration there is almost no difference between the pupils of Oriya medium schools and those of the English medium schools.

7.2.1c Process of Conceptual Extrapolation

This process is exemplified in the response to question 4 of the tool.

Q.4 depicts a simple situation of two bodies of equal mass, hanging from a frictionless pulley, by means of a weightless string. Then it is asked..., (a) Is the downward force on B more than that on A? and (b) If your answer is 'YES', explain your answer.

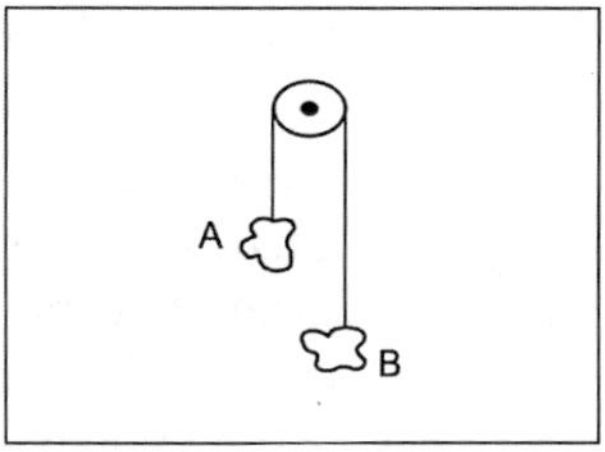

Fig. 7.5

Weight of a body is usually stated by the teacher as a common example of force. So we wanted to test students' and teachers' concepts about this force. In response to question 4(a) around 60 per cent of the pupils and also the teachers stated that the downward force on B is more than that on A, even though in the question it is clearly stated that the masses of A and B are equal. This corroborates similar observations by Gunstone and White (1981). To investigate the generative cause for this alternative conception we arranged group discussion. There was a pattern in the opinion exchanged in this discussion. We give below part of the conversation with a pupil.

Interviewer : You think that the downward force on B is more than that on A?

Pupil : Yes, Sir.

Interviewer : Why do you think it is to be so?

Pupil : Because .... (thinks)

Interviewer : Yes .... because ....?

Pupil : Sir, take the example of physical balance. (*)

Interviewer : Yes....

Pupil : The pan which has the heavier weight goes down. (*)

Interviewer : Is it always so?

Pupil : Yes.

Interviewer : So....

Pupil : In this case also, since B has gone down, it must be heavier. (*) So, the downward force on B must be more than that on A.

Interviewer : But this is not a physical balance.

Pupil : Yes...but...one can think this to be...same type.

The approach taken by the pupil is very clear from the above discussion. She associated with the physical balance the concrete (in a Piagetian sense) concept that the pan which has the heavier weight goes down. The principle of moment of forces does not strike her as the explanation of the instance under consideration. This is so because the pupil rarely has the scope to handle a faulty balance in the laboratory and in real-life situations weighing are also not done with a faulty balance. Thus, the pupil associated the concept of weight and not moment of force, with the balancing in a physical balance. This creates an IIG in her and results in the asterisked response above. Next, by conceptual extrapolation, she generalizes this IIG to all those instances which appear to her to be similar in content to a physical balance and in this particular case leads to the conclusion that B is heavier than A. Therefore, she remarks that the downward force on B is more than that on A.

This study shows that:

- Process of conceptual extrapolation leading to an IIG is also a very strong generative cause of ALCONs as it has affected a large percentage of subjects.
- The generative cause has affected the teachers.
- ALCONs generated out of this process resist modification.
- In the framework of this generative cause, there is almost no difference between the pupils of Oriya medium schools and those of the English medium school.

We note in passing that as regards the response to questions 1(b) and 2(b), it was observed that hardly 10 per cent of the pupils and teachers mentioned '*reaction of the table*' and '*tension in the string*' when they listed the names of the forces. This confirms the findings of earlier workers that '*reaction*' and '*tension*' as examples of forces rarely from usable substrates in the constructed structures of pupils. However, we demonstrated that the situation is not much different in the case of teachers. Further, we also record that about 10 per cent of the pupils and teachers cited '*inertia force*' as one of the forces in response to question 1(b). Such a terminology was difficult to comprehend and needs investigation in greater depth.

7.2.1d Process of Conceptual Myopia

Light and the phenomena associated with it are one of the basic concept domains that are taught in schools as well as in colleges. And of course without realizing the casual relation, light is perhaps the most fundamental natural manifestation, the effect of which human being has enjoyed since his/her existence, at least in the form of just being able to see objects during day time or seeing his image in a pool of water.

At the early stage of schooling the pupils are taught,

- there are sources which emit light,
- light travels from one place to another,
- light makes us see objects,
- because of light, shadows of objects are formed,
- light manifests in several colours, and
- if white light is incident on a coloured glass plate, the transmitted light has the same colour as the glass plate.

At the secondary stage they are taught about reflection and refraction of light and certain associated phenomena. These two concept domains are again discussed in greater details with more theory and applications at the +2 stage. Some of the representative studies to diagnose pupils alternative conceptions in these areas are following:

Stead and Osborne (1980) investigated pupils' views about '*light*' using a set of picture cards as the catalytic tool for conducting a flexible interview procedure which they name as "*Interview about events*". They identified several ALCONs and observed that they held very "*strange*" ideas about such issues as "Does a candle make light?", "What happens to the light?", "How far does the light from the candle go?" and "How is it that the person is able to see the candle?"

Jung (1981) enlists the ALCONs of a sample of 12-15-year olds, who suggest that their image is formed upon a mirror and not '*behind*' it. A distinctive question was asked about a completely dark room with a plane mirror fixed on a wall. A beam of light is directed at an angle on to the mirror while the interviewee is asked to imagine themselves in front of the mirror. They are then asked whether they would know there was a mirror or not. A typical response was that a small bright spot would be seen on the mirror. Jung (1981) interprets this as a "*de-coupling*" between seeing the mirror (or light lying on the mirror) and receiving light from the mirror on the eye.

Anderson and Karrqvist (1983) made a very comprehensive survey of pupils ALCONs about source of light, propagation of light, shadow formation and visibility of an object in the presence of light. Fetherstonhaugh et al. (1987) reported a comparative study of misconceptions; those pupils of Western Australia, France, New Zealand, Sweden and U.S. have about light. Osborne et al. (1983) investigated young children's (age group 7-11 years) ideas about light. An overview of the field may also be obtained from the paper by Ramadas and Shayer (1993).

However no study has been done to investigate pupils ALCONs about laws of reflection and we expect that IIG might be operative in this case. In the textbooks the laws of reflection are stated.

First Law : The incident ray, the reflected ray and the normal, at the point of incidence lie in one place.

Second Law : The angle of incidence is equal to the angle of reflection.

For this investigation the second law was chosen.

After the statement of the law, an experimental verification of the law with exact setup and prescriptive procedure to go about it using a plane mirror is presented. Observation of classroom teaching showed that the teachers faithfully explained the experiment with the plane mirror and what they will find if they performed the experiment. In the laboratory, verification of the law was also done by using plane mirror and pins.

On the other hand in the textbook and in classroom teaching of image formation in spherical mirrors, the ray diagrams are drawn where use of the second law is mentioned in passing without any specific emphasis.

So, we hypothesized that the repeated reinforcement of the proof of the validity of the second law using only plane mirror may lead the pupils to generalize incorrectly that the second law of reflection of light is valid for reflection from plane mirrors only and not from spherical mirrors. And this IIG is likely to manifest in a group of pupils exposed to the above teaching-learning process.

The investigation (Mohapatra, 1988) was conducted using the personal interview (clinical interview a la Piaget) method. The entire conversation was recorded and subsequently transcribed and analysed. The first two questions were common to every subject. They were,

(a) What is the second law of reflection of light?

(b) Is it true in the case of reflection of light from a convex mirror?

The sample consisted of 110 pupils (P1) studying in Class X and 130 pupils (P2) in the second year of the +2 programme.

The clinical interview transcript of one of the pupil is presented below as it clearly indicates IIG.

Interviewer : Is the second law of reflection of light valid in the case of reflection from a concave mirror?

Pupil : No (answer A).

Interviewer : Do you mean to say that it is not valid for reflection from either convex or concave mirror?

Pupil : Yes (answer B)

Interviewer : Why do you think it is not valid in these cases?

Pupil : Because....

Interviewer : Yes...because...?

Pupil : Because the law is true only in the case of a plane mirror (answer C).

Interviewer : Are you sure?

Pupil : Yes.

Interviewer : Why is it so?

Pupil : This has to be so (answer D).

Interviewer : But there has to be some reason....

Pupil : (Thinks) Yes.... It is given in the textbook (answer E).

Interviewer : (Astonished) What is given in the textbook?

Pupil : The section dealing with the verification of laws of reflection of light has described the verification using plane mirror only (answer F).

Interviewer : (Seeing that the student is thinking) Yes....

Pupil : And....

Interviewer : Yes...and....

Pupil : In the practical class we verified the laws of reflection of light using plane mirror only (answer G).

Interviewer : But you have also performed experiments using concave mirror.

Pupil : Yes, the aim of that experiment was to find out the focal length of the concave mirror (answer H).

Interviewer : Well! If that is so, then why don't you call it laws of reflection from a plane mirror?

Pupil : I do not know (answer I).

Interviewer : Think....

Pupil : Perhaps because of old conventions (answer J).

The above full text of the replies by a pupil has some definite points that were common to many pupils. These are the answers C, E, F, G, J. Response C is the induced incorrect generalization (IIG) and response F and G spell out the cause of this IIG. Answer J shows that this IIG has also influenced him to make some unscientific comments. He sees the nomenclature, laws of reflection of light, as an outcome of old conventions and not as a suitable name for some verifiable universal natural phenomenon. Thus the IIG has also affected his process knowledge.

We note in passing that answer D indicates the student's strong conviction about his IIG, answer C. There were also few replies such as, "The law is not valid in the case of spherical surface because one cannot draw a normal to the spherical surface at the point of incidence (answer K)." On questioning about the line joining the centre of curvature to the point of incidence, the reply in these few cases was, "it is only the radius of curvature (answer L)". The main indicators obtained from a detailed analysis of response are tabulated in Table 7.2.

Table 7.2: Per cent of subjects giving a particular answer

Subjects	Answer A	Answer C	Answer F	Answer G	Answer K	Answer L
P1	86.3	85.4	83.6	77.2	15.4	12.7
P2	84.6	82.3	83.1	76.9	13.8	10.7

We also observed that there was no perceptible variation in the response of any group of pupils due to differences in their socio-cultural background, economic status of their parents or their sex. This is perhaps because this particular IIG has been created inside the classroom, where the pupils are treated as equals. Further, one more exposure to the teaching of the same concept at the +2 stage does not seem to have produced any visible change in the ALCONs of the pupils. This is expected because the second exposure suffered from the same limitations with regards to treatment in the textbook and classroom teaching as at the secondary stage and is not likely to modify the ALCONs.

In concluding the discussion we note that although

- pupils study the laws as laws of reflection and not laws of reflection for only plane mirrors, and

- the laws are obviously valid whenever the phenomenon of reflection takes place,

the treatment in the text and the transaction in the class have induced the pupils to internalize a myopic view of the domain of the validity of the laws. As a result of which this process of conceptual myopia has led to the IIG.

7.2.2 Episodic Conceptualization

Classroom teachers are often heard to say "We have now finished '*Mechanics*'". In the next class we move on to '*Heat*', or similar statements in other discipline areas.

This atomized view is seen in the school curriculum, in teaching methods, and even in most of the textbooks. Each unit is treated as a different episode and even as a subsumption of identifiable different episodes. For example, in a physics textbook the unit on mechanics contains kinetics of linear motion, uniform circular motion and rotation of rigid bodies as different sub-episodes.

How does this format affect the construction of concepts by the pupils? In a Piagetian sense, each child internalizes a concept by going through the processes of assimilation and accommodation and arriving at a state of equilibration. With the construction of new concepts and knowledge, one of three possibilities may occur:

(a) The boundary of the earlier equilibration may change to engulf the new concept through a broader generalization. This is likely to happen when the pupil discovers a cognitive link between the new concept and an extension of the already internalized old concept.

(b) The new concept may be accommodated in the domain of the existing equilibration by developing new substrates.

(c) A new and different state of equilibration may start to be formed if the new concept is presented as being independent.

In this framework, the episodic nature of the presentation of different units and sub-units in the textbooks and the classroom is likely to induce the pupil to develop states of isolated, unconnected islands of equilibration. This form of concept construction, followed by internalization and information processing of concepts may be called '*Episodic Conceptualization*' (Epi-Con). In a similar context Tasker and Freyberg (1985) also write that in many cases lessons are frequently seen by the pupils as isolated events even though teachers saw them as building on previous lessons. In their observation a teacher was involved in a lesson where the effect of heat on the rate of dissolving of potassium permanganate crystals in water at different temperatures was to be investigated. The teacher's perception as reported was the following:

> This is the third lesson in a series aimed at developing a particular idea and going over states of matter...the first one (lesson) we did was also to do with this. It was to do with expansion and contraction of substances—today was a direct follow on from that.

However pupils' perception was totally different as is evident from the following discussion.

Interviewer : What was today's lesson about?

Pupil : What crystals can do?

Interviewer : Does today's work has anything to do with this other work you have been doing (Pointing to the pupil's open exercise book which was showing notes headed up as the "dilution of potassium permanganate crystal" and "heating and expanding liquids")?

Pupil : No, not really…no.

In view of the above framework it is hypothesized that:

(a) In the framework of such episodic cognitive structures, if a pupil is asked a question which needs the simultaneous utilization of different states of equilibration, then he/she is likely to give responses which will be categorized as manifest ALCONs.

(b) Since such an Epi-Con is likely to take place inside a classroom, it will probably affect a group of pupils simultaneously and in a similar way. Hence, an effective classroom strategy can perhaps be designed to erase/modify the consequent ALCONs.

(c) Assuming the existence of the phenomenon of Epi-Con, it is proposed that, whenever a simultaneous application of more than one episode is demanded from the pupil, there will be two processes through which the alternative conceptions may manifest because of Epi-Con. First, the 'Process of misuse': the pupil may misuse one or more of the concepts. This misuse could be in the form, structure, and/or domain of validity of the concepts. Second, the 'Process of nonuse': the pupil may not use one or more of the relevant concepts and thus arrive at a conclusion which will be regarded as an ALCON. It may be noted that these process of misuse and process of nonuse are intrinsic part of knowledge construction.

7.2.2a Some Epi-Cons in Mechanics

An investigation was conducted (Mohapatra, 1990) into the existence and operative processes of Epi-Con. The specific episodes chosen were the following:

- inertia of rest and inertia of motion (E1);
- free-fall under gravity (E2);
- projectile motion (E3);
- friction (E4); and
- conservation of momentum (E5).

The boundaries of the above episodes, as dealt with in standard texts and as usually taught in the classroom, are treated as follows. The first three episodes are simultaneously involved whenever motion in space is considered. An analysis of some textbooks (Resnick and Halliday, 1988); Weber et al., 1979) and observation of classroom teaching, demonstrates that the episode of free-fall under gravity is almost always discussed by giving examples where:

(E2.1) only the vertical motion of a body is stated;

(E2.2) bodies having zero or some finite initial velocity in the vertical direction are discussed.

Under free-fall the motion of a body under gravity, having an initial horizontal velocity, (E2.3) is never discussed. In fact, such cases are left to be discussed under the episode on '*projectiles*' with no mention being made of the term '*free-fall*'.

In the third episode:

- (E3.1) a projectile is always considered as a body projected from the surface of the earth;
- (E3.2) the case of horizontal projection from a height is usually treated in passing, mostly in the context of a numerical problem (Resnick and Halliday, 1988; Weber et al., 1978);
- (E3.3) although the constancy of horizontal component of the velocity of the projectile is discussed with emphasis, mention that this is an example of 'Inertial of Motion' in the horizontal direction, due to the absence of any unbalanced force in that direction, is rarely or never made.

In the case of friction:

- (E4.1) that friction helps and hinders motion is discussed in detail;
- (E4.2) however, that, in the absence of friction, motion cannot be transferred from one body to another through their surface-of-contact is never highlighted.

In the case of conservation of momentum:

- (E5.1) that this conservation law is applicable to only isolated systems is rarely emphasized;
- (E5.2) the problem of firing of bullet and the consequent recoil of the gun is discussed in such detail that the pupil is likely to extrapolate its conclusions to seemingly similar situations.

It was conjectured that these interrelated three episodes, with their artificially constructed rigid boundaries as stated above, are likely to generate group alternative conceptions, which will manifest, if test items, demanding simultaneous use of more than one episode, are administered to the pupils.

7.2.2b The Test

The test instrument consisted of only five items, based on the above episodes. However, as an example we discuss here only the first item to search for ALCONs generated by Epi-Con. Interested readers may refer to Mohapatra (1990) for the full text on all the items. The first item contains informative diagram of a simple pendulum in motion. A small explanatory note is given with the diagram. The subjects are then asked to draw, on the diagram, the path that the body in motion will take under given conditions.

Q1. The Fig. 7.6 depicts the oscillation of a simple pendulum. While going from A to B, when the bob has just reached the position B, the string is cut. Trace the path of the bob after that.

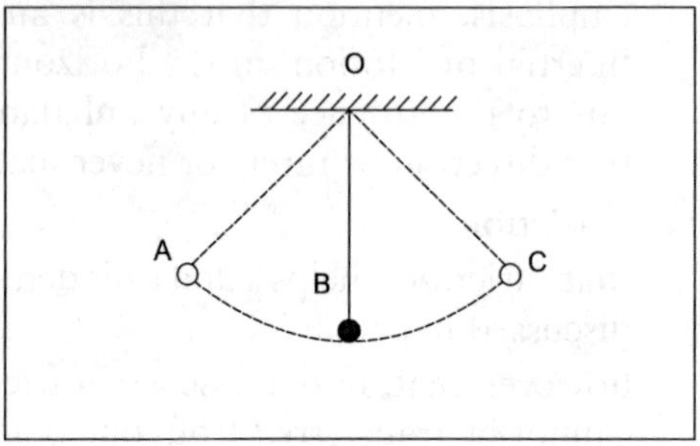

Fig. 7.6

In question 1, the pupils are likely to draw one, or simple combinations of the following basic paths in their responses (R);

(R1.1) From the position B, the bob will take a parabolic path like a projectile. This will show a proper use of the episodes E1, E2 and E3.

(R1.2) The bob will continue along the curve BC or along a horizontal straight line from B. This will demonstrate the misuse of E1 and nonuse of E2 and E3.

(R1.3) The bob will fall vertically downwards, a case of misuse of E2 and nonuse of E1 and E3. This will demonstrate a form of induced incorrect generalization (IIG) wherein the pupil has come to the conclusion that, whatever may be the initial condition, a body left to itself will fall vertically downwards. This is a consequence of E2.1 and E3.2.

(R1.4) The bob will fall along a straight line inclined to the vertical line and towards A. This will show a misuse of E5 and nonuse of E1, E2 and E3.

(R1.5) The bob will fall along a straight line inclined to the vertical line, but towards C. This will show a misuse of E3, nonuse of E1 and E2 and is a consequence of E3.2.

Since the first question is of the open-ended type, the actual responses of the pupils can show many more variations. However, most of them could be shown to be a simple combination of some of the above responses. As for example, a pupil may show that the bob will first go for some distance in a horizontal path and then fall vertically downwards. This path, though seemingly a novel and different one, is actually a combination of R1.2 and R1.3.

The subjects for this case study were both pupils and science teachers. The pupils chosen had scored more highly in formal tests conducted in schools. Students from the Andaman and Nicobar (A&N) islands, a land form in the Bay of Bengal and isolated from the mainland of India, were selected with the specific purpose of comparing their Epi-Cons with those of students of the mainland, through their responses which will reflect their personal constructs.

Table 7.3: The subjects

Subjects	Details of Subjects	Number of Subjects
Pupils		
P1	From Class IX (age group 14-15 years) D.M. School, Bhubaneswar, India	96
P2	From Class X (Age group 15-46 years) of Govt. Boys' Senior Secondary School, Port Blair, A&N Islands, India	56
P3	From Class XI (age group 16-17 years) of D.M. School, Bhubaneswar, India	67
Teachers		
T1	From secondary school of Odisha, where the medium of instruction is Oriya (one of the regional languages of India)	23
T2	From secondary schools of Odisha, where the medium of instructions is English	26
T3	From secondary schools of A&N Islands, where the medium of instruction is English	23

Results and Discussion

The responses from the various groups of subjects are presented in Table 7.4 where the starred response gives the correct response. The numbers in the table give the percentage of subjects of the particular group preferring the specific response. The table shows that

(a) Epi-Con is operative in the manifestation of similar ALCONs by a group of pupils through the processes of misuse and nonuse, as was hypothesized;

(b) there is not much of a difference between the responses of the pupils and those of the teachers, implying that the teachers also have Epi-Cons and have unknowingly transmitted them to the pupils;

(c) since the responses from the subject of the mainland and of the A&N Islands show similar structures, the forms of the Epi-Cons of the subjects from the A&N Islands perhaps do not depend upon the geophysical isolation of the A&N Islands; i.e. occurrence of Epi-Con is perhaps culture independent;

(d) the forms of Epi-Cons of pupils attending Oriya medium schools (which are schools with poor physical facilities) and those reading in schools where the medium of instruction is English (which are schools with much better physical facilities) are similar i.e. occurrence of Epi-Con is almost infrastructure facilities independent.

Table 7.4: Responses (%)

Question No.	Responses	Subjects					
		P1	P2	P3	T1	T2	T3
1	*R1.1	0.0	3.1	0.0	4.3	7.7	4.3
	R1.2	17.8	31.2	38.1	26.1	19.2	13.0
	R1.3	53.5	37.5	19.1	13.0	19.2	26.1
	R1.4	5.3	0.0	0.0	13.0	7.7	13.0
	R1.5	21.4	28.2	42.8	43.6	46.2	43.6

These general observations seem to demonstrate that Epi-Cons are almost universal phenomena. If that is so, then the ALCONs resulting because of the existence of Epi-Cons are also likely to have universal features. In that situation, universal strategies can be formulated for use inside classrooms to erase/ modify the alternative conceptions.

Apart from the above broad observations, the following specific conclusions can also be reached:

(a) The extremely low percentage of subjects giving the correct responses (R1.1) shows the inability of the subject to utilize more than one concept simultaneously, because of the episodic nature of internalization.

(b) Responses R1.3 shows the misuse of the concept of free-fall. The responses R1.3 has also been reported earlier by Mc Closkey et al. (1981). Through independent group discussions amongst the pupils and the teachers it was observed that, once the string is cut, the pupils as well as the teachers regard the bob to be a free body at rest and hence conclude that, in the absence of any support, it must fall vertically downwards. This conclusion seems to have been arrived at by the process of 'Conceptual Extrapolation' (Mohapatra et al., 1989), discussed earlier in this chapter.

(c) Responses R1.2 is a case of misuse of E1. The subsequent discussion about it, demonstrated that both pupils and teachers had yet to conceptualize in a concrete form the concept of inertia of motion. This is so perhaps because the subjects still do not realize that 'body at rest' and 'body in motion' are relative concepts. An effective way for the internalization of these concepts by the pupils could be to teach the relativistic nature of rest and motion through the demonstration and use of stroboscopes or computer generated programmes.

(d) It can be seen that in some cases (as for example the responses of subjects P1 to question 1) the sum of the percentage of various responses is not equal to 100. This is so because, in such cases, one or two pupils gave responses which do not conform to the proposed format of basic responses, but are combinations of them.

This section on Genesis of ALCONs helps the researcher and the teacher, to

- comprehend the philosophy of Research for Teaching and Teaching for Research,
- get exposed to real classroom exemplars about the genesis of ALCONs,
- appreciate the processes of conceptual reversibility, conceptual continuity, conceptual extrapolation, and conceptual myopia as generative causes of IIG during knowledge construction,
- also understand Episodic Conceptualisation (Epi-Con) as a generative cause of ALCONs during knowledge construction, and has the potential to transform the Teacher to a researcher and construct realistic tools to help her diagnose and map the processes of knowledge construction by the pupils.

7.3 Major Characteristics of ALCONs

Before the form of a holistic approach to ALCONs is agreed upon, that may lead to list the do's and don'ts of teachers, the teachers should be clear about our understanding of ALCONs in terms of their characteristics. A constructivistic analysis of extensive case studies in this field leads to the following features (Mohapatra, 1989).

(a) ALCONs exist by happening. We know they exist because they manifest. This conclusion is clearly illustrated by such evidences as the drawing of a one-line connection from the battery to the bulb (Anderson, 1986; Tiberghien and Delacote, 1976; Osborne, 1981) or the statement that the weight of a cup of ball bearings would increase if it were raised (Driver, 1983), or the expression that if a weight is dropped in a measuring cylinder full of water, the water level will not rise (Claxton, 1985), or the conviction that increase in mass due to rusting is a physical change (Mohapatra, Tripathy and Parida, 1998), or the thousands of examples in the literature. They exist inside the pupils' thoughts even though they may not match the reflections of formal science.

(b) ALCONs are real and they are physical to the extent that they have a real 'mental' existence in the minds of the pupils. In fact, in a rational sense, they are part of the search for a coordinated reality by the pupils' science. And because they are real, one has to take note of them while teaching in the classroom instead of regarding them as an outcome of the pupils' short-sighted view of natural phenomena.

(c) ALCONs have a range of convenience defined by the pupil's state of equilibration (Piaget, 1964) arrived at through endogenous reconstruction of exogenous acquisitions. Their boundaries are demarked by what is convenient to the pupil rather than what the natural phenomenon is. Thus, they are 'local' and not 'global' in their perspectives. However, in all the cases these local boundaries are not symbolized by words, because there are situations when the pupils' responses to clinical probes are only in pantomime or speechless impulses. Claxton (1985) calls these range of conveniences as "domains".

(d) ALCONs have structures and no epi-structures, i.e. they are not shadows of the pupils' thoughts. These structures appear in two forms (1) peripheral, which is construed by the range of convenience as well as by the inter-conception boundaries, and (2) internal, which is generated either by (i) affirmation or similarities, e.g. the one-way picture of source-consumer concept has in it such structures as that the current in a circuit decreases as one moves away from the cell, or the concept of conservation of volume of two bodies taken together is equal to the sum of the volumes the bodies have, has within its boundary such concept as when two equally cold liquids are mixed together, the resultant liquid will be doubly cold, or the understanding of bodies immersed in water has imbedded in it the non-unified, individualized pictures of sugar in water, boats in water, and a stone in water, or by (ii) negation, e.g. the induced incorrect generalizations in the pupils' minds, leading to the misconceptions that the laws of reflection of light are true only in the case of reflection from a plane mirror has in its domain the phenomena of reflection from spherical mirrors as a negative entity, because the pupils feel that the laws are not valid for reflection from spherical mirrors.

(e) ALCONs are modifiable, because the pupil himself/herself modifies, though, perhaps, under suitable stimulus. The modification can be produced by any of the following processes (Claxton, 1985).

(i) By integration of two or more concepts, thereby creating a new concept with a new topology. A pupil visiting a hot spring is told that the temperature of the spring is high but constant and he develops the concept that hot springs have their temperatures constant. Then in his home he acquires the concept when he changes the regulator from speed 3 to 5, making the fan rotate more rapidly, that changing the regulator from the lower mark to the higher mark results in an increase of the activity of the appliance. This he now applies to a new situation where he rotates the knob of the regulator of the cooking range with a beaker of water on the stove. But to his amazement he finds that the temperature of the water remains constant at 100 degree Celsius. He then remembers about the spring, the water in which, in his frame, was at a constant temperature because it was a hot spring. He then tries a trans-situational unification of the two phenomena. He integrates them by observing that in both the cases the water is boiling and he reaches a new concept that boiling keeps the temperature constant, although this is not necessarily the correct explanation of the constancy of the temperature of the water of the hot spring.

(ii) By the process of engulfment, where one concept appears as a part/special case of another concept. The pupil develops the concept that biology is the study of life. Then extending the concept that motion is the sign of life, he concludes that motor-car has life given to it by petrol and electricity. Now he engulfs this concept by the first concept by remarking that a study of how a car works is a study of biology (Gilbert and Osborne, 1980).

(iii) By abstraction, leading to a separation of the zone of overlap of two concepts so as to form a new domain. The pupil has the concept that (i) when a bath is heated, bubbles rise from the bottom, (ii) when a cold drink bottle is opened bubbles rise inside it, (iii) when a stone is thrown into a pond bubbles rise, and (iv) when soap solution is stirred bubbles are formed. These four different concepts have one common zone of overlap i.e. formation of bubbles. However, his failure to unify them forces him to separate the concept of formation of bubbles into a new domain. This is a process of abstraction.

(iv) By relocation, after discovering that the placement of the concept was actually a misplacement. A pupil may have one situational concept about the lowering of several solid objects into a liquid—such as a pebble into water, himself into a bath, a boat on a river and sugar into a tea-cup. But with his exposure to new experiments he learns that the last phenomenon belongs to a category other than the first three and thus puts it into a new domain of his conceptual space.

(v) By construction following the discovery of the failure of a concept to explain new phenomena. Watts (1982) and Gunstone & White (1980) have shown that the pupils have the concept that gravity operates to bring 'heavier' objects more rapidly to the surface of the earth. However, when the pupils are faced with the experiment of two bodies of different mass falling simultaneously from the same height as seen through the camera (slow motion) they are obviously forced to reconstruct their concept about the phenomenon of free-fall under gravity.

The process for achieving these modifications, through formal teaching, can be easy if the pupil is receptive or it can be difficult if the pupil, like a bad scientist (Claxton, 1985) feels no need to change (perhaps because he thinks that his concept is as good, if not better, as those of others), or may feel a need not to change (perhaps because he thinks that a change in his concept may amount to a change in himself which is not acceptable). However, there are two important outcomes of this characteristic of modifiability of alternative conceptions: (i) An effort for modification may encounter resistance. This resistance in an appropriate strength could be constructive in the same sense that friction helps motion. But too much of this resistance could be destructive as too much of friction stops all motion. On the other hand, lack of resistance may incorporate an easily deformable transient shape in the concepts of the pupil in the same way as the absence of friction makes the body change its state of motion by the application of the slightest force. This will leave the pupil with no clear, identifiable concepts to fall back upon, (ii) As the alternative conceptions are modifiable, they are expendable. This means the pupil can accept new impetus and have vertical growth.

(f) ALCONs are integral in spirit and nature. They try to integrate the world of knowledge of the child with the world outside. This integration is effected through a continuous process of bringing about a correspondence between what the pupil thinks really exists and what does really exist.

(g) ALCONs are interactive i.e. they are sensitive and not without sense. The absence of sense in them will induce in them a rigidity which will completely eliminate their character of modifiability, thus making the pupil cease to be evolving entities. This of course never happens and because of (e) and (f) above, there is always interaction in some form or other.

(h) ALCONs can be shared more freely among pupils having an age-homogeneity. This is so because in such a group the phenomenon of centrition of Piaget appears in a strong form. However, this centrition leads to a sharing of concepts between one another and results in decentrition. But such a sharing is less perceptible in a heterogeneous group. Because of the live psychological attribute of communicability the knowledge of the pupils' changes, grows and progresses.

(i) ALCONs are independent of geo-cultural boundaries, gender and perhaps of age and ability of the learner.

(j) The ALCONs sometime also offer resistance for their modification or erasement (Mc Closkey, 1983; Halloun and Hestenes, 1985; Dykstra et al., 1992; Mohapatra and Parida, 1995), whenever such an effort is made by any external agency (teacher).

We concludes this section by noting that discussions of these broad characteristics of ALCONs is likely to help the researcher to chose one of the dimensions for an intensive and extensive study and perhaps help the teacher to comprehend and appreciate the importance and pervasiveness of ALCONs and the fact that they are a reality and not a figment of high level research studies.

With similar aim to arrive at some broad features of ALCONs Wandersee, Mintzes and Novak (1994) generated eight "emerging" research-based claims about ALCONs, summaries of which are (quoted from Table 2 of Wenning, 2008):

- Learners come to formal science instruction with a diverse set of alternative conceptions concerning natural objects and events.
- The alternative conceptions that learners bring to formal science instruction cut across age, ability, gender and cultural boundaries.

- Alternative conceptions are tenacious and resistant to extinction by conventional teaching strategies.
- Alternative conceptions often parallel explanations of natural phenomena offered by previous generations of scientists and philosophers.
- Alternative conceptions have their origins in a diverse set of personal experiences including direct observation and perception, peer culture and language, as well as in teacher's explanations and instructional materials.
- Teachers often subscribe to the same alternative conceptions as their students.
- The learner's prior knowledge interacts with the knowledge, presented in formal instruction, resulting in a diverse variety of unintended learning outcomes.
- Instructional approaches that facilitate conceptual change can be effective classroom tools.

It can be easily seen that these 8 findings are a subset of our findings, enlisted and discussed in this section.

7.4 The PACT Space

Once this concretistic classification of the characteristics of ALCONs is achieved, it is worthwhile to allot the ALCONs their appropriate location in the space of TLP. Of course the first dimension of the space of TLP is the pupil (P), because in the absence of him/her the teaching process does not exist. Once the pupil is fixed, he/she carries with him/her ALCONs (A) specific to him/her. We name this A as the fourth dimension (instead of second) of TLP so as to keep record of the fact that this is the dimension that was recognized last. This is a new dimension and any teaching process has to recognize, consider, understand, interpret, and use it so as to achieve optimum functionality in the process of knowledge constructions. The second dimension is obviously the curriculum (C), which includes the totality of information and knowledge to be imparted to the pupil and may include even its hidden form. The third has to be the teacher (T), who has to transmit the knowledge to the pupil. The word "*Teacher*", however, need not strictly mean a teacher in the classroom and thus may include a whole lot of persons. We call this four-dimensional space, PACT, the space of teaching-learning process (TLP). Every point in this space defines a quantum of knowledge acquired by the pupil. At this point one comment is in order: One should not look at this space and its dimensions in exactly the same way as one does in the case of, say, the four-dimensional space of time and space. Because as contrasted with the four-dimensional physical space, each of the dimensions of the PACT space does not have a scale and none of the dimensions has the property of seriation, i.e. one cannot say that one point is higher up than another point in the coordinate of one of the dimensions.

However, the introduction of the fourth dimension does create some new ramifications in the sense that we have now six planes which need definition.

The plane defined by C and T, Fig. 7.7, is the plane of TEACHING. The various methodologies used for effective teaching may define the shapes of traces on this plane.

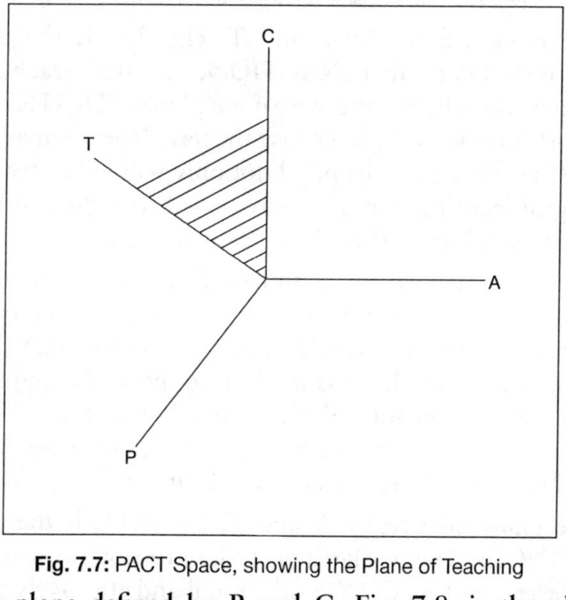

Fig. 7.7: PACT Space, showing the Plane of Teaching

The plane defined by P and C, Fig. 7.8, is the plane of LEARNING. The shapes of lines in this plane, connecting a point on P to a point on C may represent the quality and quickness of the learning process.

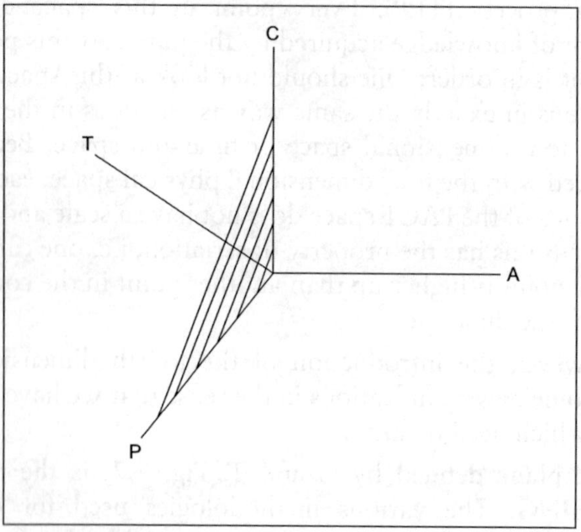

Fig. 7.8: PACT Space, showing the Plane of Learning

The plane defined by P and T, Fig. 7.9, is the plane of CONSTRUCTIVE INTERACTION, if the teaching has achieved its objectives, otherwise it is a plane of DESTRUCTIVE INTERACTION. In the later case the term 'Destructive' is used, because in such a case, the pupil not only will fail to receive any meaningful learning, but also may be led to a state of learning instability which may affect his/her further study.

The plane defined by A and C, Fig. 7.10, is the plane of OVERLAP. The commonality in phenomena and concepts, existing in the pupils' ALCONs and the curriculum, is likely to create traces in this plane. But suppose the pupil has a concept about the heating effect of electric current, and he/she is attending a class in social sciences, then in such a situation, the plane of OVERLAP remains mostly dormant.

The plane defined by A and T, Fig. 7.11, is the plane of EXCHANGES. The teacher's procedure to suitably analyse and study the relevant ALCONs of the pupil and effectively use them in the process of teaching are possible lines in this plane.

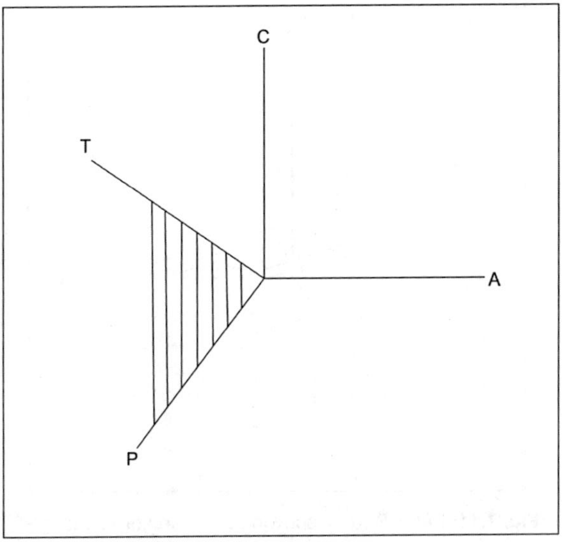

Fig. 7.9: PACT Space, showing the Plane of Constructive Interaction

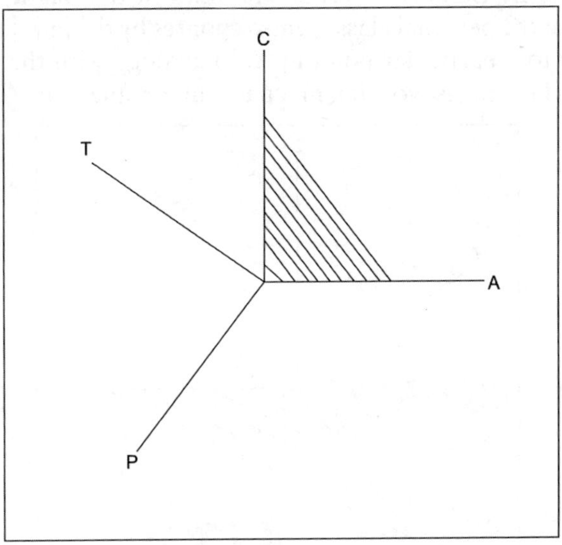

Fig. 7.10: PACT Space, showing the Plane of Overlap

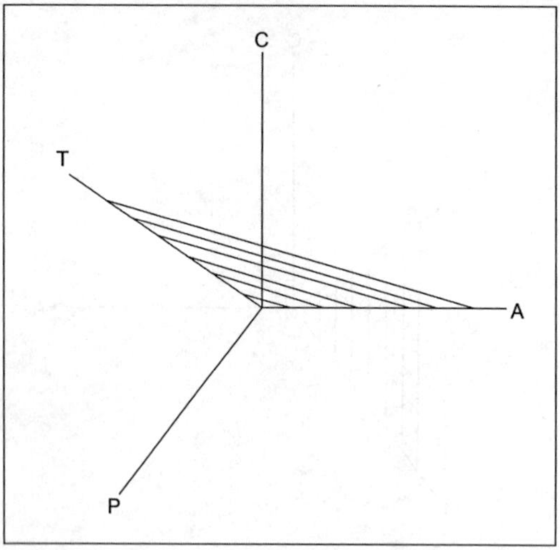

Fig. 7.11: PACT Space, showing the Plane of Exchanges

The plane defined by A and P, Fig. 7.12, is the plane of PERSONAL CONSTRUCTS. The lines in this plane perhaps represent the personal classroom-responses by the pupil that lead him/her to a particular point in A. In analogy with the physical space, when one is working in a particular plane, say C and T,

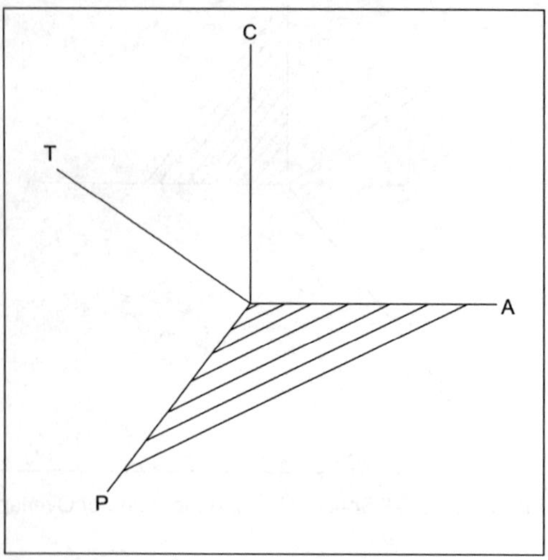

Fig. 7.12: PACT Space, showing the Plane of Personal Constructs

of the PACT space, the other five planes mostly remain dormant. But TLP is a sequential trace of a continuous line, moving from one plane to the other.

7.4.1 Implications

Before an attempt is made to study the effects of the inclusion of the fourth dimension of TLP, let us have a diagrammatic look at TLP in the conventional three-dimensional space of P, C and T, and try to answer the question: What are the paths available to the teacher in this 3-D space? The following interesting states emerge from an analysis of the various possibilities.

(a) **State of alienation:** Usually the form and structure of the teaching of an average teacher is pupil independent, i.e. if one replaces one group of pupils by another group, the teacher's style and content of teaching is not going to change much. This is so because he/she thinks that his/her responsibility is to teach and it is the pupil's responsibility to learn. This is represented in Fig. 7.13. The teacher starts from 'a' and through his teaching reaches 'b'. He expects the pupil at 'c' to make a self-effort and reach the same point 'b' and learns the content.

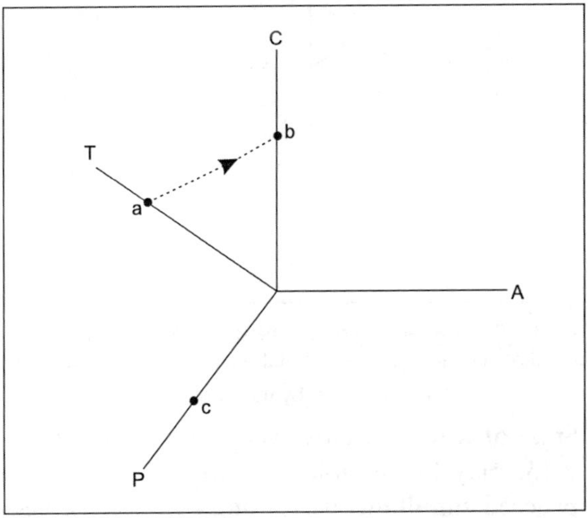

Fig. 7.13: PACT Space, showing the path leading to the State of Alienation the path taken by the Teacher Only

In this case since the teaching is 'content-centered', the pupil rarely feels the urge to reach the point 'b' and thus may develop a form of contextual alienation.

(b) **State of conditional learning:** A teacher, better than the one mentioned above, may after reaching 'b', try (Fig. 7.14) to proceed towards the pupil via the path 'bd', whereas the pupil may try to reach 'b' via the path 'ce'. If these two lines intersect, then learning occurs in a conventional sense. However, this may occur rarely. What possibly may happen is that the lines 'bd' and 'ce' may approach each other. In such a case the proximity (which will be different for different pupils) of the two lines will perhaps indicate the degree and quality of learning of the pupil.

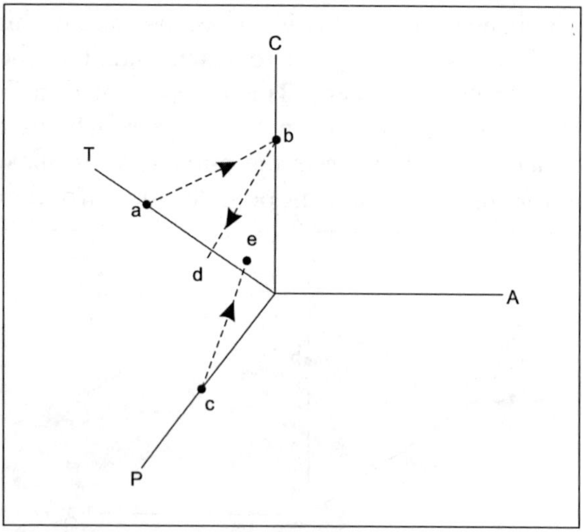

Fig. 7.14: PACT Space, showing the path leading to the State of Conditional Learning—the path taken by the Teacher only and the path taken by the Pupil Only

(c) **State of learning:** However, a good teacher at 'a', Fig. 7.15, may by suitable utilization of his competencies, proceed simultaneously along two planes, i.e. plane of PT and plane of TC. He makes an effort to reach the pupil at 'c' and the curriculum at 'b' and then guides 'c' to reach 'b'. This is a harmonious mixture of 'child-centered' teaching and is expected to produce best results in the conventional TLP.

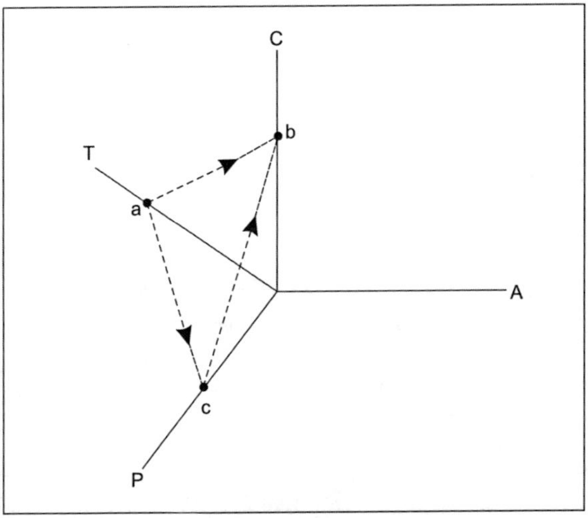

Fig. 7.15: PACT Space, showing the paths leading to the State of Learning—the path taken by the Teacher only and the path taken by Both the Teacher and the Pupil

However, the inclusion of the fourth dimension leads to a few new states. Some of the important ones are the following:

(a) **State of resistance:** Let us consider the best of the conventional teachers. When the teacher, Fig. 7.16, has simultaneously reached the point 'b' in the dimension of C and the point 'c' in the dimension of P, the child 'c' will be actually proceeding towards 'x', a point on the coordinate of his/her ALCONs. And the teacher does not have a procedure to correlate between 'b' and 'x'. The teacher obviously tries to guide the pupil along 'cb' whereas the pupil has a natural preference for the path 'cx'. Thus the effort by the teacher is met with resistance from the pupil (Driver and Easely, 1978; Gilbert, Osborne and Fensham, 1982; Fisher, 1985). Because of this inherent mismatch between the natural tendency and the imposed constraints, the pupil fails to appreciate the proposed path "cb" and accept the formal science. There may also be a new type of complicacy in the sense that the pupil might have more than one ALCON x, y, z, about the same phenomena.

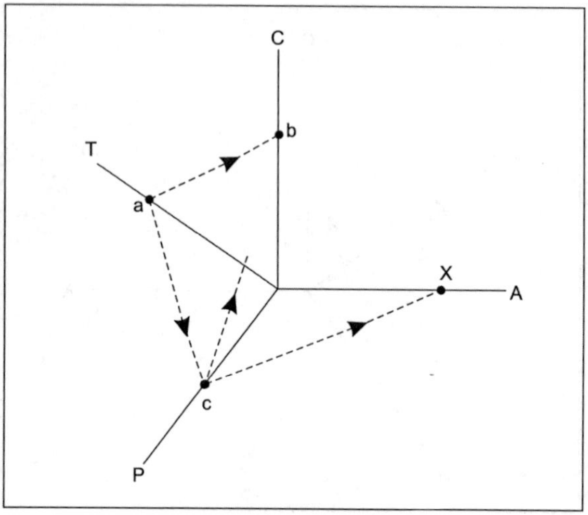

Fig. 7.16: PACT Space, showing the path leading to the State of Resistance—the path taken by the Teacher only. The path taken by the Pupil only and the path taken both by the Teacher and the Pupil

(b) **State of conceptual dichotomy:** If the teaching is effective and the ALCON is also strongly imbedded in the pupil's mind, then he/she may retain both the formal and informal notions and stay simultaneously at 'b' and 'x'. This corresponds to Fig. 8 of Gilbert and Swift's (1985) observations. However, if his/her ALCONs are weak, he/she is likely to retrace his/her path from 'x' to 'c' and start moving along 'cb' with his teacher. And if he does not have any alternative conceptions, then he will gladly travel along 'cb'. The above two cases correspond, respectively, to Fig. 7 and Fig. 6 of Gilbert and Swift (1985).

(c) **State of meaningful learning:** Perhaps, a better approach will be, Fig. 7.17, that the teacher, starting from 'a' will first try to reach the pupil at 'c' through constructive interaction (plane PT) relevant to his objectives and then enter into the plane of personal constructs (PA) to reach 'x'. For this he may use any of the following technique: (i) Cognitive conflict (Murray, 1968; Johnson and Howe, 1978; Hewson, 1981; Dreyfus et al., 1990; Mortimer and Machado, 2000; Lee et al., 2003), (ii) Concept map (Novak, 1990; Mathews, Brook and Khan-Gandapur, 1984), (iii) interview-about-instances (Gilbert and Osborne, 1980), (iv) Pencil-on-paper test, (v) Clinical interview, (vi) Dissonance through group discussion (Nussbaum and Novick, 1981a, 1981b) and other broad techniques discussed in Chapter 6. Once the teacher has reached 'x' with the pupil, and thus identified the ALCONs, he/she has to recognize the zone of overlap (plane AC) between the ALCONs and the curriculum, and move in that plane with the pupil along 'xd'. He has to then formulate his/her strategies for leaving the plane AC at some point 'd' and move to some point 'e' in the plane of learning, PC. This has to be performed smoothly and not catastrophically (Gilbert and Watts, 1983) through several quasi-equilibrium steps. After this only, he may try to effect a notional change in the pupil by guiding him to the point 'b'. This procedure looks somewhat like a spiral model. This also minimizes the resistance from the pupil and may suitably build up his psychology for a transconceptual transformation.

But this inclusion of the fourth dimension creates another new problem in a classroom-teaching situation. So far we have been discussing the learning process of a single pupil. Once a group of pupil, as that in a class, is involved, the situation changes drastically, because as emphasized earlier, the pupils in a class may have several different ALCONs about the same natural phenomena and this corresponds to several points which will become simultaneously active. Further, the mental organizations (Viennot, 1985) of the conceptions could be different for different pupils. These inherent hyperfine structures will make the problem complex for the teacher unless some regularities or group phenomena (section 7.2 of this chapter) are observed in this sensitive domain. Watts, Gilbert and Pope (1982) have reported a composite picture based on ideas shared by a number of pupils. Engel (1982) found out that the different frameworks used by pupils are finite and reasonably stable. Engel and Driver (1983) confirmed this observation of Engel. The above studies are contextual in character in the sense that the generative causes have not been identified therein. However, our search for the genesis of a group ALCON thus gains importance in this framework of PACT space if we are to take the research findings into the classroom.

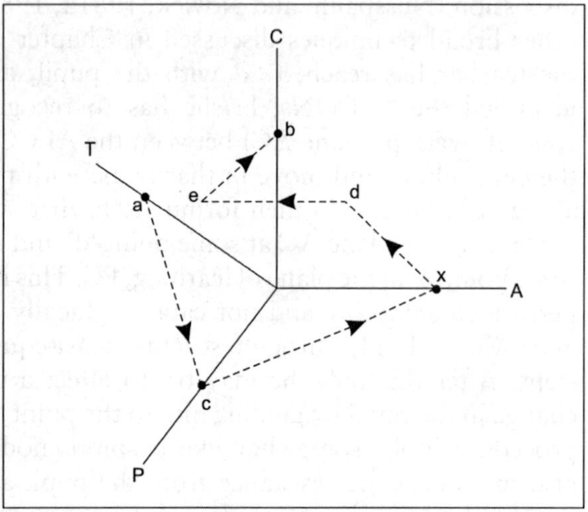

Fig. 7.17: PACT Space, showing the paths leading to the State of Meaningful Learning—the path taken by the Teacher only and the path taken both by the Teacher and the Pupil.

7.5 Role of the Teacher

7.5.1 Introduction

In spite of the fact that in the literature Constructivism appears in a plethora of forms (as discussed in Chapter 2), so that some people comment on Constructivism as a veritable jungle, there are three major tenets (von Glasersfeld, 1995; Staver, 1998) about which all the proponents of constructivism agree. They are:

1. Knowledge cannot be instructed. It is actively constructed through an autogenic process by the cognizing subject, the learner.

2. The character of cognition is functional and adaptive.
3. The purpose of cognition is to serve the learner in comprehending and organizing his/her experiential world and not to discover an objective ontological reality.

It is desirable that the contents of these three tenets be discussed in a little greater detail because only from that discussion the role of the teacher will emerge.

From the tenet-1, it is clear that learners actively construct their own knowledge whenever they learn something; also in settings that are not informed by constructivist ideas, i.e. even in strictly traditional settings that start from a passive reception view (Miller, 1989). Even when the learner rejects a concept and does not learn it, the learner still goes through a process of construction and arrives at an output of "Conceptual Rejection" (as discussed in Chapter 5) almost in the same way as Kepler went on rejecting models after models those could describe the path of a planet revolving round the sun. And when the learner constructs his/her own ALCON which is perhaps at variance with the accepted connotation of the formal concept, his/her ALCON is still real and valid for him/her in so far as organizing his/her experiential world is concerned. This picture has lots of similarity with Aristotle's ALCON that the earth is the center of the universe, because the Pope, who is the messenger of God, lives here or Lamarck's ALCON, i.e. his theory of evolution, which is based on the principle of use and misuse.

It is also possible that a learner could be able to construct new conceptions (i.e. new ALCONs) without the guidance of formal classroom teaching and solely on the basis of his/her already existing ALCONs. This involves two dimensions.

Dimension I: This dimension may appear to some as hypothetical. But research studies show that this is very much real. Every learner (even in the absence of external stimulus) observes, uses his/her already existing ALCONs, acquired through culture, language and society, to construe the observations, simplifies, interprets and re-interprets (Jung, 1986), searches for symmetry, makes cognitive adjustments and generates a new concept (nay,

ALCON) in his cognitive domain. All these sequential steps are part of a process of construction. This is possible because every learner, and for that matter every human being, is a thinking being, i.e. a homosapien.

At this point an explanatory episode is in order.

A child was stranded in the forest alone. It was winter time. Evening was fast approaching. He had the ALCON that only setting a fire can give him some relief from the cold wintery night. He had a match box with him and he had the ALCON that by using the match box he can start a fire. But, he did not have the knowledge as to what objects easily catch fire. So he collected objects those were available nearby and started the fire. He observed the fire, analysed his observations, made cognitive interpretations and arrived at the conclusion (ALCON) that cylindrical objects easily catch fire and provide a sustained fire a long period. This is so because he has accidentally collected dry twigs.

Naturally next day he started collecting only cylindrical objects. Since there was a discarded automobile and since his existing ALCONs cannot distinguish between a metal pipe and a twig in so far as it fire catching ability is concerned, the child collected twigs as well as broken metal pipes from the automobile. Needless to state that the metal pipes did not catch fire and the child developed a new cognitive structure: "Twigs catch fire, but metal pipes do not catch fire."

This micro-episode illustrates how a child constructs knowledge to comprehend and organize his/her experiential world and how he/she interprets, modifies and reinterprets his/her observations. A teacher's role in this case would have been to help him/her in his construction of knowledge. This episode also exemplifies to view learner's "self-development" and "helped-development" as complementary processes for meaningful construction of concepts as advocated by active theory (Wolze and Walgenbach, 1992; Pfundt and Duit, 1994).

Dimension II: The micro-episode, described above, also highlights that every learning and every knowledge acquisition go through a process of autogenic construction. In other words one cannot have learning without construction. Thus there is simply "learning" (Pfundt and Duit, 1994) and naming it "Constructivist Learning" is redundant, in the same way as calling "Black Crow" is redundant, because one does not ever have a "Non-Constructivist Learning", in the same way as one does not ever have a "White Crow". However, as in Literature, we will still retain the term "Constructivist Learning" only to emphasize the fact that every learning is preceded by the generic process of construction. However, there is definitely NO "Constructivist Teaching". We may at best use the term "Constructivist Teaching Approaches" with the agreed connotation that this term means "Teaching Approaches that help and promote meaningful knowledge construction by the learner."

Tenet-1 also states that knowledge cannot be instructed. In the traditional teaching-learning scenario this appears to be a very strong statement. It seems as if the teacher is not needed any more, i.e. the teacher is redundant. But that is not so. In fact in a constructivist framework the role of the teacher has become more complex and all the more important as discussed in the next sub-section.

Tenet-2 asserts that cognition is "functional" and "adaptive". These two terminologies with their inherent structure are very often heard in a discourse on Darwin's theory of evolution. This theory has three main contentions. They are:

- Struggle for existence
- Survival of the fittest
- Principle of Natural selection.

All the three principles in conjunction advocate that the organisms, provided with favourable variations succeed in the struggle for existence. These organisms are fittest for survival. Other animals are unfit to survive and they perish. The fitness or unfitness is decided by the environment. So the environment acts as the selecting force in the nature. It selects those organisms which are provided with favourable variations. This process of selection of organism with favourable variations is called natural selection. This results in progressive improvement of existing organisms.

This model of the evolution of an organism with the three basic principles can be directly transported to the cognitive evolution of the learner through knowledge construction. Because there is lots of similarity between the two processes. The prior knowledge (i.e. the host of ALCONs) of the learner is the organism with its strengths and weaknesses. When the learner encounters a new concept it is like the organism, set in a new environment. The new concept comes with many competing connotations which are based on the learner's ALCONs, the teacher's concepts, the society's concept and of course the textbook concept. And there is a struggle for existence in the cognitive space of the learner involving "meaning comprehension", "interpretation", "re-interpretation", "plausibility", "fruitfulness" (Hewson and Thornley, 1989; Schollum and Osborne, 1985; Mohapatra, 1989; Villani, 1992) within the framework of comprehending and organizing the learner's experiential environment. In this struggle for cognitive existence the learner is busy with his/her construction, deconstruction and reconstruction. The connotation (not necessarily the one approved by formal science) which survives and gets accommodated in the cognitive space of the learner is the fittest connotation. And the entire process is a process of natural cognitive selection. In this context the role of the teacher is paramount as he/she has to set the environment in such a way that the fittest one in the framework of the learner resembles closely to the one approved by formal science, as discussed in the next sub-section. This is a very complex responsibility for a traditional teacher.

The above parallelism between Darwin's theory of evolution and the cognitive evolution of the learner greatly justifies the tenet-2.

Tenet-3 is a natural corollary of tenet-2 because 'functional' and 'adaptive' demand that the construction of new knowledge must be meaningful and fruitful (Hewson and Thornley, 1989) for the learner in so far as his/her experiential world is concerned. There might be an absolute ontological reality and the purpose of acquisition of knowledge as prescribed by the society and system may be to discover and comprehend that ontological reality, but the sole purpose of acquisition of knowledge through autogenic construction by the learner is simply to comprehend and organize his/her experiential world.

This tenet-3 brings in two dimensions.

Dimension I: In a classroom teaching situation, since every learner's constructed concept about any concept, event, instance, example, is directly dependent on his/her own ALCONs and has been generated on the basis of his/her best fitment for his/her own experiential world, there is every likelihood that there will be a multiplicity of concepts about the same objective concept of formal science. Thus, constructivism advocates (von Glasersfeld, 1987) the existence of multiple truths, representations, perspectives and realities for the same ontological reality. This concept of multiplicity has important implications for teaching (Murphy, 1997). The teacher's role will be (von Glasersfeld, 1995) that of a "midwife in the birth of understanding" as opposed to being "a mechanic of knowledge transfer".

Dimension II: An outcome of the existence of monoism in the process of knowledge construction is the principle of **solipsism.** As per *Webster's Dictionary* 'Solipism' means the self is the only thing that is really existent. In this context constructivism asserts that the constructions of a learner are real and valid for him/her and those constructions constitute the reality for him/her. Von Glasersfeld (1995a) advocates that constructivism does not say there is no other world (i.e. objective, ontological reality) and no other people, it merely holds that in so far as the learner (even we) knows them, both the world and the others are mere models that the learner constructs himself/herself. Maturana (1988) and Maturana & Varela (1992) frequently assert that there is no independently existing reality (Raskin, 2002). Central to Maturana's (1988) work is the concept of **autopoiesis**—the notion that organisms (read learners) are by definition, self-creating and self-sustaining systems. Like von Glasersfeld, Maturana sees (Raskin, 2002) "Living systems as cognitively closed. When living systems think they are mapping an external world, they are simply experiencing and processing their own structurally determined responses, i.e. personal constructs." A closed system never comes into direct contact with reality. What is "outside" never gets "inside" (Raskin, 2002). These arguments clearly show that in the framework of the learner one has only the "Subjective Reality" or the "Private Reality" and no "Objective Reality" or "Public Reality". This is basis of the statement that solipisism goes side by side with the observation that reality is a personal construct.

Staver (1998) resolves this problem of solipsism (which many people think is inherent in constructivism and makes it flawed) by invoking von Foerster's postulate of relativity, which states, "a hypothesis that holds for A and holds for B will be rejected if it does not hold for A and B together" (Segal, 1986; von Foerster, 1984). Following Staver (1998) *vis-à-vis* von Foerster let us say:

- A is a solipsist.
- Then for A, his/her own consciousness is the only reality.
- There are other people, but they exist only in the mental construct of A.
- So they are only A's imagination.
- But these apparitions are also solipsist, because every human being is a solipsist by design.
- To each of these everyone else is a figment of his/her imagination.
- Thus for them A also one of the person they imagine.

Then von Foerster posed a dilemma (Staver, 1998). Can each of us be the sole reality? The answer is obviously NO. So von Foerster concludes, we cannot be solipsists imagining each other.

However, without entering into this theoretical controversy as to whether solipsism is operant or not, one is guided by the research based facts that for the learner his/her constructs are the real things for him/her and he/she is not interested in discovering any objective reality. The teacher has to redesign his/her role and activities in the framework of this truth.

7.5.2 Teacher's Role

From the discussions in the preceding sub-section it is clear that from the constructivistic point of view, where it is asserted that the "Knower constructs his/her knowledge", the teacher's role has become more complex, more demanding and more challenging with multi-layered features. Thus, the teacher's role has to be defined with a changed focus.

Before we proceed to discuss in detail this new role which will be richer in structures (Nussbaum and Novick, 1981) let us see what are the salient features of the present traditional role of a good teacher. We prefer to deviate from a normal textbook and present a checklist which is realistic and comprehensible.

A good teacher (traditional) should have:

- *Excellent professional knowledge*: Without this the situation inside the classroom will be like a blind person trying to help another blind person to search a black cat in a dark room, where it is not. Professional knowledge includes both content and pedagogical knowledge as well as 'Pedagogical Content Knowledge' (Shulman, 1987).
- *The commitment of a surgeon*: A surgeon, proceeding to the operation table, forgets whether the patient is rich or poor, educated or uneducated, an influential or a common man. His total commitment is to the operation he is going to perform.
- *The organizing ability of an executive*: An executive rarely himself does any active work. All that he does is he puts the right person at the right place, makes available the right facilities at the right time, sees the right information reaches the right worker, etc. Similarly a teacher has to properly organize the classroom, his lesson, his activities, his interactions, his time schedule, the group discussions, the question answer sessions, etc.

- *The inspiring ability of a preacher*: There are instances that on hearing a single talk by a preacher people have tried to change their lifestyle and become noble persons. History of science records that the first lecture from the first teacher inspired Madam Curie so much that she vowed to become a scientist. And the rest is history.
- *The human approach of a psychiatrist*: When a psychiatrist is treating a psychologically unstable patient he is more concerned for the mental health of the patient than for his own safety. For instance, if the patient suddenly starts rebuking him, then he does not get irritated, rather he thinks through his humane approach that unknowingly he has touched some sensitive center of the patient's mind. Similarly, if a teacher finds that a pupil is behaving awkwardly or giving meaningless, error prone responses, he should with all humane patience searches for the cause of such a response and try to help the pupil come out of that depressive state, and not reprimand the pupil.
- *The friendly approach of a salesperson*: A salesperson has always a smiling friendly approach. Even when the house lady is very angry and cross with him and says a strong 'no' to the commodity, the salesperson is selling, the salesperson smiles and says, "Madam, I will take only 2 minutes of your valuable time. I am not insisting that you buy it. I am only requesting you please see its performance, in our door to door campaign, because we are conscious of your busy schedule."
- *The audience contact of an actor*: When a drama is being staged, for the success of the show, it is imperative that every actor must be able to have iconic contact with every person, present in the audience. If an actor fails to do so, then a group from the audience will definitely start gossiping among themselves and the show will be disturbed and become a flop. Similarly, in a classroom the teacher's presentation should be such that every

pupil must feel that he/she is the focus of attention of the teacher.

- *The ability to execute all these abilities in a classroom situation*: This is in fact the most important ability. Without this, to expect a teacher to become a good teacher is like professing that library is the wisest entity in the world as it contains within its system books of all forms of wisdom.

It may be noted that each of the above 8 ability statements carries with it a corresponding example which may help the teacher to concretise the concept in his/her cognitive domain.

The above list of 8 necessary abilities of a traditional good teacher may appear a bit challenging, but it also provides a check-list to assess one's efficiency as a teacher. Further one should not lose sight of the fact that

> To practise his art, a poet needs a pen, a painter needs a brush, but a teacher needs an army of knowledge, ideas, skills, techniques, strategies, and...and....

With the advent of constructivism, these 8 abilities have to be redefined, refined and new roles which are, out of necessity, richer in structures, have to be added (Nussbaum and Novick, 1982b).

Links (2000) states, "The teacher's role in a constructivist classroom is not so much to lecture at students but to act as an expert learner who can guide students into adopting cognitive strategies such as self-testing, articulating, understanding, asking probing questions, and reflection. The role of the teacher in constructivist classrooms is to organize information around big ideas that engage the students' interest; to assist students in developing new insights and to connect them with their previous learning. The activities are student-centered and students are encouraged to ask their own questions, carry out their own experiments, make their own analogies and come to their own conclusions. Becoming a constructivist teacher may prove a difficult transformation, however, since most instructors have been prepared for teaching in the traditional, objective manner." (www.questia.com/ constructivism_Edu)

This suggests that the teacher's role will be to 'guide', 'organise' and 'develop'.

"Understanding the role of the teacher in the constructivist classroom provides a useful vantage point from which to grasp how the theory impacts on practice" (Murphy, 1997).

"The role of the authority figure (teacher) has two important components. The first is to introduce new ideas or cultural tools, where necessary and to provide the support and guidance for students to make sense of these for themselves. The other is to listen and diagnose the ways in which the instructional activities are being interpreted to inform further action. Teaching from this perspective is also a learning process for the teacher" (Driver et al., 1994).

This suggests that the teacher's role will be to 'provide', 'listen' and 'diagnose'.

One of the six underpinnings derived by Ernest (1995) after a critical analysis of radical and social perspectives of constructivism is:

"An awareness of the social construction of knowledge suggests a pedagogical emphasis on discussion, collaboration, negotiation and shared meanings...."

This suggests that the teacher's role will be to 'discuss', 'collaborate', 'negotiate' and 'share'.

Von Glasersfeld (1996) opines that the teacher's role is not to dispense knowledge but to provide students with opportunities and incentives to construct knowledge. For him the classroom is not a dispensary and the teacher is not the pharmacist.

This suggests that the teacher will be to 'provide'.

Mayer (1996) suggests that the teacher's role will be to 'guide' and the learners will be 'sense makers'.

In Gergen's (1995) view, teachers are 'coordinators', 'facilitators', 'resource adviser', 'tutors' and/or coaches.

Jonassen (1994) summarizes what he refers to as "the implications of constructivism for instructional design". He lists the flowing principles as to how knowledge construction can be facilitated.

- Provide multiple representations of reality.
- Represent the natural complexity of the real world.
- Focus on knowledge construction, not reproduction.
- Present authentic tasks (contextualizing rather than abstracting instruction).
- Provide real-world, case-based learning environments, rather than predetermined instructional designs.
- Foster reflective practice.
- Enable context-and-context dependent knowledge construction.
- Support collaborative construction of knowledge through social negotiation.

This list envisages that the teacher's role will be to 'facilitate', 'guide', 'innovate' and 'negotiate'.

Brooks and Brooks (1993) state twelve cardinal principles essential to constructivist teaching *vis-à-vis* the teacher's role. They are the following:

- Encouragement and acceptance of student autonomy and initiative.
- Utilization of raw data and primary sources along with manipulative, interactive and physical materials.
- When planning, teachers use cognitive terminology such as "classify", "analyze" and "create".
- Allowance of student responses to drive lessons, shift instructional strategies and alter content.
- Inquiry concerning students' understanding of concept before sharing their own understanding of those concepts.
- Encouragement of students to engage in dialogue, both with the teacher and with one another.
- Encouragement of students' inquiry by asking thoughtful, open-ended questions and encouraging students to ask questions of each other.
- Pursuit of elaboration of students' initial responses.

- Engagement of students in experiences that might engender contradictions to their initial hypothesis and then encourage discussion.
- Allowance of wait time after posing questions.
- Providing time for students to construct relationships and create metaphors.
- Nurturing students' natural curiosity through frequent use of the learning cycle model.

  This list suggests that the teacher's role will be to 'encourage', 'diagnose', 'promote reflective thinking', 'elaborate', 'nurture'.

The following synthesis of constructivist learning and teaching is from Murphy (1997):

"Multiple perspectives, authentic activities, real world environments these are just some of the themes that are frequently associated with constructivist learning and teaching. There were many similarities between the perspectives of different researchers." The following presents a synthesis and summary of the characteristics of constructivist learning and teaching. These are not presented in a hierarchical order.

- Multiple perspectives and representations of concepts and content are presented and encouraged.
- Goals and objectives are derived by the student or in negotiation with the teacher or the system.
- Teachers serve in the role of guides, monitors, coaches, tutors and facilitators.
- Activities, opportunities, tools and environments are provided to encourage meta-cognition, self-analysis-regulation, reflection and awareness.
- The student plays a central role in mediating and controlling learning.
- Learning situations, environments, skills, content and tasks are relevant, realistic, authentic and represent the natural complexities of the 'real world'.
- Primary sources of data are used in order to ensure authenticity and real-world complexity.

- Knowledge construction and not reproduction is emphasized.
- This construction takes place in individual contexts and through social negotiation, collaboration and experience.
- The learner's previous knowledge constructions, beliefs and attitudes are considered in the knowledge construction process.
- Problem-solving, higher order thinking skills and deep understanding are emphasized.
- Errors provide the opportunity for insight into students' previous knowledge constructions.
- Exploration is a favoured approach in order to encourage students to seek knowledge independently and to manage the pursuit of their goals.
- Learners are provided with the opportunity for apprenticeship learning in which there is an increasing complexity of tasks, skills and knowledge acquisition.
- Knowledge complexity is reflected in an emphasis on conceptual interrelatedness and interdisciplinary learning.
- Collaborative and cooperative learning are favoured in order to expose the learner to alternative viewpoints.
- Scaffolding is facilitated to help students perform just beyond the limit of their ability.

  This collated list suggests that the teacher's role will be to 'negotiate', 'guide', 'monitor', 'tutor', 'facilitate', 'collaborate' and 'promote reflection'.

We synthesize the salient features of the above diverse suggestions, which are engulfed within individualism, and present a model of roles for a classroom teacher. The model is very pragmatic and within the avowed philosophy of 'Research for Teaching and Teaching for Research'. It is hoped that this model will provide the necessary scaffolding for the young researcher to make some intensive case studies and the girders to teachers to try, experiment and then transform themselves to adopt constructivist teaching approaches.

The various roles are the following:

As Diagnostician

In the wake of pupils ALCONs and the constructivism informed situation this is a new role added to the mosaic of earlier roles of the teacher. Since ALCONs have a major influence on the degree of learning the teacher has to:

- be aware of this influence.
- be sensitive to pupils' ALCONs.
- ascertain them through the use of question answer discussion, structured interview, concept maps, micro-computer-based strategies, analogies, cognitive conflict, etc.
- classify them as useful or detrimental ones.
- appreciate the fact that in so far as pupils are concerned there is a multiplicity of realities.

This demands a quantum change in the attitude and approach of the teacher. Whereas under the traditional conditions the inappropriate answer given by a pupil is ignored and the teacher moves the question on to another pupil in a relentless pursuit of the "*tailored right*" answer, now in the changed scenario the teacher has to take careful note of each inappropriate answer, interesting unconventional comments by the pupils, dwell a little on them through discussion with the aim in view to find out why the pupil gave that answer/comment, then suitably change his instructional path and not follow the regimented path, prescribed by the curriculum.

An Example

The following is the text of a conversation that took place in one of the Standard II primary class of D.M. School:

Teacher : What is the colour of a leaf?

Pupil 1 : Sir, Brown.

Teacher : (Taken aghast) What?

Pupil 1	:	Sir, Brown. (entire class starts laughing at Pupil 1)
Teacher	:	You do not know the answer to even such a simple question. Sit down. (Then whispers) useless fool. Yes.... You tell (pointing at another pupil with the aim in view to obtain the 'tailored right' answer)
Pupil 2	:	Sir, Green.
Teacher	:	Very good. (Looking at Pupil 1) Could you understand?
Pupil 1	:	Yes, sir (actually he did not very much agree with the answer of Pupil 2, but still said 'Yes' because of the authority of the teacher).

At this point a little conceptual discussion on the dialogue between the pupil and the teacher is in order, because the dialogue demonstrates the manifestation of Hermeneutic Constructivism. As per Oxford dictionary Hermeneutic means "relating to the meaning of written text". Chiari and Nuzzo (1996), the proponent of Hermeneutic constructivism emphasize that reality as constituted in language exemplifies hermeneutic viewpoint. From this angle language is not only a means for communication; it is also a vehicle of constructing cognitive structures through brain maps. Now if one considers two interlocutors, say A and B, then the verbal information sent out by A is interpreted by B in his/her framework. The response of B is then interpreted by A in a totally different framework, i.e. that of A. This circle of interpretation, i.e. A – B – A, is called the "circle of interpretation", or, Hermeneutic Circle, justifying the Greek origin of the word "Hermeneutic", i.e. "interpretative".

From this point of view if one analyses the above dialogue between the teacher and the pupil 1, when the teacher asks, "what is the colour of a leaf?", he/she has a definite cognitive structure about the concepts 'colour' and 'leaf' in his/her mind. The pupil 1 receives the question and interprets it as per his/her cognitive structures, i.e. ALCONs and replies, "Brown". This response is interpreted by the teacher in his/her framework of personal constructs and is taken aghast because the response of the pupil 1 is completely in dissonance with the teacher's personal constructs. This 'Hermeneutic Circle' is repeated in the dialogue again, this time through the consonance between the cognitive structure of the pupil 2 and that of the teacher.

However, if the TLP would have been a constructivist informed process, the conversation would have gone the following way:

Teacher : What is the colour of a leaf?

Pupil 1 : Sir, Brown.

Teacher : Why do you say so?

Pupil 1 : Sir, because in our house there is a decorative plant whose leaves are brown.

Teacher : Very good.

And suddenly the teacher has become a diagnostician, because he/she has been able to diagnose the cause of the unusual reply by Pupil 1.

As Motivator

Traditionally, one of the widely accepted, but little explicitly adopted, role of a teacher is that of pupil motivator.

Motivation has been defined as an "internal state that activates, guides and maintains behavior" (Green, 2002). From a pedagogical point of view the term 'motivator' can be applied to a person (read teacher) who can create situations those activate and maintain the learning process. In fact Pintrich and Schunk (1996) opine that motivational beliefs can be significantly influenced by aspects of the classroom context. This indicates that classroom strategies can be used to optimize student motivation.

Motivation has been classified into two types, 'Intrinsic' and 'Extrinsic'. Deci (2001) defines, "Intrinsic motivation...refers to doing something because it is inherently interesting or enjoyable, and extrinsic motivation...refers to doing something because it has a separable outcome." Extrinsic motivation is mostly used by the behaviouristic psychologists. In fact Deci et al. (2001)

observed that intrinsic motivation is directly related to the task being performed and has a positive influence, in the sense that it promotes learning and achievement.

Palmer (2005) states, "According to intrinsic motivation theory (White, 1959), a person feels instinctive pleasure when he/she learns something new or succeeds in a challenging tasks. This creates feeling of confidence and mastery that are self-reinforcing, so the student will be more inclined to engage in future learning activities, simply for the enjoyment of succeeding."

Lepper and Hodell (1989) proposed that by providing challenge, curiosity, fantasy and control, intrinsic motivation can be enhanced. The details about the factors, those control the above four critical parameters, can be obtained from Lepper and Hodell (1989) as well as Palmer (2005).

Palmer (2005) writes:

> According to constructivist theory, learning is an active process requiring effort, so students need to be motivated to make that effort. In a constructivist classroom, teachers should therefore aim to arouse students and maintain their intrinsic motivation at optimum levels throughout the learning process. However, motivation by itself only means that students are willing to engage in learning—it does not ensure that they will develop scientifically acceptable knowledge structures. (Pintric et al., 1993)

Strategies for intrinsic motivation therefore need to be integrated with teaching techniques that can reduce the status of students' misconceptions and increase the status of scientific concepts.

This is obviously a difficult but not impossible proposition.

In this framework the teacher should try to—

- select concepts that represent appropriate and achievable challenge, considering the conceptual ecologies (including the epistemological and ontological ALCONs) of the students,

- avoid extended sequence of step-by-step procedure,
- present multiple opportunities to apply the concept so as to foster long-term memory (Nuthall, 1999),
- use "dual-purpose" teaching technique (such as, class discussions, appropriate hand-on practice, computer simulation, application to real-life contexts),
- create variety, as studies show students like variety,
- avoid over-reliance on any one technique because even highly motivating experiences, like discrepant events demonstrations can become monotonous (Loughran et al., 1994),
- praise improvement,
- provide detailed assessment feedback, given privately, and
- be supportive, reassuring and attentive as students participate in the learning process.

In the framework of pupils' ALCONs the teacher has to now motivate the pupils to:

- express their personal constructs about any event/concept,
- ask themselves and each other, questions with focus on the personal constructs, such as, Why do you say so? What does that suggest you? What could we use that for? Is there any other way we could have done that? Can we apply it to any other real-life situation?,
- argue about the justifiability of their own personal constructs,
- reflect on their own ideas (Osborne and Wittrock, 1983 have shown that pupils of all ages are very interested in other children's ideas),
- clarify their own ideas (of course, in a non-threatening environment),
- design and try out novel and challenging activities (obviously prompted by the teacher),
- try out their constructed concept in multiple situations,

- Experiment with computers simulation,
- Work in peer group collaboration,
- Chose exciting task formats,
- Develop self-confidence to work at a higher level, and
- Enjoy the entire learning process.

An Example

The following example have been used by us in several regional workshops of TGTs (Trained Graduate Teachers) and PGTs (Post Graduate Teachers) and has also been tried out on Standard X students in various states of India. The intrinsic motivational effects on all subjects have been astounding.

We report here the activity as performed with students of Standard X.

In the entire process of motivation (which resulted in a meaningful construction of concept) the teacher,

- started with a simple conversation (which was intended to diagnose students' ALCONs),
- then created cognitive conflict (the function of which was to initiate intrinsic motivation),
- presented an out of the blue surprise (intended to accentuate the motivation),
- asked the students to collect specific materials (motivated individuals will perform this task with eagerness and sincerity, since each student will feel that he/she is going to make a breakthrough),
- suggested the design of the activity (intended to activate the cognitive apprentices),
- demonstrated the visible result (intended to resolve the cognitive conflict),
- created excitement among students (this motivated state will help in correct construction of the concept), and
- built up self-confidence of the students (intended to promote self-development and continued interest in forthcoming classes).

The session was as follows:

Teacher	: (looking at the whole class with a quizzical smile) Suppose the electrical connection goes from this room to the next room. There is a switch here in this room and the corresponding bulb is in the other room. If you put on the switch what do you think will happen? [The simplicity of the question was expected to put the students at ease and there would be high probability that they will voice (Mohapatra, 1997) their ALCONs without any inhibition.]
All students	: (simultaneously) Bulb in the other room will start glowing immediately.
Teacher	: Are you sure?
All students	: Yes, Sir.
Teacher	: But, why will the bulb glow? (No response came immediately).
Student 1	: Sir, the bulb will glow because current will flow from the switch to the bulb. (The evidence of an ALCON).
Student 2	: Current will of course flow and that is why bulb will glow. But Sir, current will not flow from the switch.
Teacher	: Why do you say so?
Student 2	: Sir, a switch cannot be a source of current. Because if that be so, then if we carry a naked switch in our hand we should get shock (Shows the process of knowledge construction).
Teacher	: (Without dwelling much on the ALCON, proceeds forward) When you say current flows, what actually flows? (Step for diagnosis)

All students : Sir, electrons flow through the wire. They carry the current to the bulb.

(Evidence of another ALCON)

Teacher : Are you sure?

All students : Yes, Sir.

Teacher : Why do you say so?

Student 3 : Sir, we have been taught that 'Current is the rate of flow of charge'. And here the charge is carried by electrons.

(Evidence of another ALCON generated through IIG.) (Teacher thinks, so far so good. Now let me ask the critical question. The timing of the next question is crucial or else the lesson may fall flat.)

Teacher : What will be the speed of the charges when the current is flowing?

(Silence descends on the classroom. Perhaps each student is prepared to advance his/her response. But he/she is not very sure of his/her ALCON. Therefore, he/she cannot muster enough courage to answer. The teacher provides the prop to take the students cognitively forward.)

Teacher : Let me give you options. Very Fast, Fast, Medium speed, slow. Those who feel the speed is 'very fast' please raise your hands.

(All students raise their hands. This is a case of manifest mass ALCON. In fact in the case of teachers, 90 per cent of them gave the same answer.)

Teacher : Sure.

All students : Yes, Sir.

Teacher : Why are you so sure?

Student 3 : (Stands up and tells in a confident tone) Sir, the bulb glows up the moment the switch is put on. There is almost no time gap. This is a fact. So speed must be very fast.

Teacher : But, (remains dramatically silent for few seconds to arouse the curiosity of the students and this dramatization initiates motivation) scientist do not agree with your conclusion. They say the speed of the charges is very very slow. They report that it is only one tenth of a millimeter per second.

All students : (Strongly) It cannot be so. Or else how does the bulb glow immediately?

(Thus a severe cognitive conflict has been generated, between their ALCONs and Scientists' viewpoint.)

Teacher : You people say the speed is very fast. Scientists say the speed is very slow. How do we know who is correct?

(Silence falls over the entire class. Students are unable to suggest any method to resolve this conflict.)

Teacher : The only way to resolve this conflict is to experiment and find out the speed of these charges when a current is flowing.

Student 3 : But Sir, I have read somewhere that experiment on these charges are performed only in special laboratories using sophisticated instruments.

Teacher : Yes, you are right. But, you can also measure the speed of these charges in this classroom.

(This statement from the teacher was a pleasant surprise and a source of excitement for the students.)

All students : (With disbelief) Sir, is that possible?

Teacher : (With assurance) It is quite possible. But, each of you has to collect certain materials.

All students : Sir, whatever you say, we will collect.

(They were in a state of intense motivation and excitement and were prepared to do whatever the teacher suggests.)

Teacher : Ok, then. Each of you please collect a 4″ × 3″ blotting paper, two gem clips, two pieces of flexible wire, each 6″ to 8″ long, a torch battery.

All students : (With disbelief) We will bring tomorrow all these. But only with these we can measure the speed of the charges when current flows!!

Teacher : I assure you that you can yourself do this measurement.

(The class disperses)

(Next day the students reached the class 5 minutes before the scheduled time, with lots of excitement and curiosity, which was visible on their faces. This was a clear indication of their increased involvement and intensity of motivation. Each of them had brought all the articles as asked by the teacher.)

(The teacher came on time and asked.)

Teacher : Now connect the articles and complete the circuit as shown on the black board, Fig. 7.18.

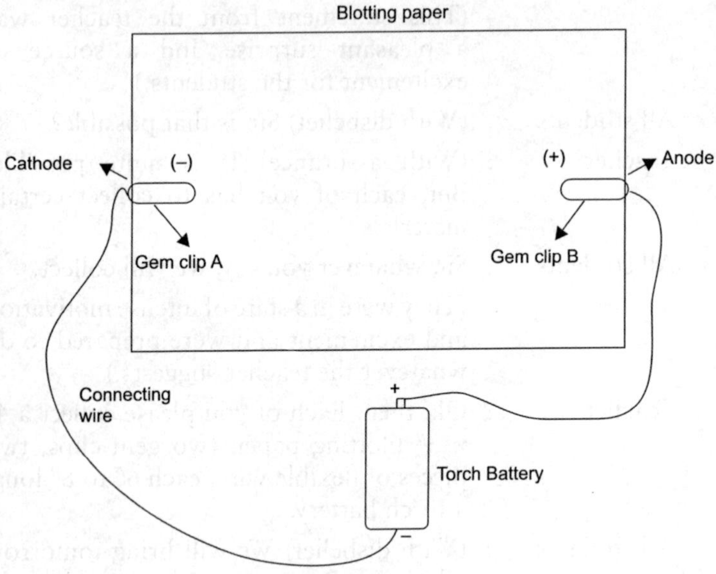

Fig. 7.18

(The students sat down on their respective seats and arranged the circuit on their respective tables.)

Teacher	:	Is the circuit closed now?
Student 4	:	No, Sir.
Teacher	:	Why you say so? Because to me, the circuit seems to be closed.
Student 5	:	Sir, the blotting paper is an insulator.
Teacher	:	(To the entire class) Do you agree with him.
All students	:	(In a single voice) Yes, Sir.
Teacher	:	This plate contains common salt and there is water in this beaker. (He calls one student and says) Please prepare a solution of salt in water.
		(The student does it eagerly.)
Teacher	:	Now you take this beaker containing salt solution and make the blotting paper of

each of your classmates wet with this solution.

(The students promptly completed the activity.)

Teacher : (asks) Can you tell me whether the circuit is now closed?

All students : Sir, the circuit is now closed, because common salt solution conducts electricity.

Teacher : Very good.

[These little words of appreciation sometimes work as agents for 'extrinsic' motivation (Deci, 2000)]

(Teacher then shows them some violet coloured crystals in a watch glass and asks)

Teacher : Can you tell me what this substance in the watch glass is?

(One student comes forward, observes the crystals from very close quarters and tells)

Student 6 : Sir, it looks like potassium permanganate crystals.

Teacher : (Smiles) Yes, they are potassium permanganate crystals. What is its chemical formulae?

Many students : Sir, $KMnO_4$.

Teacher : Good, Now if you take a crystal and put it on your wet blotting paper, what will happen?

Some students : Sir, it will go into solution.

Teacher : And will it still remain $KMnO_4$?

Few students : No, Sir. It will dissociate into potassium ion and permanganate ion.

Teacher : And what are the charges of these ions?

Few students : Sir, potassium ion is +vely charged and permanganate ion is –vely charged.

Teacher	:	Take one crystal each and put it on the blotting paper, near the cathode (Gem Clip A).
		(Each student does that.)
Teacher	:	Now observe the area of blotting paper near the cathode for 5 minutes and tell me what you find.
		(Each student starts intently looking near the cathode with curiosity. Only after 2 minutes there was muffled hissing sound of excitement as if something unexpected is happening. Then)
Entire Class	:	Sir, Sir, A violet line is moving out from the cathode. (This statement was more or else like soliloquy.)
		(Teacher does not give any comment. After 5 minutes)
Teacher	:	5 minutes have elapsed. Now measure the length of that violet line and then disconnect the circuit.
		(Each student with his/her own scale measures the length of the violet line)
Student A	:	Sir, it is almost 3 cm.
Student B	:	Sir, it is 3.1 cm.
Student C	:	Sir, it is 3 cm.
Teacher	:	So the length of the line is about 3 cm.
All students	:	Yes, Sir,
Teacher	:	What is cause of this line?
All students	:	We do not know Sir.
Teacher	:	In fact you know everything.
All students	:	(Looking at the violet line and in disbelief) Sir,
Teacher	:	You said permanganate ion is there. You said it is –vely charged. Cathode is also –vely charged. So what will happen?

Students : Sir, the permanganate ion will be repelled.

Teacher : Anode is +vely charged. So what will happen?

Students : Sir, it will attract the permanganate ion.

Teacher : So, what is the cause of the line?

Students : (in disbelief on realizing the exciting discovery) It is created by the motion of the permanganate ion.

Teacher : Exactly. But why should they move?

Students : Because there is a current.

Teacher : Exactly. Now calculate the speed of the permanganate ions.
(Students calculated and said)

Students : Sir, it is about 0.1 mm/sec.

Teacher : That is exactly what scientists had found out. When there is a current the speed of the charges is very slow. And when there is a current, always electron is not the charge carrier in motion. In this case what is the charger carrier?

Students : (With extreme cognitive satisfaction) Sir, permanganate ion.
(The lesson ends here.)

This lesson has been taught in a purely constructivist environment with the teacher as the prime motivator.

In this lesson,

- The novelty and excitement (Gay, 1987; Palmer, 2005) of the innovative activity provides the strong intrinsic motivation.
- Teacher was able to diagnose the ALCONs of the students. They are:
    - o When the circuit is closed current flows from the switch to the bulb.
    - o Whenever there is a current, electrons flow through the wire.
    - o The speed of the electrons is very fast.

- A strong cognitive conflict between students' views about the velocity of charges in a wire and those of the scientists was generated.
- Ingenuity and simplicity of the activity generated excitement and challenge.
- Students' self-confidence was enhanced as they could measure speed of the charges, which they were convinced is performed only in big laboratories by scientists.
- All the students' ALCONs got either erased or suitably modified.

As Facilitator

Opportunities for taking false steps abound in most science lessons. Often we are in a hurry to get across facts and to complete the syllabus, rather than taking time to develop sound thinking procedures which will help pupils make better sense of the world around them. In other words a traditional teacher has been giving the pupils "*fishes to eat*" and not teaching them "*how to catch a fish*".

In the changed role, the teacher has to now help the pupils **learn how to learn** (Novak, and Gowin, 1984), because it is the pupil who constructs his/her own knowledge. Under the dimension, the teacher could be a guide and/or an innovator and/or negotiator and/or catalyst.

As Innovator

Traditionally a good teacher has been providing materials resources and creating an effective (in the old sense) learning environment. In addition, now with ALCONs entering the scene, the teacher should be seen by the pupils as a human resource—a **source of ideas.**

- on how to do things,
- about where to find things,
- about what could have gone wrong,
- for generating alternative ways of doing things,

- to find new ways which will help to perceive the ideas of others as perhaps more intelligible, possible and potentially useful, and
- to arrive at the valid concept rather than the viable concept.

The teacher has to be also an innovator to new and uncharted strategies for how best to go about erasing/modifying/absorbing pupils ALCONs.

At this point it may also be kept in mind that the knowledge of the ALCONs of the pupils of their own classes places the teachers in a potentially better position and makes them functionally better instruments than the authors of textbooks, teachers' guide, resource materials, reference modules, to advise and implement ways of modifying pupils' ideas about any specific event or topic.

As Guide

The traditional role has been (Ogborn, 1977) the **Alpine Guide** approach to teaching. The teacher leads the pupils through a reasoned argument, interspersed with lecture and demonstration, or towards the solution of a problem using a step-by-step series of questions. Each step in the exploration is turned into a question, the answer to which provides the basis for the next step. A question which is not answered, or is answered incorrectly, is regarded as inadequate and the guide attempts to replace it with a less difficult, clearer or simple question which will lead to the expected, and needed answer. This last step of the approach has enough basic similarity with the Baconian Philosophy that—We search for evidences which are likely to substantiate our hyopotheses.

The pitfall in the growth of knowledge through Baconian philosophy is that we may in the process turn a blind eye to glaring evidence which in all probability contradict our hypothesis. Similarly, the pitfall in the Alpine Guide approach, as in most mountain climbing lessons, is that the teacher may feel elated when the top of the mountain is reached and assume, without any logic, that the pupils must be feeling the same. The pupils in reality may feel no real sense of achievement, more so in the new context of their existing ALCONs.

The changed role then demands that the teacher should

- encourage the pupils to attempt to climb their own mountains (in a modified Alpine Guide approach),
- provide them with useful skills regarding how to select more gentle slopes and to climb,
- gently point out to the pupils the logical errors, inconsistencies, and unjustifiable reasoning in their thinking,
- teach them to become receptive to other ideas, possibilities and to suspend judgment,
- show them where they have over or under-generalised because of IIG, Epi-Con or connotative relativity,
- provide them with many examples and applications of a new idea,
- present the same matter in several different ways and formats, and
- help them to consider the new idea from a number of points of view.

An Example

In this session class IX students were involved. The students were divided into four groups, A, B, C, D. Each group was given a set of everyday objects, namely, a small plastic comb, a small wooden plank, a 2″ nail, a piece of paper, a one rupee coin, a razor. Now the teacher says,

Teacher	:	Using your educated guesses pick out the conductors of electricity out of these six items. (The students use their personal constructs to list the conductors only.)
Teacher	:	Now set up an experiment to check whether your guesses are right or wrong.
Group A	:	Sir, we will need a battery and some connecting wires to set up a circuit. (Soon other group demands the same articles.)

Teacher : In that case, each group draw the circuit diagram first and show it to me.

(Each group draws a circuit diagram and brings it to show to the teacher. The diagrams they draw are given below.)

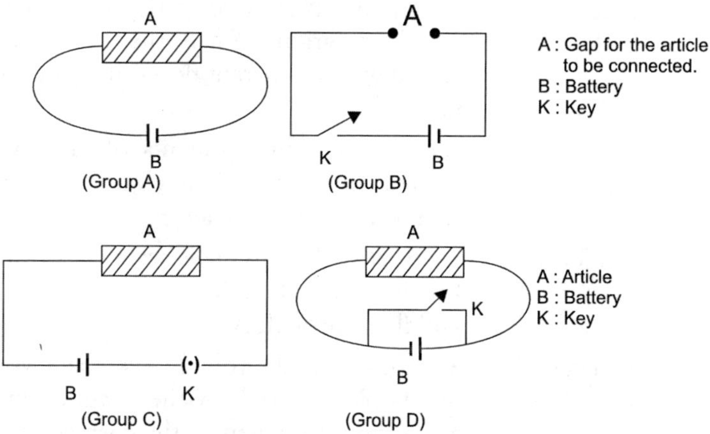

Fig. 7.19

(Teacher now points at Group A and asks)

Teacher : What is this item 'A' in your circuit diagram?

Leader A : Sir, that is the position where we will connect any of the items given to us.

Teacher : Then you should have labeled as other group have done in their diagrams.

Leader A : It was so obvious that we missed to label it.

Teacher : The rest three groups have connected a key in their circuit. You don't need a key in your circuit?

Leader A : Yes, Sir. We need a key. We have forgotten to connect a key.

Teacher : Is a key necessary in any electrical circuit?

Leader A : Without the key the circuit will remain closed all the time and the battery will be unnecessarily drained out soon. With the key there in the circuit, we can close the circuit only when it is needed.

Teacher : Very good. Now Group D, look at your circuit diagram. When the key is not closed will the current flows through A or not?

(On hearing this, students of Group D started examining their circuit diagram with keen interest. Then,)

Leader D : Sir, Sorry. Our circuit is wrongly drawn, because even when the key is open current will flow through A.

Teacher : So Group A and Group D, take back your notebooks and redraw the circuit, which as per your judgment is the correct one.

(Both the groups redrew the circuit and the redrawn circuits were similar to those drawn by Group B and Group C.)

(The teacher handed over the circuit diagrams to respective groups and asked.)

Teacher : Each group, examine your circuit diagram and tell us how are you going to find out whether the object A is a conductor or not. You have five minutes time for this.

(Each group examined their circuit diagram and got engaged in intense discussion and arguments.)

Leader C : Sir, it is easy. If A is a conductor and we switch on the circuit then current will flow through A and we will know that A is a conductor. But if current does not flow through A then we will know A is not a conductor.

Teacher : But how will you know that current is flowing through A?

Leader C : Sir!! (And starts thinking and discussing with his group mates. This question did induce all the groups to be engaged in vigorous discussion.)

Teacher : So, how will you know that current is flowing through A?

(On repetition of the question, silence falls over the entire class)

Leader D : (Says in a meek tone) Sir, we cannot know.

Teacher : Exactly. So your circuit is incomplete. Now let us see. Suppose in this room there is no bulb and we switch on that switch on the wall, can we know whether current is flowing through the wires or not?

Leader B : No, Sir. We cannot know. But if a bulb is there we can know current is flowing or not.

Teacher : Exactly. Bulb is the simplest appliance to know whether current is flowing in a circuit or not.

Leader A : Yes, Sir. We have seen Electrical Lines man, using a bulb with two wires connected to it, to test whether there is current or not.

Teacher : Exactly. So....

(Teacher dramatically stops his talk and looks at each of the groups. This had an exciting effect on the entire class. Soon the four group leaders raised their hands to make a statement.)

All leaders : Sir, here also we will need a bulb in the circuit.

Teacher : What type of bulb?

All leaders : Sir, a torch light bulb, because we are using a torch battery.

Teacher : So redraw your circuit using the standard symbol of a bulb and submit for examination.

(Each group took around 5 minutes to redraw the circuit, because there was hushed argument in each group as to where to connect the bulb. They each redrew the circuit on a white drawing sheet and submitted for check up by the teacher. The circuits were—

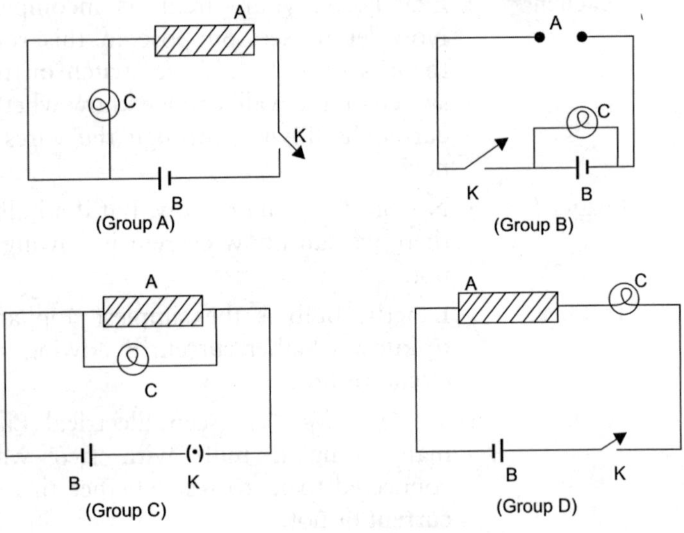

Fig. 7.20

(Teacher fixed the circuit diagrams on the black board with cello tape so that the entire class can see them. Then,)

Teacher : Although the circuit diagrams drawn by Group B and Group C look different, do you think they are different?

(The entire class examines the circuit diagrams)

Student 6 : No, Sir. The circuit diagrams are not different.

Teacher : Do all of you agree with Ravi?

(All students consider the statement for some time.)

All students : Yes, Sir. Ravi is right.

Teacher : Now look at the circuit diagram of Group C. If we switch on the circuit, and A is an insulator, will the bulb C glow or not?

(After considering for sometime)

Leader C : Sir, the circuit is wrong. Whether A is conductor or insulator does not make any difference. The bulb will glow all the time if the switch is on.

Teacher : Now, let us consider the circuit diagram of Group A. Do the part of the connection which is to the left of the bulb serve any purpose?

(After considering for sometime)

Leader A : No Sir. It does not serve any purpose.

Teacher : Now, let us consider the circuit diagram of Group D. If A is an insulator and we switch on the switch, will the bulb glow?

All students : No, Sir.

Teacher : If A is a conductor and we switch on the switch, will the bulb glow?

All students : Yes, Sir.

(Teacher then hands over to each group a torch bulb. The students start doing the experiment and successfully identify the conductors from among the objects given to them. They then match their results with the guesses they made at the beginning of the session.)

The teaching session ends.

In this session, the teacher has,

- nowhere imposed his/her ideas on the students,
- trained the students to go one simple step at a time,
- through the four diagrams provided the students with multiple, but manageable number of options,
- allowed the students to commit errors naturally and then through open discussions modify them,
- implemented the process of learning through doing,
- showed them the pitfalls arising out of over or under-generalisation, and
- pointed out to them inconsistencies and unjustifiable reasoning in their thinking.

In other words he/she worked as a true guide for the students.

As Negotiator

Cognitive negotiation is one of major tenets of constructivist informed classroom teaching, because

- pupils offer strong resistance for modification or erasement of their ALCONs (as discussed earlier in this chapter Mc Closkey, 1983; Halloun and Hestenes, 1985; Dykstra et al., 1992; Mohapatra and Parida, 1996) whenever such an effort is made by an external agent (teacher), and
- pupils are cognitive apprentices.

However, the positive indicators are,

- ALCONs are still modifiable, because the pupils themselves modify them, and
- Pupils' natural tendency is to construct knowledge, which needs cognitive accommodation.

Under these evidences the teacher's role as a negotiator is clearly demarked.

The teacher should

- recognize and accept resistance from pupils when a new concept, which affects pupils' ALCONs, is introduced,

- not harp on his/her presentation, for which there is resistance,
- search for alternative pathways, approaches, activities, techniques to bypass the resistance,
- negotiate conceptual adjustments,
- help the pupils discover that their ALCONs need modifications,
- help the pupils realize the cognitive futility of their resistance,
- realize that his/her traditional role of a salesperson and/or psychiatrist will come handy in this regard.

An Example

In this case the subjects are pupils of Class VIII.

In Class VIII the concepts of 'rest' and 'motion' are taught. In this context pupils have the ALCON that bodies can remain in a state of 'Absolute' rest, like the tree, hill, school building, road, etc. and in a state of 'Absolute' motion, like the earth revolving round the sun, the birds flying in the sky, the river flowing down, the train running on the rails.

This ALCON is very strongly imbedded in their cognitive domain.

But the scientific stand is,—There is no absolute rest or absolute motion.

Teacher's job was to resolve this conflict between pupils' concept and scientific concept.

Teacher : If you are sitting in a moving train and you look outside, to you the trees outside appear to move or really move?

(Immediately all the students raised their hands. Teacher pointed his/her finger towards some students.)

Student 1 : Sir, to me the trees, outside appear to move.

Teacher : Are you sure?

Student 1	:	(Laughs, because Sir is doubting his/her statement) Yes, Sir. I am very sure.
Teacher	:	(Persistently) Why are you so sure?
Student 1	:	Sir, I have been seeing that the tree is at rest, because it is strongly fixed to the earth with its roots. (This shows a very strong ALCON.)
Teacher	:	But how do you know, whether the motion of the trees is an appearance or a reality? (Silence falls over the class. In fact the cognitive negotiation has started with this question because it tries to resolve the cognitive conflict.)
Some students	:	But Sir, how can trees move? They are after all rooted to the earth. (They forget that even the earth moves, i.e. revolution round the sun. But, that is another concept.)
Teacher	:	I agree with what you say, i.e. the trees are rooted to the earth. But being students of science you must have a scientific method to know, whether the motion of the tree is a reality or an appearance, for you when you are sitting in a moving train. (This is a way of diverting their mind from their strong attachment to their ALCON. This is essential for cognitive negotiation as it reduces resistance.)
Students	:	(After a little lapse of time) Sir, we do not know any such method. But can there be such a method?
Teacher	:	Yes, there can be such methods. You know that the image in a plane mirror is not real, it is virtual. And the method for differentiation is that a real image can

be caught on a screen but a virtual image cannot be caught on a screen.

Students : Yes, Sir. That we know.

(Their thought process is entirely diverted now. When there is strong resistance, cognitive diversion is an essential technique for cognitive negotiation.)

Teacher : Do you know Galileo?

Students : Yes, Sir. He was a famous scientist of the 16th century.

Teacher : Galileo had established a principle to differentiate between 'reality' and 'appearance'. He had stated, "If you perform more than one independent experiments and each of them give you the same conclusion, then that is a 'reality' for you. If they give different conclusions, then they are 'appearances' for you."

(This approach shows the ingenuity of the teacher to operationalise cognitive negotiation. Silence falls on the class, because the students try to comprehend the principles.)

Teacher : Could you understand the principle?

Students : No, Sir.

Teacher : Let me give you an example. Satish sees that I am teaching you. His seeing me is an experiment. Mary also sees that I am teaching. Satish's seeing does not influence Mary's seeing. Both are independent experiments. And the conclusion for both is I am teaching here. So I am teaching is a reality for Satish and Mary. Is this clear now.

Students : Yes, Sir.

Teacher : I dream that fairies have wings. Madhu dreams that fairies have tails likes fishes and they swim in water. Two independent experiments are giving different conclusions. So fairies having wings or tails are appearances. Is this clear now.

Students : Yes, Sir.

Teacher : Now, suppose all of you are standing near the school gate and you see that a car passes you. How will you know whether the car moving is a reality or an appearance for you?

Student 1 : Sir, since each of sees that the car is moving, so, that car is moving is a reality for us.

Teacher : Very good. But, can you think of any other experiment which will tell us about the status of the motion of the car?

(Students start thinking. Inducing such reflective thinking is one of the main processes of cognitive negotiation.)

Student 2 : We can measure at regular time intervals the distance of the car from us. If the distance is changing then the car is moving.

Teacher : Any other method.

(Students remain silent.)

Teacher : I am suggesting a thought experiment. If you take a roll of twine, tie one end of it to the back of the car and hold the roll in your hand, what will you see if the car is moving?

(Exposing students to thought experiments is an excellent technique to expand the cognitive domain of the

		pupils. It is also an effective tool for cognitive negotiation.)
Student 3	:	We will see that the roll in our hand will open out.
Teacher	:	Exactly. Now sitting inside the moving train if you perform this last experiment what will you observe? (There was total silence in the class. Realisation of the truth has put them in a state of total disbelief.)
Student 4	:	Sir, we will see that the roll will open out.
Teacher	:	So...?
Students	:	(In a hushed tone) For us sitting in the train the trees moving outside is a reality.
Teacher	:	Good. But for the persons on the platform, the trees are....
Students	:	At rest.
Teacher	:	So a body is in rest or motion, depends solely on the observer. Nobody is in absolute rest or in absolute motion.

(Lesson ends)

In this single lesson based on constructivist approaches the teacher achieved many objectives, such as

- creation and resolution of cognitive conflict,
- expansion of the cognitive domain of the pupils,
- exposition to functional thought experiment,
- generation of meaningful and functional participation by pupils,
- modification/erasement of pupils ALCONs,
- construction of scientifically viable concepts,

and all these through the process of cognitive negotiation and not transmission of knowledge.

As Catalyst

In the process of knowledge acquisition through knowledge construction one of the basic ground realities is the following:

The pupil has his/her Cognitive Domain, C, Fig. 7.21, well defined. Inside the domain the density of concepts is very LOW because it consists of only his/her ALCONs. This density is in a fluid state in the sense that the ALCONs are getting regularly constructed and reconstructed, modified, refined, changed or erased through cognitive construction by the pupil. Thus the density of concepts inside the domain is regularly changing. The cognitive membrane defining this domain is

- elastic, because its shape changes due to erasement of ALCONs and/or inclusion of new concepts, and
- permeable, because through this new concepts enter into C or undesirable ALCONs are removed from C.

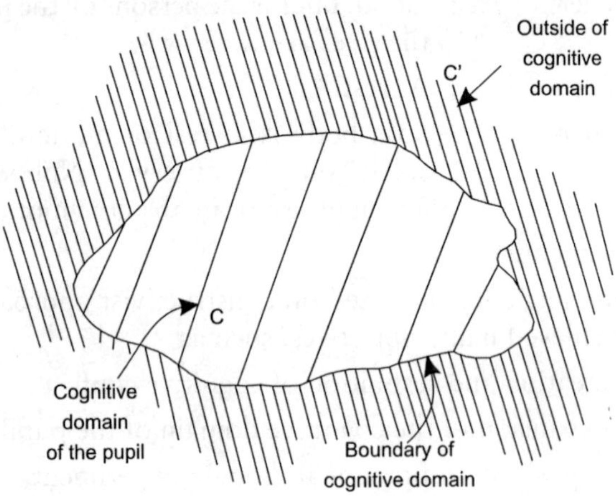

Fig. 7.21

The cognitive space, C′ outside this domain is filled with innumerable new concepts and so in C′ the density of concepts is very HIGH.

Thus if a new concept in C′ is meaningful, plausible and fruitful (Hewson and Thornley, 1989) then the concept is either accepted into C through the membrane by Cognitive Osmosis or the ALCONs inside C get suitably modified so that the boundary of the domain, C, gets changed so as to include the new concept through the process of Cognitive Reverse Osmosis.

For both these processes the teacher has to act as a catalyst so that (a) the process remains active till completion of Osmosis or Reverse Osmosis and (b) the Osmosis and Reverse Osmosis may get accelerated.

This role of the teacher as a catalyst is particularly needed when knowledge construction takes place through revolutionary conceptual change (Kuhn, 1970).

As Experimenter

This role of the teacher as an experimenter is not concerned with only demonstration of activities/experiments or design of projects. It is also concerned with the philosophy of '*teaching for research*'.

In this new role, the teacher is to seek answer to the important question—"*How could I have taught more effectively keeping in view the ALCONs of the pupils?*"

The testing of pupils at the end of a lesson is frequently used to assess how much they know about the topic which has been taught. The results of such tests should not be confused; however, with how much the pupils have learnt or modified their ALCONs as a result of the lesson. The degree of modification of the ALCONs and not necessarily the learning of the exact formal science concept/view gives a measure of the effect of the lesson. An example (Osborne and Freyberg, 1985) is in order.

Before the lesson was delivered, the pupil was presented with a card showing a player hitting the golf ball with a club. The interviewer desired to discuss the situation after the ball has been hit.

Before the Lesson

Interviewer : Is there a force on the golf ball?

Pupil : Gravity pulling it downwards—and the force of the hit.... No, there is not the

		force of the hit...because.... Oh yes, the force of the hit.... And....
Interviewer	:	So which way is that one (the force of the hit)?
Pupil	:	That way (gives the direction of the ball's flight).
Interviewer	:	Are there any other force?
Pupil	:	I cannot think any more.

After the Lesson

Interviewer	:	Can I talk to you again about the force of the hit (on the golf ball), because you said to me...there is the force of the hit on it... no, there isn't the force of the hit on it... yes, there is a force of the hit. Can you tell me what are you thinking about it now?
Pupil	:	I think the teacher told me that the force of the hit stops the instant the golf club does not touch the ball.
Interviewer	:	After it has been hit?
Pupil	:	Yes, I think.
Interviewer	:	You think...but that is not the way you thought about it before?
Pupil	:	No.
Interviewer	:	Do you like to think of the force of the hit being still in the ball?
Pupil	:	Yes.

This conversation shows:

- some modification in the existing ALCON has been effected because of the teaching, and
- the pupil prefers to keep with him/her both the view i.e. the formal view given by the teacher and his/her own personal view, and thus generate the state of 'conceptual dichotomy', as discussed in Chapter 3.

This situation now demands on the teacher as an experimenter to develop new techniques and reporting procedures to assess.

- the coherence of pupils' ALCONs and their reasons for holding them,
- the degree to which pupils understand and accept the scientific perspective,
- what attempts they have made to relate the two view points where these differ,
- how successful a teaching sequence has been in erasing/ modifying/absorbing the ALCONs, and
- the nature and quality of the learning experience itself for the child.

As Researcher

The role of the teacher as a teacher-researcher demands that he/she be in contact with other teachers and not remain in a self-satisfied state of 'Splendid Isolation'. To be an effective researcher in most fields it is important and essential to have the opportunity to report one's findings to other researchers and to have their comments. Hence, to become a functional researcher, the teacher-researcher should:

- share his findings about pupils' ideas, ways of thinking and why do they think so (genesis),
- share the successes and failures of innovative teaching strategies and sequences,
- make a cold and dispassionate analysis of the context in which any strategy, developed as a part of action research, has been used,
- assess the weaknesses as well as strengths, and the limitations as well as the potential of the strategy, and
- present his/her 'new' idea to others for constructive criticism and not to be keen only to 'sell' it to others.

All these roles of a teacher are presented diagrammatically in Fig. 7.22.

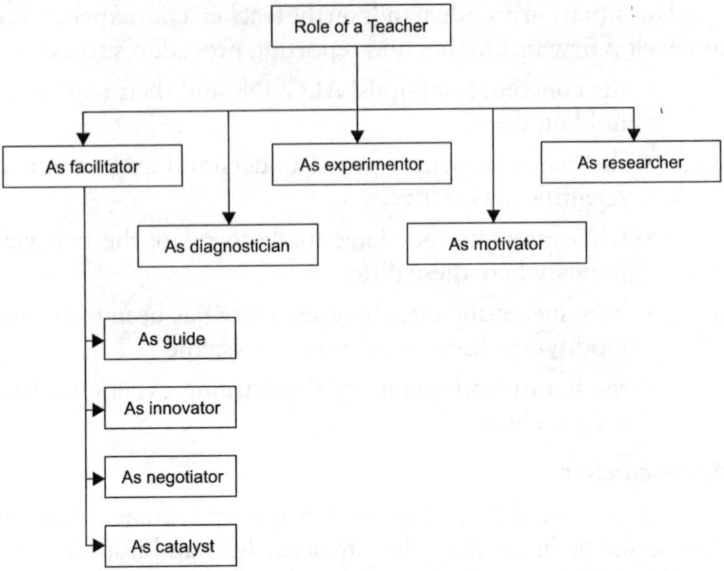

Fig. 7.22

7.6 Do's and Don'ts for Teachers

All constructivist-informed teaching aims at reducing the status of pupils' ALCONs and increase the status of scientific concepts. To achieve this objective the only human input is the teacher. So with all the theoretical models, research results as well as examplars presented so far in all the chapters, it is essential that to make the principles of constructivism really operational in a classroom situation, one needs to provide the teacher a checklist of Do's and Don'ts which are realistic, operationally implementable and plausible in the cognitive domain of the teacher. We provide such a list in this section under two headings.

- Do's and Don'ts in the framework of ALCONs.
- Holistic Do's and Don'ts.

7.6.1 Do's and Don'ts in the Framework of ALCONs

Do's	Don'ts
1. Before teaching any concepts try to learn about the concept putting yourself in the position of the learner. Because every teacher is first a learner.	Do not think teaching is simply transmitting/reproducing the contents of the book in the class.
2. Try to make educated guess as to what perhaps the pupils think about the concept because of their own experiences and consequent personal constructs.	Do not assume that the learner has no role in the teaching process, and his/her role is confined to the learning process only.
3. Try to establish what the pupils think.	Do not appear to judge the pupils meaning of the concept in terms of your meanings.
4. Make the pupils realize that their ideas are important and are being explored for functional consideration.	Do not give any indication to the pupils about your meaning for the concept.
5. Try to ascertain the genesis of the ALCONs. This will help you to identify any pattern/symmetry and design prescription.	Do not be satisfied by just diagnosing the ALCONs.
6. In the steps 3, 4, 5 above the techniques used could be structured interview, question as a pencil-on-paper test, display of cards containing diagrams about instances or events followed by questions, group discussion, innovative demonstrations, bridging analogies, cognitive conflict, challenging activities or even interactive computer programme. In using any of these strategies try to bring a balance between open-ended component (questions) and closed-ended components (questions).	Do not keep components with a YES/NO type, agree/disagree type or fixed recall type output. Do not lose sight of multiplicity of realities, representation, truths, connotations and concept of concepts.
7. Analyse pupils' responses carefully and then plan the design of the interaction step.	Do not rush the pupil for responses otherwise one will be enmeshed in 'noises' and not indicators.
8. Whenever a doubt or a hesitation is spotted in any pupil's mind while expressing his/her ideas helps him/her to share it with his/her classmates.	Do not ever generate an atmosphere where any pupil may think that only the right answer is required from him/her.
9. Be sensitive and receptive to unanticipated responses which were not part of your educated guess and explore them systematically and carefully.	Do not ignore responses which you do not understand. Rather follow them up carefully until you understand because therein may lie the indication about the strategy you are going to use for teaching.
10. Pupils may give self-contradictory statements, give due weightage to all of them.	Do not forget earlier statements made by the pupils.
11. Encourage and respect pupils' attempts to make queries. This will generate a healthy, informal atmosphere.	Do not let your strategy for diagnosis become a process of formal testing, examination or interrogation.
12. Some queries may be ridiculous and inconsistent. But still take note of them and generate innovative situations where the pupils may realize the lacunae in their queries.	Do not outright reject ridiculous/ inconsistent queries.

Do's	Don'ts
13. Carefully check that the language you are using is conveying the same meaning to the pupil as you intend it to convey.	Do not assume that what you intend to convey is conveyed to the pupils.
14. Be careful while investigating connotative relativity, because pupils might be very sensitive to such a probe.	Do not let the pupils realize that such an effort is on.
15. Try to recognise the situation when a pupil is giving a response only for the purpose of giving a response i.e. simply to fill a 'silence'.	Do not just accept such an answer without exploring the reason behind it.
16. Maintain a record of all that is done in this diagnostic process so that logical interlinking is maintained.	Do not hesitate to go back to earlier responses as those in juxtaposition with the recent one may indicate the genesis.
17. Encourage group interaction so as to help the pupils retain only the useful ALCONs and reject the detrimental ALCONs.	Do not reject the detrimental ALCONs in an ad-hoc way.
18. If your strategy fails to develop pupil's confidence abort it and plan for an alternative approach.	Do not religiously stick to your strategy or else it may lead the pupils to a state of total resistance and alienation.

7.6.2 Holistic Do's and Don'ts

Do's	Don'ts
1. Always put emphasis on intrinsic motivation.	Do not use the technique for extrinsic motivation.
2. For concept construction by the pupil use cognitive negotiation.	Do not use regimented transmission of knowledge or imposition of knowledge.
3. Be a sensible guide.	Avoid over indulgence of guidance and prescriptive guidance.
4. Try to use cognitive conflict as and when opportunity arises.	Do not use cognitive conflict on a regular basis, because then it generates monotony and demotivation.
5. Whenever there is cognitive resistance try out other forms of acceptable strategies.	Do not go on harping on your own views.
6. Provide opportunity for cognitive apprenticeship learning.	Avoid prescriptive learning modes.
7. For authenticity use real-life experiences of the pupils.	Do not faithfully follow only those experiences or instances described in the textbook.
8. Goals and objectives may be arrived at through cognitive negotiation.	Goals and objectives should not be authoritatively stated.
9. Emphasize on knowledge construction.	Do not emphasize on mechanical knowledge acquisition and reproduction.
10. Brain storming sessions may be judiciously used for creating intrinsic motivation.	Mechanical statement of facts and questions with fixed responses should be avoided.
11. Steps be undertaken to expand the cognitive domain of the pupils.	Do not discourage many pupils when he/she, out of his/her own volition, is trying to go beyond the periphery prescribed by you or the textbook.

Do's	Don'ts
12. Try to explore the zone of proximal development of every pupil by providing suitable scaffoldings.	Do not confine your instruction within the perceptible limits of pupil's cognitive boundary.
13. Allow the pupils even to commit mistakes in his/her efforts for cognitive growth. Search for the cause of those mistakes.	Do not degrade pupils even if they commit mistakes. Do not decry them on the basis of their mistakes.
14. Provide pupils with access to IT and internet so that they can expand their experimental information world and will have the opportunity to apply their ALCONs in this expanded domain to test the viability of ALCONs.	Do not by authority confine the pupils to their text books and whatever transpires in the classroom.
15. Encourage pupils to define, refine and conceptualize the interrelations between concepts. Construction of proper conceptual interrelatedness leads to functional, meaningful learning.	Do not introduce concepts, topics and chapters as isolated islands. Because this may lead to Epi-Con.
16. Do change your technique if assessment shows that your teaching has not resulted in proper knowledge construction.	Do not rigidly adhere to your teaching technique as it may result in cognitive resistance from the pupils.
17. Teach the pupils to learn how to learn.	Do not teach the pupils with the sole objective of doing well in the examination.
18. Do recognise the truth that every teacher is first a learner, then a teacher and every learning is preceded by a process of unlearning.	Do not ever think that you have nothing more to learn.

7.7 Conclusion

Consequent upon the exponential rise (Duit, 1993) in the number of research studies on pupils' ALCONs since 1980, the dominance of constructivist school of thought on researches in the areas of epistemology, in general, and science education, in particular, have become so pronounced that in the view of Lyotard (1984) it has acquired implicitly the status of a meta- or "grand theory" and Tobin et al. (1994) name it as the new paradigm for science education.

Another school of thought (details are in Chapter 9) argues that constructivism:

- is a flawed epistemological theory, because it fails to elaborate any methodology of theory adjudication (Osborne, 1996),
- replaces "truth" by "viability" and hence is in contradiction with the objectivity and rationality of science,

- replaces objective reality by solipsism,
- fails to elaborate any objective and repeatable mechanism by which one theory can be considered more "viable" than the other,
- is more a referent than a method (Tobin and Tippins, 1993), and
- does not predict as to what material will or will not be accessible to the learners.

In spite of these and other dialectical and philosophical criticisms (see for example Suchting, 1998; Rowlands, 2009; Irzig, 2000; Larochelle and Bednarz, 1998; Phillips, 1998; Lerman, 1994) it is most plausible that constructivism, with its major three tenets (spelled out in the beginning of this chapter) is going to stand the test of time as well as the umpteen future studies to probe its reliability and validity, because it answers two critical questions:

- How does a child learn a concept?
- Why does a child learn a concept?

However, keeping in tune with constructivism's intrinsic philosophy of change through construction,

- constructivism may get refined,
- its conceptual structures may get restructured,
- its emphasis may change,
- out of the very large numbers of constructivisms, several may have a natural death under the principle of struggle for existence and survival of the fittest,
- radical constructivism and social constructivism may converge on some common zone of overlap, and
- the boundaries between social negotiation, individual creativity (Confrey, 1991), language individuality and subjective experience based cognitive construction (Von Glasersfeld, 1998) may get diffused and become more porous for cognitive osmosis, resulting in improved viability and sense making, because constructivism, as a school of thought has also to go through the

evolutionary process of struggle for existence, survival of the fittest and principle of natural selection.

However, we advocate that with all its modifications, improvements and refinements, Constructivism, for surviving the process of natural selection, must stand up to the touchstone of its applicability in real life situations and transportability into the classroom.

Herein comes the important role of multiplicity of truths, representations, realities and concepts in the form of pupils' ALCONs in a classroom situation. To handle this situation, which is formidable, we look for analogies in the history of science. In the beginning man also faced the problem of multiplicity of matter, from leaf to iron ore, from water to hills. Man tried to look for pattern and symmetry so that the properties of the huge number of seemingly different matter can be explained by only a few parameters. Thus developed the models of living, non-living, solid, liquid and gas, elements and compounds and finally atoms and molecules, and then elementary particles and quarks.

Similarly, in this case we hypothesize that if we can diagnose the genesis (supposedly few in number) of ALCONs, then a pattern will emerge and the handling of the multiple ALCONs will reduce to handling only a few generic processes. This we presented in this chapter where the generic processes diagnosed by us are:

- Induced Incorrect Generalization (IIG)
    - (i) Conceptual reversibility
    - (ii) Conceptual continuity
    - (iii) Conceptual extrapolation
    - (iv) Conceptual myopia
- Episodic conceptualization (Epi-Con).

Literature shows that there have been other attempts to look for such a set a optimal number of parameters to meaningfully operationalize the multitude of ALCONs. Niedderer (2001) proposes that cognitive structures can be described by means of Cognitive Atoms, or, building blocks. His arguments is based on (a) the fact that ALCONs form stable elements in the cognitive system (Pfundt and Duit, 2000), (b) the idea (generated by neurobiological views of structure and function of the human brain) that these stable ALCONs are stored in the brain like goods in a departmental store (Aufsch Naiter and Welzel, 1997). He then states (Niedderer, 1996; 1997) that certain more elementary and basic "cognitive tools" are represented in the mind, and they, in interaction with the particular situation, produce these conceptions.

On the other hand di Sessa (1993) introduced the model of Phenomenological Primitive, acronymed as "P-prims" and states, "P-prims are rather short knowledge structure (typically involving configurations of only a few parts) that acts largely by being recognized...in the system's behaviour or hyothesised behaviour...p-prims become the intuitive equivalent of physics laws; they may explain other phenomena, but are not themselves explained with the knowledge system."

Minstrell's (1992) model introduces the idea of "facets of student's knowledge and reasoning". For him a "facet" is a convenient unit of thought, a piece of knowledge or a strategy seemingly used by the student in addressing a particular situation. However, the "grain size of knowledge" conceptualized by Minstrell (1992) usually has the pitfall of a long list of facets.

In a parallel modeling Wittmann (1988) proposes the entity—"Reasoning Primitives". He states, "In this sense, a primitive is a common and small logical building block that lets us describe basic elements of common events in many different situations."

Tirosh, Stavy and Cohen (1988) talk of 'intuitive rules' as elementary building blocks.

But all the above efforts to search for or hypothesize the minimum number of parameter to handle the problem of multiple ALCONs will be operationally viable only when one has knowledge about the broad characteristics of ALCONs, which we present in the section 7.3.

Thereafter we place ALCONs in their rightful place in TLP by proposing a hypothetical PACT space with implications for classroom practices.

Then the myth that 'since knowledge cannot be instructed and hence the role of a teacher is minimal or redundant' is demystified by discussing nine major roles, those the teacher has to perform in a classroom situation. In this context life centered exemplars have also been given to infuse realism into the various roles of the teacher.

Once this background framework is completed we give a list of Do's and Don'ts for the teachers so that it can always work as referring sign post whenever TLP is in operation.

We assert that this chapter is a complete package in itself for a classroom teacher who can go through only this chapter and be empowered enough to adopt constructivism in TLP.

References

Anderson, B. (1986). Pupils' reasoning in science—Theoretical background, examples and implications for teaching. Invited paper. *ICASE symposium "Science Education and the Researcher"*. Annual meeting of the Association for Science Education, University of York, York, January, 1986.

Aufshnaiter, S.V., and Welzel, M. (1997). Wissen svermittlung dursh Wissensntwick-lung. Das Bremer Komplex it atsmodell zur quantitative Beschreibung von Bedeutungsentw-icklung und Lernen. *Zeitschrift fur Didaktik der Natur wissen schaften*, Vol. 3(2): 43-58.

Ausubel, D.P. (1968). *Educational Psychology: A Cognitive View*. New York: Holt, Rinehart and Winston.

Brooks, J.G., and Brooks, M.G. (1993). *In Search of Understanding: The Case for a Constructivist Classroom.* Alexandria, VA: Association for Supervision and Curriculum Development.

Champagne, A.B., Klofer, L.E., Solomon, C., and Cahn, A. (1980). *Technical Report*, Pittsburgh: University of Pittsburgh Press.

Chiari, G., and Nuzzo, M.L. (1996). Psychological constructivism: A meta theoretical differentiation. *Journal of Constructivist Psychology*, Vol. 9, pp. 163-84.

Claxton, G. (1983). *School Science: Falling on stony ground or choked by thorns?* Mimeograph, Centre for Science and Mathematics Education, Chelsea College, University of London.

—— (1985). Teaching and acquiring scientific knowledge. In T. Keen and M. Pope (Eds.), *Kelly in the Classroom: Practical Applications of Personal Construct Psychology.*

Clement, J. (1982). Students' perceptions in introductory mechanics. *American Journal of Physics*, Vol. 50(1): 66-71.

—— (1988). Observed methods for generating analogies in scientific problem-solving. *Cognitive Science*, Vol. 12(4): 563.

Confrey, J. (1991). Learning to listen: A student's understanding of powers of Ten. In E. von Glasersfeld (Ed.), *Radical Constructivism in Mathematics Education*. Dordrecht: Kluwer.

De Vires, R. and Kohlberg, L. (1987). *Programs of Early Education: The Constructivist View*, New York: Longman.

Deci, E.L., Koestner, R., and Ryan, R.M. (2001). Extrinsic rewards and intrinsic motivation in education: Reconsidered once again. *Review of Educational Research*, Vol. 71, pp. 1-27.

di Sessa, A.A. (1993). Towards an epistemology of physics. *Cognition and Instruction,* Vol. 10 (2-3): 105-25.

Dreyfus, A., Jungwirth, E., and Eliovitch, R. (1990). Applying the "Cognitive Conflict" strategy for conceptual change—some implications, difficulties, and problems. *Science Education*, Vol. 74(5): 555-69.

Driver, R. (1973). *The representation of conceptual frameworks in young adolescent science students*. Ph.D. dissertation, University of Illinois, Urbana, IL.

—— (1983). *The pupils as scientists?*. Milton Keynes: Open University Press.

—— (1989). Students' conception and the learning of science. *International Journal of Science Education,* Vol. 11(5): 481-90.

Driver, R., and Easley, J. (1978). Pupils and paradigms: A review of literature related to concept development in adolescent science students. *Studies in Science Education*, Vol. 5, pp. 61-84.

Driver, R., Asoko, H., Leach, J., Mortimer, E., and Scott, P. (1994). Constructing Scientific knowledge in the classroom. *Educational Researcher*, Vol. 23(7): 5-12.

Duit, R. (1993). Research on students' conceptions—development and trends. Paper presented at the *Third International Seminar on Misconceptions in Science and Mathematics Education*. Cornell University, Ithaca, NY.

Dykstra, D.J., Boyle, C.P., and Monarch, I.A. (1992). Studying conceptual change in learning Physics. *Science Education*, Vol. 76(6): 615-52.

Engel, C.E. (1982). The development of understanding of selected aspects of pressure, heat and evolution in pupils aged between 12 to 16 years. *Unpublished Ph.D. thesis*, Leeds: University of Leeds.

Engel, C.E., and Driver, R. (1983). Stability and charge in children's conceptualization of scientific phenomena. *Unpublished paper*, Leeds: University of Leeds.

Ernest, P. (1995). The One and The Many. In L. Steffe and J. Gale (Eds.), *Constructivism in Education*. New Jersey: Lawrence Erlbaum Associates, Inc.

Fisher, K.M. (1985). A misconception in Biology: Aminoacids and translations. *Journal of Research in Science Teaching*, Vol. 22, pp. 53-62.

Gay, L.R. (1987). *Educational Research: Competencies for analysis and application*. Columbus, OH: Merrill.

Gergen, K. (1995). Social construction and the education process. In L. Steffe and J. Gale (Eds.), *Constructivism in Education*. New Jersey: Lawrence Erlbaum Associates, Inc.

Gilbert, J.K. and Swift, D.J. (1985). Towards a Lakatosian analysis of the Piagetian and Alternative conceptions research programmes. *Science Education*, Vol. 69, pp. 681-96.

Gilbert, J.K., and Osborne, R.J. (1980). "I understand, but I don't get it": Some problems of learning science. *School Science Review*, Vol. 61, pp. 664-74.

Gilbert, J.K., and Watts, M. (1983). Concepts, misconceptions and alternative conceptions: Changing perspectives in Science education. *Studies in Science Education*, Vol. 10, pp. 61-98.

Gilbert, J.K., Osborne, R.J., and Fensham, P.J. (1982). Children's Science and its consequences for teaching. *Science Education*, Vol. 64(4): 623-33.

Green, S.K. (2002), Using an expectancy-value approach to examine teachers' motivational strategies. *Teaching and Teacher Education*, Vol. 18, pp. 989-1005.

Gunstone, R.F., and White, R.T. (1980). A matter of gravity. Paper presented at *Australian Science Education Research Association Conference*, Melbourne, May, 1980.

—— (1981). Understanding gravity. *Science Education*, Vol. 65, pp. 2291-99.

Hammer, D. (1996). More than misconceptions: Multiple perspectives on student knowledge and reasoning, and an appropriate role for education research. *American Journal of Physics*, Vol. 64(10): 1316-25.

—— (2000). Student resources for learning introductory Physics. *American Journal of Physics. Physics Education Research Supplement*. Vol. 68(51): 552-59.

Harrison, A.G., Grayson, D.J., and Treagust, D.F. (1999). Investigation a grade 11 students' evolving conceptions of heat and temperature. *Journal of Research in Science Teaching*, Vol. 36, pp. 55-87.

Haslam, F., and Treagust, D.F. (1987). Diagnosing Secondary Students' misconceptions of photosynthesis and respiration in plants using a two tier multiple choice test instrument. *Journal of Biological Education*, Vol. 21, pp. 203-11.

Hewson, P.W. (1981). A conceptual change approach to learning science. *European Journal of Science Education*, Vol. 3(4): 383-96.

—— (1982). A case study of conceptual change in special relativity: The influence of prior knowledge in learning. *European Journal of Science Education*, Vol. 4(4): 61-78.

Hewson, P.W., and Thornley, R. (1989). The conditions of conceptual change in the classroom. *International Journal of Science Education*, Vol. 11(5): 541-53.

Irzig, G. (2000). Back to basics: A philosophical critique of constructivism. *Science & Education*, Vol. 9(6): 621-39.

Johnson, J.K., and Howe, A.C. (1978). The use of cognitive conflict to promote conservation acquisitions. *Journal of Research in Science Teaching*, Vol. 15, pp. 239-47.

Jonassen, D. (1994). Thinking technology. *Educational Technology,* Vol. 34(4): 34-37.

Karplus, R. (1981). Education and formal thought—A modest proposal. In I.E. Sigel, D.M. Broadzinsky and R.M. Golinkoff (Eds.), *New Directions in Piagetian Theory and Practice*. Hillsdale, NJ: Lawrence Erlbaum and Associates.

Kelly, G.A. (1955). *The Psychology of Personal Constructs*. Vols. 1, 2. New York: W.W. Norton.

Kuhn, T. (1970). *The Structure of Scientific Revolution*. Chicago: University of Chicago Press.

Larochelle, M., and Bednarz, N. (1998). Constructivism and education: Beyond epistemological correctness. In M. Larochelle, N. Bednarz and J. Garrison (Eds.), *Constructivism and Education*. Cambridge: Cambridge University Press.

Lee, G., et al. (2003). Development of an instrument for measuring cognitive conflict in Secondary—Level science classes. *Journal of Research in Science Teaching*, Vol. 40(6): 585-603.

Lepper, M.R., and Hodell, M. (1989). Intrinsic motivation in the classroom. In C. Ames and R. Ames. (Eds.), *Research on motivation in Education*, Vol. 3, San Diego. CA: Academic Press.

Lerman, S. (1994). Articulating theories of mathematics learning. In P. Ernest (Ed.), *Constructing Mathematical Knowledge: Epistemology and Mathematical Education*. London: Falmer.

Links (2000). www.questia.com/constructivism_edu.

Loughran, J., Northfield, G., and Jones, C. (1994). Deriving public knowledge from self study experience. Paper presented at the *Australian Science Education Research Association Conference*, Hobart, Tasmania.

Lyotard, J.F. (1984). *The postmodern condition: A report on Knowledge.* Minneapolis, MN: University of Minnesota Press.

Mathews, G.P., Brook, V.G., and Khan-Gandapur, T.H. (1984). Cognitive structure determinations as a tool in science teaching, Part-1: A new method of creating concept maps. *European Journal of Science Education*, Vol. 6(2): 169-77.

Maturana, H.R. (1998). Reality: The search for objectivity or the quest for a compelling argument. *The Irish Journal of Psychology*, Vol. (9): 25-82.

Maturana, H.R., and Varela, F.J. (1992). *The tree of knowledge: The Biological roots of human understanding.* (rev. ed.: R. Paolucci, Trans). Boston: Shambhala.

Mayer, R. (1996). Learners as information Processors : Legacies and limitations of educational psychology's second metaphor. *Educational Psychologists*, Vol. 31(3/4): 151-61.

McCloskey, M., Carmazza, A., and Green, B. (1981). Curvilinear motion in the absence of external forces: Naïve beliefs about the motion of objects. *Science*, Vol. 210, pp. 1139-41.

McCloskey, (1983). Naïve theories of motion. In D. Genter and A.L. Stevans. (Eds.), *Mental Models*, Hillsdale, NJ: Lawrence Erlbaum.

McDermott, L.C. (1984). Research on conceptual understanding in mechanics. *Physics Today*, July, pp. 24-32.

Miller, R. (1989). Constructive criticisms. *International Journal of Science Education*. Vol. 11, pp. 587-96.

Ministrell, J.A. (1989). Teaching Science for understanding. In L. Resnick and L. Klopter (Eds.), *Towards a Thinking Curriculum: Current Cognitive Research*. Alexandria: VA: Association for Supervision and Curriculum Development.

Minstrell, J. (1982). Explaining the 'at rest' condition of an object. *Physics Teacher,* Vol. 20, pp. 10-14.

—— (1992). Facets of students' knowledge and relevant instruction. In R. Duit, F. Goldberg, and H. Niedderer (Eds.), *Research in Physics Learning: Theoretical Issues and Empirical Studies*. Kiel: IPN, Kiel.

Mohapatra, J.K. (1988). Induced incorrect generalization leading to misconceptions—an exploratory investigation about laws of reflection of light. *Journal of Research in Science Teaching*, Vol. 25(9): 777-84.

—— (1989). The fourth dimension of the teaching-learning of science—its characteristics and implications. *Indian Educational Review*, Vol. 24(8): pp. 1-17.

—— (1990). Episodic conceptualization: A possible cause of manifest alternative conceptions amongst group of pupils in some Indian schools. *International Journal of Science Education*, Vol. 12(4): 417-27.

Mohapatra, J.K., and Bhattacharya, S. (1989). Pupils, teachers, induced incorrect generalization and the concept of force. *International Journal of Science Education*, Vol. 11(4): 429-36.

Mohapatra, J.K., and Parida, B.K. (1995). The location of alternative conceptions by a concept graph technique. *International Journal of Science Education*, Vol. 17(5): 663-81.

Mohapatra, J.K., Tripathy, H.H., and Parida, B.K. (1998). Pupils' alternative conceptions about rusting of iron—A concept map analysis. *Indian Educational Review*, Vol. 34(2): 22-37.

Mortimer, E.F., and Machado, A.H. (2000). Anomalies and conflicts in classroom discourse. *Science Education*, Vol. 84(4): 429-44.

Murphy, E. (1997). http:/www.cdli.ca/-elmurphy/emurphy/cle2b.html

Murray, F.B. (1968). Cognitive conflict and reversibility training in the acquisition of length conservation. *Journal of Educational Psychology*, Vol. 59, pp. 82-87.

Niedolerer, H. (1997). Learning process studies in physics: A review of concepts and results. Paper presented at *AERA*, Chicago, USA. (http://diclaktik. physik. uni-bremen. de/niedderer/pubs. htm).

—— (1996). Uberblick ueber Lempro Zesstudien in Physik. In R. Duit, and C. von Rhoeneck (Eds.), *Lernen in den Natur wissen Schaften*. Kiel: IPN, Kiel.

—— (2001). Physics learning as cognitive development. In R.H. Evans, A.M. Anderson, and H. Sorensen (Eds.), *Bridging Research Methodology and Research Aims*. ESERA Summer School in Gilleleje, Denmark.

Novak, J.D. (1990). Concept maps and Vee diagrams: Two meta-cognitive tools to facilitate meaningful learning. *Instructional Science*, Vol. 19, pp. 1-25.

Novak, J.D., and Gowin, D.B. (1984). *Learning how to learn*. Cambridge: Cambridge University Press.

Nussbaum, J., and Novick S. (1982a). Alternative frameworks, Conceptual conflict and accommodation: towards a principled teaching strategy. *Instructional Science* Vol. 11, pp. 183-200.

—— (1982b). A study of conceptual change in the classroom. Paper presented at the *Annual Meeting of the National Association for Research in Science Teaching*, Lake Geneva, Chicago.

—— (1981a). Brainstorming in the classroom to invent a model: a case study. *School Science Review*, Vol. 62 (221): 771-78.

Nuthall, G. (1999). The way students learn: Acquiring knowledge from an integrated science and social studies unit. *The Elementary School Journal*, Vol. 99, pp. 303-42.

Ogborn, J. (1977). Questions, questions, questions. In J. Ogborn (Ed.). *Small group teaching in Undergraduate Science*. London: Heinemann.

Osborne, J. (1996). Beyond constructivism. *Science Education*, Vol. 80(1): 53-82.

Osborne, R., and Freyberg, P. (1985). *Learning in Science: The Implications of Childrens' Science*. London: Heinemann.

Osborne, R., and Wittrock, M.C. (1983). Learning Science : A generative process. *Science Education*, Vol. 67(4): 489-508.

Palmer, D. (2005). A motivational view of constructivist—informed teaching. *International Journal of Science Education,* Vol. 27(15, 16): 1853-81.

Peterson, R.F., Treagust, D.F., and Garnet, P. (1986). Identification of secondary students' misconception of covalent bonding and structure concepts using a diagnostic test instrument. *Research in Science Education*, Vol. 16, p. 40-48.

Pfund, H., and Duit, R. (2000). duit@ipn.uni-kiel.de

Pfundt, H., and Duit, R. (1994). *Bibliography: Students' Alternative Frameworks and Science Education*. Institute for Science Education at the University of Kiel. Kiel: Germany.

Piaget, J. (1964). Cognitive development in children: Piaget Part I: Development and learning. *Journal of Research in Science Teaching*, Vol. 2, pp. 176-86.

Pintrich, P.R., and Schunk, D.H. (1996). *Motivation in Education: Theory, Research and Application*. Englewood Cliffs, NJ: Prentice Hall.

Pintrich, P.R., Marx, R.W., and Boyle, R.A. (1993). Beyond cold conceptual change: The role of motivational beliefs and classroom contextual factors in the process of conceptual change. *Review of Educational Research*, Vol. 63, pp. 167-99.

Posner, G.J., Strike, K.A., Hewson, P.W. and Gertzog, W.A. (1982). Accommodation of a Scientific Conception: Towards a theory of conceptual change. *Science Education*, Vol. 72(1): 103-13.

Raskin, J.D. (2002). Constructivism in Psychology: Personal construct psychology, Radical constructivism and Social constructivism. In J.D. Raskin and S.K. Bridges (Eds.), *Studies in Meaning: Exploring Constructivist Psychology*. New York: Pace University Press.

Resnick, R., and Halliday, D. (1988). *Physics*. New Delhi: Wiky Eastern.

Rowlands, S. (2009). The contradictions in the constructivist discourse. *Philosophy of Mathematic Education Journal*, Vol. 14, pp. 1-11.

Schollum, B., and Osborne, R. (1985). Relating the new to the familiar. In R. Osborne and P. Freyberg. (Eds.), *Learning in Science: The Implications of Children's Science*. London: Heinemann.

Segal, L. (1986). The dream of reality: Heinz von Foerster's constructivism. New York: Norton.

Shulman, I.S. (1987). Knowledge and teaching: Foundations of the new reform. *Harvard Educational Review*, Vol. 57, pp. 1-22.

Smith, J., di Sessa, A., and Roschelle, J. (1993/94). Misconceptions reconceived: A constructivist analysis of knowledge in transition. *Journal of Learning Science*, Vol. 3(2): 115-63.

Staver, J.R. (1998). Constructivism: Sound theory for explicating the Practice of Science and Science teaching. *Journal of Research in Science Teaching*, Vol. 35(5): 501-20.

Suchting, W.A. (1998). Constructivism deconstructed. In M.R. Matthews (Ed.), *Constructivism in Science Education*. Dordrecht: Kluwer.

Tasker, R., and Freyberg, P. (1985). Facing mismatch in classroom. In R. Osborne and P. Freyberg (Eds.), *Learning in Science: The Implications of Children's Science*. London: Heinemann.

Thomas, R.S.D. (1994). Radical constructive criticisms of von Glasersfeld's Radical constructivism. In P. Ernest (Ed.). *Constructing Mathematical Knowledge: Epistemology and Mathematical Education*. London: Falmer.

Thornton, R.K. and Sokolof, D.R. (1990). Learning motion concepts using real-time Micro-computer-based Laboratory Tools, *American Journal of Physics*. Vol. 58(9): 858.

Thornton, R.K. (1987). Tools for Scientific Thinking: Micro-Computer-based Laboratory. *Physics Education*, Vol. 22(4): 230-38.

Tiberghien, A., and Delacote, G. (1976). Manipulation et representations de circuits electrique simples chez des enfants de za izans. *Review Francaise de Pedagogie*, Vol. 34, pp. 32-44.

Tirosh, D., Stavy, R., and Cohen, S. (1998). Cognitive conflict and intuitive rules. *International Journal of Science Education*, Vol. 20(10): 1257-69.

Tobin, K., and Tippins, D. (1993). Constructivism as a referent for teaching and learning. In K. Tobin (Ed.), *The Practice of Constructivism in Science Education*. Washington, D.C.: AAAS Press.

Tobin, K., Tippins, D., and Gallard, A. (1994). Research on instructional strategies for teaching science. In D.L. Gabel (Ed.). *Handbook of Research in Science Education and Learning*. New York: Macmillan.

Tobin, K.G., and Capie, W. (1981). The development and validation of a group test of logical thinking. *Educational and Psychological Measurement*, Vol. 11, pp. 413-23.

Treagust, D.F. (1988). Development and use of diagnostic tests to evaluate students' misconception in Science. *International Journal of Science Education*, Vol. 10(2): 159-69.

Trowbridge, D.E., and Mc Dermott, L. (1980). Investigation of student understanding of the concept of velocity in one dimension. *American Journal of Physics*, Vol. 48(12): 1020-28.

—— (1981). Investigation of student understanding of the concept of acceleration in one dimension. *American Journal of Physics,* Vol. 49(3): 242-53.

Viennot, L. (1979). Spontaneous reasoning in elementary dynamics. *European Journal of Science Education*, Vol. 1(2): 205-21.

—— (1985). Analysing student's reasoning in science: A pragmatic view of theoretical problems. *European Journal of Science Education*, Vol. 7, pp. 151-62.

Villani, A. (1992). Conceptual change in Science and Science education. *Science Education*, Vol. 76(2): 223-37.

von Foerster, H. (1984). *Observing Systems* (2nd. ed.). Seaside, CA: Intersystems Publications.

von Glasersfeld, E. (1995a). *Radical Constructivism: A Way of Knowing and Learning*. Washington. D.C.: Falmer Press.

—— (1996). Introduction: Aspects of Constructivism. In C.T. Fosnot (Ed.), *Constructivism: Theory, Perspectives, and Practice*. New York: Teachers College Press.

—— (1987). *The Construction of Knowledge.* Seaside, CA, Systems Inquiry Series, Intersystems Publication.

—— (1995). A constructivist approach to teaching. In L.P. Steffe and J. Gale (Eds.), *Constructivism in Education.* Hillsdale, NJ: Lawrence Erlbaum.

Watts, M. (1982). Gravity—do not take it for granted. *Physics Education*, Vol. 17(5): 116-21.

Watts, M., Gilbert, J.K., and Pope, M. (1982). Alternative frameworks: representations of school children's understanding of science. Paper presented at the *First International Symposium on Representing Understanding*, London, Feb. (1982).

Weber, R.L., Manning, K.V., White, M.W., and Weygand, G.A. (1979). *College Physics*. New Delhi: Tata McGraw.

Wenning, C.J. (2005). White boarding and Socratic dialogues: Questions and answers. *Journal of Physics Teacher Education Online*, Vol. 3(1), September 2005, pp. 3-10.

—— (2008). Dealing more effectively with alternative conceptions in Science. *Journal of Physics Teacher Education, Online*, Vol. 5(1): 11-19.

Wenning, C.J., Holbrook, T.W., and Stankevitz, J. (2006). Engaging students in conducting Socratic dialogues: Suggestions for Science teachers. *Journal of Physics Teacher Education. Online*, Vol. 4(1), Autumn 2006, pp. 10-13.

White, R.W. (1959). Motivation Reconsidered: The concept of competence. *Psychological Review*, Vol. 66, pp. 297-333.

Wiser, M. and Amin, T. (2001). "Is heat hot?" Inducing conceptual change by integrating everyday and scientific perspectives on thermal phenomena. *Learning and Instruction*, Vol. II(4-5): 331-55.

Wittmann, M.C. (1988). *Making sense of how students come to an understanding of Physics : An example from Mechanical waves*. Doctoral Dissertation, Department of Physics, University of Maryland, College Park, Maryland.

Wolze, W., and Walgenbach, W. (1992). Naturwissenschaftliche Bildung als System bildung. In P. HauBler (Ed.), *Physikunterrichi und Menschenbildung*. Kiel, Germany: IPN at the University of Kiel, pp. 163-86.

8 Teacher Education in Constructivism

8.1 Introduction

With changing times there has been a paradigm shift in the comprehension about the nature and process of human learning. This shift has been engineered through (i) a natural process of cognitive evolution, (ii) a necessity to meet the challenges of new and demanding experimental evidences, and (iii) a desire to optimize the degree and quality of meaningful learning by the learner. As a result the shift has slowly but conclusively moved from behaviourism to cognitivism and now to constructivism (Cooper, 1993). This latest approach in the thinking about the nature of human learning leads to a metamorphosis in the classroom teaching-learning process (TLP) and designed instruction, because it dramatically puts emphasis solely on the learner's autogenic effort to construct and internalise knowledge. Thus constructivism has emerged as the new encompassing epistemology. Parallelly, pedagogical researchers (Carlin and Ciaccio, 1997; Deeds and Allen, 2000; Vaughan, 2002; Emmer and Gerwels, 2002; also see references on Teaching Models in Constructivist Framework in chapter 6) show that teachers with functional and skill based knowledge about constructivism can become better agents to help the learner to construct meaningful knowledge with 'validity' and not 'viability' as the discerning criteria.

However, to achieve this desired result constructivism puts a non-negotiable premium on the teacher, as discussed in Chapter 7. This premium, in brief, manifests in broadly two forms; (a) Absolute necessities, and (b) Operational necessities.

Absolute Necessities

The implementation of constructivist principles in a classroom transaction so as to maximize meaningful learning through autogenic construction by the learner demands an attitudinal change in the teacher, which was never emphasized before. The teacher should realize that

- he/she is always first a learner and then a teacher,
- every learning is preceded by a spate of unlearning, because that is one of the basis of cognitive evolution through self-constructivism, and
- to internalize the above two basic essentials he/she must be prepared to change, i.e. changeability with the associated flexibility and not rigidity has to become an integral component of his/her cognitive space.

Such an attitudinal change is difficult, but not impossible.

Operational Necessities

Many of these necessities have been discussed in the earlier chapters keeping in view the focus of each chapter. However, we enlist here some of the primary ones so as to infuse completeness into this chapter. The teacher, empowered with the above three absolute necessities, must stop committing the mistake of assuming that

- every concepts has a unique objective existence,
- concepts can be instructed,
- empiricist/inductivist approach is the correct technique to teach a concept,
- every concept can be learnt by a learner if the teaching is good,
- concepts are like commodities which can be transported and delivered using communication techniques as conveyances,
- the entire teaching-learning activity is like a "banking process" where the teacher fills the learners with deposits of information, considered by the teacher to be true knowledge, and the learners store these deposits intact until needed (Oldfather, Bonds & Bray, 1994),

- memorizing through practice is the fruitful way of learning,
- the purpose of learning is to regurgitate in the examination,
- performance in an examination (which believes in regurgitation) is a measure of learning,
- the unanticipated/wrong responses by a learner are all trash and better be put in a trash can,
- his/her strategy/method to teach is best even if it does not produce the desired learning outcome,
- purpose of learning a concept by a learner is to have the knowledge of some natural truth/process or to discover/learn an ontological reality,
- acquiring knowledge is a passive process and can be imposed by the teacher using his/her authority,
- improving the content knowledge, pedagogical knowledge and honing the teaching skills of a teacher will necessarily improve the learning outcome, and
- if the teacher is satisfied with his/her teaching then everything of the TLP is well-taken care of.

The teacher has to also recognize, study, reflect, comprehend and appreciate the background results that led to the emergence of constructivism and the basic influences of constructivism on the teaching approaches, some of which are presented below as a compactified list.

- Research in parts of philosophy, psychology, linguistics, even art, history and science, all converge to suggest that the traditional epistemological paradigm is somehow asked and faulted (Kuhn, 1970). And by default corresponding teaching approaches are blind and error ridden.
- The epistemological base of constructivist teaching approaches comes from an epistemological difference between the traditional epistemology of knowledge and the constructivist epistemology of knowledge (Kim, 2005).

- Traditional epistemology views knowledge as an objective phenomena, while the constructivist epistemology views knowledge as a subjective construct of the person.

Though this drastic conclusion was an outcome of the synthesis of von Glasersfeld (1984), its legacy started very early when Vico (1710) stated, "*verum ipsum factum*", i.e. "God knows the world because he created it, human beings can know only what they themselves have made."

A different way of stating the same idea is that epistemic agents can know nothing but the cognitive structures they themselves have put together, which Vico (1710) states succinctly as "God is the artificer of Nature, man the God of artifacts."

- As a result of the above the connotation of every concept has a relativistic situatedness (von Glasersfeld, 2006) in the context of the cognitive space of each learner. Thus from the learner's point of view each concept loses its unique objective existence.
- The purpose of acquiring knowledge is not a quest for discovering Immutable Objective Truths/Ontological Realities (von Glasersfeld, 1989a, 1989b).
- Knowledge is not a representation of an observer-independent world-in-itself and in the framework of the learner, the conceptual construct, that is called the learner's knowledge, is actually a viable structure consistent with the learner's experiential world, and used to comprehend and organize it (Staver, 1998).
- Concepts and knowledge are autogenically constructed by the cognizing subject, learner, using such processes as assimilation, trial and error, fitment, reflection, accommodation, test of viability, equilibration (Piaget, 1967).
- Though 'Viability' is the discerning criteria used by the learner to construct a concept, still this constructed concept of a concept is real and valid for the learner whenever he/she applies it to any familiar or unfamiliar situation.

- The teacher job is to provide necessary facilities, cognitively viable multiple situations, peer discussion, brain storming and cognitive conflict sessions, bridging analogies, exciting and innovative challenges based on real life experiences, opportunities for reflection, analysis, self-evaluation of one's own ALCONs, encouragement to learners to ask question, to assess and criticize others views, reference and ancillary reading materials of interest.
- And all the above activities has to be executed through the process of Cognitive Negotiation and not cognitive imposition.

To comprehend, internalize and functionally operationalize all the above imperatives imposed on the teaching approaches by constuctivism, in the new paradigm, the teacher has to become (refer Chapter 7) not a/an

- lecturer delivering the contents of the textbook, but a provider of novel situations, activities, conflicts, possibilities, and alternative cognitive pathways,
- transmitter of immutable objective truths but a negotiator of ideas, concepts and knowledge,
- alpine guide who takes the tourist is enjoying it, but a facilitator to help the learner to climb one step at a time of the cognitive hill and enjoy it through self-reflection,
- enforcer of prescriptive learning on the entire class irrespective of the individualized ALCON and mental level of each learner, but a promoter of group discussion and self-analysis,
- stickler of using faithfully the textbooks, the curriculum, prescribed teaching techniques and included activities but an innovator of new and challenging ideas,
- person who spoon-feeds the learner, but a motivator to generates interest and curiosity in the mind of the learner,
- provider of pre-fabricated knowledge but a catalyst to help the learner construct knowledge in a way the teacher expects him/her to construct,

- critic of the mistakes committed by a learner but a diagnostician of the ALCONs of a learner and their genesis,
- robotic teacher but a researcher to understand learner's ALCONs, to provide alternative pathways to reassess the viability of ALCONs, to operate as a resource adviser, and as a coordinator,
- snobbish rejecter of learner's questions but an encourager to make the learner learn how to frame a question and ask it,
- avoider of new experiments, but a designer of new, challenging and exciting experiments,
- believer in one-way teaching-learning process but an implementer of collaborative teaching-learning process,
- protagonist of "what is relevant for examination is relevant for education" but a believer in "what is relevant for learning is relevant for education",
- designer of test to assess the ability of the learner to regurgitate but an evaluator to monitor the degree of meaningful learning by the learner and to nurture his/her talent so that he/she approaches his/her zone of proximal development (Vygotsky, 1978),
- assumer of the view that learning/acquisition of knowledge is a routine, mechanical activity meant to meet the demands of parental aspirations, in particular and social expectations in general but an implementor of the view that learning/acquisition of knowledge is an adaptive activity meant to meet the demands of cognitive evolutions, and
- practitioner of traditional teaching methods in a classroom situation but a creator of learning friendly classroom environment (Mahapatra and Mohapatra, 2008) geared to foster meaningful construction of concepts by the learner.

The discussions above about the non-negotiable premium on the teacher in the form of absolute necessities, the basic influences on the teaching approaches, and the defining indicators about the role of the teacher, as imposed by the philosophy and principles of constructivism, necessitates that

- the teacher education programme (both for pre-service and in-service teachers) has to be reexamined,
- new thrust areas have to be included,
- some of the old thrust areas, which are now obsolete except for historical record, have to be deleted,
- the basic structure, approach and emphasis in the curriculum have to be redefined and reformulated, and
- most importantly teacher educators have to be oriented and geared to meet this challenge.

However, from a constructivist point of view one must take note of the fact that in any teacher education programme

- the teacher are the learners and the teacher-educators are the teachers,
- being learners, the teachers carry with them their own ALCONs about constructivism into the classroom,
- these ALCONs will control the degree of meaningful learning of the principles and philosophy of constructivism by the teachers, hence
- these ALCONs will ultimately decide the quality and ability of the teacher to become instrumental in helping the pupils to construct their knowledge in a desirable way.

Thus it is imperative that every discourse on Teacher-education should be preceded by a knowledge list of ALCONs of teacher about constructivist approaches for teaching. This is presented in section 8.2.

8.2 Teachers' ALCONs About Constructivist Pedagogy

It is now established that every person's experiences and exposures are perceived and autogenically organized into complex mental constructs such as ideas, concepts, relationships and phenomena (Jonassen et al., 1999). These subjective unique constructions (ALCONs), as has been already discussed in earlier chapters are used to comprehend, explain, predict or make inferences about phenomena or the subjective ontological world and also to extend his/her cognitive space by further learning. Therein lies the importance of ALCON in constructivism.

ALCON 1: Since knowledge cannot be instructed, the role of the teacher in a classroom is minimal or redundant.

De-ALCONisation: If one analyses from a constructivist point of view then the role of a classroom teacher, who implicitly and explicitly puts his/her faith in the transmissionist approach i.e., the empiricist/inductivist philosophy, is actually minimal or, redundant, because he/she cannot help the learner to construct concepts/knowledge meaningfully.

As compared to the mundane role of such an inconsequential teacher, the new role of a teacher, who believes and makes a sincere effort to implement constructivist approach, is more demanding, more encompassing, more challenging, and more exciting. Because such a teacher has to be (refer Chapter 7) a researcher, a diagnostician, a motivator, a negotiator, a facilitator, an innovator, an experimenter, a guide and a catalyst. Thus to create a purposeful, focused, constructivist learning friendly environment the role of the teacher is really critical and crucial. The teacher does not have to and cannot follow any rule, specific strategy or prescriptive method for teaching. As a result, on the one hand his/her job and role become more difficult, and on the other hand he/she has more freedom for operation based on his/her content knowledge, pedagogy knowledge, pedagogical content knowledge (Shulman, 1987), as well as characteristics of learner, learner's ALCONs, social, cultural and linguistic influences (Vygotsky, 1978) on the learner. Such a freedom for operation in the context of learners and hence for the teachers as well, is strongly advocated by Constructivism. However, to meaningfully operationalise this freedom, the teacher has to be more ingenious, more skillful, more reflective, more resourceful and more spontaneous for facilitating the construction of knowledge by the learner. For this, the path he/she has to tread in unknown, un-prescribed and uncertain.

ALCON 2: Constructivist based instruction cannot be preplanned because there is an unpredictability about the ALCONs the learners bring with them and hence an unpredictability about the constructed learning outputs.

De-ALCONisation: It is a fact that a conventional, regimented Lesson Plan (based on transmissionist approach) before a lesson is delivered will not serve the purpose, because at any point of the cognitive negotiation it may become necessary to explore new angles, look for new activities, create new situations, and charter new path.

However, because of this inherent uncertainty, a constructivist based instruction needs much more meticulous planning, more carefully selected diverse and multiferous activities. Once the students are presented with a learning focus; a challenge; a conflict; an issue or a situation for discussion; an interactive computer programme; an exciting problem, which could be simple, like, why do the hairs of a painting brush get squeezed when the brush is dipped in water and then taken out, or, which could be complex, like why on the body of a fluorescent tube it is written 6,500^{0}K, or for that matter, from which surface, the upper or the lower one, of a leaf there is greater evaporation of water; an opportunity to test the validity of their ALCONs; and/or an instance to try out new ideas; there will be

- unexpected questions,
- unexpected responses,
- unexpected suggestions,
- unexpected arguments,
- unexpected comments,
- unexpected criticisms,
- unexpected explanations,
- unexpected clarifications,
- unexpected ideas,
- unexpected real-life experiences,
- unexpected rationalizations, and/or
- unexpected conclusions.

from them. Successfully handling of such a situation needs a plethora of structured mini-plans ensconced within a world of fine tuned knowledge, skills, constructs and innovations so that real and purposeful knowledge can be negotiated through an actual teacher-learner collaboration for achieving the desired performance criteria, visualized for the learner.

ALCON 3: Since constructivism espouses relativity of concept (read concept/knowledge is subjective) it is not possible to fix a specific objective or a learning outcome within the confines of a classroom instruction.

De-ALCONisation: Relativity always manifest whenever there is acquisition of knowledge, because knowledge is constructed by the subject and is hence subject specific. In fact, if one talks of science (which is one domain of knowledge, where concepts are supposed to have agreed upon connotations), one has, in a broader framework, the learner's science, the textbook science, the teachers' science, the scientists' science and of course the indigenous science. At the individual learner's level, since each learner construct his/her knowledge/concept, primarily on the basic of his/her personal ALCONs, it is obvious that each concept will have a learner specific, individualized connotation. Hence, the principle of relativism of concepts. And one cannot escape this cognitive reality.

But, every concept has two characteristics, One; just the word, on which there is universal linguistic agreement, and Two; the cognitive image/connotation associated with the word and this image/connotation is culture specific, subject specific, experience specific, and ALCON specific. It is in this characteristic Two that relativism appears and operates, for which examples are abounding in literature (refer Chapter 7).

Thus, relativity of concepts/knowledge is inherent in the process of knowledge acquisition through construction. In fact for epistemologists' relativism of concepts is a controversial, problematic and almost non-acceptable notion (Staver, 1998).

Critics (Matthews, 1992, 1994; Osborne, 1996; Phillips, 1995) reject relativism. For example, Osborne (1996) comments:

> A full consideration of how we adjudicate between theories would require an acknowledgement that our language and our ideas are constrained by reality, to

> real references that do exist, and thus, while there may be no ultimate check that any construction is right, there are checks that one construction is better than another. The failure to recognise this important practice of science leads implicitly towards a relativist ontology where viability is equated with validity so that any viable theory is considered worthy of consideration.

Realist, on the other hand, regard (Searle, 1995) relativity of concepts as an acceptable concept. According to him we create systems of representations and any one or more of these mental constructions can viably represent the same reality. Searle (1995) called this cognitive ground reality as "Conceptual relativity". He further opined that we may view the external world as our representations of it and we can use incommensurable vocabularies to describe different components of reality.

In the brief discussion, above, about 'relativism' both the "critics" and "realist" are of the view that from the learner's framework, and hence for all practical purposes (because each of us is a learner) relativity of concept is implicitly contained in the very process of knowledge acquisition *vis-à-vis* constructivism.

We note in passing that Segal (1986) opines that constructivists do not criticize the process by which scientists adjudicate theories (compare this with Osborne's Statement, quoted above). As an epistemology, constructivism should be preferred to science on grounds of parsimony (Staver, 1998) because it contains one less assumption—the realist presupposition; it does not assume a priori the existence of an external world which is separate from human perception, and this non-assumption result in relativity of concept/knowledge.

One of the basic principles of constructivism is

- not to regard every ALCON as a misconception and wrong,
- consider every ALCON on merit, because therein lies the seed for knowledge construction, and
- some of the ALCON may really be correct, partly or fully, and hence can be retained in the knowledge structures with/without modification.

Incidentally, in this case ALCON 3 is mostly correct because,

- there is relativity of concepts, and so
- in a traditional sense one cannot design a regimented Lesson Plan and state there in the learning of a concept as the specific objective.

However, in a constructivist based pedagogy a teacher will have to keep in focus a specific concept which he/she has to negotiate with the learners within the constructivist based objectives of helping the learners

- to learn how to learn (Novak and Gowin, 1984),
- to effectively perform parallel processing instead of series processing,
- to meaningfully transform the purpose of construction from "Recall" to "A Search for Principle", and
- to learn how to search for "Validity" and not "Viability" when comprehending and organizing one's experiences and environment,

all of which are part of teachers' effort to help the learner construct knowledge the way the teacher expects the learner to construct.

ALCON 4: In constructivist based instruction, there is no focus for learning and no clear goal.

De-ALCONisation: A prototype of a clear goal based on traditional teaching methods, bonded to the transmissionist approach is of course absent in the constructivist-based instruction.

But, it is also true that in the constructivist framework, instruction is always purposeful, intentional and collaborative (Scardamalia and Bereiter, 1991) and that learners are guided to actively strive to achieve a cognitive objective through meaningful knowledge construction.

Constructivism does not prescribe a fixed set (compare with the traditional behaviouristic approach) of activities, strategies, options, pathways, but it does not mean that it is not leading towards the visualized construction of intended learning.

Constructivism also does not offer any clear guidelines for a regimented sequence of operations, a prescriptive set activity, action plan and strategies, a fixed so-called learning outcome in a set time frame and environment nor does it assure an expected performance at the traditional annual examination. But this does not at all mean that constructivism-based teaching is aimless and is not leading towards an intended knowledge construction *vis-à-vis* learning. What constructivism does is it gives primacy to and sets up a construction friendly learning environment, because the crucial focus of constructivism is on knowledge construction instead of rote learning and regurgitation (Duffy and Jonassen, 1992). Jonassen (1990) describes very succinctly the characteristics of such environment as to what they are not. He states, they "are not unregulated, anarchic, sink-or-swim, open discovery learning cesspools that many fear".

To create such an environment the effort lies with the teacher. The diversity of learner's ALCONs, the complex process of cognitive negotiation, the onerous effort of knowledge construction and the associated uncertainty about the form, structure and validity of the outcome make the task that much more difficult, but enjoyable, challenging but exciting, daunting but desirable, and ill-defined but well-directed so that every TLP under constructivism is as much a learning situation for a learner as it is a learning situation for the teacher also. That is the basic philosophy of cooperative and collaborative teaching-learning.

ALCON 5: In a constructivist learning friendly environment there is an absence of structures for learning.

De-ALCONisation: As a discussion progresses in a learning environment, because of the prolification of learners' ALCONs as well as unpredictability of the type, degree and quality of knowledge construction, it is commonly alleged by teachers that structures of learning are obviously absent in constructivist informed teaching approaches.

Nothing can be farther from the truth because in a constructivist learning environment a learner is tactfully and tacitly helped to construct a concept, a topic, a principle, a law which is contained in the curriculum and a curriculum has a organized structure. Further in a broader instructional strategy within the framework of constructivism the learner is provided with

- Seminal learning experiences (like, if one mixes two volumes equally cold water, the volume becomes double but why not the coldness becomes double?),
- decision-making learning experiences,
- relational learning experiences, (like relation between concepts, relation between definitions, relation between concepts and definitions),
- causal learning experiences (like why there are lightening only when there are clouds in the sky?),
- additional learning experiences (like when the learner is constructing his/her knowledge about 'friction', as a necessary evil, he/she can have the additional learning experience of a rain drop, freely falling from a cloud at a height of 2 km, does not kill a man when it hits the man's head although simple calculation shows that it is expected to have a momentum of the order of that of a bullet fired from a revolver),
- analogical learning experiences (like, in the process of constructing his/her knowledge about electric current the learner can have the learning experience of flow of natural wind, flow of heat, flow of water),
- open-ended learning experiences (like, the learner may be guided to explore as to what will happen if all the cows stop giving milk from today or using ten points draw as many geometrical figures as possible),
- hierarchical learning experiences (like, the learners may be given a set of related concepts and asked to arrange them in a hierarchy, starting with the most basic concept. This will help them to functionally construct and comprehend the relations between concepts and learn a cognitive truth that 'concepts never exist in isolation').

The eight experiences above and such other holistic learning experiences are structures for learning, which are absent in the transmissionist approach for teaching but are girders on which constructivist informed teaching is planned and executed. Further, such structures of learning helps the learner to construct and internalize higher order structures for learning, like, classification, seriation, identification, search for attributes and non-examples.

Thus, a teacher practicing teaching approaches based on constructivism is continuously engaged in a complex planning process to generate novel structures for learning.

ALCON 6: Constructivism emphasizes that discussion and interaction are two essential processes for knowledge construction by learners. Absence of them will reduce learning.

De-ALCONisation: This ALCON is both true and false. Involvement in discussion and interaction is essential for knowledge construction by the learner, because it helps the learner to

- reexamine his/her ALCON,
- defend his/her ALCON when it is challenged/criticized by peer group, teacher, or in a social environment,
- modify/erase his/her ALCON,
- develop an unbiased attitude towards others views,
- be more receptive to new ideas if they seem to be more viable, and
- reduce 'centration' (Piaget) and resistance.

These six are very crucial parameters for acceptable and valid knowledge construction by the learner. However, for the discussions and interactions not to go off the track or create new misunderstandings as well as new ALCONs the teacher

- has to be omnipresent, yet not to develop an atmosphere of authority or, self-imposition,
- need to tactfully intervene and tacitly realign the discussion on the correct path (Brown, 1994),

- need to stimulate consideration of critical points, key issues and desirable perspectives,
- help to arrest and minimize the construction of new ALCONs, and
- has to silently monitor group work and whole class discussions.

In the absence of such guided discussion and interaction there will still be knowledge construction but such constructions are likely to be off the mark as they will be controlled by spontaneous reasoning by the learner, himself/herself.

To discharge this important responsibility of a guide for meaningful discussion and interaction a teacher has to have

- sophisticated abilities,
- fine tuned judgement as to when, how and where to intervene, and
- clear understanding and internalization of constructivist principles, philosophy, and pedagogy.

ALCON 7: In a constructivist pedagogy a structured learning environment cannot be maintained within the given timeframe of a classroom transaction.

De-ALCONisation: This ALCON 7 is more perception-based than research-based. Planning, organizing and executing a constructivism-based instruction schedule is definitely a difficult proposition for the teacher, but not necessarily a time consuming one. It of course demands a lot of teacher's time in the planning phase. Without field trial, the teacher has a perception that since in this approach the students have the freedom to follow and hence to spend time in designing their own investigation, search for answer for their cognitive queries and take active part in discussions to thrush out the limitations in their constructions and ALCONs, and since the teacher needs to judiciously facilitate and streamline the thought process and activities of the students, there will obviously paucity of time for the teacher to keep all the students of a class focused towards a learning goal, visualized and planned by the teacher. This apprehensive conclusion is arrived at by the teacher because he/she is trying to examine a constructivist-based instruction schedule using his traditional/behaviouristic eye.

However, if the situation is analysed from a constructivist perception, the teacher will observe that

- although the students are allowed free movement (physically and cognitively) inside the classroom to discuss with the peer group/collect materials/design and demonstrate experiments, the teacher is still in active control of the structured learning environment and hence wasteful use of time can be minimized (i.e. save wastage),
- instead of receiving tailored correct response from few students and assume that the lesson delivered under the transmissionist approach has been a successful one (which in fact, it is not if one takes the whole class into consideration and/or measures the learning outcome in a scale for assessing meaningful knowledge construction) in the constructivist framework the teacher has the ability to attend to the ALCONs and the knowledge construction process of all the students simultaneously and thus save time in the context of the whole class,
- by cogently improving the ability of all students to analyse a situation from all angles and to synthesize information by self-reflection, the teacher can, in a single class, plan to achieve more than one interrelated learning goals by gradually infusing parallel processing ability amongst the students, thereby save time, and still maintain sustainable structured learning environment, and
- once the thinking and reflecting abilities of the students to search for regularities, similarities, principles get fine tuned then the construction of knowledge by the students in the subsequent classes will take much less time than a traditional teaching schedule.

At this point an example is in order.

In a Traditional Class: In a conventional mathematics class, based on transmissionist approach, the teacher, while teaching multiplication tables, say involving the digit 9, writes down the table on the blackboard as,

$9 \times 1 = 9$	$9 \times 6 = 54$
$9 \times 2 = 18$	$9 \times 7 = 63$
$9 \times 3 = 27$	$9 \times 8 = 72$
$9 \times 4 = 36$	$9 \times 9 = 81$
$9 \times 5 = 45$	$9 \times 10 = 90$

Then he/she asks the students to take it down in their notebooks and memorise it (i.e. rote learning). In this process the students

- try mechanically to cram the table,
- do not know the purpose, i.e. for recall, or for search of a principle or for just future use,
- are blind followers of teacher's direction, nay, authority,
- miss any regularity inherent in the table, and
- are bored by the rigmarole.

Thus, the entire process do not lead to construction of knowledge.

In a Constructivist Oriented Class: In such a learning friendly classroom environment the students have autonomy for thinking, freedom for discussion and reflection as well as selection and use of independent cognitive approaches. In such a class may develop their own pathways (to interpret the table and remember it), some of which are the following:

A: They may look at the table and discover that in the 9th table, $9\times1=9$ & $0+9=9$, $9\times2=18$ & $1+8=9$ and so on. So, if we want to find out, say, 9×5 then the product is obtained as, the ten's place number is $5-1=4$ and the one's place number is $9-4=5$, i.e. the number is 45.

Thus, the student does not have to cram the table, he/she has to remember the above stated regularity. This process

- is enjoyable, because the student discovers a regularity,
- results in permanent retention of knowledge and not temporary rote learning for regurgitation in the examination, and
- helps the student to comprehend the causal relation between cognitive process and cognitive output, i.e. learning.

B: By examining the table they may discover that,

$$9 \times 1 = 9$$
$$9 \times 2 = 18$$
$$9 \times 3 = 27$$
$$9 \times 4 = 36$$
$$9 \times 5 = 45$$

and the rest of the table can be created by interchanging the position of the ten's place and one's place digit and reversing the order of the above product one can recreate the 2nd half the table as,

$$9 \times 6 = 54$$

(ten's place and one's place of the digit for the product of $9 \times 5 = 45$ have been interchanged)

$$9 \times 7 = 63$$
$$9 \times 8 = 72$$
$$9 \times 9 = 81$$
$$9 \times 10 = 90$$

By this process

- the learning is enjoyable, because the student discovers a symmetry, and
- helps the students to learn that search for symmetry reduces the number of independent parameters.

In the above context of knowledge construction by using such valid (not viable) tool as search for regularity and symmetry, it is worthwhile to recount an episode from the early childhood days of Gauss, the Prince of Mathematics. He was a brilliant child studying in Standard II. In a mathematics class the teacher was busy in evaluating their term papers and had not assigned any specific work to the students to keep them busy. Thus the students were gossiping amongst themselves and creating disturbing murmuring sound. The teacher got vexed with as the situation affected his valuation of papers. So he assigned the students to complete a task. He asked them to add all the integers from 1 to 100. He was sure, this task will keep them busy for quite sometime and he will be able to evaluate the term papers, undisturbed. But after only a minute or two he again heard whispers and murmurs. He scanned the class and found that the source of disturbance is Gauss. He asked in a rude tone, "Gauss, have you solved the problem?" Gauss said calmly, "Yes, Sir." The teacher was surprised and asked, "What is your answer?" Gauss replied, "Sir, it is 5050". The teacher could not understand how Gauss was able to do the repeated addition within a minute or two. He again asked, "How did you get your answer?" Gauss smiled and replied, "Sir 100 plus 1 is 101. 99 plus 2 is 101. We will have 50 such 101s. So, 50 × 101 i.e. 5050 is the answer."

The above episode from the life of Gauss demonstrates several issues based on constructivism. They are:

- Through his own construction of knowledge Gauss could complete the task in much shorter time than the time it would take to complete the task by using the traditional approach based on regimented learning, i.e. there is a saving of learner's time.
- By his construction, he could locate, comprehend and learn the existence of regularity and symmetry in the task and such a construction is a higher order cognitive activity which can be meaningfully used in other learning situation and thereby save time.
- Construction of such higher order constructs by the learner helps the teacher to reschedule his/her teaching design so as to save time, because he/she can cover many analogous situations in a single stroke.

ALCON 8: It may not be possible on the part of the teacher to complete the curriculum within the scheduled timeframe if he/she implements the constructivist approach for teaching.

De-ALCONisation: Like ALCON 7, this ALCON is also perception based and is not research based. There is no report in the literature which mentions that a teacher actually tried over a period of one year to complete the curriculum by using the constructivist approach and failed.

From the learner's point of view, one has to seek answer to the question: Whether the objective of the learner, coming to the school to study, is to complete the curriculum and appear at an examination, or, to meaningfully learn the concepts incorporated in the curriculum? Pitiably, in the social context, if a student forgets everything one day before the examination, he/she is branded as a bad student. In so far as learning is concerned, this societal outlook and operational philosophy towards education have to change. Because after all education is a food that society creates to eat, grow and procreate itself. Thus for the success of the implementation of constructivism the societal attitude towards and demands on education need a quantum change.

One point has to be made clear that constructivist informed teaching approaches put their emphasis not one how much of the curriculum is covered but on how much the students learn how to learn, how to construct valid constructs and how to meaningfully cognize. This does not necessarily imply that by teaching in a constructivist informed way the curriculum cannot be completed in time.

It only implies that constructivist informed teachers will try to accentuate the goal of achieving depth of learning through valid construction rather than breadth of learning through across the board memorization (Brooks and Brooks, 1993).

It is a fact that every curriculum can be broken down to concepts, sub-concepts, sub-sub-concepts and specific examples. It has been discussed under ALCON 7 that during a constructivist transaction of a sub-concept in a classroom there is a high possibility that the teacher is going to save time if he/she follows constructivism in true form, structure and spirit. Therefore, logically he/she is going to complete the curriculum in time, or, may be before time, if he/she faithfully follows the constructivist approach. However, to achieve this, the teacher has to

- plan the lesson more carefully, so that the transaction will involve very little direct, regimented involvement by him/her,
- succinctly monitor learning activities, discussions, arguments and counter argument, innovations, i.e. the cognitive thought process and construction of the students,
- more efficiently generate and maintain a learning friendly environment, and
- make the learning more carefully and validly structured.

But for the teacher to develop and implement these abilities a properly tuned teacher education programme is an absolute necessity.

ALCON 9: The student has to struggle a lot in the process of learning in the constructivist approach.

De-ALCONisation: In this context two features have to be kept in view.

One: In traditional classroom the students rarely get any opportunity to ask, to explore, to discuss, to voice their views and are thus constantly under cognitive tension and struggle because in any case they have to cram the concepts (sometimes without comprehension) to pass the once-in-a-year examination.

Two: Every construction, be it art and painting or music, building, cognitive structure involves struggle, because it is

- preceded by some form of deconstruction,
- a search for acceptability (read for cognitive construction acceptability by the existing ALCONs), and
- an effort for excellence, not necessarily perfection (read for cognitive construction best fit to comprehend and organize one's experimental world).

However, in constructivist informed teaching approaches the students get the opportunity

- to think and not to struggle passively,
- to work independently and not to mimic authority meekly,
- to be receptive and not stubborn,
- to interact for clarity and not for dissonance, and
- to search for consensus and not to demonstrate superiority.

Thus, although there will be cognitive struggle during knowledge construction, it becomes an enjoyable experience in a constructivist informed classroom.

ALCON 10: Constructivism visualizes the learner as a lonely voyager.

De-ALCONisation: Such an ALCON stems from the all-important statement: Knowledge is constructed by the cognizing subject through an autogenic process.

Whenever a construction is being affected, the person who is constructing is both a lonely voyager and not a lonely voyager. An example will clarify this dichotomy.

When the famous painter Michelangelo was painting the roof of the dome of a chapel by sleeping on his back for months together on a makeshift bed, hanging from scaffoldings, he was a lonely voyager. He himself has to chose the right combinations of paints for every micro spots of the painting, select the right type of brushes, conceptualise the right structures for every micro space within the framework of the whole painting and finally keep in mind a stable, holistic, mental image of the painting as visualized by him.

But he was also not a lonely voyager, because, there was somebody who was busy in maintaining the supply of right amount, right quality, and right type of paints as well as brushes to him at the right moment. There was also somebody to provide him with right quality and intensity of lighting system so that he receives just enough light to do his painting but the light is not strong enough to damage the painting. Finally, there was somebody to keep the scaffoldings intact and introduces changes in them as and when it is needed by Michelingelo.

Exactly, in the same way a learner is a lonely voyager in so far as constructing cognitive structures to conceptualise a concept is concerned.

But he/she is also not a lonely voyager because,

- the teacher is always there to help, to guide, to facilitate, to check, to question, to catalyse so that the construction remains on track,
- the peer group is there for constructive discussion, self-reflection, self-regulation, self-modification and self-realization, and
- of course the society is there to throw up constraints which challenge individual perceptions (Jaworski, 1993), to offer discussion or argument so that the learner negotiates new positions which leads to the development of shared meanings (Vigotsky, 1978), to demand individual perspectives and meanings to match with the community of practices (Lave and Wenger, 1991) and to set up an environment of evolutionary adaptivity (Matthews, 2003) so that reality in socially constructed, constituted only through language and organized and maintained through narratives (Gergen, 1985, 1991; Kavale, 1992).

The above ten ALCONs are the principal ones those the teachers have about constructivism. They are critical information, necessary for a functional teacher education curriculum in a constructivist framework. The De-ALCONisations are expected to optimize the operationalization of any teacher education programme.

8.3 Priority Areas for Teacher Education

A teacher needs to be prepared in relation to the needs and demands of learner and learning process in the school context. With the changing scenario of education a teacher to be a facilitator of children's learning in a manner that helps children to construct knowledge and the teacher is also a co-constructor of knowledge. The teacher also needs to get opportunity to participate in development of textbooks, syllabi and teaching materials. To get acquainted with such aspects the teacher is supposed to be equipped with understanding of curriculum, subject content and pedagogy along with school management, school structure and society. Thus the overarching challenge constructivism presents to teachers and teacher educators is the formidable task of translating a learning theory into a theory of teaching (Mackinnon and Scarff-Seatter, 1997), which in turn fixes the priority about what teachers need to know and be able to do. As mentioned in this chapter, the absolute necessities, operational necessities and the ten ALCONs related to constructivism should be considered as the basics for developing all teacher education programmes.

The priority areas for teacher education needs to incorporate the emerging demands from the school system and prepare teachers (NCF 2005) for the roles of being an:

- supportive, encouraging human facilitator in teaching-learning situations to enable learners to discover their talents, realize their physical and intellectual potentialities to the fullest and to develop character and desirable social and human values to function as responsible citizens; and
- active member of a group of persons who makes a conscious effort for curricular renewal so that it is relevant to changing societal needs and the personal needs of learners.

To realize the above, the teacher-education programme must contain the following to enable the student-teachers (NCF, 2010) who:

- Care for children and love to be with them, understand children within social, cultural and political contexts, develop sensitivity to their needs and problems, treat all children equally.
- Perceive children not as passive receivers of knowledge, augment their natural propensity to construct meaning,

discourage rote learning, make learning a joyful, participatory and meaningful activity.

- Critically examine curriculum and textbooks, contextualize curriculum to suit local needs.
- Do not treat knowledge as a 'given', embedded in the curriculum and accepted without question.
- Organize learner-centered, activity-based, participatory learning experiences—play, projects, discussion, dialogue, observation, visits and learn to reflect on their own practice.
- Integrate academic learning with social and personal realities of learners, responding to diversities in the classroom.
- Promote values of peace, democratic way of life, equality, justice, liberty, fraternity, secularism and zeal for social reconstruction.

This can only be achieved if teacher education curriculum provides appropriate and critical opportunities for student teachers to:

- Observe and engage with children, communicate with and relate to children.
- Understand the self and others, one's beliefs, assumptions, emotions and aspirations; develop the capacity for self-analysis, self-evaluation, adaptability, flexibility, creativity and innovation.
- Develop habits and the capacity for self-directed learning, have time to think, reflect, assimilate and articulate new ideas; be self-critical and to work collaboratively in groups.
- Engage with subject content, examine disciplinary knowledge and social realities, relate subject matter with the social milieu of learners and develop critical thinking.
- Develop professional skills in pedagogy, observation, documentation, analysis and interpretation, drama, craft, storytelling and reflective inquiry.

The above priorities may change according to practical situations encountered by different educational institutes throughout the world.

Besides the above factors there are other priority areas like pedagogical content knowledge (PCK) and evaluation procedures in constructivist framework, which should also be taken into consideration while developing the teacher education curriculum.

8.3.1 Pedagogical Content Knowledge (PCK)

Constructivism brings important connection between pedagogical approaches to learning content. Lee S. Shuleman (1986) introduced the term pedagogical content knowledge as "the ways of representing and formulating the subject that make it comprehensible to others". This goes beyond knowledge of the content per se to include issues of teaching the content, including typical curricular choices, powerful ideas, common learning difficulties, and student conceptions in the specific subject. PCK involves the transformation of content knowledge from the understandings of content, their own teaching practice and their own schooling experience. PCK is closely intertwined with both content knowledge and pedagogical process knowledge (Van Driel, Verloop and De Vos, 1998). PCK connects research on teaching with research on learning, helping to determine constructivist approaches to learning content for teaching. All researchers agree that PCK differs considerably from content knowledge and that is developed through an integrative process during classroom practice (Van Driel, Verloop and De Vos, 1998). PCK has been renamed as pedagogical content knowing (PCKg) based on a constructivist view of teaching and teacher education (Cochran, De Ruiter and King, 1993). Their model (PCKg) includes subject matter content and specific pedagogical knowledge but adds teachers' understanding of students and of the environmental context of learning. Understanding students includes student abilities and learning strategies, developmental levels, attitudes, motivations, and prior conceptions. Context includes teachers' understanding of political, socio-cultural and physical environment. Teachers experience these four components simultaneously as they prepare for and progress in their prospective career.

Teacher education programmes can enhance the development of PCK in prospective teachers by modeling and sharing teaching decisions and strategies with students, both by education and content-area faculty. Teacher educators/faculty should have opportunities to demonstrate and reflect on how they use PCK in their own teaching (Cochran, De Ruiter and King, 1993). Contexts that promote many components of teaching within the content area allow for the development of PCK. These contexts should be similar to incorporation of multiple field based experiences along with classroom environment within the teacher education programmes. Field based experiences include real teaching, contact with experienced teachers and feedback and reflection (Hausfather, Outlaw and Strehle, 1996).

Thorough and coherent understanding of content is necessary for effective PCK as it is difficult to separate PCK from content knowledge (Van Driel, Verloop and De Vos, 1998). Under the umbrella of PCK teacher education programme can assist pre-service teachers in constructing a deep understanding of disciplinary content from a teaching perspective so it can be used to help specific students understand specific concepts (Cochran, De Ruiter and King, 1993). This involves both working closely with arts and science faculty to understand pedagogical perspectives as well as integrating methods, courses with or alongside content courses and it emphasizes interdisciplinary approach. Generally content is taught without any attention to process or process is taught without a deep understanding of the nature of the content involved. Hence, an effective teacher education programme needs to balance the process of learning with the content of what is being learned in ultimately result in helping teachers to better understand both content and learning of their students.

8.3.2 Evaluation Procedures in Constructivist Framework

Assessment is an essential ongoing component of instruction that guides the process of learning. Ongoing assessment uses exhibitions, student explanations of concepts, the writing of a poem or any other thought—demanding performances to evaluate and reflect on students' work.

According to Jonassen (1991b), evaluating how learners go about constructing their knowledge is more important than the resulting product, suggesting that evaluative procedures must become a part of the instructional process. Thus, constructivist evaluation procedure emphasizes the process of knowledge acquisition but not any product or observable behaviour. Jonassen feels that goal free evaluation could be an important part of constructivist assessment, since that would allow the evaluator to be unbiased by the goal of instruction. Cole (1992) disagree with Jonassen (1991b) statement about goal free evaluation by stating that in most authentic tasks, there are very measurable goals which can be used to identify successful completion of that task.

Constructivist learning is an active process and alternative assessment celebrates this active process (Herman, Aschbacher and Winters, 1992). Instead of testing for the "presence or absence of discrete bits of information", alternative assessment provides a means to understand whether "students organize, structure and use information in context to solve complex problems", thereby measuring the holistic picture of the students understanding emerges.

Assessment can be used to build understanding through reflection and iteration. There is great promise for deeper understanding and appreciation of the creative, generative process called learning, when a student is aware of scholastic expectations and understands how to effectively review and critique his/her own work. Simmons (1994) outlines this process in three steps:

1. The teacher must help students understand from the outset the standards by which their work will be judged.
2. Students must document their work process for the duration of the unit or project.
3. Through performance and feedback, students come to understand the complex nature of judging and improving upon ones work.

The last point is very crucial as "taking the time and energy to reflect on and improve one's work is essential to the understanding process itself". Single score assessments meted out by traditional instructor is replaced by alternative assessment as outlined by Simmons (1994) which is indeed difficult to practice.

In a constructivist classroom autonomy is given to the students as well teachers to have a choice for evaluation like which tasks are evaluated. Students often participate in the decision-making process of establishing the criteria to be used in the evaluation process. The students are engaged in peer and self-evaluation which help them in making decisions about what they know and what they need to learn and what task they need to complete next.

Binz (1991) outlines the philosophical beliefs and theoretical assumptions of traditional assessment and alternative assessment which is depicted in Fig. 8.1.

Traditional Assessment

- Assumes knowledge has universal meaning.
- Treats learning as passive process.
- Separates process from product.
- Focuses on mastering discrete, isolated bits of information.
- Assumes the purpose of assessment is to document learning.
- Believes that cognitive abilities are separate from affective and conative abilities.
- Views assessment as objective, value-free and neutral.
- Embraces a hierarchical model of power and control.
- Perceives learning as an individual enterprise.

Alternative Assessment

- Assumes knowledge has multiple meanings.
- Treat learning as an active process.
- Emphasizes process and product.
- Focus on inquiry.

- Assumes the purpose of assessment is to facilitate learning.
- Views assessment as subjective and value laden.
- Embraces a shared model of power and control.
- Perceives learning as a collaborative process.

Thus alternative assessment/portfolio assessment is in direct contrast to what is known as performance evaluation or traditional assessment or summative assessment. Alternative assessment is also known as holistic assessment, formative assessment or integrative assessment. One can elaborate and explain the philosophical beliefs and theoretical assumption cited above as follows:

Assumes Knowledge has Universal Meaning. One assumption of traditional assessment is that knowledge has a single consensual meaning. It is possible for everyone to reach a consensus about meaning because knowledge has "the same meaning for all individuals everywhere" (Berlak, 1992).

Treats Learning as a Passive Process. In traditional assessment, the metaphor of "empty vessel" is often used to talk about learners. Students are treated as if they do not possess prior knowledge about a topic. The instructor's role is "to 'fill' the students by making deposits of information which the instructor considers to constitute true knowledge" (Freire, 1990). This passive process involves students (novices) memorizing the knowledge dispensed by the text or instructor (expert).

Separates Process from Product. Generally in traditional assessment, students' final products are evaluated based on some sort of test. The final outcomes of students' efforts are assumed to be representative of their learning. The how and why of student learning is not taken into consideration.

Focuses on Mastering Discrete, Isolated Bits of Information. These bits of information basically represent lower-level thinking skills (Herman, Aschbacher, and Winters, 1992), believed to exist in a hierarchical form. Students are expected to master and demonstrate specific skills at one level before moving on to the next.

Assumes the Purpose of Assessment is to Document Learning. Typically, traditional assessment is used only to monitor students' learning. Under this model, students who "know" are separated by those who "do not know". In other words, traditional assessment creates a system that classifies and ranks students (Berlak, 1992).

Believes that Cognitive Abilities are Separated from Affective and Conative Abilities. The focus of traditional assessment is primarily on cognitive abilities. The values and interests that students have about the activity being undertaken are not considered to be connected to their competence in carrying out the task (Raven, 1992). Little, if any attention is given to students' disposition to use the skills and strategies taught or their ability to apply them (Herman, Aschbacher, and Winters, 1992).

Views Assessment as Objective, Value-Free, and Neutral. Traditional assessment assumes that facts and values are distinct and separable entities that can be measured objectively (Berlak, 1992). Decisions about what to teach and test are not considered to be value-laden.

Embraces a Hierarchical Model of Power and Control. In traditional assessment, generally the instructor alone has the power to make decisions about what is learned and how it is assessed (Heron, 1988; Sessions, 1995). Students do not participate in making decisions about what is important for them to learn or in determining how well they are learning.

Perceives Learning as an Individual Enterprise. Traditional assessment focuses on an individual student's performance. Students are generally expected to accomplish tasks without the assistance of others, and if they get help they are cheating. Students often work against one another in a competitive manner. "In competitive contexts, learners do not consider their own performance, and they concern themselves less with the process than with the outcome" (Johnston, 1992).

Philosophical Beliefs and Theoretical Assumptions of Alternative Assessment. The underlying assumptions of traditional assessment are now being challenged by advocates of alternative assessment practices. Alternative assessment is based on an entirely different set of philosophical beliefs and theoretical assumptions than traditional assessment (Bintz, 1991), as outlined in Fig. 8.1. Alternative assessment has the following beliefs and assumptions:

Assumes Knowledge has Multiple Meanings. One assumption of alternative assessment is that knowledge has "multiple realities with accompanying multiple meanings" (Roderick, 1991). It is impossible for everyone to reach a consensus about meaning because each individual brings his or her own diverse interpretation to an ever-changing situation.

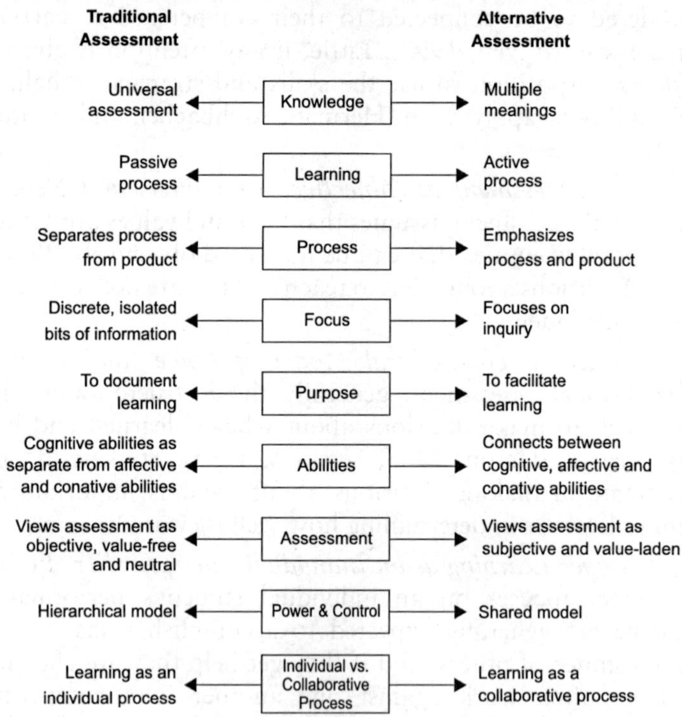

Fig. 8.1: Comparison of Philosophical Beliefs and Theoretical Assumptions of Traditional and Alternative Assessment.

Treats Learning as an Active Process. "Learning is a natural, integral, and ubiquitous part of living" (Bintz, 1991). It is not something that is given to someone else. Rather, students actively search for new meanings to transform their present understanding (Greene, 1988). In other words, learning entails "producing, rather than reproducing knowledge" (Newmann and Archbald, 1992).

Emphasizes Process and Product. In alternative assessment practices, the process is valued as well as the product. What, how, and why students learn is taken into consideration (Hutchings, 1993; Johnston, 1992).

Focuses on Inquiry. The focus of alternative assessment is on developing real-world problem-solving skills that will lead people to observe, think, question, and test their ideas (Herman, Aschbacher, and Winters, 1992).

Assumes the Purpose of Assessment is to Facilitate Learning. The purpose of alternative assessment is to enhance students' learning (Johnston, 1989; Short and Burke, 1991; Wolf, 1990). When students receive feedback about their learning, they gain new direction and are able to progress in their learning. Clearly, the purpose of assessment is not to sort or classify the students.

Recognizes a Connection Between Cognitive, Affective, and Conative Abilities. When students care about the activity they are engaged in, they are more likely to invest their time and effort in it, and, as a result, they learn more from it. An assumption of alternative assessment is that "it is meaningless to attempt to assess a person's abilities except in relation to their valued goals" (Raven, 1992).

Views Assessment as Subjective and Value-Laden. Advocates of alternative assessment practices believe that decisions about what to teach and assess are subjective and value-laden (Bintz and Harste, 1994). "Indeed, value systems not only influence decisions about what assessment questions get answered, but also about what assessment questions get asked in the first place" (Bintz, 1991).

Embraces a Shared Model of Power and Control. An assumption of alternative assessment is that instructors should share the power with students to make decisions about what they learn and to determine how well they are learning. Alternative assessment embraces a democratic decision-making process (Heron, 1988).

Perceives Learning as a Collaborative Process. In contexts that use alternative assessment practices, students and instructors are co-learners, freely expressing and testing their ideas together. In this social milieu, collaborative learning is valued, and instructors and students "are intellectually responsible to each other for creating a substantive curriculum in the classroom" (Bintz, 1991). Advocates of the social constructivist theory of learning view assessment as part of the curriculum; they believe assessment should be guided by the same principles that guide our work in developing curriculum (Johnston, 1992; Short and Burke, 1991).

In constructivist assessment paradigm students often participate in the decision-making process of establishing the criteria to be used in the evaluation process. They establish rubrics for rating the criteria and engage in peer and self-evaluation. Constructivist assessment paradigm needs practices, which involves (i) instructional strategies, (ii) formative and summative evaluation, (iii) rubrics, and (iv) teacher, peer and self-evaluation.

- An instructional strategy which promotes constructivist assessment involves small group work, various writing assignments and inquiry projects.
- Both summative and formative evaluation procedures should be included in the constructivist assessment. Feedback on their work must be given before the final product is completed and sufficient time must be given to engage the students in the revision process.
- Students need to participate in developing the criteria and creating the rubric that is used to grade their work. The teacher should formulate tentative criteria before negotiating with students so the teacher/instructor can make suggestions in case students are slow to identify criteria.
- A balance is needed between teacher, peer and self-evaluation. The teacher does not take the sole responsibility of determining the grade of the students. The students can gain multiple perspectives on their work by engaging in peer and self-evaluation.

The teachers need to be trained in alternative assessment procedures. The in-service and pre-service teacher education programmes for all levels of schooling should emphasize this component of teaching-learning process. In moving towards alternative assessment the teachers should listen to students, negotiate with them and ask for their feedback. This enables teachers to gain insight into how the alternate assessment is working. Such assessment connects teaching, learning and assessment. It is a teaching tool that promotes students' learning and is a significant and powerful tool that assists teachers in being fair, thoughtful and creative when assessing students' work. Thus keeping in view the importance of constructivist assessment practices this need to be an important part of all teacher education programmes.

Each of the priority area can be incorporated to the teacher education course through a carefully designed curriculum that draws upon theoretical and empirical knowledge as well as student teachers' experiential or practical knowledge.

8.4 The Conceptual Framework for Teacher Education (Global)

Many teacher education programmes throughout the world have identified constructivist principle as fundamental to their teacher education mission and goals. These programmes worked to understand and create the links between content and process that are fundamental in constructivist approaches. Some of the important teacher education programmes with their underlying priority are as follows:

8.4.1 Cleveland State University (CSU) Teacher Education Programme

The conceptual framework for teacher education programme emphasizes "The teacher as a Reflective Responsive Professional—A Partner in Learning". CSU teacher education graduates have the ability to reflect the four knowledge bases

- Inquiry,
- Partnership,
- Contexualism, and
- Professionalism.

Figure 8.2 indicates the four elements of the conceptual framework are related and emanate from our common beliefs about learners and teaching-learning process. Inquiry, contextualism and partnership are encircled by the concept of professionalism. The conceptual framework assumes that professionalism is not a plateau but rather a career-long process of reflection and growth, an ongoing process whereby teachers constantly enhance their understanding of how Inquiry, contextualism and partnership relate to the teaching-learning process. At the very center of the conceptual framework is the learner.

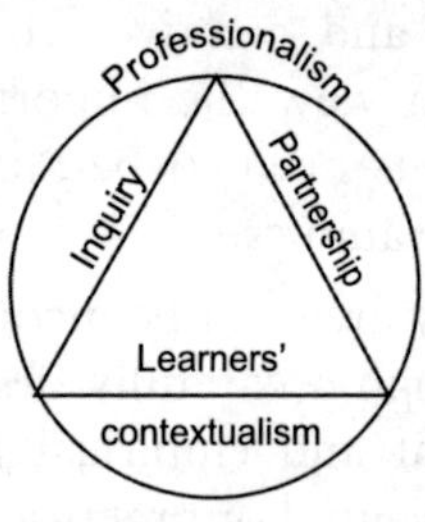

Fig. 8.2: The Teacher Education Conceptual Framework

CSU teacher education programme ensures implementing and adapting the conceptual framework to a variety of instructional environments, urban and suburban, where learner diversity-measured in terms of gender, race, ethnicity, socio-economic status. This contextual approach accounts for the unique challenges faced by the educators of today.

Inquiry: Inquiry is a recursive process of teaching and learning that incorporates aspects of constructivism, reflective practice and a socio-cultural perspective. Constructivism may be individualist constructivism (Piaget's, 1974) or social constructivism (Vygotsky's, 1962) but all types of constructivist approach generally agree that the learner constructs knowledge through his/her own action in the world (Richardson, 1997; Walker, 2002). Reflective practice involves teachers who review, reconstruct, reenact and critically analyze their classroom teaching an learning often through dialogue with colleagues (Bullough and Gitlin, 2001, Ancess, 2003). The socio-cultural view of teacher inquiry as articulated by Weade and Green (1989), sees reflection as an individual act set within the larger cultural system of the school and the community beyond. Moreover, as students participate in the inquiry process, they also review, critically analyze and self-evaluate their learning and become produces of knowledge within the social context of the classroom.

Rationale: Inquiry is an important knowledge base for the teacher education programme for two reasons—teacher growth and student growth. First, teachers who understand and engage inquiry are more likely to support student inquiry (Keene and Zimmerman, 1997; Bullough and Gitlin, 2001). Second, students who engage in inquiry actively construct knowledge by posing questions, seeking answers, evaluating results, and asking new questions both individually and collaboratively (Brooks and Brooks, 1993; Davydov, 1995; Dewey, 1910; Walker, 2002). Teachers, who engage in inquiry and encourage their students to be inquirers, also, recognize dissonance between theory and practice as an opportunity to grow. Their reflections, self-evaluations, observations, and researches provide a basis for genuine change rooted in questions and problems they have identified themselves (Bullough and Gitlin, 2001). The signature of the professional teacher is the continual practice of comparing personal knowledge with other educators' experiences (i.e. theory, ethical principles, as well as strategies and techniques), taking into account the needs and backgrounds of the students, then making decisions about instruction based upon a synthesis of these factors (Wells, 1994; Richardson, 1997; Walker, 2002).

Relation to Content: The inquiry approach informs the content of study, which primarily involves process strategies, at two levels: the teacher teaches students how to engage in inquiry and at the same time engages in it her/himself (Ancess, 2003; Lambert, 2003). Inquiry may incorporate elements constructivist and socio-cultural pedagogy including problem-posing curriculum, shared responsibility for learning, assessment integrated with instruction, collaborative discourse and reflective practice (Morrison and Collins, 1996; Bullough and Gitlin, 2001). Using a thematic unit on weather as an example, teachers establish a developmentally appropriate environment for learning, select resources, and engage with students working individually and in small groups to ask questions about the weather, record observations, create graphs, analyze data, and make predictions. Concurrently, the teacher documents both individual learning and group interaction for the purposes of evaluating students' cognitive and social development, and then uses the results to inform planning for subsequent learning experiences. As teachers reflect upon and revise their own practice, they help students critically evaluate their work (Ancess, 2003; Brooks and Brooks, 1993; Bullough and Gitlin, 2001).

Relation to Process: The process elements of inquiry mirror the content elements. When an inquiry approach is taken, teachers and learners share responsibility for learning. The students' prior knowledge, their questions and interests, and their developmental levels help shape instruction. For example, thematic units or projects that integrate students' individual and cultural patterns of learning, their questions, and their interests with curricula, goals provide opportunities for students to learn how to conduct research, select appropriate materials, and reflectively evaluate process and outcomes. In addition, an inquiry approach supports students' comprehension of challenging text material as they are guided to consider what they already know about the topic, ask questions, read the material, and determine for themselves what they have learned. Often inquiry is supported by group discussion built around higher order questioning and evaluative thinking. Reflective journals are another means of sustaining self-evaluation for both students and teachers.

Partnership

Definition: The concept of partnership has a dual meaning as a key element in the CSU teacher education conceptual framework. First, it encompasses the notion of individuals working together to learn as students in cooperative and/or cohort groups, or as students and their teacher(s) learning with and each other. Second, partnership refers to the notion of individuals' organizations, or social structures collaborating to facilitate and enhance the achievement of learning outcomes. Such partnerships include teachers working with colleagues, parent and community involvement in schools, and business/school and university/school collaborations.

Rationale: Partnership is important to the educational enterprise for a number of reasons. Foremost among these is that the achievement of learning outcomes is enhanced when students work in cooperation with each other and their teachers (Johnson and Johnson, 1990; Slavin, 1990) and when collaborative relationships are established to provide for the combination of resources and efforts (Zacchei and Mirman, 1986; Gross, 1988; Sirotnik and Goodlad, 1988; Epstein, 1984, 1991; Marjoribanks, 1979). In addition, when students share learning with others, their social skills and interpersonal interactions improve, they learn the value of working together toward common goals, and they often enjoy the Teaming experience more (Johnson and Johnson, 1990; Slavin, 1990; McGrath, 1984; Black and Ammon, 1992; Lanier and Little, 1986; Howey and Zimpher, 1989; Little, 1982). Finally, collaborative relationships can enhance teacher morale and professional development (Lieberman and McLaughlin, 1992; Baker, 1994) and can provide a variety of economic and social benefits to the businesses, universities, or communities involved (Zacchei and Mirman, 1986; Gross, 1988; Sirotnik and Goodlad, 1988).

Relation to Content: The teacher who comes through the CSU teacher preparation programme must be ready to work in partnership with others and to facilitate cooperative and team learning experiences among students. Components of a variety of courses in the CSU programme therefore focus on such content as: (a) the importance and benefits of partnership and collaboration; (b) social aspects of learning; (c) techniques for structuring learning experiences that involve partnerships; (d) methods for encouraging students to work together effectively; and (e) procedures for establishing and maintaining collaborative efforts with parents, community members, colleagues, businesses, and universities.

Relation to Process: Students in the CSU teacher preparation programme will learn about partnership by dealing with relevant content. In addition, as they move through the programme, they will learn about partnership, learn to value it, and learn how to incorporate it in their own teaching by experiencing it and seeing it in action as they: (a) work together in small group projects and discussions; (b) move through parts of their programmes in cohort groups; (c) meet expectations to assist and provide feedback to each other; (d) see faculty working together in teaching teams, conducting research and writing grants together, and serving together on committees; (e) develop files of professional, community, and organizational resources; (f) and encounter partnerships in their field experiences.

Contextualism

Definition: Teaching and learning do not occur in isolation. Context as a conceptual framework includes the entire range of influences surrounding and infusing the teaching-learning process. One important context is the individual learner and the background she or he brings to the classroom. It is an acknowledgement that children and adolescents come to the learning situation with prior knowledge and understandings and that the teacher's capacity to build these prior experiences is an essential element in successful teaching. In this connection the idea of diversity is of central significance, particularly in urban settings where issues surrounding race, multi-culturalism, socio-economic status, and exceptionality are in higher focus than in the larger society. Then, too, understanding the various contexts of education means understanding multiple ways in which broad historical, social, economic, political, and technological forces shape—for better or worse—educational priorities and policies at the national, state, and local level. (Dewey, 1938; Bruner, 1996; Plucker, 2002; Moore, 1998).

Rationale: The emphasis on context comes from the recognition that learning is contextually situated, that is to say, it is inextricably intertwined and informed by the developmental, socio-cultural and institutional contexts in which it is being constructed and internalized. A comprehensive understanding of the multiple contexts of the teaching-learning process enables the teacher to incorporate into their teaching the cultures and background that students bring to the classroom, helping learners bridge connections between home, school, and the larger society. Similarly, teachers need to understand how the culture of the school and specific teaching practices may support or undermine students' motivation to learn. Finally, in a time of immense social, economic, and technological change, it is imperative that teachers engage in an ongoing examination of the possible ways in which their students' educational futures are either constrained or enhanced by existing curricular priorities and classroom strategies as well as continuing proposals for educational reform (Aronson, 2002; Au and Kawnkami, 1994; Dweck, 2000; Ladson-Billings, 2001; Neisser, 1998; Hunt, 1995; and Reich, 1992).

Relation to Content: As a model for teacher preparation, contextualism implies three major strands of content—(1) First, there is that body of knowledge related to learners and the learning process. In this connection the teachers must acquire an understanding of how learners develop physically, cognitively, socially and emotionally. Toward this end, teachers need to know how new learning is constructed, what learners bring to the teaching-learning process, and how teachers might incorporate the learner's background and interest into their instructional practices. (2) Second, teachers will need to understand the nature and significance of diversity in all its multiple forms. Toward this end the role of gender, culture, race, socio-economic status, and exceptionality in shaping students' school experience must be given careful attention. Also important are the implications of diversity for choosing curriculum objectives, instructional methodologies, assessment strategies as well as ways of creating patterns of positive social interaction in classrooms where all learners are respected for their unique contributions to a multicultural learning environment. Finally (3) teachers need to understand how historical, political, economic forces and structures influence all levels of the educational enterprise. In this respect, teachers must comprehend how such diverse factors as the global economy, racism, poverty, changing family structure, definitions of equity, the growing influence of popular culture, and the politics of school reform shape not only the decisions of educational policy-makers but also the quality of life in every classroom. (Lareau, 2000; Tatum, 1992; Vygotsky, 1963; Hidalgo, Chavez-Chavez, and Ramage, 1996; Ducette, Sewell, Shapiro, 1996; Flynn, 2003; Cole, 1998; Gerstle, 2001; Lowry, 2002; Ogbu, 2003; Patterson, 2001; Rothstein, 2002; Ravitch and Viteritti, 2001; Suarez-Orozco, 2001; and Zimmerman, 2002).

Relation to Process: Arguing this, knowledge must necessarily be an active not passive process. Because the purpose of CSU's teacher education conceptual framework is to prepare teachers who are reflective inquirers, so the content of their coursework must provide a forum for constructive engagement and analysis. Whatever the format of instruction—lecture, Socratic dialogue, reading essays or texts, cooperative learning, or reflective essays—the spirit and essence of instruction should be an invitation to improve upon one's professional knowledge and identity in an ever-changing society.

Professionalism

Definition: Broadly defined as the distinguishing features of an occupation that generally requires advanced knowledge or training, the concept of professionalism presupposes the existence of a clearly defined knowledge base that has been codified and, is, therefore, accessible to guide and support informed decision-making and practice (Goodlad, 1990). Hence, as manifest in this conceptual framework, professionalism is viewed as an overarching construct which further assumes that teachers can and should assume greater collective responsibility for defining, transmitting, and enforcing standards of professional practice so that their clients or students are well served (Burbules and Densmore, 1991; Case, Lanier, and Miskel, 1986; Conley and Muncey, 1999; Haberman, 1986; Lewis, 2002).

Rationale: The challenges and rewards of teaching have never been greater. The range and type of information that students need to know far exceeds that of previous decades such that academic expectations are increasing in virtually every state and community. Similarly, educators are being urged to teach higher-order thinking skills and creative problem-solving strategies in much more inclusive and diverse classroom settings to ever increasing numbers of children whose social, economic, and/or emotional difficulties place them at risk academically (Darling-Hammond and Cobb, 1996). Given these and other societal changes that are having a profound impact on education, the nation-wide movement to restructure schools continues to gain momentum as have concomitant efforts to reform teacher education; to further professionalize teaching; and to reformulate the standards and procedures by which states and school districts license, hire, induct, support, assess, and provide for the continual learning of teachers (Wise and Darling-Hammond, 1987; Darling-Hammond and Berry, 1988). Nevertheless, when issues of inequity are not directly addressed, the positive effects of teacher leadership and school reform would appear to be largely doomed as a means of raising the academic achievement of students in under resourced schools (Delpit, 1995; Ladson-Billings, 2001; Lipman, 1999; Wynne, 1999).

Recognizing that the promise of a high quality education for all children is dependent not only on a total restructuring of schools, but also on the knowledge and commitment of practitioners to that restructuring, current efforts to strengthen professional accountability are indicative of a deepening commitment to client-oriented practice as the primary means of transforming and revitalizing education. Assuming that instructional decisions about different learners' needs are too complex and individualistic to be prescribed from afar, "teachers must be prepared to address the substantial diversity in experiences that children bring with them to school: the wide range of languages, cultures, learning styles and challenges, talents, and intelligences that require in turn an equally rich and varied repertoire of teaching strategies" (Darling-Hammond and Cobb, 1996: 16). To this end, new entrants to the profession as well as veteran practitioners will need to develop deeper understandings of their disciplines, of interdisciplinary connections, and of inquiry-based learning and teaching. They will need skills for creating learning experiences that enable students to construct their own knowledge and will need to understand and use a variety of more authentic, performance-based means for assessing students' knowledge and understanding, their approaches to learning, and their prior experiences (Hawley and Valli, 2001; Wilson and Berne, 2001). In sum, this mission for teaching defies any single, formulaic approach to instructional delivery, calling instead for thoughtful, adaptive teaching that is learner-centered. As a result, professional development should be linked to student learning and emphasize subject-specific pedagogical content knowledge. Likewise, it should apply findings of cognitive research by providing active intellectual engagement, sustained collaboration, and ongoing support (Fickel, 2002).

Relation to Content: Recognizing that teacher education is a career-long process beginning with undergraduate studies and culminating in retirement (Burke, 1987; Steffy, Wolfe, Pasch, and Enz, 1999), CSU's program aims to provide an ongoing range of opportunities for continuous development that promote systemic reform initiatives in subject matter teaching, equity, assessment, and school organization. Without denying that there are times when technical skill training is appropriate, the programme primarily serves to promote self-reliance in instructional decision-making by providing a rich learning environment that stimulates meaningful engagement with ideas, with materials, and with colleagues; takes explicit account of the experience, interests and developmental needs of teachers and their students; offers support for informed dissent as a vehicle for examining alternative approaches to instruction; places classroom practice in the larger contexts of school and societal reform; prepares teachers to engage in inquiry as a means of generating knowledge and assessing the knowledge claimed by others; and helps ensure a balance between the interests of individuals and the interests of institutions when planning for and delivering instruction (Little, 1993). As a result, the programme promotes both professionalism and the further professionalization of teaching such that graduates may successfully assume positions of ever-increasing leadership both within and beyond the classroom.

Relation to Process: The view of teaching as intellectual work is at the heart of the restructured school, where practice is not prescribed and where considerable responsibility is placed on teachers for making judgments based on the best available information and a sound knowledge base. Given this imperative, CSU's teacher education programme seeks to provide prospective and practicing teachers, problem-based learning experiences that are situated in the context of practice and that further serve to promote partnerships, critical inquiry, reflection, and resilience. Extended clinical and site-based field experiences that are interwoven with coursework that incorporates microteaching, simulations, role playing, and well-designed case studies are a fundamental means of achieving this end (Carter and Anders, 1996; Darling-Hammond, 2000; Rentel, 1992); yet another is the conduct of action research. Specifically designed to promote critical inquiry, action research encourages teachers to make meaning of their own situational contexts by systematically engaging in analytical and reflective practice (Fueyo and Koorland, 1997; Zeichner and Noffke, 2001). Such reflection anticipates a career-based model of teacher development grounded more persuasively in the ongoing pursuit of knowledge than its transmission and thereby contributes to the development and refinement of a personal philosophy of education. Still other means for promoting reflection—student journals and professional portfolios—as they are used in CSU's programme, encourage teachers to examine their beliefs, knowledge, and performance over time; to better understand their strengths and weaknesses; and to establish meaningful goals for continued development (Howey and Zimpher, 1996; Hurst, Wilson, and Cramer, 1998).

Looking to the future, the college hopes to further its involvement with projects that help to develop teachers' abilities to examine teaching and learning from the perspective of diverse learners as has been recommended by Darling-Hammond (2000). In addition, plans are underway to maintain and expand its network of professional development or partner schools which hold particular promise for the improvement of practice and student achievement while simultaneously providing for the induction and cognitive apprenticeship of novice teachers as well as the continued advancement and renewal of practicing teachers and teacher educators (Clark, 1999; Cobb, 2000, 2001; Darling-Hammond, 1994; David, 2000; Levine, 1996; Pritchard and Ancess, 1999).

Applications of The Conceptual Framework

Curriculum organization: In terms of the professional education curriculum organization (i.e. core, specialty, fieldwork, etc.), the student outcomes will be accomplished and the four knowledge bases themselves will be emphasized at different levels of intensity depending upon the stage of the programme. For example, basic information about diversity and technology may be gained during the core and applications developed during the special methods courses. Teacher Education Curriculum needs to determine the undergraduate and graduate cores that adequately reflect the knowledge bases.

Further, it must be determined where and how the four knowledge bases will be established and used in the curriculum. For example, partnership may be applied to the curriculum by both establishing basic information about learning partnerships in the core as well as having students learn in cooperative groups. Additional study of partnership could occur throughout the programme as students reflect on their own learning experiences and develop learning strategies for their own students.

8.4.2 Berry College's Teacher Education Programme

Berry College is situated in northwestern Georgia, USA, established in 1902. The programme is developed keeping in view the teachers as developer of Human Potential. The teacher education mission believe the role of excellent teachers is to develop the potential of every student has to gain a lifelong appreciation of learning; to acquire the basic skills and wide repertoire of thinking strategies with which to construct and evaluate knowledge; to become morally responsible and fully participating partners in a democratic society within an ever-changing world, develop and enhance positive self-esteem; and to work cooperatively with others to foster changes in society. The teachers trained in Berry college needs to

- Promote Reflection and Decision-making capabilities (head),
- Facilitate learning (hands), and
- Enhance self and social awareness (heart).

Berry College's undergraduate teacher education programme tries to continually mix content with process, so as theories are discussed, applications can be modeled. The programme is structured to involve a back and forth between college classroom and field experience, allowing students opportunities to continually test the content of teacher education against the process of teaching in real classrooms. There are aspects of the theoretical content where mastery is expected, both in demonstrations to faculty and on the national certification tests. Assessments are constructed which allow demonstration, both authentic and traditional.

Subject-matter content (math, science, social studies, phonics, etc.) is a clear part of the responsibility of an undergraduate teacher education programme. Faculty strive to model the way they want students to teach this content while at the same time teaching them the content. Because they cannot teach all the content teachers should know, the emphasis goes more to big ideas, inquiries, and the attitudes necessary to help our students become lifelong learners.

This starts with an understanding of the nature of knowledge and how knowledge changes through time. It is important to give credence to students' preconceptions while at the same time understanding the currently accepted conceptions. Teacher education students must understand how to use the tools given to them to continue to learn. They must understand the content deeply in order to teach it. For teacher educators, paying attention to deep understanding of content means you cannot cover everything you hope to. Teachers and teacher educators should not be afraid of exploring their own understandings and delving on their own to understand further. The tools at our disposal are powerful to do this, with the web, electronic encyclopedias, linked communications, etc. Faculty expects students to do the self-learning necessary to prepare well to teach others, both in college classrooms and in their field experiences. Faculty models for students their own attempts to keep up with the burgeoning knowledge in their fields and their continual revision and updating of courses. One group of faculty began a self-study of their attempts to integrate technology in their teacher-education courses. They openly shared with college students their challenges and learning as they attempted to use technology in constructivist ways. And faculty honour student expertise as they learn from student explorations into particular content. Content and process become as inseparable as teacher and learner.

What about the teaching of particular content? College faculty depends on their colleagues in the arts and sciences for the content background of teacher education students. Faculty from across the campus were brought together to design the teacher-education curriculum. Discussion and debate helped all faculties understand the perspectives each brought on the role of content and process in teacher education. At first, arts and sciences faculty questioned the content and rigour of education courses. As they participated in the deconstruction and recreation of the teacher education courses, they participated in and came to understand the links between content and process that exist in education courses. Constructivist teacher education cannot occur in a vacuum. Too often students move from teacher education classes to arts and sciences classes where behaviourist techniques prevail. Teacher education faculty continues to struggle with the role of helping colleagues across campus understand changes in pedagogy. Historically teacher education has held a low status within colleges and universities, viewed as a professional school committed to practice instead of research (Schneider, 1987; Goodlad, 1999). This is beginning to change as calls for reform of both teacher education and general undergraduate education are opening to view the entire higher education experience. In smaller institutions such as Berry College, the commitment to teacher education has allowed for long-term curricular and budgetary investments. We continue to struggle with working with our arts and sciences colleagues to understand the process aspects of their content teaching.

Teacher education faculty also deals with teacher education students as we expect them to deal with their own pupils. This involves surfacing students' alternative conceptions or misconceptions, and then building understanding of the alternative conceptions pupils will bring to the classroom. Content is thus revealed, making it approachable but challenging. In the teacher education classroom, an approach to teaching content is modeled that begins with experiences orienting students to a content issue. Student ideas are then elicited, and a process of restructuring ideas is modeled which challenges student ideas and introduces accepted ideas. Students then have the chance to apply their ideas through experience, and review their change in thinking. This "constructivist teaching model" (Scott, 1987) is taught not as a pattern to be reproduced but as a way of understanding constructivist teaching, allowing for variety based on context. Students then explore the understanding of the pupils they may teach. In science methods for example, students are given the assignment of interviewing a child about conceptions in one area of science. The instructor models surfacing alternative conceptions in several science content areas, providing experiences that challenge student conceptions and then discussing current scientific views. Students then watch and discuss videos of child interviews that reveal specific content misconceptions. Students research a science concept and interview a child. They videotape their interview and write a reflective summary on what they learned about student understandings of science concepts. College students are amazed at how differently children think about everyday phenomena.

Although there is clear need for understanding of disciplinary content, that understanding must become a part of interdisciplinary thinking. Once one steps outside the classroom, there is little in life that narrowly follows disciplines. Berry College is in the process of breaking down course walls, moving all courses to become "blocks" team taught by professors bringing different perspectives together. A literacy block will bring together reading, language arts, and literature. An inquiry block will share math and science. An integrated arts block will allow social studies, art, music, and PE to create integrated units. A foundations block will bring together psychology and education. Curriculum brokers will ensure that technology, child development, special education, and second-language learners are integrated throughout all blocks. Blocks will be integrated vertically through faculty sharing of expertise and the development and modeling of interdisciplinary units, with faculty time and expertise choreographed to "dance" through disciplinary walls. In this way, content areas will be given meaning within integrated blocks emphasizing active/inquisitory approaches to knowledge.

8.4.3 Mills College Teacher Education Programme

The School of Education at Mills College, established in 1920, located in Oakland, California, USA is a leader in the preparation of future teachers, leaders and early childhood education professionals. The Mills College School of Education is built on the concept of principled practice which is reflected in core belief that learning is developmental and constructivist and guided by developmental conceptions of how learners come to know.

Inherent in the concept of constructivism are the notions of content and process. The teacher education programme at Mills College strives to help students think about this dichotomy as complementary. One programme principle articulates this area as "Teaching for the acquisition and construction of subject matter knowledge." A primary focus of the Mills College graduate-level credential programmes is to help candidates think in different ways about the subject-matter knowledge they already possess. Opportunities are provided for students to transform their content knowledge into working knowledge often referred to in the literature as pedagogical content knowledge. That is, students analyze and reorganize their subject matter knowledge in ways that will make it possible for them to provide similar opportunities for their students to organize knowledge. In addition, candidates construct and reconstruct their own subject-matter knowledge where necessary as a means to obtain and develop more pedagogical content knowledge in the future.

To emphasize the contrast and dichotomy of process and content, students engage with content at an adult level while thinking about the teaching of that content (or process) at the instructional level—whether it be for a child or an adult. For example, all elementary-education students participate in Writers' Workshop during the second semester. The semester ends with a publishing party where a collection of writing with a contribution from each class member is published. By participating in writers' workshop, student teachers think about content and process in several ways.

First they think about the nature of learning to write; we might consider this content about learner development. Second they think about different aspects of writing, like genre, writing conventions, the process of writing and rewriting. Here, process is the content. Third they think about writers' workshop as an instructional technique, from the perspective of the learner and the perspective of the teacher. As learners, they connect this aspect with the developmental content, and as teachers they connect this aspect with the process of writing and the pedagogy of writing instruction. This "activity" helps clarify the dichotomy and overlap of content and process.

In both the methodology classes and in child development classes, students examine children's learning of mathematics and literacy and apply that understanding to thinking about how best to teach the content. Thus, throughout the program there is a goal of coordinating the nature of the discipline, children's learning, instructional practice and an overall view of the curriculum.

8.5 Conceptual Framework for Teacher Education in India

In India, the National Curriculum Framework (NCF), 2005 was developed to reform the traditional school practices. It emphasized constructivist perspective into the school education system. It recognized learners as active constructor of knowledge within the context of social, political and environmental situations. The NCF (2005) places different demands and expectations on the teacher, which leads to the reform of the existing pre-service and in-service teacher education programme.

This resulted in the development of National Curriculum Framework for Teacher Education (NCFTE), 2009. Keeping the priority areas for teacher education as mentioned earlier the teacher education programme is redesigned to focus on the learner, to provide a greater 'space' for the personal social and professional development of the teacher and to equip him/her to evolve pedagogic practices and create a learning environment that addresses the needs of learners.

As outlined in NCFTE (2009) the curriculum for teacher education can be conceived as comprising three broad curricular areas:

A. Foundations of Education
B. Curriculum and Pedagogy
C. School Internship.

The Fig. 8.3 depicts the main curricular areas along with potential courses.

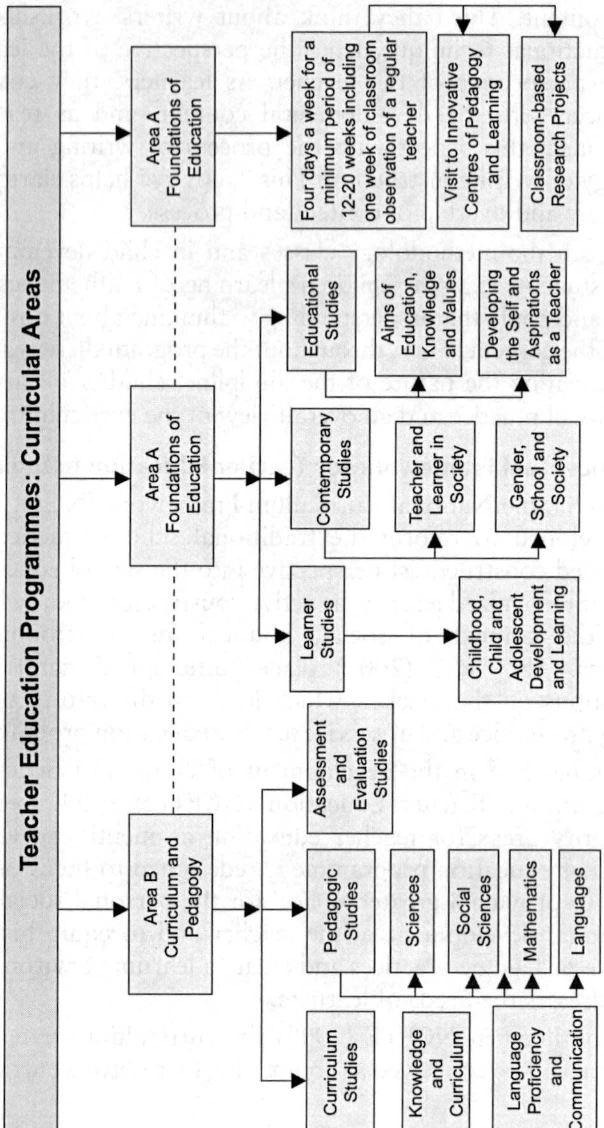
Teacher Education Programmes: Curricular Areas
Area A Foundations of Education
Area A Foundations of Education
Area B Curriculum and Pedagogy
Four days a week for a minimum period of 12-20 weeks including one week of classroom observation of a regular teacher
Visit to Innovative Centres of Pedagogy and Learning
Classroom-based Research Projects
Educational Studies
Aims of Education, Knowledge and Values
Developing the Self and Aspirations as a Teacher
Contemporary Studies
Teacher and Learner in Society
Gender, School and Society
Learner Studies
Childhood, Child and Adolescent Development and Learning
Assessment and Evaluation Studies
Pedagogic Studies
Sciences
Social Sciences
Mathematics
Languages
Curriculum Studies
Knowledge and Curriculum
Language Proficiency and Communication

Fig. 8.3

8.5.1 Curricular Area-A: Foundations of Education

Learner Studies: Childhood, Child and Adolescent Development and Learning

Rationale: The courses on Learner Studies are visualized as the first systematic introduction to the study of childhood, child development and adolescence. Beginning teachers need to engage with and understand children of different ages by interacting with them and observing them in diverse social, economic and cultural contexts rather than through an exclusive focus on psychological theories of child development. This would include a close study of adolescence in contemporary India as it poses several new challenges that emerge from the personal as well as social turmoil characteristics of societies in transition. It is equally important for teachers to engage with the social construct of childhood and adolescence, the various socio-cultural and political dimensions associated with its positioning and development in society.

Foundational learning in this area involves establishing links between developmental constructs and principles in psychological theory and the larger socio-political realities in which children grow and develop. Understanding the development of children in diverse contexts is necessary to equip student teachers to address diversity in the classroom and to teach within the frame of inclusive education. Pre-service teacher education programmes at all levels (including senior secondary) should be designed to include the observation and study of young children in order to appreciate the developmental process as a continuum.

An adequate opportunity for this can be provided through courses designed around key concepts and research from the disciplines of Psychology, Philosophy as well as Sociology.

Understanding children's (of diverse age groups) questions, their observations of natural and social phenomena; enquiring into children's thinking and learning and learning to listen to children with attention and empathy are necessary pre-requisites to develop teachers who are learner sensitive. Such engagement will help teachers to understand that learning is not a linear process; that it is a divergent process, essentially spiral in nature, and takes place in a variety of situations, including everyday contexts. Exclusive engagement with theories of learning fails to provide this perspective.

Every child needs to be made aware of the importance of healthy living and preventing disease. There is an urgent need, therefore, to generate health awareness and cultivate habits conducive to healthy living. It is suggested that comprehensive, systematic and scientific approaches to health education and health awareness be included in teacher education curricula. The contents proposed include: nutrition, personal and environmental hygiene, family and *school health*, disease prevention and control including HIV/AIDS, mental health, prevention of accidents, health information, use of health services, *physical health and sports*.

Curricular Provision—Theory and Practicum: *Theory Course Work*: 2 to 3 theory courses designed around key concepts and research from psychology, philosophy and sociology to engage student teachers with theoretical concepts and frameworks. These would include a critical reading of theories of child and adolescent development; context and processes of socialization; social and emotional development; self and identity; cognition and learning; language acquisition and communication; constructs of childhood and child-rearing practices; school and physical health and inclusive education. Each of the theory courses should have *in-built field-based units of study* leading to projects and assignments focusing on observations and interaction with children and adolescents, their conceptions and learning of natural and social phenomena and examining issues of school health and related social constructions.

Practicum Course Work: The aim is to provide hands-on experience with children of diverse ages and contexts as children and as learners; and to enable a back-and-forth movement between theory and the field. Student teachers need to be given opportunities to be with children of diverse contexts such as first generation learners and street children, interact with them, organize creative activities for them with the aim to learn to communicate and relate with them. While engaging with developmental theories and constructs, many of the experiences they have had with children during this practicum are consciously brought into the classroom discourse to draw interconnections, verily and evolve theory and help those articulate, new ideas.

Using the mode of group and individual field-based assignments followed by workshops and seminar presentations, specific practicum courses should be designed for student teachers to:

- Observe, interact with and study children and adolescents of different ages in natural settings in and outside the school, in diverse socio-economic, cultural, linguistic and regional contexts.
- Observe and analyse learning and thinking processes of children of different age groups, including adolescents.
- Examine their thoughts, questions and observations of natural and social phenomena in order to appreciate the developmental process as a continuum.

Contemporary Studies

(a) **Teacher and Learner in Society**

Rationale: There is a need to shift the focus from an overwhelming emphasis on psychological characteristics of the individual learner to his/her social, cultural, economic and political contexts. Therefore, a rigorous engagement with issues of *contemporary Indian society* must necessarily be examined through an engagement with concepts drawn from a diverse set of disciplines including sociology, history, philosophy, political science and economics. Courses under this rubric are likely to provide space for engagement with issues and concerns of India's pluralistic nature; issues of identity, gender, equity, poverty and diversity. This would enable teachers to *contextualize education* and evolve a deeper understanding of its purpose and its relationship with society and humanity. It is also important to understand the *classroom as a social context*, as it provides a setting for interaction, generation of dialogue and the opportunity to appreciate diverse perspectives on a given issue.

Critical awareness of *human and child rights* equips the teacher with a proactive perspective and a sense of agency. Respect for human rights cannot be seen in isolation from an analytical awareness of the contexts in which human rights are to be observed, starting from Constitutional provisions (e.g. reservation and the right to education), the institutional context, extending to the social, national and global contexts. Teachers also need to be aware of children's rights, the role of the NCPCR in protecting these lights, rights for gender equality and their implications for social change. The critical perspective of *environmental education* also falls within the rights' perspective that asserts the role of education in sustaining a democratic social order.

Curricular Provision—Theory: *Theory Course Work*: One or two courses to engage learners with social science concepts and specific issues critical in contemporary Indian society. Concepts from across a range of social science disciplines such as civilisation and democracy, nation-state, Constitutional values and provisions, culture and societal stratification are likely to equip the teacher with tools of analysis and a perspective on social reality. An engagement with issues and concerns of contemporary Indian society: pluralistic culture, identity, gender, equity, poverty and diversity would provide a social, cultural and political context to locate education and its practice. This is likely to help student teachers understand the classroom as a social context where learning is greatly influenced by the social context from which learners and teachers come. It provides a, setting for interaction, generation of dialogue and the opportunity to appreciate diverse perspectives on given issues.

Each course would have an *in-built field-based unit of study*. Student teachers study the major characteristics of India's pluralistic make-up with the help of field interviews while studying the issue of reservation as an egalitarian policy, collate people's experiences of such a provision and examine policy and theory. Through such a pedagogic process, the onus of drawing connections between experience and theory is not left to the student teacher alone. Learning spaces are structurally provided in the design of teacher education programmes for drawing such connections.

Student teachers can undertake *projects* such as tracing the process by which a consumer product is made available from its raw form to a finished product and studying the various factors of geography, economics, politics, history and sociology that may have influenced it in one way or another. Projects can be complemented with workshops, seminars, assignments and group discussions around issues and concepts studied in theory.

(b) **Gender, School and Society Rationale**

Rationale: Developing a gender perspective through teacher education necessarily requires a pedagogic approach that allows riot just systematic study of gender theory but also an engagement within their own position in society *vis-à-vis* gender roles. Student teachers also need to do a critical reading of the existing literature that draws linkages between democracy and education from the perspective of gender. Space needs to be provided within such courses to build teachers' abilities to make linkages between theory and real life situations. This implies rigorous systematic theoretical study as well as intensive observation and analysis of field realities. This approach is likely to strengthen teachers' ability to conceptualise from a given experience.

Curricular Provision—Theory: *Theory Course Work*: A single course that deals with theoretical perspectives in gender studies, questions of identity and self; examining their positions in society; curriculum and text analysis from the gender lens, critically analysing disciplinary studies, analysing school cultures, engaging in debates associated with professional education and the feminisation of the teaching profession and strategies of creating change. Hands-on experience with examining textbooks, curriculum framework and syllabi from a gender lens would provide immense opportunities to develop critical perspectives. These can be *in-built, field-based units of study* in the course on gender.

Although this course will provide necessary focus on the theory and construct of gender, all other courses would require an engagement with gender perspectives whether in understanding the development of children and adolescents or in understanding issues of society, culture, equity arid diversity.

Educational Studies

(a) **Aims of Education, Knowledge and Values Rationale**

Rationale: Basics of education like the meaning of education, curriculum, teaching, learning and school need to be discussed with a view to providing a sound foundation for advanced discussions on issues relating to the theory and practice of education. Among the many questions that contemporary educational discourse excludes are substantive philosophical questions about the fundamental aims and values that should provide the intellectual basis of contemporary education policy and practice. Student teachers need to engage with issues in a manner that makes them sensitive to the fact that educational debate is never neutral; it always tends to promote certain educational values while marginalizing others.

True education is a process of developing the human personality in all its dimensions—intellectual, physical, emotional, social, moral and spiritual. Peace provides an integrating principle for the value-orientation of education. Education for peace is education for life, not merely training for a livelihood. Equipping individuals with the values, skills and attitudes, they need to be wholesome persons who live in harmony with themselves and others and are responsible citizens is the goal of education for peace. Ideas of educational thinkers such as Gandhi, Tagore, Dewey, Krishnamurti, Montessori and others examined in their socio-historical contexts would provide the philosophical basis to engage with these questions.

Curricular Provision—Theory: *One or more courses* focused on philosophical thinkers in education, theoretical constructs that help to question and debate issues around aims of education and questions of epistemology. Philosophical and sociological probing into the idea of knowledge, morality and values; status, problems and concerns of school education in India; frames and persuasions of peace education within the national and international contexts would be some of the critical units of study; engagement with school culture and school as a learning organization. Apart from lectures and discussions, a close reading of original writings, seminar/term paper presentations and self-study of select units of study must be encouraged.

(b) **Developing the Self and Aspirations as a Teacher**

Rationale: Teacher trainees need to study issues related to self and identity, human relationships, adult-child gaps, assumptions, beliefs and attitudes. They could explore the meaning of ethics and values, observe and understand feelings of fear and trust and their influences in personal and social attitude, attitudes towards competition and co-operation, analyse and observe the impact of competition in personal and social life, observe the role of listening, attention and empathy and the role of a teacher in establishing relationship with children and as a communicator. A greater insight into one's aims of life, one's strengths and weaknesses and the dynamics of identity formation provides the base for developing a professionally competent teacher who is sensitive to issues of equity, democracy and social justice.

Curricular Provision—Theory: *Theory Course Work: One course* with focused workshops through link with theory that would require specific inputs from professionals engaged with self-development, theatre and creative drama. These often provide non-threatening and non-judgmental learning environments that enable the participants to reflect on their own positions in society with ease. Theoretical study on issues of identity, interpersonal relations, adult-child gaps, personal and social constructs, schools as sites for struggle and social change; complementary workshops with focus on identity development; recognising one's own strengths and limitations and developing social sensitivity; and the capacity to listen and empathies.

Practicum Course Work: Student teachers need to engage with their childhood experiences, personal aspirations and aspirations to become teachers, their views on issues of gender and identity, personal, familial and social conflict. This can be best done through workshops in drama, art, music and craft. They need to be encouraged to record and analyse observations to interpret reality within varying theoretical and experiential frameworks.

8.5.2 Curricular Area-B: Curriculum and Pedagogy

Curriculum Studies

(a) **Knowledge and Curriculum**

Rationale: It is important to engage prospective teachers with the conceptual knowledge they have gained through general education. Most teacher education courses focus exclusively on the methodology of teaching individual school subjects. It is assumed that the teacher trainees have the subject-content knowledge which they would draw upon when required. Hence, teacher education curricula do not engage teacher trainees with subject-content. However, if we want to prepare teachers to present subject-content in developmentally appropriate ways and with critical perspectives it is essential that several theoretical concepts learnt during general education in school and college be revisited and reconstructed. This course also aims to engage student teachers with epistemological and ideological assumptions about knowledge, learner and learning; their implications for curriculum, pedagogy and assessment in school education.

Although much learning and teaching takes place at home, within the neighbourhood and communities of rural and tribal India, the school introduces the child to an environment of teaching and learning that, quite by design, marks itself off from the rest of the child's environment. Schools need to facilitate the creation of vital links between children's experiences at home and in the community and what the school offers them.

Curricular Provision—Theory: *Theory Course Work*: *Four to six courses* with units of study that are designed along the syllabi of plus two and graduation level as the case may be in each of the major disciplines of language, mathematics, social sciences and natural sciences. The concepts studied by student teachers in their general education are revisited and reconstructed using several hands-on activities. This will enable a deep engagement with concepts and sub-concepts, thus enabling many misconceptions to come to the fore for interrogation, and thus enabling clarity.

Understanding School Curriculum: Philosophical and ideological basis of curriculum design, selection of knowledge; critical examination of curriculum, design and analysis of textbooks, negotiating curriculum; linking school knowledge with community life: examining textbooks to contextualize school knowledge, learning to draw upon resources other than textbooks, including local oral histories.

In-built field-based units of study can provide sustained engagement with content through the close examination of select concepts. Science, for example, can involve laboratory work, library and reference, field surveys, group discussions, seeking expert opinion to investigate into questions that children often ask such as, Why is the sky blue? Why do stars twinkle? Similarly, mathematical concepts and operations can be reconstructed, through activities and problems using concrete materials from everyday experiences as well as from mathematical kits, to arrive at solutions or conduct investigations. These need to be followed by reflective discussion on the concepts, solutions, results and the methods used, both 'right' and 'wrong'. A variety of investigative projects can be designed for this purpose. Reconstructing concepts helps student teachers and teacher practitioners to appreciate the nature of subject knowledge and to link it with appropriate pedagogic processes that communicate meaningfully with children. Student teachers can undertake projects in oral history; alternative medicine; appropriate technologies; pedagogies of informal learning situations in order to grasp the diverse nature of knowledge.

(b) **Language Proficiency and Communication**

Rationale: Language cuts across the entire school curriculum and hence, the role of language as a medium and tool of communication assumes great importance. A teacher talks, explains, narrates, asks questions, illustrates, translates, guides, instructs, cautions, motivates, encourages and plays various other roles. All of these imply an appropriate and context-specific use of language. Concepts, constructs, examples are the building blocks of knowledge and all these are language-based. This makes the teacher's language proficiency and communication skills critical factors in school education, apart from a sound knowledge-base, pedagogical and other professional capacities.

Curricular Provision: *Course Work*: *Once course* that focuses on developing the proficiency levels of student teachers in the appropriate language. This should be the language in which the teacher would teach. Irrespective of stage specificity and subject specialisation, all teacher education programmes must focus on and accord high priority to the development of student teacher's language competence and communication skills. This course should be designed to include hands-on experience in using the language in different contexts, meta-linguistic awareness with a focus on listening, speaking, reading, comprehension and writing for varying contexts.

Pedagogic Studies

School Knowledge, Learner and Pedagogy

Rationale: The purpose of pedagogic study is to understand school subjects and their pedagogic approaches in the concrete context of the school and the learner by forging linkages among learner, context, subject discipline and the pedagogical approach. The key departure of pedagogical courses from conventional teacher education would involve shifting the focus from pure disciplinary knowledge and methodology to the learner and his/her context as well. For instance, a course on language pedagogy would promote an understanding of the language characteristics of learners, language usage, socio-cultural aspects of language learning, language as a process and the functional use of language across the curriculum. This would mean moving away from the conventional focus on language as a subject, which emphasizes its grammatical structure rather than usage.

Pedagogic study of school subjects such sciences, social sciences, languages and mathematics needs to be organized as such rather than for individual school subjects of history, geography or chemistry. This would facilitate a teacher to draw upon epistemological insights while teaching any of the key disciplines that fall under one rubric-sciences or social sciences. This approach also has the advantage of preparing teachers for teaching integrated courses in sciences and social sciences.

Curricular Provision—Theory and Practicum: *Theory Course Work*: *Two to four courses* on Pedagogy: Knowledge as construction through experiences, nature of disciplines, critical understanding of school curriculum; and pedagogy as the integration of knowledge about the learner, the discipline and the societal context. This would include separate courses on languages, mathematics, social sciences, sciences and environmental sciences at the primary, upper primary, secondary and senior secondary stages of education.

For instance, a pedagogy course on EVS should include the following: philosophical and epistemological basis of EVS as a composite area of study that draws upon the sciences, social sciences and environmental education; acquainting student teachers with children's ideas of their physical and social world so that these can later be interpreted for classroom instruction; helping student teachers develop the ability to plan comprehensive units that do not compartmentalize knowledge but view it holistically.

Engagement with research relating to different aspects of young children's learning in languages, mathematics, environmental education, history, geography, followed by reflective discussion, records of observation, analysis can form an important part of developing sound pedagogic understanding of the elementary school teacher. A critical examination of and engagement with teaching methods such as concept formation, enquiry-based teaching, problem-solving, discovery and activity-based learning and related terms can go a long way in making him/her a reflective teacher.

The secondary and senior secondary school teachers will need to engage with deeper epistemological questions of the disciplines they specialize in. Specific tasks related to, how learners engage with school subject-content misconceptions need to be addressed through a rigorous study of disciplinary knowledge, besides a specific focus on content area literacy and tasks of writing observations and analysis for enhancing conceptual understanding.

Pedagogy courses will need to be designed to address different stages of education: preschool, elementary (primary and upper primary), secondary as well as senior secondary.

Practicum Courses Work: Practicum courses can be designed on themes of classroom management, material development and block teaching in schools. Student teachers learn to integrate ideas, experiences and professional skills through hands-on experience of developing curriculum and learning materials, designing appropriate activities for children of different age groups and formulating questions to facilitate learning. Teachers also need to learn to prompt children to ask questions and to learn to collate these to further processes of learning. For instance, for a language pedagogy course, student teachers would need to engage with projects involving listening to children's reading, observing and analysing reading difficulties, observing and identifying mismatches between school language and home language, analysing textbooks and other materials used in different subjects in terms of presentation, style and language used.

Practicum activities for social sciences could be based on organizing and planning for excursions, drawing upon local sources of evidence in history, projects on oral history, collection and presentation of specimens of rocks, leaves, stamps, flags, using reports, newspapers, documents, local maps, atlas, map drawing and reading in the classroom. These could be followed by reflective discussion, learning how to make observations, record them and analyse them. Such an approach would help forge linkages between the learner and his/her context, disciplinary content and the pedagogical approach.

Placing student teachers with learners of secondary and senior secondary classes will help them design developmentally appropriate projects. This would necessarily require deeper and wider engagement with disciplinary knowledge. Practicum of this nature can help teachers develop a repertoire of skills for reflective practice, such as critical reading of school textbooks, making pedagogical sense of learner errors and learning styles.

Assessment and Evaluation Studies

Perspective and Practice of Learner Assessment

Rationale: An important role that every teacher has to play is that of assessing children's progress, both in terms of their psychological development and the criteria provided by the curriculum. The scope of learner assessment and evaluation needs to be broadened to go beyond the limited context of syllabus-based achievement testing; achievement scores in a subject need to be linked with the child's overall development; testing should cover higher level of learning objectives, not just information. The NCF proposes school-based evaluation as a long-term goal of examination reform. For this goal to be attained, teacher education programmes will need to build capacity to introduce student teachers to the history of evaluation and current practices, including contemporary debates on perspective and the practice of testing. There is a need to emphasise on the need to view assessment as an aspect of learning. Teachers must recognise the role evaluation plays in motivating children to learn. This is particularly crucial to achieve the goals of the right to education and to bring every child into the fold of quality education. The current system of evaluation as a means to select by failing is not consistent with the goal of universalizing education. A rigorous informed understanding of assessment has become even more important in the current global context of laying undue stress on student performance.

Curricular Provision—Theory and Practicum: *Theory Course Work*: Theoretical engagement with learner assessment needs to be integrated with courses in pedagogic studies and curriculum studies. This engagement should include a rigorous critical reading of perspectives that regard learner assessment as the panacea of school and teacher reform; examining the history of evaluation and current practices; place of evaluation in learning and development of the learner, and broadening the scope of assessment beyond achievement testing to cover child's overall development.

Practicum Course Work: Student teachers need to get hands-on experience of designing assessment methods that are qualitative in nature and assess children's developing capacities to think and solve problems rather than to recall. Tasks of formulating different types of questions, studying their impact in terms of learner performance and learning grasp in the classrooms could be undertaken consistently. Systematic recording of learners' errors, examining them in the light of empirical research and attempts at leading learners towards newer ways of thinking need to be closely recorded and discussed with faculty.

8.5.3 Curricular Area-C: School Internship

Rationale: It is common knowledge that practice teaching which constitutes the most functional part of the teacher preparation has suffered severe neglect and dilution in quality. The common complaint is that theory dominates the curriculum and practice teaching continues to suffer from inadequacies of different kinds such as: it follows a mechanical routine (observation, micro teaching, teaching practice and examination), operates with rigid lesson plan formats, inadequate mentoring and supervision; exhibits no original thinking, lacks variety and context specificity in teaching. There is no attempt made towards comprehensive, qualitative evaluation covering professional attitudes and values and provision of sustained engagement with schools. The major drawbacks of the current model of practice teaching are:

- Current practices in teacher education take the school curriculum and textbooks as 'given' and train teachers to adjust to the needs of the existing school system through fastidious planning of lessons in standardized formats, fulfilling the ritual of delivering the required number of lessons.
- Repeated 'practice' in the teaching of a specified number of isolated lessons is considered a sufficient condition for professional development.
- There is no opportunity for teachers to examine their own biases and beliefs and reflect on their own experiences as part of classroom discourse and enquiry.
- Theory courses have no clear articulation with practical work and ground realities.
- The evaluation protocol is too theoretical, excessively quantitative and lacks comprehensiveness.

Situating the practice of teaching in the broader context of the vision of the role of the teacher: It is obvious that in imparting professional rigour to the preparation of a teacher, the practice of teaching and associated rigorous theoretical study play a crucial part. It is the effectiveness with which the multiple components of field learning—getting to know the school, observing children, observing teaching and learning in real classroom contexts, practicing teaching, developing capacities to think with educational theories and applying concepts in concrete teaching-learning situations, managing classroom learning, evaluating learners and providing feedback, learning to work with colleagues, reflecting on one's own professional practice—are drawn upon to provide appropriate learning experiences for the student teacher that is critical to the education of teachers.

At the outset, it can be seen that any attempt towards reform of current practices and design of innovative approaches in practice teaching should begin with an understanding of the place of teaching practice in the overall scheme of things. The first thing to be noted is that the practice of teaching constitutes the hub of the multiple and varied activities comprising the total programme of teacher education. It is interconnected with theoretical study, field work and practicum and a wide range of institutional experiences involving school students, teachers, student teachers, mentor teacher educators. In a way, it acts both as the evaluation tool for effective teacher education as well as its critical quality indicator.

Curricular Provision—Sustained engagement with learners and the school: The School Internship programme needs to have the following critical components:

- Visits to Innovative Centres of Pedagogy and Learning, wherever feasible;
- Classroom-based Research Project;
- Internship in schools for a continuous period of 4 days a week and a minimum duration of 6-10 weeks for a two-year programme and 15-20 weeks for a four-year programme, including an initial phase of one week for observing a regular classroom with a regular teacher;
- Developing Unit Plans and maintaining Reflective Journals; and

- Creating and maintaining resources for teaching-learning in the Internship schools.

While functioning as a regular teacher for a sustained period of a minimum of 12-20 weeks, the intern would get an opportunity to learn to set realistic goals in terms of learning, curricular content and pedagogic practice. A sustained contact through internship would help teachers to choose, design, organize and conduct meaningful classroom activities, critically reflect upon their own practices through observations, record keeping and analysis and develop strategies for evaluating students' learning for feedback into curriculum and pedagogic practice.

The school would benefit from such an alliance in terms of witnessing possibilities of unconventional pedagogies. In this process of internship, teacher trainees develop new materials for teaching-learning which can become valuable resource for the regular teachers of the school.

The internship needs to be worked as a partnership model with the school rather than a continuation of the current model of practice teaching during which the trainees merely 'use' the school for their own 'formal degree requirements'.

The feature distinguishing the proposed process-based teacher education from conventional teacher education is that of bringing the learners' own experiences centre-stage. Engagement with theoretical concepts and frameworks takes place within the learner's experiential and larger social realities. The structural provision for such opportunity is to be made in the design of the teacher education programme structure and within each area of study. By structural provision we mean the positioning of areas of study/inquiry in a manner that allows an easy flow of movement from experience to theory and theory to field experiences.

A back-and-forth movement between theory and the field could be provided through inbuilt field-based units of study, in each theory course as well as specially designed practicum as has been indicated in each of the curricular areas presented in Fig. 8.3.

The school internship programme provides the platform for the interns to give expression to their learning while planning and reflecting on their own practice.

8.6 Conclusion

Constructivist teacher education programmes followed world wide deal with the issues of content and process acknowledging the vital link between content and its acquisition. Such type of innovative teacher education programmes are characterized by the following features:

(i) Context-sensitive
(ii) Purposeful and articulate
(iii) Participatory and collaborative
(iv) Knowledge-based
(v) Ongoing
(vi) Developmental, and
(vii) Analytic and reflective.

Teacher education programme based on these seven features ensures teacher growth and development; acknowledge the complexity of classroom; school and community; sensitive to the ways teachers think, feel and make meaning from their experiences and inculcate pedagogical content knowledge. The constructivist teacher education programmes are essential for leading the students at all level of schooling to better appreciate the world around them.

References

Ancess, J. (2003). *Beating the odds: High schools as communities of commitment*. New York: Teachers College Press.

Aronson, J. (Ed.) (2002). *Improving academic achievement: Impact of psychological factors on education*. New York: Academic Press.

Au, K.H., and Kawakami, A.J. (1994). Cultural congruence in instruction. In E.R. Hollins, J.E. King, and W.C. Hayman (Eds.), *Teaching Diverse Populations: Formulating a Knowledge Base*. Albany, NY: SUNY.

Baker, W.E. (1994). *Networking smart: How to build relationships for personal and organizational success*. New York: McGraw-Hill.

Banks, J.A. and Banks, C.A. (1997). *Multicultural education: Issues and perspectives* (3rd Ed.), Boston: Allyn & Bacon.

Berlak, H. (1992). The need for a new science of assessment. In Berlak, H., Newmann, F., Adams, E., Archbald, D., Burgess, T., Raven, J. and Romberg, T. (Eds.) *Toward a New Science of Educational Testing and Assessment*. Albany: NY.

Bintz, W.P. (1991). Staying connected—Exploring new functions for assessment. Contemporary Education, 62(4): 307-12.

Bintz, W.P. and Harste, J. (1994). Where Are We Going with Alternate Assessment? And Is It Really Worth Our Time? *Contemporary Education*, 66(1): 7-12.

Black, A., and Ammon, P. (1992). A developmental-constructivist approach to teacher education. *Journal of Teacher Education*, 43: 323-35.

Brooks, J.G. and Brooks, M.G. (1993). *The Case for Constructivist Classroom*. Alexandria, Va: Association for Supervision and Curriculum Development.

Brown, A.L. (1994). The advancement of learning. *Educational Researcher*, 23(8): 4-12.

Bruner, J. (1996). *The Culture of Education*. Cambridge: Harvard University Press.

Bullough, R.V., Jr., Young, P., Erickson, L., Birrell, J.R., Clark, D.C., Egan, M.W., Berrie, C.F., Hales, V., and Smith, G. (2002). Rethinking field experience: Partnership teaching versus single-placement teaching. *Journal of Teacher Education*, 53(1): 68-80.

Bullough, R.V., Jr. and Gitlin, A.D. (2001). *Becoming a student of teaching: Linking knowledge production and practice* (2K> ed.). New York: Routledge Palmer.

Burbles, N., and Densmore, K. (1991). The limits of making teaching a profession. *Educational Policy*, 5(1): 44-63.

Burke, P.J. (1987). *Teacher development: Induction, renewal and redirection*. New York: Palmer Press.

Carlin, M.B. and Ciaccio, L. (1997). Improving high school students' performance via discovery learning, collaboration and technology. *THE Journal*, Vol. 24(10): 62-66.

Carter, K., and Anders, D. (1996). Program pedagogy. In F.B. Murray (Ed.), *The teacher educator's handbook: Building a knowledge base for the preparation of teachers* (pp. 557-92). San Francisco, CA: Jossey Bass.

Carvan, M.T., Nolen, A., and Yinger, R. (2002). Power through partnership: The Urban Network for the Improvement of Teacher Education (UNITE). *Teacher Education and Practice*, 75(1-2): 88-101.

Case, C.W., Lanier, J.E., and Miskel, C.G. (1986). The Holmes Group report: Impetus for gaining professional status for teachers. *Journal of Teacher Education*, 37(4): 36-43.

Cibulka, J.G. (2003). Introduction: The evaluation of Baltimore's city-state partnership to reform BCPSS: Framing the context, national trends, and key findings. *Journal of Education for Students Placed at Risk*, 8(1): 1-14.

Clark, R.W. (1999). *Effective professional development schools.* San Francisco, CA: Jossey-Bass.

Cobb, J.B. (2000). *Critical themes in teacher education: The impact of a professional development school on preservice.*

—— (2001). Graduates of professional development school programs: Perceptions of the teacher as change agent. *Teacher Education Quarterly*, 28(4): 89-107.

Cochran, K.F., De Ruiter, J.A. and King, R.A. (1993). Pedagogical content knowing: An integrative model for teacher preparation. *Journal of Teacher Education*, 41: 32-43.

Cochran-Smith, M., and Lytle, S.L. (1993). *Inside/Outside: Teacher Research and Knowledge.* New York Teachers College.

Cole, M. (1992). Education in the market place: A case of contradiction, *Educational Review*, 44: 335-43.

—— (1998). Can cultural psychology help us think about diversity? *Mind, Culture, & Activity*, 5: 291-305.

Conley, S., and Muncey, D. (1999). Teachers talk about teaming and leadership in their work. *Theory Into Practice.* 38(\): 46.

Constructivist learning environments: Case studies in instructional design (pp. 107-20). Englewood Cliffs, NJ: Educational Technology Publications.

Cooper, P.A. (1993). Paradigm shifts in designed instruction: from behaviourism to cognitivism to constructivism. *Educational Technology*, Vol. 33, pp. 12-19.

Darling-Hammond, L. (1994). *Professional development schools: Schools for developing a profession.* New York: Teachers College Press.

—— (2000). How teacher education matters. *Journal of Teacher Education*, 51(3): 166-73.

Darling-Hammond, L., and Berry, B. (1988). *The evolution of teacher policy.* Santa Monica, CA: RAND.

Darling-Hammond, L., and Cobb, V. L. (1996). The changing context of teacher education. In F.B. Murray (Ed.). *The teacher educator's handbook: Building a knowledge base for the preparation of teachers* (pp. 14-62). San Francisco, CA: Jossey Bass.

David, T. (2000). Programs in practice: Teacher mentoring-benefits all around. *Kappa Delta Pi Record*, 36(3): 134-36.

Davydov, V.V. (1995). The influence of L.S. Vygotsky on education theory, research, and practice. *Educational Research*, 24: 12-21.

Deeds, D. and Allen, C.S. (2000). A new paradigm in integrated math and science courses. *Journal of College Science Teaching*, Vol. 30(3): 178-84.

Delpit, L. (1995). *Other People's Children.* New York: The New Press.

Dewey, J. (1916). *Democracy and Education.* New York: Macmillan.

—— (1910). *How We Think*. Lexington, MA: D.C. Heath.

Ducette, J.P., Sewell, I.E., and Shapiro, J.P. (1996). "Diversity in Education: Problems and Possibilities." In F.B. Murray (Ed.), *The Teacher Educator's Handbook: Building a Knowledge Base for the Preparation of Teachers*. San Francisco: Jossey-Bass.

Duffy, T.M. and Jonassen, D.H. (1992). *Constructivism and the Technology of Instruction*. New Jersey: Educational Technology Publications.

Dweck, C.S. (2000). *Self-theories: Their role in motivation, personality, and development*. Philadelphia. PA: Psychology Press.

Edens, K., Shirley, J, and Toner, T. (2001). Sustaining a professional development school partnership: Hearing the voices, heeding the voices. *Action in Teacher Education*, 23(3): 27-32.

Emmer, E.T. and Gerwels, M.C. (2002). Cooperative learning in elementary classrooms: Teaching practices and lesson characteristics. *The Elementary School Journal*, Vol. 103(1): 75-92.

Epanchin, B.C. and Colucci, K. (2002). The professional development school without walls: A partnership between a university and two school districts. *Remedial and Special Education*, 23(6): 349-58.

Epstein, J.L. (1984). Effects of Teacher Practices and Parent Involvement on Student Achievement. Paper presented at the annual meeting of the *American Educational Research Association*, New Orleans, LA.

Epstein, J.L. (Ed.) (1991). "Parental involvement: A special section." *Phi Delta Kappan*, 72(5): 344-88.

Fickel, L.H. (2002). Quality professional development: Suggestions about process and content. *Educational Forum*, 57(1): 47-54.

Flynn, J.R. (2003). Movies about intelligence: The limitations of g. *Current Directions in Psychological Science*, 12: 95-100.

Freedman, J. and Goolishian, H. (1988). Human systems as linguistic systems. *Family Process*, Vol. 27: 271-393.

Freire, P. (1990). Pedagogy of oppressed. New York: Continuum.

Fueyo, V., and Koorland, M.A. (1997). Teacher as researcher: A synonym for professionalism. *Journal of Teacher Education*, 48(5): 336-44.

Galassi, J.P., White, K.P., Vesilind, E.M., and Bryan, M.E. (2001). Perceptions of research from a second-year, multisite professional development schools partnership. *Journal of Educational Research*, 95(2): 75-83.

Gergen, K. (1985). The social constructionist movement in modern psychology. *American Psychologists*, Vol. 40, pp. 266-75.

—— (1991). The *Saturated Self*. New York: Basic Books.

Gerstle, G. (2001). *American Crucible: Race and Nation in the Twentieth Century*. Princeton: Princeton University Press.

Goodlad, J. (1990). *Teachers for our nation's schools*. San Francisco, CA: Jossey-Bass.

Gordlad, J.I. (1999). Rediscovering Teacher Education: School renewal and educating educators. *Change*, 31(5): 28-33.

Greene, M. (1988). *The Dialectic of Freedom*. New York: Teacher College Press.

Gross, T.L. (1988). *Partners in education: How colleges can work with schools to improve teaching and learning*. San Francisco: Jossey-Bass.

Haberman, M. (1986). Licensing teachers: Lessons from other professions. *Phi Delta Kappa*, 67: 719-22.

Hausfather, S.J., Outlaw M.E. and Strehle, E.L. (1996). Relationships as a foundation: emerging field experiences within multiple college school partnerships. In T. Warren (Ed.), *Partnerships in teacher education: schools and colleges working together*, 27-41, Lanham, Md: University Press of America.

Hawley, W.D., and Valli, L. (2001). The essentials of effective professional development: A new consensus. In D. Boesel (Ed.), *Continuing professional development: Improving teacher quality: Imperative for educational reform* (pp. 1-17). Washington, D.C.: U.S. Department of Education, Office of Educational Research and Improvement. Retrieved July 16, 2003, from http://www.ericsp.org/ pages/digests/ConProfDev.pdf

Herman, J.L. Aschbacher, P.R., and Winters, L.A. (1992). *A Practical Guide to Alternative Assessment*. Alexandria, Va: Association for supervision and curriculum development.

Heron, J. (1988). "Assessment Revisited". In D. Boud (Ed.), *Developing Student Autonomy in Learning* (2nd ed.). New York: Nichols.

Hidalgo, F., Chavez-Chavez. R., and Ramage, J. (1996). "Multicultural Education: Landscaped for Reform in the Twenty-First Century." In J. Sikula (ed.), *Handbook of Research on Teacher Education*. New York: MacMillan.

Howey, K.R., and Zimpher, N.L. (1989). *Profiles of Pre-service Teacher Education: Inquiry into the Nature of Programs*. Albany: State University of New York Press.

Hunt, Earl B. (1995). *Will we be smart enough?: A cognitive analysis of the coming workforce*. New York: Russell Sage Foundation.

Hurst, B., Wilson C., and Cramer, G. (1998). Professional teaching portfolios. *Phi Delta Kappan*, 79(8): 578-82.

Hutchings, P. (1993). "Principles of Good Practice for Assessing Student Learning", Assessment Update, 5(1): 6-7.

James, C.E., and Haig-Brown, C. (2001). "Returning the dues": Community and the personal in a university-school partnership. *Urban Education*, 36(2): 226-35.

Jaworski, B. (1993). Constructivism and Teaching—The socio-cultural context: Paper presented at the Seminar on *Mathematics Teaching and Learning Enquiry Group*, Manchester, January, 1993. (http://www.grout.demon.co.uk/Barbara/chreods.htm)

Johnson, D.W., and Johnson, R.T. (1990). Social skills for successful group work. *Educational Leadership*, 47(4): 29-33.

Johnston, P.H. (1989). "Constructive Evaluation and Improvement of Teaching and Learning". *Instructors College Record,* 90(4): 509-28.

—— (1992). Constructive Evaluation of Literate Activity. *White Plains*, N.Y.: Longman.

Jonassen, D.H. (1990). Thinking technology: Towards a constructivist view of instructional design. *Educational Technology*, 30(9): 32-34.

—— (1991b). Objectivism Versus Constructivism: Do we need a new philosophical paradigm? *Educational Technology*, 39(3): 5-14.

Jonassen, D.H., Peck, K.I. and Wilson, B.G. (1999). *Learning with technology: A constructivist perspective.* NJ: Prentice Hall Inc.

Kavale, S. (1992). Postmodern Psychology: A contradiction in terms? In S. Kavale (Ed.), *Psychology and Postmodernism.* Newbury Park, CA: Sage.

Keene, E.O. and Zimmerman, S. (1997). *Mosaic of thought: Teaching comprehension in a reader's workshop.* New York: Heinemann.

Kim, J.S. (2005). The effects of a Constructivist teaching approach on student academic achievement, self-concept and learning strategies. *Asia Pacific Education Review*, 6(1): 7-19.

Kuhn, T.S. (1970). *The Structure of Scientific Revolution.* Chicago: University of Chicago Press (2nd Edition).

Ladson-Billings, G. (2001). *Crossing Over to Canaan: The Journey of New Teachers in Diverse Classrooms.* San Francisco: Jossey-Bass.

Lambert, L. (2003). *Leadership capacity for lasting school improvement.* Alexandria, VA: Association for Supervision and Curriculum Development.

Lanier, J.E., and Little, J.W. (1986). Research on teacher education. In M.C. Wittrock (Ed.), *Handbook of Research on Teaching* (3rd ed.). New York: Macmillan.

Lareau, A. (2000). *Home Advantage: Social Class and Parental Intervention in Elementary Education.* New York: Roman and Littlefield.

Lave, J. and Wenger, E. (1991). *Situated learning: Legitimate Peripheral Participation.* New York : Cambridge University Press.

Lee, S. Shuleman (1986). Paradigms and research programs for the study of teaching. In M.C. Wittrock (Ed.), *Handbook of research on teaching* (3rd ed.). New York: Macmillan.

Levine, M. (1996). Educating teachers for restructured schools. In F.B. Murray (Ed.), *The teacher educator's handbook: Building a knowledge base for the preparation of teachers* (pp. 620-47). San Francisco, CA: Jossey-Bass.

Lewis, A.C. (2002). School reform and professional development. *Phi Delta Kappan*, 83(1): 488-89.

Lieberman, A., and McLaughlin, M.W. (1992). Networks for educational change: Powerful and problematic. *Phi Delta Kappan*, 73(9): 673-77.

Lipman, P. (1999). *Race, class and power in school restructuring*. Albany, NY: State University of New York Press.

Little, J.W. (1993). Teacher's professional development in a climate of education reform. *Educational Evaluation and Policy Analysis*. 15(2): 129-51.

—— (1982). Norms of Collegiality and Experimentation: Workplace Conditions of School Success. *American Educational Research Journal*, 19: 325-40.

Loury, G. (2002). *The Anatomy of Racial Inequality*. Cambridge: Harvard University Press.

Mackinnon, A. and Scarff-Seatter, C. (1997). Constructivism: Contradictions and confusion in teacher education: In V. Richardson (Ed.), *Constructivist Teacher Education: Building New Understandings* (pp. 38-55), Washington D.C., Ealmer Press.

Mahapatra, M. and Mohapatra, J.K. (2008). Criteria for generating learning friendly classroom environment—Science teachers' perception under Indian conditions. *Indian Educational Review*, 44(2): 17-43.

Marjoribanks, K. (1979). *Families and their Learning Environments: An Empirical Analysis*. New York: Routledge and Kegan Paul.

Mathews, M.R. (1992). Old wine in new bottle: A problem with constructivist epistemology. Paper presented at the *National Association for Research in Science Teaching* (NARST) annual meeting. Cambridge, MA.

—— (1994). *Science teaching: The role of history and philosophy of science*. London: Routledge.

Mathews, W.J. (2003). Constructivism in the classroom: Epistemology, History and Empirical Evidence. *Teacher Education Quarterly*, Summer 2003.

McGrath, J.E. (1984). *Croups: Interaction and Performance*. Englewood Cliffs. N.I: Prentice Hall.

Mitchell, S. (Ed.) (2002). *Effective educational partnerships: Experts, advocates, and scouts*. Westport, CT: Praeger.

Moore, B.J. (1998). Situated cognition versus traditional cognitive theories of learning. *Education*, 119: 161-71.

Murray (Ed.). *The teacher educator's handbook: Building a knowledge base for the preparation of teachers* (pp. 465-505). San Francisco, CA: Jossey-Bass.

Murrell, P.C. (2001). *The community teacher: A new framework for effective urban teaching*. New York: Teachers College Press.

Negroni, P. (2002). A network of relationships. *Phi Delta Kappan*, 84(4): 284-85.

Neisser, U. (Ed.) (1998). *The rising curve: Long-term gains in 1Q and related measures*. Washington, DC: American Psychological Association.

Newmann, F.M. and Archbald, D.A. (1992). "The Nature of Authentic Academic Achievement." In H. Berlak et al. (Eds.), *Toward a New Science of Educational Testing and Assessment*. Albany: State University of New York.

Novak, J.D. and Gowin, D.B. (1984). *Learning how to learn*. Cambridge: Cambridge University Press.

Ogbu, J. (2003). *Black American Students in an Affluent Suburb: A Study of Academic Disengagement*. Mahwah: Lawrence Erlbaum.

Oldfather, P., Bonds, S. and Bray, T. (1994). Drawing the circle: Collaborative mind mapping as a process for developing a constructivist teacher education programme. *Teacher Education Quarterly*, 21(3): 5-13.

Osborne, J.F. (1996). Beyond constructivism. *Science Education*, Vol. 80: 53-82.

Patterson, J. (2001). *Brown v. Board of Education: A Civil Rights Milestone and It's Troubled Legacy*. New York: Oxford University Press.

Phillips, D.C. (1995). The good, the bad and the ugly: The many faces of constructivism. *Educational Researcher*, Vol. 24, pp. 5-12.

Piaget, J. (1967). *Six Psychological Studies*. New York: Vintage Books.

—— (1974). *To Understand is to Invent*. New York: Viking.

Plucker, J.A. (2002). Smart people or smart contexts? Cognition, ability, and talent development in an age of situated approaches to knowing and learning. *Educational Psychologist*, 37: 165-83.

Pritchard, F., and Ancess, J. (1999). The effects of professional development schools: A literature review. Washington, D.C.: U.S. *Department of Education, Office of Educational Research and Improvement*. (ERIC Document Reproduction Service No. ED448155)

Raven, J. (1992). A model of competence, motivation, and behaviour and a paradigm of assessment. In Toward a New Science of Educational Testing and Assessment. Albany, NY: SUNY Press.

Ravitch, D. and Viteritti, J. (Eds.) (2001). *Making Good Citizens: Education and Civil Society*. New Haven: Yale University Press.

Reich, Robert B. (1992). *The work of nations: Preparing ourselves for 21st century capitalism*. New York: Vintage Books.

Rentel, V.M. (1992, May). Preparing clinical faculty: Research on teacher reasoning. *Paper presented at a conference on faculty development*, Washington, DC.

Richardson, V. (1997). Constructivist teaching and teacher education: theory and practice. In V. Richardson (Ed.), *Constructivist teacher education: Building new understandings* (pp. 3-14). Washington, DC: Falmer Press.

Roderick, J.A. (1991). Context-Responsive Approaches to Assessing Children's Language, Urbana, III: National conference on Research in English.

Rothstein, R. (2002). *Out of Balance: Our Understanding of How Schools Affect Society and How Society Affects Schools*. Chicago: Spencer Foundation (30th Anniversary Essay).

Scardamalia, M. and Bereiter, C. (1991). Higher levels of agency for children in knowledge building: A challenge for the design of new knowledge media. *The Journal of the Learning Science*, Vol. 1, pp. 37-68.

Schnneider, B. (1987). Tracing the provenance of teacher education. In T. Popkewitz (Ed.), *Critical studies in teacher education: Its folklore, theory and practice* (pp. 211-41). New York, Falmer Press.

Scott, P. (1987). *Children learning in science project: A constructivist view of learning and teaching in science.* Leeds, England: University of Leeds. Centre for Studies in Science and Mathematics Education.

Seagal, L. (1986). *The dream of reality: Heinz von Foerster's Constructivism.* New York: Norton.

Searle, J.R. (1995). *The construction of social reality.* New York: Free Press.

Sessons, R. (1995). "Education is a Gift not a Commodity". Paper presented at the *National conference of the community colleges Humanities Association*, Washington, D.C.

Short, K.G. and Burke, C. (1991). *Creating Curriculum: Instructors and Students as a community of Learners.* Postsmouth, N.H.: Heinemann.

Shulman, I.S. (1987). Knowledge and teaching: Foundations of the new reform. *Harvard Educational Review*, Vol. 57, pp. 1-22.

Simmons, R. (1994). The Horse before the Cart: Assessing for understanding. *Educational Leadership*, 51(5): 22-23.

Sirotnik, K.A., and Goodlad, J.I. (Eds.) (1988). *School-university partnerships in action: Concepts, cases, and concerns.* New York: Teachers College Press.

Slavin, R.E. (1990). Research on cooperative learning: Consensus and controversy. *Educational Leadership*, 47(4): 52-55.

Smith, W.F., and Fenstermacher, G.D. (eds.) (1999). *Leadership for educational renewal: Developing a cadre of leaders.* San Francisco: Jossey-Bass.

Staver, J.R. (1998). Constructivism: Sound theory for explicating the practice of science and science teaching. *Journal of Research in Science Teaching*, 35(5): 501-20.

Steffy, B.E., Wolfe, M.P., Pasch, S.H., and Enz, B.J. (Eds.) (1999). *Life cycle of the career teacher.* Thousand Oaks, CA: Corwin Press.

Suarez-Orozco, C. and Suarez-Orozco, M. (2001). *Children of Immigration.* Cambridge: Harvard University Press.

Tatum, B.D. (1992). Talking about Race, Learning about Racism: The Application of Racial Identity Development Theory in the Classroom. *Harvard Educational Review*, 62: 1-24.

Teacher preparation, in-service teachers' professionalism, and children's achievement: Perceptions of in-service teachers. *Action in Teacher Education*, 22(3): 64-76.

Van Driel, J.H., Verloop, N. and de Vos, W. (1998). Developing Science teachers' pedagogical content knowledge. *Journal of Research in Science Teaching*, 35(6): 673-95.

Vaughan, W. (2002). Effects of cooperative learning on achievement and attitude among students of colour. *The Journal of Educational Research*, 95(6): 359-64.

Vico, G. (1710). *De Antiquissima Italarum Sapientia* (with translation by F.S. Promodoro, Stamperia de' Classici Latini, Naples, 1858).

von Glasersfeld, E. (1984). An Introduction to Radical Constructivism. In P. Watzlawick (Ed.), *The Invented Reality.* London: W.W. Naughton & Co.

—— (1989a). Cognition, construction of knowledge and teaching. *Synthese*, 80(1): 121-40.

—— (2006). http://Srri.nsm.umass.edu/vonGlasersfeld/onlinePapers/html/geneva/

—— (1989b). http://Srri.nsm.umass.edu/vonGlasersfeld/onlinePapers/html/117.html.

Vygotsky, L.S. (1962). *Thought and Language*. Cambridge, MA: MIT.

—— (1963). "Learning and Mental Development at School Age." In B. Simon and J. Simon (Ed.), *Educational Psychology in the U.S.S.R.* Stanford: Stanford University Press.

—— (1978). *Mind in Society*. Cambridge, MA: Harvard University Press.

Walker, D. (2002). Constructivist leadership: standards, equity, and learning-weaving whole cloth from multiple strands. In L. Lambert, D. Walker, D. Zimmerman, J. Cooper, M. Gardner, M.D. Lambert and M. Szabo (Eds.), *The Constructivist leader* (2nd ed.). New York: Teachers College Press.

Weade, R. and Green, J.L. (1989, March). Action research and the search for meaning. Paper presented at the *Annual Meeting of the American Educational Research Association*, San Francisco, CA.

Wells, G. (1994). *Changing Schools from Within*: Creating Communities of Inquiry. Portsmouth, NH: Heinemann.

Wilson, S.M., and Berne, J. (2001). Teacher learning and the acquisition of professional knowledge: An examination of research on contemporary professional development. In D. Boesel (Ed.), *Continuing professional development: Improving teacher quality: Imperative for educational reform* (pp. 19-50). Washington, D.C.: U.S. Department of Education, Office of Educational Research and Improvement. Retrieved July 16, 2003, from http://www.ericsp.org/pages/digests/ConProfDev.pdf

Wise, A.E., and Darling-Hammond, L. (1987). *Licensing teachers: Design for a profession*. Santa Monica, CA: RAND.

Wolf, D.P. (1990). "Assessment as an Episode of Learning". Paper presented at the *Conference of Constructive Response*, Princeton, N.J.

Wynne, J.T. (1999, April). The elephant in the living room: Racism in school reform. Paper presented at the *Annual meeting of the American Educational Research Association*, Montreal, Canada. (ERIC Document Reproduction Service No. ED436614)

Zacchei, D.A., and Mirman, J.A. (1986). *Business-Education Partnerships: Strategies for School Improvement*. Andover, Mass.: Regional Laboratory for Educational Improvement.

Zeichner, K.M., and Noffke, S.E. (2001). Practitioner research. In V. Richardson (Ed.), *Handbook of research on teaching* (4th ed., pp. 298-330). Washington, DC: American Educational Research Association.

Zimmerman, J. (2002). *Whose America: Culture Wars in the Public Schools*. Cambridge: Harvard University Press.

9 Beyond Constructivism

9.1 Introduction

Over the years, constructivist thinking has permeated many diverse fields such as art, history, communication, ethnology, industrial management, law, linguistics, and psychotherapy, etc. Constructivism has also enjoyed considerable success in the domains of science and mathematics education. It has been instrumental in generating a considerable amount of research based empirical data (e.g. Irzik, 2001), which has led to a greater understanding of the characteristics of learner, the process of learning, and the general problems of teaching learning (e.g. Solomon, 1994). The many advantages/positive outcomes of constructivism including innovative pedagogical strategies have been discussed in the previous chapters of the present book. In spite of the successes, constructivism is said to have a number of shortcomings which have been viewed rather seriously by experts (e.g. Suchting, 1992; Matthews, 1992, 1994; Phillips, 1995; Osborne, 1996; Kozloff, 1998; McCarty and Schwandt, 2000; Fox, 2001; Meyer, 2009; Rickert, 2009; Rowlands and Carson, 2009) although some of them do acknowledge the usefulness of constructivism. Those who oppose constructivism have come to be known as 'realists'. Proponents as well as supporters of constructivism in their turn have tried to answer the critics (e.g. Glasersfeld, 1992; Staver, 1998; Quale, 2010).

As we have seen in Chapter 2 of the present book, there is a large variety of constructivism available in the literature. Though the commonly used term *constructivism* is a generic name, it appears to be strongly influenced by the two major varieties: *radical constructivism*, and *social constructivism*.

The former is also sometimes called *cognitive constructivism*, or *personal constructivism* and the latter *realist constructivism* (Liu and Matthews, 2005). However, in our discussion we shall use their more familiar names, radical constructivism, and social constructivism respectively.

In this chapter, the last one of the book, we shall first have a glimpse of the overall criticism of constructivism (section 9.2) before taking a look at the main controversies associated with constructivism in general, and its radical and social versions in particular and how some researchers have attempted to address them (section 9.3). We shall also speculate what might lie beyond constructivism in the rapidly evolving teaching learning scenario (section 9.4). Section 9.5 contains our conclusion along with a flow-chart summary (Fig. 9.1) of the various controversies that we have discussed. To facilitate the understanding of general readers/non-experts, appropriate meanings of typical terms associated with constructivism have been given at the end (Appendix).

Though a considerable amount of literature exists concerning the pros and cons of constructivism, we only consider a small sample of the same here. We shall also avoid delving into deep philosophical dimensions of the arguments involved. In order to minimize the problem inherent in the process of paraphrasing and with a view to retain the authenticity of arguments and counter-arguments, we shall try to quote the authors, sometimes directly and sometimes through other authors.

9.2 A First Account of Criticism

Before going on to review the various charges levelled against constructivism in general and radical constructivism and social constructivism in particular, let us note a few overall critical perceptions, which may often be considered as unkind to the supporters of constructivism. We hope these initial observations will make the reader more interested in the various controversial issues involving constructivism, to be presented later.

The main points of criticism of constructivism may be stated in the following form (Staver, 1998): (i) constructivism is a flawed instrumental epistemology; (ii) it leads to subjectivism, relativism, and solipsism; (iii) it fails to break away from a traditional empiricist view; and (iv) it does not accurately portray the practice of science.

Matthews (1995: 125) opined that in constructivist epistemology,

> knowledge is degraded to whatever makes sense to you, or whatever suits your person or class interest.

It has been also alleged that constructivism does not recognize its own shortcomings, which is reflected in the following statement by Osborne (1996):

> The failure of constructivism to recognize its own limitations has led to it enjoying a hegemony in the research community which is undeserved.

Continuing, let us quote from an article titled 'Constructivism in Education: Sophistry for a New Age' by Kozloff (1998) (the emphasis marked by **bold** fonts here and in subsequent quotations is due to Kozloff):

> "Even a cursory reading of Ernst von Glasersfeld, Brian Cambourne, Jacqueline Brooks, Catherine Fosnot and other 25 watt illuminaries reveals their ignorance and/or misrepresentation of their created foe." The foe here refers to instructivism.
>
> **"Constructivist "philosophy", research, and pedagogy rest almost entirely on fanciful presumptions about learning."**
>
> **"Constructivist "theory" is a mishmash of overlapping platitudes and absurdities—"empty words and poetic metaphors"** (Aristotle, *Metaphysics*). Taken separately, constructivist "propositions" are merely simpleminded. Taken together, they are indistinguishable from the verbal behavior of a person suffering from chronic schizophrenia."
>
> **"Of course, the claim that truth is relative ought to put an end to constructivism as a serious contender for anyone's attention."**

"…a case can be made that constructivists' inability to be concrete, means that constructivists literally do not know what (behavior, learning, meaning, knowledge, construction) they are talking about."

"Constructivist's empty talk about knowledge construction is easily revealed."

"Constructivist writing is laced with informal fallacies identified by logicians–"

"Constructivism is perhaps best seen as the anarchical utopianism of a socially privileged class (academics) fueled by fake neo-Romantic sentimentality."

"Constructivists are at least consistent in one regard. They do not "evaluate", "judge", and reject their own "theory (interpretation) of learning" and constructivist pedagogy on the basis of hard data, experimentation, and logic, any more than they expect students to submit their interpretations to verification by traditional methods."

"….However, judging by book sales, speaker engagements, and teacher training programs, **constructivists have turned skillful duplicity and smarmy pseudo-liberationist cant into a thriving industry accountable to no one.**"

"Would an x-ray "showing" a large mass in a constructivist's lung be seen by the constructivist as merely the radiologist's construction (idea)? In other words, when it comes to serious (personal) matters, constructivists suddenly reveal that they see the world as real (out there) enough, and that they want to hear statements that are true, not a physician's "construction"."

Kozloff has of course tried to justify his allegations with observations and arguments drawn from various authors. Some of his observations are derived from Suchting (1992) wherein the latter examined von Glasersfeld's doctrine of constructivism (1989) in a paper titled 'Constructivism deconstructed'. Suchting's main finding is

> "that the basic concepts and theses of constructivism are, mostly, at best very obscure, that there is very little argument involved, and that where there is it is quite unsatisfactory."

Von Glasersfeld (1992), of course, published his reply to Suchting in quick time (in the next issue of the same journal) in a paper called 'Constructivism reconstructed: A reply to Suchting' in which he points out the lacunae in Suchting's process of 'deconstruction', Suchting's futile attempt to prove that constructivists dabble with a correspondence theory of truth, Suchting's misrepresentation of the term 'knowledge' used by von Glasersfeld, etc.

In 1998, M.R. Matthews edited a volume titled *Constructivism in Science Education: A Philosophical Examination*. It had a number of articles giving a critical appraisal of constructivism in science education and philosophy including that of Suchting referred to above. This work was reviewed by Irzik (2001) who considers that "the critical articles in *Constructivism in Science Education* present a penetrating attack against constructivism both in science education and in philosophy". In course of the review Irzik discusses a taxonomy of constructivism which includes varieties such as cognitive constructivism, epistemic constructivism, semantic constructivism, and metaphysical constructivism. Some of the concluding remarks of Irzik (2001) are:

> Once the ontological, epistemological and semantical claims of constructivism are differentiated and made explicit, I believe that their weaknesses, flaws and limitations become apparent both in themselves and in terms of their implications for science education. At least this is the overall message I received reading *Constructivism in Science Education*. It seems to me that with the exception of noncontroversial cognitive constructivism, there is little to be gained by the existing constructivist theory and pedagogy. I urge the science educators, especially those who have constructivist inclinations, to read this book. For I claim that once

> they give it the serious consideration that it well deserves, they will start thinking differently about constructivism.

In an appreciative commentary on the abovementioned review paper of Irzik, Matthews (2001) made a scathing remark implying that most science educators and researchers including constructivists lack even the working knowledge of philosophy, which might be the reason for the weaknesses of constructivism. Let us quote a sample from Matthews (2001):

> The most influential constructivists in science education—Ernst von Glasersfeld, Rosalind Driver, and others—have little, or no, training in philosophy, yet their work is replete with philosophical claims, allusions and arguments. Von Glasersfeld is quite frank about having no formal training and being an autodidact in the subject. It is not surprising then that research literature is full of conceptual confusions and non-sequiturs. Irzik in his review has drawn attention to a number of the endemic ones: the confusion of epistemological questions with psychological ones; the casual substitution of 'belief' for 'knowledge'; the confusion of semantic with psychological issues; the illogical move from fallibilism to relativism; the incorrect identification of realist epistemology with didactic pedagogy; the conflation of representative realism with modest realism; and so on. The late Rosalind Driver, in one publication, made the breath-taking claim that 'The authority for truth lies within each of us.' One cannot imagine anyone who has completed even first year philosophy saying such a thing. Yet it was written, and it influences hundreds of research students.
>
> Not only do conceptual confusions and non-sequiturs abound, but also gross distortions of the history of philosophy are commonplace in constructivist writing. In other publications I have attempted to show how the basic tenets of educational constructivism (we know only our experimental world, knowledge of the

> real is beyond our capacity, knowledge is individually constructed), when added together, actually define philosophical positivism—the supposed *bête noire* of constructivism!

In another critique, Meyer (2009) observes that the

> "basic assumptions of constructivism are flawed" and that
>
> "the implications of constructivism for future generations may be both profound and non-benign".

The level of misunderstanding of constructivism may be gauged by an observation made by a pre-service student teacher, as reported by Garbett (2011: 38) with reference to a work by Korthagen and Lunenberg (2004):

> Constructivist has taught me I do not need to know any science in order to teach it. I will simply allow my students to figure things out for themselves, for I know that there is no right answer.

With the above observations forming a kind of backdrop, we shall now take a closer look at the main controversies surrounding constructivism.

9.3 The Controversies

The allegations against constructivism and the corresponding replies may be broadly classified into the following issue based categories though we realize that these cannot be put in watertight compartments. We shall include observations on radical constructivism and social constructivism in the following sub-sections and sub-sub-sections. The scheme of our presentation is depicted in a flow-chart in Fig. 9.1.

9.3.1 Constructivism vs. Instructivism

Let us start with the issue of constructivist vs. instructivist (behaviourist) approach to teaching learning process, which is still a matter of debate, though root of constructivism may be traced to the education community's disenchantment with instructivism. We shall mostly refer to the website http://

inclusionclub.s3.amazonaws.com/learning_theory.pdf for the following discussion.

The dynamic principles underlying constructivism (sometimes called *progressivism*), whose origins are credited to such luminaries as Dewey ('experience through action', 'emphasis on situated learning'), Piaget ('stages of cognitive development', 'internal motivation', 'spiral curriculum'), Vygotsky ('social context of learning', 'collaborative learning', 'student centeredness'), and von Glasersfeld ('radical constructivism') may be summarized as:

- The focus of education should be on the learner who constructs her own knowledge.
- Teacher plays the role of a facilitator by providing necessary situations and resources.
- There is no entity called knowledge, lying out there to be acquired, apart from the constructed experiences of the learners or communities of learners.

The general components of constructivism include *metacognition*, *active learning*, *contextual learning*, *collaborative learning*, *spiral curriculum*, and *authentic assessment*.

On the other hand, the dynamic principles underlying instructivism (sometimes called *objectivism*) whose foundations are ascribed to great names such as Skinner ('stimulus response theory', 'behaviourism'), Merrill ('programmed instruction'), and Carrol ('pacing', 'grouping', 'teacher centeredness') may be written down as follows:

- An external reality exists and the objective of learning is to reach it.
- Teachers primarily control the process of teaching learning using the general principles of psychology and instruction.
- Education results in changes in the behaviour (learning) of the learner.

Some of the components of instructivism are: functional relationships between learners, teachers, and learning materials, precision teaching, mastery learning, and standardized assessment.

It may be pointed out that instructivist's idea of teaching learning is *not* the same thing as the one comprising reading and lecture only; it rather includes more beneficial strategies such as precision teaching, and mastery learning.

A specially designed direct instruction (DI) model developed by S. Engelmann and W. Becker was tried out quite successfully in the USA in perhaps the biggest ever education initiative called 'Project Follow-Through' spanning the period 1967-95 and involving almost 700,000 students at the cost of $ 1 billion (http://www.projectpro.com/icr/research/di/summary.htm). The main objective of the project was to reduce the disparity between the low and high achievers by improving the performance of the former. The DI model involved highly structured and elaborately specified instruction, high degree of pupil-teacher interaction with feedback mechanism, behavioural practices, and mastery learning. The basic guiding principle was, 'anything presumed to be learned by students must first be taught by the teacher'. The results showed that the students did much better in the domains of basic skills, cognitive-conceptual skills, and affective/cognitive skills when the DI scheme was used than when constructivist methods were used.

Muthukrishna et al. (1993) claim that in the domain of earth sciences, an approach based on explicit instruction with a laser videodisc could eliminate alternative frameworks of students to the extent of more than 90 per cent compared to 28-69 per cent success rates achieved by others who addressed the alternative frameworks directly. They concluded that the

> common hypothesis that meaningful learning cannot result from explicit instruction may possibly be an overstatement.

It may be noted that alternative frameworks of learners constitute a central theme of constructivist pedagogy. We shall see more of this later.

Notwithstanding the success of instructivism, it is slowly yielding place to constructivism which is supposed to be more conducive to meaningful learning. Brooks and Brooks (1993) for instance observe:

> A constructivist framework challenges teachers to create environments in which they and their students are encouraged to think and explore. This is a formidable challenge. But to do otherwise is to perpetuate the ever-present behavioural approach to teaching and learning.

But the constructivism vs. instructivism debate is still alive. For example, Rickert (2009) contends:

> Within the field of education, the question arises, whether children's "ways of knowing" should be considered formative for the classroom and curriculum or whether classroom or curriculum should form the student's "ways of knowing". Essentially the question is reduced to asking whether history, academic fields, and culture should be instructive of the student (an objectivist approach), or whether the student should fit these ideas into his or her thinking to transform information (a constructivist approach). The answer is determined by one's presuppositions not only about the nature of truth, but also by the current understanding of how learning occurs. The first part is philosophical, the second is functional.

Kozloff (1998) (referred to above) joins the debate by observing that:

> **Constructivist writing typically begins with an intellectually dishonest and shallow critique of the "instructivist" (Finn and Ravitch, 1996)—sometimes called "behavioural"—approach.**
>
> Even a survey-level understanding of the instructivist approach and its history enables one to see the constructivist critique as an **inept caricature that reveals constructivists' stunning ignorance** of the approach whose alleged failings constructivists claim to remedy, or **outright manipulation** of naïve consumers by withholding information.

Also, constructivist's dismissal of the role and importance of such processes as passive perception, and memorization and activities as demonstrating, showing, or telling in knowledge acquisition has been criticized on the ground that students are not likely to gain the understanding of a scientist without them (e.g. Osborne, 1996). In the domain of mathematics education, Rowlands and Carson (2009) observe:

> Constructivism seems to be the anxiety not to transmit anything. Yet concepts have to be defined, explained, elaborated, etc. if there is to be a 'cognitive response' to what is taught. We would argue that the fundamental question for mathematics educationalists has to be 'what is the best way to enable a class to understand—to make their own—a framework of concepts that constitutes the subject-matter'? By 'understand' we mean in the manner of Skemp's (1971) relational understanding of mathematics as a body of knowledge.

Related to the above observations is the question, how about the knowledge constructed by others previously and accepted as authentic? Should it not be considered as a referent for the current learners? Do we want the learners to construct/discover it all on their own initiative? It is difficult to visualize how children can construct the history and civilizations of a bygone era, or geography of different regions of the world, or the life histories of great personalities without being told about them. These are some of the points raised by those who do not favour constructivism. Another observation derived from research studies on learning styles (Pask, 1976; Entwistle, 1981; Kempa and Martin-Diaz, 1990a, 1990b) is that different categories of students prefer different approaches including self-learning as well as didactic (intended to convey instruction and information) teaching. As constructivism values learner autonomy, it needs to accommodate their diverse learning styles.

It goes without saying that basically learners do build up or construct their knowledge edifices both in instructivist and constructivist scenarios (this is called trivial constructivism as we shall see later) though details of the processes involved may differ. Also, a constructivist learner demonstrates changes in behaviour, overtly as well as covertly, owing to changes in her knowledge structure. Even a constructivist class cannot begin without some amount of instruction from the teacher. It is difficult to imagine practical classes or laboratory sessions where the teacher leaves the students without instructions. On the home front, most of our childhood learning is based on instructions which are meant to facilitate the entry of the young ones to the world in general. Everyday life of most men and women, scientists included, is influenced by religious practices, which often amount to following certain instructions. In case of physical ailments we need to follow the advice and instruction of the doctor. In a civil society citizens are supposed to follow rules, regulations, and guidelines framed by the authorities from time to time. Manufacturers warn the customers not to start using a new gadget/appliance without first going through the relevant instruction manual. Thus, the role of instruction in our everyday life cannot be ignored or trivialized.

Further, in the present age of e-learning, online courses, and workplace learning, instructivism and constructivism both are relevant and they coexist with a new mode of learning called connectivism (e.g. Tracey, 2011). For example, a new employee to an organization initially needs to be instructed by a supervisor on bare essentials before she can take advantage of constructivism and connectivism in her work. Here, 'connectivism' amounts to building a network of knowledge sources and accessing them when needed. This is considered to be important as it is not possible to know everything in this digital era with a huge abundance of ever changing information. Further, in recent years, the various tenets of constructivism *vis-à-vis* instructivism have come under scrutiny for designing of online learning resources and environments (e.g. Dalgarno et al., 2010).

9.3.2 Cognitive Issues

There is a central cognitive aspect on which constructivists and realists agree (e.g. Osborne, 1996; Irzik, 2001) according to which cognition comprises mental representations which are not passively received but actively constructed by individuals as members of a community through mutual interactions. This is called trivial constructivism (Glasersfeld, 1995) and is supported by the fact that learning basically amounts to construction of knowledge in instructivism as well as constructivism although the details involved may differ.

9.3.3 Epistemological/Philosophical Issues

Under this heading we propose to discuss the following aspects of constructivism in general and radical constructivism and social constructivism in particular.

9.3.3.1 Is constructivism a theory?

Recognizing that *epistemology* basically means 'theory of knowledge' we may start with the question, 'Is constructivism a theory?' The answer seems to vary. According to Fosnot (1996), constructivism is both a 'paradigm' as well as a 'theory'. Osborne (1996) says that as a theoretical referent (Tobins and Tippins, 1993) constructivism "suffers from a flawed instrumental epistemology which is a misrepresentation of the views and practice of science and scientists" and that "it offers no guidance on adjudication between theories". According to Staver (1998), "constructivism is a sound theory with which to explain the practice of science and science pedagogy". Irzik (2001) observes that constructivism in science education is essentially a 'theory of learning (knowing) and teaching'. Rowlands and Carson (2009) opine that constructivism, which encompasses ethics, politics, ethnography, and curriculum design and development, is 'more a belief system than it is a theory'. In another view, constructivism is the dominant 'theoretical paradigm associated with teaching and learning today' (Dalgarno et al., 2010). Perhaps the existence of a large variety of constructivism (see Chapter 2 of the present book) is not favourable to a unique theoretical status of constructivism. Another important point is, unlike most scientific theories, constructivism does not prescribe a set of rules or activities to be followed in a classroom though several constructivist teaching learning models are available in the literature (see Chapter 6 of the present book). There is of course no single/unique constructivist approach to teaching learning; it is primarily context specific.

9.3.3.2 The critique of radical constructivism

The center of criticism of constructivism by realists is radical constructivism. Let us therefore start with the main ideas of radical constructivism. The radical constructivist epistemology, which was formulated by von Glasersfeld, has been discussed in some detail in Chapter 2 of the present book. However, it may be worthwhile to recount the basic tenets here (Glasersfeld, 1995: 51; as quoted in Irzik, 2001 and Rowlands and Carson, 2009):

1a. Knowledge is not passively received either through the senses or by way of communication;

1b. Knowledge is actively built up by the cognizing subject.

2a. The function of cognition is adaptive, in the biological sense of the term, tending towards fit or viability;

2b. Cognition serves the subject's organization of the experiential world, not the discovery of an objective ontological reality.

E. von Glasersfeld considers radical constructivism as a 'theory of learning and knowledge' (von Glasersfeld, 1995), whereas others view it as a 'theory of epistemic and ontological relativism' (e.g. Quale, 2010) on account of its implications. The stipulations 1a and 1b together constitute the familiar trivial constructivism, which is said to be non-controversial and accepted by the realists. E. von Glasersfeld recognized the importance of social interaction in the construction of knowledge by individuals. The concepts of fit and viability are similar to those in the theory of evolution of species: only the fit or viable ones survive. E. von Glasersfeld coined the term 'radical' because his constructivism rejected the traditional philosophical materialism/realism. The other terms used by von Glasersfeld, which became the bone of contention along with their interpretations and implications include construction, knowledge, viability, and objective ontological reality. These in turn are said to lead to the ideas of relativism, anything goes, solipsism, etc. which are also criticized vehemently.

In the context of natural science, Quale (2010) categorizes the objections against radical constructivism (RC) under the following four headings before attempting to refute them.

1. *existential* – the charge of solipsism;
2. *logical* – allegations of self-refutation;
3. *social/moral* – the claims that RC supports reactionary social and political structures;
4. *ontological* – the "miraculous match" that is sometimes claimed to be manifest between science and the experiential world.

Here, however, we shall take a look at a few of the many criticisms available in the literature along the following lines centered around the various concepts inherent in or implied by the pronouncements of radical constructivism.

I. *The question of construction*

It is alleged by the critiques of constructivism (including radical constructivism) that what constructivists mean by *construction*, the central idea of constructivism, is not clear. Kozloff (1998), for example, poses:

> ...one does not know what counts as knowledge, construction, experience or meaning. For example, what processes are signified by the word "construct"? When does this constructing occur? Before we think? Before we act? Afterwards? And does this not lead to an infinite regression? That is, when do we construct the tools by which we construct knowledge? And how could we possibly do so? Such constructing would require an even more primitive tool-tool constructing process. But if it is claimed that we are somehow taught the tools for constructing knowledge, or that we come equipped with them then that invalidates the major premise that we construct knowledge—for surely, the tools for constructing knowledge world have to count as knowledge.

Schmidt (2010) poses another version of the question related to construction:

> Does "construction" solely denote cognitive processes, or are material constructions also included? What are the presuppositions and regulations of constructions

and what are the criteria for success or failure? To what degree must constructions be performed consciously, and must actors be able to report on their constructions consciously?

As discussed later on, constructivists do distinguish between knowledge, construction, and experience. The tools to be used for knowledge construction are based on the experience and choice of the constructor. Radical constructivism assigns the entire responsibility of construction to the constructor of knowledge or the knower herself. It is possible for the constructor to build several constructs out of which she is likely to retain the one which is in consonance with her experience. Radical constructivism being a theory of learning that deals with mental representations, material construction as such is not in its purview. However, the constructor has the freedom to use material objects for construction of knowledge.

II. *The question of truth, objective ontological reality, viability, relativism, etc.*

'What ought to be the nature of knowledge *vis-à-vis* truth' appears to be the central issue of controversy between constructivists and realists. Epistemologists are in general concerned with two views of truth (Staver, 1998; Quale, 2010):

(i) *Truth as correspondence*: In order to appreciate the meaning and ramification of this version of truth, we shall directly quote from Mautner (2010: 627): "The oldest theory is the Correspondence Theory. Aristotle's early formulation in *Metaphysics* 1077^b26 was: 'to say of what is that it is, or of what is not that it is not, is true'. Contemporary versions phrase it as '"p" is true if and only if p'. The intervening period usually preferred to hold that something is true if it corresponds with something else. Controversy about the theory has usually been three-fold: what is it that is true—is it a belief, proposition, statement, sentence, or what?; what is it that this corresponds with—is it a state of affairs, situation, reality, fact, or what?; and what exactly is the relation called 'correspondence' between what is true and what makes it true?"

(ii) *Truth as coherence*: We shall again quote from Mautner (2010: 627): "According to the Coherence Theory the truth of a proposition consists in its being part of a comprehensive system in which it (according to certain idealist theories) entails every other proposition, or (according to certain positivist theories) it is consistent with every other proposition. For the rationalists the system constitutes the whole of reality; for some logical positivists it is the system accepted by contemporary scientists."

We note that the first view (truth as correspondence) assumes the existence of objective ontological reality. [*Ontology*: (Gr, *on*, being + logos, logic). The theory of being (Runes, 1960: 219).] Radical constructivism ignores the first view and chooses to consider knowledge as a coherent system that is actively built up by the constructor of knowledge (radical constructivism tenets 2b and 2a above). Staver (1998) attempts to justify this stand of constructivists by referring to what is called *root paradox* of the ancient Greek philosophy. According to Staver (1998):

> Put simply, the so-called root paradox holds that we humans, individually or collectively, possess but a single lens, that of experience, with which we can learn of the world about us. To independently check any knowledge claim, we, individually or collectively, must check it through a lens independent of experience.

It thus follows that we can claim our knowledge, gathered through experience, to correspond to objective ontological reality only if we can verify it in another way which is independent of experience. This apparently has not happened over the last several thousand years since the original Greek proposal, thereby leaving the root paradox unresolved. This, according to Staver (1998), has led constructivists to ignore the question of objective ontological reality and go for coherence. It may be recognized that for theory/model building in science, internal consistency is of primary importance.

Thus the assertions of radical constructivism imply that the knowledge constructed by an individual does not have to represent the reality or truth but needs to be viable or fit with the knower's experience. The requirement of viability implies that any viable construction is acceptable, which in turn makes knowledge relative and leads to the idea of relativist ontology. As regards 'realism' in science, Osborne (1996) gives a nice review by referring to authorities like Harre and others. He quotes Matthews's argument (1994): "*Modest realism* is enough to go on with, and it is incompatible with constructivism." According to modest realism, scientists do not ask, "Are statements of this theory true or false?" but instead ask, "Do things, properties, processes of this sort exist?" and do their best within human limitations to find exemplars (Osborne, 1996). Modest realism recognizes the existence of an ontological reality and believes that scientific theories lead us progressively towards it. It is further contended that since modest realism implies verification of knowledge claims against reality, it goes against the relativist criterion of radical constructivism according to which any viable theory resulting from personal experience is valid. It is said that whereas modest realism suggests which aspects/contents of science should or should not be included in a curriculum, constructivism is silent about it. However, it may be worthwhile to recall what von Glasersfeld had said in the area of training, learning, and curriculum (Glasersfeld, 1986):

> It would help to separate the acquisition of skills, i.e. patterns of action, from the active construction of viable conceptual networks, i.e. understanding. Hence it would encourage educators to clarify the particular goals they want to attain. Curricula could be designed with more internal coherence and, consequently, would be more effective, once they deliberately separated the task of achieving a certain level of performance in a skill from that of generating conceptual understanding within a given problem area. There is no question that the old stand-bys "rote learning" and "repeated practice" have their value in training, but it is naïve to expect that they must also generate understanding.

Though realists such as Osborne (1996) consider relativism as a weak point of the constructivist epistemology, there are other realists such as Searle (1995) who accept relativity arguing that it is consistent with realism. Needless to say, modern physics has embraced relativity in an essential way in its theoretical framework, thanks to Einstein, perhaps the greatest scientist of the twentieth century.

Rickert (2009) compares the positions of *naïve realism* and *creative anti-realism* on the basis of Naugle's work (2002: 322-24) to clarify the stand of radical constructivism on the issue of realism and relativism. Rickert's observations are as follows:

"*Naïve Realism*

1. an objective, independent reality exists;
2. the character of this reality is fixed and independent of any observer;
3. human knowers have trustworthy cognitive capacities by which to apprehend this fixed reality unencumbered by personal prejudices and traditions;
4. truth and knowledge about the world are discovered and certain, not invented and relative.

Creative Anti-Realism

1. while an external world may, and probably does exist, its objective character remains forever obscure;
2. human knowers lack epistemic access to apprehend the world as it is in itself;
3. what poses as reality is linguistically constructed, an idealistic product of the human mind;
4. consequently, truth and knowledge about the world are not discovered and certain, but invented and relative."

The tenets of creative anti-realism as given above are similar to those of radical constructivism; in fact, some criticisms of the latter can be countered by the tenets of the former.

III. *The question of personal construct*

The requirement of viability seems to imply that the learner or the constructor of knowledge is never wrong. Some allege that constructivists' confusion of knowledge with belief and substitution of truth by viability imply that they "have lost the idea of a right and wrong answer in science and science education" (Irzik, 2001). In this connection, Osborne (1996) cites an example:

> ...the child's common conception that the sun moves round the earth clearly satisfies the radical constructivist's epistemological criteria that it is both viable and fits with experience.

Let us recognize that this is an example of personal construct or alternative conception of the child, which is just opposite of the accepted empirical fact. Though the child's idea fits with her everyday observation, i.e. it is valid in her cognitive framework, it is the duty of the elders including the teachers to make the child modify the notion using suitable means. Talking a little more about personal constructs, which play a central role in constructivism, even adults are known to have common sense ideas which are widely different from the standard or accepted knowledge, and they live comfortably with them without any apparent harm. As an example, let us quote from a survey based article titled "That's Incredible" published in a recent issue of the widely circulated and popular magazine, *Reader's Digest* (Caporimo et al., 2013):

> 20 percent of people polled think that the sun revolves around the earth.
>
> Less than half (47 percent) of them don't know how long it takes the earth to revolve around the sun. We'll give you 365 guesses.

Let us make a couple of guesses regarding the above findings of the survey. (i) Most likely, no other persons or sources of information have given the respondents these ideas explicitly. (ii) Even if they went through normal classroom processes, these ideas persisted with them most likely because these were not discovered and addressed by the teachers.

Personal constructs by individual learners are accepted in radical constructivism as a matter of fact, which makes knowledge true or false depending upon the learners. Thus the concept of true/false becomes relative. But, then through interpersonal communication which is allowed in constructivism, it is possible to refer to the established knowledge base (as in science for example) and decide the truth or falsity of a personal construct. Constructivist pedagogy says that it is most important for the teacher to discover and address learners' personal constructs or alternative conceptions to make teaching learning meaningful. In this connection, it may be worthwhile to recount the famous Ausubelian dictum (Ausubel, 1968):

> If I had to reduce all of educational psychology to just one principle, I would say this: The most important single factor influencing learning is what the learner already knows. Ascertain this and teach him accordingly.

This has been found to be a useful approach to teaching learning by many (e.g. Garbett, 2011).

IV. *The question of solipsism*

Another charge against constructivists is that they are *solipsists* as they choose to ignore the existence of ontological reality and give primacy to one's own perception. Staver (1998) refers to Lacey (1996) on the concept of solipsism, according to which, 'Solipsism is the view that nothing exists, or can be shown to exist, beyond one's own mind.' Stated differently, 'there is no good reason to believe that anything exists other than oneself' (Ahmad, 2008: 478). This has led some critiques to declare that constructivists believe everything outside one's consciousness to be only one's imagination. However, some realists such as Osborne (1996) and Steffe (1999) deny this charge. Staver (1998) tries to justify why solipsism does not apply to constructivism with the help of von Foerster's *postulate of relativity* (Foerster, 1984) according to which "a hypothesis that holds for *A* and holds for *B* will be rejected if it does not hold for *A* and *B* together". Staver then describes von Foerster's way of rejecting solipsism, which may be expressed in the following way: Suppose a person *P* is a solipsist. Therefore, *P* considers her consciousness to be the only reality and the rest of the world exists in *P*'s imagination, which includes another person *Q*. Granting that *Q* is also a solipsist, *Q*'s imagination may include other persons one of whom may be *P* herself. This leads to a dilemma that every person who is solipsist has real as well as imaginary existence at the same time. Another form of the dilemma is that each solipsist is a sole reality. The dilemma can be resolved by applying von Foerster's postulate of relativity to the persons P and Q. Thus, the conclusion is, individuals are not solipsists and a world exists outside individual consciousness. It follows that constructivists are not solipsists and though they are silent about ontology, they do not deny the existence of a world beyond their perceptions. This is how Staver (1998) exonerates constructivism of the charge of solipsism.

Quale (2010) talks about two kinds of solipsism: (i) *ontological solipsism*, "defined as the view that *nothing exists* outside one's own self and the contents of one's own mind", and (ii) *epistemological solipsism*, "which holds that *nothing can be known* except one's own self and mind". He claims that ontological solipsism does not exist in radical constructivism and, though epistemological solipsism exists in radical constructivism, it poses no problem. He refutes the charge of ontological solipsism by analyzing a point raised by McCarthy and Schwandt (2000) according to which if solipsism were true then a person has no way of knowing that there is a world outside his consciousness. Quale (2010) addresses this serious problem by stating that radical constructivism does not deny the existence of world outside our consciousness. According to him, one of the fundamental ontological premises of radical constructivism is that "the world is indeed there, not as a territory to be discovered and mapped, but as a shared resource for individual learners/knowers to experience and construct their knowledge of". He rejects the ontological solipsist fallacy on the basis of this assertion. Quale (2010) further says that though the world is shared by individuals, their individual experience/knowledge of the world constructed by them individually is not shared. This leads to the question as to how one's knowledge can be shared with another person. The problem is resolved by Quale (2008, 2010) by asserting that "Knowledge may be considered to be shared between two persons only in so far as *they can agree that they share it*, i.e. to the extent that their actions with respect to this knowledge are at best compatible." Thus, though radical constructivism allows epistemological solipsism, it is not a problematic issue as interpersonal sharing is allowed and this sharing may lead to changes in the persons' experiences. This of course presupposes that the persons involved interact with each other using a common language. Teaching is a good example of this state of affairs. The 'world' in this case becomes the collection of knowledge available till date generated through construction, negotiation, and social acceptance, etc.

V. *The question of self-refutation*

Self-refutation is an interesting allegation often made against radical constructivism. Self-refutation means falsifying one's own position or proposition. To give an example, "I don't speak the truth" is a self-refuting statement. This is because if the speaker is indeed a liar, her statement makes her truthful, and if she is actually speaking the truth, the statement makes her a liar! Quale (2010) recognizes that the charge of self-refutation on radical constructivism is of two types: (i) *logical self-refutation*, and (ii) *epistemic self-refutation* and attempts to refute them both.

The charge of logical self-refutation concerns the basic claim of radical constructivism (RC): 'There is no true knowledge.' This statement is self-refuting as explained above, which implies that the theory of radical constructivism cannot be right! However, Quale (2010) argues against this kind of allegation through the following observation:

> RC does not claim to represent "truth", neither in a logical nor an ontological sense. In other words, the theory of RC is not regarded as a set of logical propositions, each having a binary truth value (i.e. *true* XOR *false*) to be deduced from an axiomatic base; and (more importantly) this theory does *not* pretend to give an objectively true representation of "the way the world is"!

The concept of relativism accepted by radical constructivism makes the truth value of a proposition dependent upon context. Hence, the propositions of radical constructivism cannot be categorized as either true or false. The conclusion is that radical constructivism is *not* logically self-refuting.

Epistemic self-refutation implies that if a proposition is considered to be true by one person and false by another person, then the two perceptions of true knowledge ought to be mutually incompatible. This position holds if one accepts the correspondence theory of truth, as stated above: how can the same proposition describing the same reality have two truth values, true and false? In order to solve the problem, Quale (2010) points out that radical constructivism rejects the correspondence theory of truth and accepts the coherence theory of truth which implies that propositions can be considered to be true or false depending upon the context. Therefore, when two persons perceive the same proposition differently, it only means that their knowledge of the proposition is based on different contexts that are mutually incompatible. Quale then illustrates the context dependence of propositions with examples from mathematics, science, and religion, which in turn justifies the viability requirement of radical constructivism.

VI. *The question of dualism*

Constructivism has also been criticized on the principle of dualism. According to Liu and Matthews (2005), the constructivist metaphor of cognitive psychology emerged in the 1970s to overcome the 'Cartesian mind-body dualism' and the 'well-rehearsed debates between empiricism and rationalism'. Their main observation is,

> The irony now appears to be that from the divergence of constructivist views has emerged a dualist position—the very position constructivism came into being to avoid. By arguing for individual or social construction of knowledge a Cartesian parallelism between individual and social idiosyncrasy has arisen. This is most clearly seen in popular accounts of constructivists and their recent critics.

Cartesian dualism means the idea that the mind and body are entirely separate, distinct entities, with neither influencing the other except in voluntary action (Ahmad, 2008: 66). The authors, Liu and Matthews have examined the underlying epistemological beliefs of the many variants of constructivism (in the authors' language, 'a church of theoretical accounts') and the criticisms thereof on the basis of (a) Vygotsky's perspective on education including the role of the social and the collective in learning, the role of language, and consciousness, and (b) the central tenets of Vygotsky's philosophy including history, dialectics, monism, and paradigmatic philosophy. The authors distinguish between the traditional monist philosophy (according to which 'the universe consists of a singular substance') from Vygotsky's 'functional monism where all living factors exist in interdependency and form a dialectic organic whole'. They

> "argue that Vygotsky's educational theory is guided by an alternative epistemological paradigm—that of historical-dialectical-monism. This philosophical rigour has not been widely recognized in popular literature."

Their conclusions may be stated as follows:

> (i) There has been a move from behaviourism to constructivism in educational psychology, but philosophically there has not been a shift from dualism.
>
> (ii) Confusions about Vygotsky's theory often arise from concepts taken literally and from the lack of appreciation of the general philosophical orientation underpinning his works.

VII. *The question of empiricism*

'Empiricism' is a theory according to which all knowledge originates in experience. Experience is a crucial factor in constructivism through which knowledge is constructed. Some realists claim that constructivism is just a form of empiricism with its inherent weaknesses; for example, in the classical form of empiricism, mind is considered to be a blank slate that can receive information from the external world. This seems to follow the principle of truth as correspondence (Staver, 1998). But the fact is that constructivism relies on the principle of truth as coherence which implies that mind is never blank or devoid of experience/perception. Some also allege that terms like 'experience' and 'knowledge' are used by constructivists in a confusing and synonymous manner (Kozloff, 1998, as noted above). Staver (1998) clarifies the situation by noting that experience provides the basis for the construction of knowledge (experience acting as a 'lens' through which knowledge about the world is gathered, see above) and is not the same thing as knowledge. In fact, there may not be a one-to-one correspondence between one's experience and knowledge, or even the same experience may lead to different knowledge bits in case of different knowers.

VIII. *The question of instrumentalism*

This is another bone of contention between realists and constructivists. According to Lacey (1996), 'instrumentalism' is a doctrine in philosophy which advocates the provision that scientific theories, principles, and laws should be considered as mechanisms for observing, predicting, and explaining natural phenomena; but we should refrain from categorizing such propositions as true or false (as described in Staver, 1998). Constructivist's stance that the basic purpose of knowledge construction is to explain the human experience makes constructivism instrumental in nature. This follows from its principle of accepting truth as coherence. Clearly, this is not appreciated by the realists who tend to accept truth as correspondence.

IX. *The question of ethics, political stance, etc.*

In another form of controversy, radical constructivism is "accused of encouraging (or even implying) support for reactionary social and political views and of leading to ethical corruption" (Quale, 2010). As an example, Quale quotes McCarty and Schwandt (2000):

> there can be no commitment to democratic values [...and that this theory] seems far more at home with non-democratic forms of educational and governmental practices.

Quale argues that this position is not tenable because radical constructivism is basically a theory of cognitive knowledge and it addresses the epistemic and ontological status of this knowledge besides discussing how learners construct their knowledge. On the other hand, ethical considerations, moral values, political or ideological stances, religious beliefs, etc. reflect personal beliefs, feelings, values, emotions, and preferences and may be devoid of logical or rational thinking which is supposed to be the basis of cognitive knowledge. These constitute knowledge of a non-cognitive kind that belongs to affective domain and forms the knower's personal ontological space, which is beyond the purview of radical constructivism. Thus, radical constructivism (RC) enjoys a 'cognitively neutral' or 'agnostic' status in the matter of ethics. Quale sums up the position thus:

> RC rejects the idea that there exists a true code of ethics lying somewhere out there for us to discover. For any individual knower, her ethical knowledge must be constructed by herself; how that is to be done is left entirely up to her! One might describe this as a position of *ethical and political/ideological agnosticism*.

Accordingly, radical constructivism cannot be faulted for people's own perceptions in their affective domains comprising ethical and other matters, and consequences thereof.

A similar position is announced by Rickert (2009) by referring to White (2006: 99):

> Constructivism asserts that the "powerful cannot criticize the oppressed, because the central epistemological categories are inexorably tied to particular perspectives". It also follows that the oppressed cannot criticize the powerful...unless we allow a "double standard: allow a questionable idea to be criticized if it is held by those in a position of power—Christian creationism, for example—but not if it is held by those whom the powerful oppress—Zuni creationism, for example".

We may look at the situation in another way and remark that individual choices/preferences of a person in matters of ethics, religious beliefs, political thinking, etc. are indicative of some kind of constructivism at work in her non-cognitive domain.

X. *Constructivism and the practice of science*

Realists in general contend that constructivism goes against the practice of science (e.g. Osborne, 1996, quoted earlier) as it rejects the theory of truth as correspondence. However, constructivists claim that this is not so. For example, after doing a comprehensive analysis of the various controversies surrounding constructivism (as may be seen in our discussions above), Staver (1998) says:

> The practice of science does not change when one rejects truth as correspondence and embraces truth as internal coherence. Only the wishes of science change. Science should give up the hot pursuit of the independence, discovery, lawfulness, and certainty of nature via the correspondence theory of truth. Why? Because the independent comparison required to establish that a knowledge claim corresponds to the facts of reality must be done outside another act of knowing. Until now, no one has offered such a comparison.

The question of whether science corresponds to reality or supports relativism has also been analyzed at some length by Quale (2010). He quotes the philosopher Putnam (1975) as supporting scientific realism according to which, "well-developed theories of science do in fact refer to real (i.e. objectively existing) entities and processes in the physical world". Putnam argued that if science does not correspond to reality then the "success of science would indeed be a miracle..." though, according to Quale, "in later years Putnam revised his viewpoint on this issue". Nonetheless, the basic question is, if scientists (practitioners of science) construct their knowledge of science in a relative manner with no access to reality as suggested by constructivism, then how are their theories turning out to be successful in describing natural phenomena? Quale (2010) attempts to answer this dilemma with a brief summary of radical-constructivist position on this issue:

1. Nature is *not* assumed to possess any pre-existing identifiable intrinsic structure that is person-independent.

2. A scientific theory is a *model* of some domain of natural phenomena, constructed by scientists and *imposed* on the phenomena. This construction can be done in many ways, depending on which questions the constructors (scientists) want to address; it is not possible to identify one such model as giving "the objectively correct" description.
3. It (i.e. the model) should be formulated in *mathematical* terms.
4. It should yield *predictions* that agree with observation.
5. It should fit with the *ontological preferences* of its practitioners (the scientists).

Clearly, points 1 and 2 are not accepted by realists, whereas points 3 and 4 are universally acceptable as a part of sound policy of scientific pursuit. Point 5 refers to the practitioner's personal attributes such as her previous experience, preferences, attitude to science, etc. which, according to Quale, constitutes her personal *ontological perception* of science. Thus, according to radical constructivism, a scientist constructs a model or tool with the specific purpose of answering a question in a specific domain on the basis of her ontological perception. She may make several attempts with appropriate modifications, within her grasp, to arrive at a suitable model or theory. One essential requirement of course is that the scientist's construction be internally consistent. The resulting theory/model may answer the particular question or describe the particular phenomenon well and there is no miracle in it. Of course, the ontological perceptions of a scientist as well as her questions are likely to change with time.

Even if we accept that in scientific pursuits, theories and models are constructed, and experiments conducted in an attempt to understand what 'reality' might be, there is no way of knowing what that reality or truth is in an absolute sense. In modern physics, for example, there are highly sophisticated and mathematically consistent theories, such as *string theory*, *supergravity*, *super unification*, *theory of everything*, etc. which so far have no empirical support (e.g. Hawking, 2007).

Therefore, it cannot be said to what extent they represent the truth or reality they intend to explain. Another example is the use of a highly speculative proposal called the '*anthropic principle*' in cosmologists' attempt to understand the origin and evolution of the universe (e.g. Hawking, 1994). In a simple language, the anthropic principle states that, "We see the universe as it is because we exist; if it were different, we wouldn't be here to observe it." In other words, according to this principle, the universe started and evolved so that intelligent beings capable of making such queries would emerge at a point of time. This appears to be a philosophical statement rather than an established/physically verifiable assertion. Unlike classical physics which is deterministic in nature, quantum mechanics (e.g. Omnes, 2001), the modern theory of the structure of matter, is probabilistic in nature and this was 'socially' accepted by scientists after much debate and deliberation led by great scientists and thinkers like Born, Einstein, and others in the early part of twentieth century. In quantum mechanics, there is a fundamental principle known as the Heisenberg 'uncertainty principle' or 'indeterminacy principle' according to which some physical properties of elementary particles cannot be simultaneously determined with full certainty. This means that the exact reality or truth about the elementary particles cannot be revealed no matter how hard we try. Even the laws/principles in the domains of the three 'pillars' of deterministic classical physics namely mechanics, thermodynamics, and electrodynamics, apply to 'ideal' situations. To apply them to real situations several assumptions are invoked. Then, in all kinds of measurements (measurement being an essential tool of science), there are limits of accuracy owing to the inherent characteristics of the measuring instruments and other factors. Such limits affect our knowledge about 'real' objects/situations.

All said and done, we may say that at a given point of time, there exists a well-established system of concepts and principles in science found by scientists, which forms a benchmark of our understanding and knowledge about nature within the corresponding limits of accuracy/validity. The role of a science teacher then is to guide the learners towards this benchmark using suitable means and media. The role of a scientist is to try to establish newer and sharper benchmark thereby expanding the domain of our knowledge of the nature.

XI. *von Glasersfeld's anguish*

The most prominent proponent of radical constructivism, von Glasersfeld, might have felt aggrieved at the criticisms, sometimes quite harsh (as we have seen above), his theory has attracted since its inception. He must have given rebuttal to his critics a number of times in different forms/forums. In perhaps the last paper of his life (see 'Afterword' in Riegler, and Quale, 2010), titled 'Why People Dislike Radical Constructivism' (Glasersfeld, 2010) laid out three possible reasons for the situation:

(1) *Shirking responsibility*: In general, people are averse to the implication of radical constructivism according to which, "we are all responsible for what we say and do in any situation".

(2) *The thirst for certainty*: The thinking that our actions and experiences are linked to the existence of an *independent reality*, something denied by radical constructivism.

(3) *The stickiness of beliefs*: "The belief that what we call knowledge must by definition reflect aspects of a real world ignoring the fact that all our knowledge is abstracted from experience, pertains to experience, and has no demonstrable relation to anything beyond the experiential interface."

It is interesting to note, however, that Jack Lochhead, in an 'Afterword' appended to the above-mentioned paper of von Glasersfeld, observes that

> ...right up to his final days Ernst held strongly to those elements of radical constructivism that are most radical and most difficult for us to fully accept. While Ernst has never challenged the notion that there must be some relationship between our constructions and the external reality we believe exists, he strongly denies the

possibility of our knowing what that relationship might be or how the term "exists" should be interpreted.

9.3.3.3 Critique of social constructivism

Interesting criticisms have also been leveled at social constructivism (see Chapter 2 of the present book), which we shall outline now. Social constructivism avers that the concept of truth is 'socially constructed', and in this process, language plays a vital role (Gregen, 1985, 1995). Thus, whereas knowledge is 'subjective' in radical constructivism, it is 'intersubjective' or 'consensual' in social constructivism. Just as individual and cognition are central to radical constructivism, society and language are central to social constructivism. The knowledge may be originally constructed by an individual; it can then become the knowledge of the society to which the individual belongs through the vehicle of social interaction driven by language. This immediately leads to the following kinds of uncomfortable implications (http://en.wikipedia.org/w/index.php?title=Constructivist_epistemology&oldid=566253716). Truth becomes socially relative, which in turn reduces social constructivism to relativism (similar to what happens in radical constructivism) and leads to the charge of self-refutation, i.e. social constructivism may be true in one social system and false in another social system at the same time. Relativism also connotes that the concepts of two different social systems about the same thing may be entirely different and incommensurate. Then, how to establish communication between them about the truth or falsity of any given statement? This may make different social systems, with their own worldviews constructed according to their own interests, isolated groups of individuals without any inter-society communication. Had this been the real situation, the human society as a whole won't have reached where it is now. Kitching (2008) traces another contradiction with social constructivism on the basis of the deterministic view of language which severely constrains the minds of the members of a society: while other members of the society are constrained/controlled by the dominant concepts of the society, the advocate of constructivism is somehow not similarly constrained and can transcend these concepts!

As regards the standing of scientific knowledge in relation to society, the basic fact is that the idea of a scientist starts as a personal construct and its subsequent fate depends upon its acceptance or otherwise by the community of scientists who are supposed to critically examine its pros and cons. It is of course not mandatory that the same be accepted by all scientists; a consensus however is required. Any number of examples may be cited: Darwin and Wallace's *Theory of Evolution* (1859), Kekule's *Idea of Benzene Ring* (1865), Planck's *Concept of Quantum* (1900), Ehrenhaft's *Idea of Subelectrons* and its refutation by Millikan (1910), Einstein's *Theories of Relativity* (early part of 20th century), de Broglie's *Idea of Wave-Particle Duality* (1924), Dirac's *Concept of Antimatter* (1930), Watson and Crick's *Double Helix Structure of DNA* (1953), Gell-Mann and Zweig's *Idea of Quarks* (1964), Higgs and Englert's *Concept of the Mass Giving Quantum Field Higgs Boson* (proposed in 1964 and tentatively discovered in 2013 that earned Higgs and Englert the 2013 Nobel Prize in Physics), and so on. Gerald Holton, an eminent physicist and historian of science, makes this pertinent observation (Holton, 1978: viii):

> ...I tend to look on any product of scientific work, whether published or not, as an "event" that stands at the intersection of certain historical trajectories, such as of the largely private or personal scientific activity; of the shared, "public" scientific knowledge of the larger community; of the sociological setting in which a science is being developed; and indeed of the cultural context of the time.

A similar view is expressed by Driver et al. (1994):

> ...scientific knowledge is symbolic in nature and socially negotiated. The objects of science are not the phenomena of nature but constructs that are advanced by the scientific community to interpret nature.

Thus, according to social constructivists, "scientific theory does not describe the world, but on the contrary, constitutes it"

(Osborne, 1996). But a realist tends to term this as a kind of confusion between the way of knowledge generation and the objects of knowledge, and believes that the findings of scientists are not limited by their imagination or social factors but by the nature itself through its specific dispositions which may or may not be revealed to the scientists. Again, the constructivist's connection between the knowledge constructed individually (mental representation) and socially (consensual domain) seems unclear to some. For example, Rowlands and Carson (2009) say, "Even social constructivists are unsure as to what constitutes the 'social' and how it relates to the individual.... We suggest that if knowledge is seen in terms of something over and above mental representation and consensus then the contradiction between the individual meaning-maker and the 'social' might be resolved."

9.3.4 Pedagogical Issues

In the field of pedagogy, especially related to science, constructivism has been acknowledged as the source of many new insights and methodologies, even by its bitter critics (e.g. Matthews, 1992, 1994; Phillips, 1995; Osborne, 1996). Besides producing a large body of research on how children learn and their learning difficulties, constructivism has suggested a variety of learner centered teaching learning models; redefined learners' mistakes or misconceptions as alternative conceptions or alternative frameworks; highlighted the usefulness of tools like concept mapping (Chapter 4 of the present book, and e.g. Novak, 1998), collaboration, cognitive conflict, cognitive negotiation, cognitive apprenticeship, multiple interpretations, multiple manifestations, etc. and approaches such as collaborative learning (Tobin, Tippins, and Gallard, 1994). There are also attempts to provide valuable guidelines, practical tips, and models to help both pre-service and in-service teachers to set up and sustain constructivist classrooms (e.g. Marlow and Page, 2005; Garbett, 2011).

Highlighting the constructivist perspective of science pedagogy, Irzik (2001) writes:

> It is essential in this process that "the teacher not tell students what concepts to construct or how to construct

> them", nor tell them that they are "wrong", but simply prevent them from going in futile directions (Glasersfeld, 1995: 184). After all, there is no fixed body of truths to be transmitted, but only "conceptual constructs" that are "viable". Indeed, the aim of science education, according to this picture, is not to help students learn or (re)construct the concepts and views that scientists have formulated and tested as a result of long and arduous cooperative work, but to "enable [them] to function effectively in their world". (Gunstone, 1988: 89)

Though constructivism enunciates certain epistemological principles to guide knowledge construction by students, as is well-known, it does not seem to specify teacher's knowledge base required for successful implementation of constructivism in the classroom. For example, for teaching science, whether the teacher's knowledge base should correspond to the well established formal wealth of science. If yes, then this formal science becomes indirectly the goal of science learning by the students and, in this case, the scope of students to construct knowledge through viability, etc. becomes limited or constrained, which probably a staunch constructivist won't like. If no, then how does the teacher prevent the students from taking 'futile directions' referred to by von Glasersfeld in the above quotation or, how does the teacher set up a constructivist scenario in the classroom? Moreover, if the teacher is allowed to use her personal constructs/idiosyncrasies in guiding students' learning, then it might lead to a cognitive catastrophe with serious consequences for the future of science, especially if the teacher's perceptions do not correspond to standard or established science. Further, the place of curriculum/textbook in the constructivist teaching learning process is not clear. Thus, the recommendations of constructivists pose a series of dilemma for the practicing teacher. Continuing the discussion, let us quote from Irzik (2001) again:

> Few constructivists take head on cases where a student's understanding does not match the teacher's. What then? Do we explain to the student why she is wrong or not? As Grandy says, "if we are unwilling to evaluate representations, unwilling to judge some

> representations and understandings as more accurate, more general, more consistent than others, then there is no need to teach 'science'" (116). It goes without saying that as teachers it is our responsibility to teach our students the very best. Finally, it is naïve to expect the students to discover all or most of the relevant scientific truths by themselves. Even with much guidance some students will fail for various reasons, as every teacher knows.... Not being able to tell the student what concepts to construct or how to construct them is not a virtue but a vice of the constructivist theory.

But, once we accept the radical constructivist stand that there is world outside the learner's consciousness and that interpersonal sharing of knowledge is possible, comparison of representations becomes possible. Similarly, as radical constructivism supports truth relativism instead of objective truth, the scenario of students discovering scientific 'truths' by themselves does not occur.

9.4 Future Possibilities/Beyond Constructivism

We have seen above that most criticisms are directed at radical constructivism. On account of its philosophical and epistemological assumptions, radical constructivism has not been accepted as a mainstream theory. In 2010, an on-line journal, *Constructivist Foundations* brought out a special issue (Vol. 6, No. 1) devoted to the pertinent question: 'Can radical constructivism become a mainstream endeavour?' which was answered by both detractors and admirers of constructivism in their own ways. Noting its potential and usefulness in diverse disciplines, some thinkers have suggested how radical constructivism can improve its standing. We shall take a look at a few of them before speculating on possible future educational scenario *vis-à-vis* constructivism.

In order to improve the acceptability of radical constructivism, Schmidt (2010) advises constructivist scholars to (i) do more introspection and address the weaknesses inherent in constructivism, (ii) be more receptive to the views of critics, (iii) "improve their strategic orientation, i.e. participate in the non-constructivist academic discussion instead of sitting on the fence and criticizing all other positions as inadequate", (iv) use constructivism to solve definite problems across disciplines, and (v) "realize the insight into the finality of transience: the times of master narratives have gone—for ever."

Regarding the future of radical constructivism (RC), Riegler and Quale (2010) say, with optimism:

> Even if RC cannot or should not become a mainstream endeavour, it will further develop. Although the fundamental questions and disputes within RC might never stop, radical constructivists should attend to more specific tasks within their (scientific) disciplines. If radical constructivists manage to demonstrate how effective RC can be at explaining specific phenomena, RC has the potential to become a helpful tool for solving specific research problems.

There are also attempts to revisit radical constructivism in terms of new ways of looking at the old philosophical problems related to action, communication, knowledge, language, reality, truth, etc. by shifting from object (ontological entity) orientation to process orientation (Schmidt, 2011, including open peer commentaries followed by Schmidt's response).

Be that as it may, in the current educational scenario, constructivism has been accepted as a more relevant view of learning than instructivism though neither can claim to be exclusively right or wrong (Brown, 2005). Even their relative merits may have to be examined in situations involving different types of learners (e.g. Ellis, 2005). However, educational programmes, planning, and practices are starting to be influenced by constructivism. Educational authorities are trying hard to implement constructivism at all levels of school education and teacher education in different countries. In the Indian context, the National Council of Educational Research and Training (NCERT), an apex body in matters relating to school education, has come out with a constructivism-based curriculum framework for the school system in the country, the *National Curriculum Framework 2005* (NCERT, 2005). Different states are trying to put it into practice in their own ways. A recent example is that of the state of Maharashtra, where the Maharashtra Knowledge Corporation Limited is planning a 40-episode television serial in Marathi titled *Mazhi Shala (My School)* to empower students, teachers and parents to recognize the importance of constructivism and implement it in day-to-day learning in school as well as at home (Pune Mirror Bureau, 2013).

We have to accept the fact that internet is opening up new and popular avenues of learning through free courses and support materials offered by best educators from around the world, both for learning new subjects as well as upgrading one's knowledge base. The internet based education has both instructivist and constructivist components put together in an essential manner. Examples of such courses include Coursera (coursera.org), OpenCourseWare Consortium (ocwconsortium.org), Khan Academy (khanacademy.org), Wikiversity (en.wikiversity.org), TED Talks (ted.com), iTunes U (apple.com/education/itunes-u), Oresoft Live Web Class (contact.oresoft@gmail.com) and many others. Some of them are interactive in nature, and support collaborative learning communities. Experts are even talking about 'flipped classroom' (e.g. Cummings, 2013). In this scenario learners take instruction online outside of class and do their 'homework' in the classroom. Though internet surfing is considered by many to discourage deep and original thinking, some experts (e.g. Margolis, 2013) are of opinion that it can actually make children more clever and creative, and wean them away from rote learning. The internet based education is obviously going to be more popular and widespread in days to come, it being a more viable vehicle to reach those who cannot be reached through direct face-to-face means.

Enhancing teaching learning experience at different levels through technology in many different forms has become/is becoming a prime activity of professional bodies around the world. Mention may be made of a couple of such initiatives. The Australian Society for Computers in Learning in Tertiary Education (ascilite), founded in 1985, is a professional community of innovators, leaders, and scholars engaged in improving higher education through technology driven activities such as e-learning research and development, instructional design, web applications, web services, and interactive multi-media (http://www.ascilite.org.au). Another global initiative called WISE (World Innovation Summit for Education), launched in 2009 by Qatar Foundation, provides an international and multi-sectoral platform with the purpose of building the future of education through innovation (http://www.wise-qatar.org/content/wise-initiative). The 2013 WISE Summit was held between October 29-31, 2013 on the theme 'Reinventing Education for Life', which was attended by more than 1200 prominent educators, entrepreneurs, political leaders and social leaders from over 100 countries. The summit addressed the question of how to close the "widening gap between the learning we have and the learning we need to meet the challenges and aspirations of societies and individuals around the world" (http://www.wise-qatar.org/wise-summit-2013). Clearly, as these initiatives indicate, in the emerging times, new approaches to teaching learning are likely to emerge by subsuming instructivism and constructivism, and perhaps going beyond them.

9.5 Conclusion

In this chapter, we have attempted a review of the various objections to constructivism in general and radical constructivism in particular and how they have been countered by supporters of constructivism. For the purpose of summary, the broad framework of our presentation on the controversies is given in Fig. 9.1. We have been able to accommodate only a few of the authors working in this domain. Given below is our concluding observation in brief.

Looking at the overall structure of constructivism, especially its radical version, its practical aspects seem to be more acceptable than the underlying philosophical assumptions. Constructivism may be considered as a viable alternative to instructivism in spite of its controversial theoretical underpinnings. Its pedagogical significance has been appreciated even by its hardcore critiques. It can be practised by teachers in classrooms using the various resources and a variety of constructivism inspired teaching learning methods/models available today. If required, a suitable amalgamation of constructivism and instructivism may also be used to good effect. Such a combination might work better in India where the academic set-ups are not conducive to the practice of full-fledged constructivism. This is not unlike the case of curing a patient using any system of therapy or a combination of more than one.

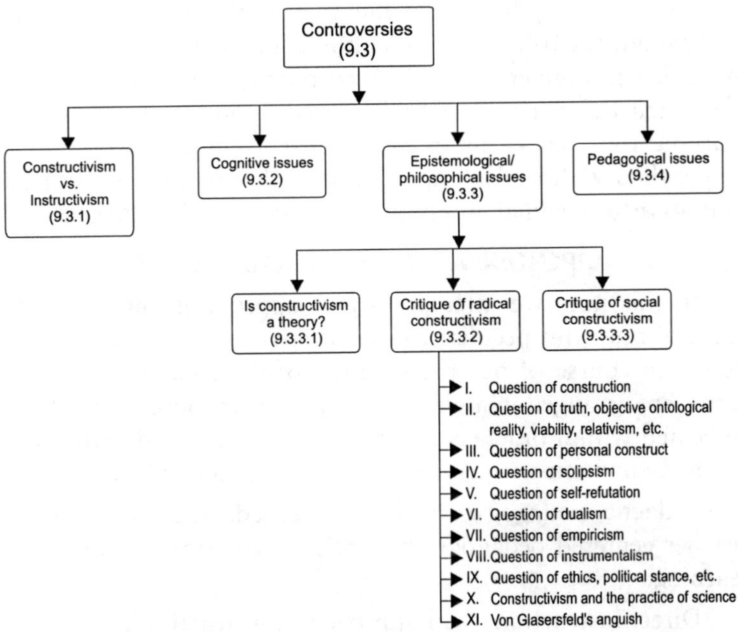

Fig. 9.1

Let us further recognize that constructivism and its criticisms are replete with typical terms (such as knowledge, truth, realism, relativism, empiricism, ontology, etc.) taken from mainstream philosophy, psychology, sociology, etc. which usually have multiple meanings, and more often than not, are difficult for non-specialists to follow. If a teacher is required to understand all the underlying theoretical dimensions of constructivism before using it in classroom, she may run away from it all. It is not unlike a situation where a young man wants to marry a woman whom he considers to be beautiful, but instead of going by what he sees/perceives, he decides to find out what 'beauty' actually means in all its dimensions by carrying out relevant research before marriage. The end result might be that the man would lose the woman he wanted to marry in the first place. Let us therefore ensure that with a little orientation and training the teachers are able to put constructivism to good use without having to worry about the theoretical underpinnings. In this connection it may be worthwhile to note the title of the paper by Schmidt (2010), referred to above: 'Radical Constructivism: A Tool, not a Super Theory!' Accordingly, it would be enough if constructivism could be widely used as an effective teaching learning tool across disciplines even if it could not become a 'super theory'. It is also important to realize that no tool is final and no theory is final and both are likely to evolve further.

APPENDIX: A NOTE ON TERMINOLOGY

In this note we attempt to give appropriate meanings of some of the terms peculiar to constructivism that we have come across in course of our presentation of the controversies. The terms are arranged in alphabetic order. Their sources have been indicated within brackets following the respective descriptions. We hope non-experts/general readers will find this helpful.

Didactic pedagogy: Instruction based, textbook driven, teacher centered pedagogy that includes transmission and rote learning.

Direct instruction: "An approach to instruction that uses a variety of techniques (brief explanations, teacher questioning, rapid pacing, guided and independent practice) to promote learning of basic skills. Presentation of factual information by lecture, demonstration, and rote practice. Systematic instruction for mastery of basic skills, facts, and information. Is a model of teaching, generally described as the didactic method. It generally involves an important amount of teacher talk. This method has origins with Rousseau and Dewey" (Ahmad, 2008: 155).

Dualism: "A theory that has at its basis *two* radically distinct concepts or principles." There various forms of dualism such as religious dualism (good and evil), metaphysical dualism (two kinds of reality: finite and infinite, matter and form, matter and spirit, relative and absolute, etc.), psychophysical dualism (body, constituted by matter and immaterial mind or soul) (Mautner, 2010: 170).

Empiricism: "The view that all knowledge is based on or derived from experience." Though useful in explaining how most of our knowledge is generated, empiricism has no explanation for the *a priori* nature of parts of human knowledge and of the truths of logic, mathematics, and ethics (Mautner, 2010: 186). "The permanent strand in philosophy that attempts to tie knowledge to experience. Experience is thought of either as the sensory contents of consciousness, or as whatever is expressed in some designated class of statements that can be observed to be true by the use of the senses. Empiricism denies that there is any knowledge outside this class, or at least outside whatever is given by legitimate theorizing on the basis of this class. It may take the form of denying that there is any *a priori* knowledge, or knowledge of necessary truths, or any innate or intuitive knowledge or general principles gaining credibility simply through the use of reason; it is thus principally contrasted with rationalism" (Blackburn, 2008: 114).

Fallibilism: The term 'fallibilism' basically means that "all knowledge-claims are provisional and in principle revisable", or "the view that the possibility of error is ever-present" (Mautner, 2010: 216). Stated in another way, fallibilism implies that "no belief (theory, view, thesis, and so on) can ever be rationally supported or justified in a conclusive way; always there remains a doubt about the truth of the belief" (IEP, 2005). Also, fallibilism is "the doctrine that knowledge gained empirically can never be certain" (*Chambers Dictionary*, 1995: 605).

Instrumentalism: "1. The view that theories, especially in the sciences, are not strictly speaking true or false but are to be regarded as tools. There main use is in predictions, in making the transition from one set of data to another. Some theories prove more useful for this purpose than other ones and this, rather than their supposed truth, is why they can justifiably be accepted. 2. The view that statements about a certain kind of entities M can be true, although strictly speaking there are no Ms. The suggestion is that the truth of such statements consists in their usefulness as instruments for predictions. Of these two views, the first seems to reject truth in favour of usefulness, whist the second seems to identify truth with usefulness (Mautner, 2010: 306). "The view that a scientific theory is to be regarded as an instrument for producing new predictions or new techniques for controlling events, but not as itself capable of literal truth or falsity" (Blackburn, 2008: 187).

Materialism: Materialism is "a proposition about the existent or the real: that only matter is existent or real; that matter is the primordial or fundamental constituent of the universe; that only sensible entities, processes, or content are existent or real" (Runes, 1960: 189). It is "the theory that matter alone exists. It immediately implies a denial of the existence of minds, spirits, divine beings, etc., in so far as these are taken to be non-material" (Mautner, 2010: 378).

Metaphysics: "(Gr. *ta meta ta physica* what comes after the Physics; but it can also mean 'what lies beyond nature')". This is "the inquiry into or theory of that which lies *beyond nature* and transcends the limits of ordinary knowledge and experience" (Mautner, 2010: 387). "Originally a title for those books of Aristotle that came after the *Physics*, the term is now applied to any enquiry that raises questions about reality that lie beyond or behind those capable of being tackled by the methods of science" (Blackburn, 2008: 231-32).

Modest realism: This is the view that "the world has numberless organizations of its own; the world contains infinitely different kinds of objects; the world has more objects than we usually talk about, not fewer" (www.trinity.edu/cbrown/papers/internalrealism.html). In the context of science, modest realism "insists that the goal of science is to find out how things really are and which asserts we are making progress in that direction but which recognizes that this goal will always be incompletely achieved and which is aware of the principal obstacles" (www.physics.nyu.edu/sokal/bielefeld_final_rev.pdf; 23 September 2001).

Ontological realism: "A theory of what there is. Realists accept the idea that we live in a world that exists independently of us and our thoughts, and hence that some facts may be beyond our grasp, in the sense that we are unable to confirm that they obtain. *Syn*. Metaphysical realism" (Mautner, 2010: 520).

Ontology: "Ontology is the general theory of being as such, and forms the general part of metaphysics, or theoretical philosophy. In the usage of analytical philosophy, ontology is the general theory of what there is" (Mautner, 2010: 442).

Positive philosophy: It is based upon "the doctrine that man can have no knowledge of anything but phenomena, and that the knowledge of phenomena is relative, not absolute" (*Chambers Dictionary*, 1995: 1333).

Positivism: Positivism holds that "the highest or only form of knowledge is the description of sensory phenomena" (Blackburn, 2008: 283). "According to positivist theories of knowledge, all knowledge is ultimately based on sense-experience. There cannot be different kinds of knowledge. All genuine inquiry is concerned with the description and explanation of empirical facts" (Mautner, 2010: 482). "Positivism is a philosophy of science based on the view that information derived from logical and mathematical treatments and reports of sensory experience is the exclusive source of all authoritative knowledge, and that there is valid knowledge (truth) only in scientific knowledge" (en. wikipedia.org/wiki/Positivism). Positivism is the "philosophical system recognizing only facts and observable phenomena" (*Oxford Dictionary and Thesaurus*, 2005: 577).

Realism: Realism is "a theory that entities of a certain category exist mind-independently, i.e. independently of what we believe or feel about them—in short, a *realist* theory" (Mautner, 2010: 520). "In philosophy, any viewpoint that accords to the objects of human knowledge an existence that is independent of whether they are being perceived or thought about; it asserts the independent existence of material objects and their qualities" (*Britannica*, 2006, Vol. 8, p. 131). It is "the philosophical doctrine that in external perception the objects immediately known are real existences; the tendency to regard, accept or represent things as they really are" (*Chambers Dictionary*, 1995: 1434).

Realist epistemology: "A realist epistemology would be the position that we have *direct access* to the objects of the world, such that our representations of objects are *exactly like* these objects themselves. Here mind is treated as a *passive* recipient of the world that merely *receives* data from objects as they are from the world and then dutifully reports them" (larvalsubjects.wordpress.com/2009/11/04/realism-epistemology-science-and-scientism/).

Relativism: Relativism is the view that truth is relative and may vary from individual to individual, from group to group, or from time to time, having no objective standard (Runes, 1960: 269). Also, relativism is the "permanently tempting doctrine that, in some areas at least, truth itself is relative to the judging subject ('beauty lies in the eyes of the beholder')" (Blackburn, 2008: 313). Expressed in another way, relativism is "the view that accepted standards of right and good vary with environment and from person to person" (*Chambers Dictionary*, 1995: 1453).

Representative realism: "According to representative realism, we do not perceive objects directly. Rather, objects cause us to have certain experiences, sense-data, and it is these to which we have direct access" (www.theoryofknowledge.info/theories-of-perception/representative-realism/). Representative realism thus introduces a distinction between our experience of objects, which is based upon the secondary qualities of the objects, and the objects themselves, which are characterized by their primary qualities. Representative realism is also called 'representationalism' or 'indirect realism'.

Scientific realism: "The view that most of the theoretical entities, such as electrons and quarks, which are postulated in a true scientific theory to explain observable phenomena are real, independently existing things. This in opposition to operationalism and instrumentalism. Some writers use 'scientific realism' in a more general sense, for various kinds of realism that are in harmony with a scientific world-view" (Mautner, 2010: 521).

Solipsism: The metaphysical meaning of solipsism (Lat. *solus*, alone + *ipse*, self) is that it is a "Subvariety of idealism which maintains that the individual self of the solipsistic philosopher is the whole of reality and that the external world and other persons are representations of that self having no independent existence" (Runes, 1960: 295). "The belief that only oneself and one's experience exists. Solipsism is the extreme consequence of believing that knowledge must be founded on inner, personal states of experience, and then failing to find a bridge whereby they can inform us of anything beyond themselves" (Blackburn, 2008: 343).

References

Ahmad, M. (2008). *Comprehensive Dictionary of Education* (New Delhi: Atlantic Publishers & Distributors (P) Ltd.).

Ausubel, D.P. (1968). *Educational Psychology: A Cognitive View* (New York: Holt, Rinehart, and Winston).

Blackburn, S. (2008). *The Oxford Dictionary of Philosophy*, 2nd edition revised. (Oxford University Press).

Britannica (2006). *Ready Reference Encyclopedia* (New Delhi: Encyclopædia Britannica (India) Pvt. Ltd. and Impulse Marketing).

Brooks, J.G., and Brooks, M.G. (1993). *In search of understanding: The case for constructivist classrooms* (Alexandria, VA: Association for Supervision and Curriculum Development).

Brown, T.H. (2005). Beyond constructivism: Exploring future learning paradigms. *Education Today*, 2. (Thames, New Zealand: Aries Publishing Company).

Caporimo, A., Dreher, B., and Simmons, A. (2013). That's Incredible. *Reader's Digest*, September 2013, 49-59.

Chambers Dictionary (1995). (New Delhi: Allied Chambers Dictionary (India) Limited).

Cummings, Pip (2013). The Khan Academy. *Reader's Digest*, September 2013: 98-103.

Dalgarno, B., Kennedy, G.E., and Lee, M.J.W. (2010). Critiquing constructivist theory: (Mis)aligned (mis)application of constructivism in online learning environment. In C.H. Steel et al. (Eds.), *Curriculum, technology and transformation for an unknown future*. Proceedings Ascilite Sydney 2010: 266-68.

Driver, R., Asoko, H., Leach, J., Mortimer, E., and Scott, P. (1994). Constructing scientific knowledge in the classroom. *Educational Researcher*, 23: 5-12.

Ellis, Louise A. (2005). Balancing approaches: revisiting the educational psychology research on teaching students with learning difficulties. *Australian Education Review*. Australian Council for Educational Research. Victoria: ACER Press.

Entwistle, N. (1981). *Styles of learning and teaching* (Chicester: Wiley).

Finn, C.E., and Ravitch, D. (1996). Educational Reform 1995-1996. A Report from the *Educational Excellence Network*. http://www. edexcellence. net/library/ epciv.html.

von Foerster, H. (1984). *Observing systems* (2nd ed.) (Seaside, CA: Intersystems Publications).

Fosnot, C.T. (Ed.) (1996). *Constructivism: Theory, Perspectives and Practice* (New York: Teachers College Press).

Fox, R. (2001). Constructivism Examined. *Oxford Review of Education*, 27(1): 23-35.

Garbett, D. (2011). Constructivism Deconstructed in Science Teacher Education. *Australian Journal of Teacher Education*, 36(6): 36-49.

Gregen, K.J. (1985). The social constructionist movement in modern psychology. *American Psychologist*, 40: 266-75.

—— (1995). Social construction and the educational process. In L.P. Steffe and J. Gale (Eds.), *Constructivism in Education* (17-39) (Hillsdale, NJ: Earlbaum).

Gunstone, R.F. (1988). Learners in Science Education. In P. Fensham (Ed.), *Development and Dilemmas in Science Education* (73-95) (London: The Falmer Press).

Hawking, S.W. (1994). *A Brief History of Time* (Bantam Books).

—— (2007). *The Theory of Everything* (Jaico Publishing House).

Holton, Gerald (1978). *The Scientific Imagination: Case Studies* (Cambridge: Cambridge University Press).

IEP (2005). *Internet Encyclopedia of Philosophy* (A peer-reviewed academic resource). www.iep.utm.edu/.

Irzik, G. (2001). Back to basics: a philosophical critique of constructivism. *Studies in Philosophy and Education*, 20(2): 157-75.

Kempa, R.F., and Martin-Diaz, M. (1990a). Motivational traits and preferences for different instructional modes in science. Pat 1: Student motivational traits. *International Journal of Science Education*, 12: 194-203.

—— (1990b). Student's motivational traits and preferences for different instructional modes in science. Pat 2: *International Journal of Science Education*, 12: 205-16.

Kitching, G. (2008). *The Trouble with Theory: The Educational Costs of Postmodernism* (Pennsylvania: Penn State University Press).

Korthagen, F.A.J., and Lunenberg, M. (2004). Links between self-study and teacher education reform. In J.J. Loughran, M.L. Hamilton, V.K. LaBoskey, and T. Russell (Eds.), *International handbook of self-study of teaching and teacher education practices*, 1: 421-51 (Dordrecht: Kluwer Academic Publishers).

Kozloff, Martin A. (1998). *Constructivism in Education: Sophistry for a New Age*. http://people.uncw.edu/kozloffm/ContraConstructivism.html.

Lacey, A.R. (1996). *A Dictionary of Philosophy* (3rd ed.) (London: Routledge).

Liu, C.H., and Matthews, R. (2005). Vygotsky's philosophy: Constructivism and its criticisms examined. *International Education Journal*, 6(3): 386-99.

Margolis, J. (2013). The good, the bad and the unexpected. *Reader's Digest*, September 2013: 111-14.

Marlowe, B.A., and Page, M.L. (2005). *Creating and Sharing the Constructivist Classroom*, 2nd edition (Thousand Oakes, California: Corwin Press).

Matthews, M.R. (1995). *Constructivism and New Zealand Science Education* (Auckland: Dunmore Press).

—— (1992). Old wine in new bottles: A problem with constructivist epistemology. Paper presented at the *National Association for Research in Science Teaching* (NARST) annual meeting. Cambridge, MA.

—— (1994). *Science teaching: The role of history and philosophy of science* (New York: Routledge).

—— (1995). *Challenging New Zealand science education* (Palmerston North: Dunmore Press).

—— (Ed.) (1998). *Constructivism in Science Education: A Philosophical Examination* (Kluwer Academic Publishers).

—— (2001). Back to basics: a comment on Irzik. *Studies in Philosophy and Education*, 20(2): 177-80.

Mautner, T. (2010). *The Penguin Dictionary of Philosophy*, 2nd edition. (Penguin Books).

McCarty, L.P., and Schwandt, T.A. (2000). Seductive illusions. In D.C. Phillips (Ed.), *Constructivism in education* (41-85) (Chicago: University of Chicago Press).

Meyer, D.L. (2009). The poverty of constructivism. *Educational Philosophy and Theory*, 41(3): 332-41.

Muthukrishna, N., et al. (1993). Children's alternative frameworks: Should they be directly addressed by science instruction. *Journal of Research in Science Teaching*, 30: 233-48.

Naugle, D.K. (2002). *Worldview: The history of a concept* (Grand Rapids, MI: William, B. Eerdmans).

NCERT (2005). *National Curriculum Framework 2005* (New Delhi: NCERT).

Novak, J.D. (1998). *Learning, Creating, and Using Knowledge: Concept Maps™ as Facilitative Tools in Schools and Corporations* (Mahwah, New Jersey: Lawrence Erlbaum Associates, Publishers).

Omnes, R. (2001). *Understanding Quantum Mechanics* (New Delhi: Prentice-Hall of India Private Limited).

Osborne, J.F. (1996). Beyond constructivism. *Science Education*, 80(1): 53-82.

Oxford Dictionary & Thesaurus (2005) (New Delhi: Oxford University Press).

Pask, G. (1976). Styles and strategies of learning. *British Journal of Educational Psychology*, 46: 128-48.

Phillips, D.C. (1995). The good, the bad, and the ugly: The many faces of constructivism. *Educational Researcher*, 24: 5-12.

Pune Mirror Bureau (2013). Serial to create awareness about holistic education. *PuneMirror*, Oct. 19, 6. www.punemirror.in/city.

Quale, A. (2008). *Radical constructivism.* Rotterdam: Sense.

—— (2010). Objections to Radical Constructivism. *Constructivist Foundations*, 6(1): 12-18.

Rickert, Paul R. (2009). A Presuppositional Critique of Constructivism. *Christian Perspectives in Education*, 3(1).

Riegler, A. and Quale, A. (2010). Editorial: Can Constructivism Become a Mainstream Endeavor? *Constructivist Foundations*, 6(1): 1-5.

Rowlands, S. and Carson, R. (2009). The contradictions in the constructivist discourse. *Philosophy of Mathematics Education Journal*, 14; http://people.exter.ac.uk/PErnest/pome14/rowlands.htm.

Runes, D.D. (Ed.) (1960). *Dictionary of Philosophy* (New York: Philosophical Library).

Schmidt, S.J. (2010). Radical Constructivism: A Tool, not a Super Theory. *Constructivist Foundations*, 6(1): 6-11.

—— (2011). From Objects to Processes: A Proposal to Rewrite Radical Constructivism. *Constructivist Foundations*, 7(1): 1-9 and 37-47.

Searle, J.R. (1995). *The construction of social reality* (New York: Free Press).

Skemp, R.R. (1971). *The Psychology of Learning Mathematics* (Middlesex: Penguin).

Solomon, J. (1994). The rise and fall of constructivism. *Studies in Science Education*, 23: 1-19.

Staver, J.R. (1998). Constructivism: Sound theory for explicating the practice of science and science teaching. *Journal of Research in Science Teaching*, 35(5): 501-20.

Steffe, J.P. (1999). Intersubjectivity in Mathematics Learning: A Challenge to Radical Constructivist Paradigm? *Chreods*, 13, February. The Manchester Metropolitan University. (http://s13a.math.aca.mmu.ac.uk).

Suchting, W.A. (1992). Constructivism deconstructed. *Science and Education*, 1(3): 223-54.

Tobin, K. and Tippins, D.J. (1993). Constructivism as a referent for teaching and learning. In K. Tobin (Ed.), *The practice of constructivism in science education*, 3-21 (Washington DC: AAAS Press).

Tobin, K., Tippins, D.J., and Gallard, A. (1994). Research on instructional strategies for teaching science. In D. Gabel (Ed.), *Handbook of research on science teaching and learning* (45-93) (New York: Macmillan).

Tracey, Ryan (2011). *E-Learning Provocateur,* Vol. 1; http://ryan2point0.wordpress.com.

von Glasersfeld, E. (1987). Learning as a constructive activity. In C. Janvier (Ed.), *Problems of representation in the teaching of mathematics.* (Hillside, NJ: Lawrence Erlbaum), 3-17.

—— (1989). Cognition, Construction of Knowledge, and Teaching. *Synthese*, 80(1): 121-40; www.univie.ac.at/constructivism/EvG/papers/118.pdf.

—— (1992). Constructivism Reconstructed: A Reply to Suchting. *Science and Education*, 1(4): 379-84.

—— (1995). *Radical Constructivism: A Way of Knowing and Learning* (London: The Falmer Press).

—— (2010). Why People Dislike Radical Constructivism. *Constructivist Foundations*, 6(1): 19-21.

White, H. (2006). *Postmodernism 101* (Grand Rapids, MI: Brazos Press).

Index

R

S

T

U

V

W

Z